Hillel Steiner and the Anatomy of Justice

Routledge Studies in Contemporary Philosophy

1. Email and Ethics
Style and Ethical Relations in Computer-Mediated Communication
Emma Rooksby

2. Causation and Laws of Nature
Max Kistler

3. Internalism and Epistemology
The Architecture of Reason
Timothy McGrew and Lydia McGrew

4. Einstein, Relativity and Absolute Simultaneity
Edited by William Lane Craig and Quentin Smith

5. Epistemology Modalized
Kelly Becker

6. Truth and Speech Acts
Studies in the Philosophy of Language
Dirk Greimann and Geo Siegwart

7. Fiction, Narrative, and Knowledge
A Sense of the World
Edited by John Gibson, Wolfgang Huemer, and Luca Pocci

8. A Pragmatist Philosophy of Democracy
Communities of Inquiry
Robert B. Talisse

9. Aesthetics and Material Beauty
Aesthetics Naturalized
Jennifer A. McMahon

10. Aesthetic Experience
Edited by Richard Shusterman and Adele Tomlin

11. Real Essentialism
David S. Oderberg

12. Practical Identity and Narrative Agency
Edited by Catriona Mackenzie and Kim Atkins

13. Metaphysics and the Representational Fallacy
Heather Dyke

14. Narrative Identity and Moral Identity
A Practical Perspective
Kim Atkins

15. Intergenerational Justice
Rights and Responsibilities in an Intergenerational Polity
Janna Thompson

16. Hillel Steiner and the Anatomy of Justice
Themes and Challenges
Edited by Stephen de Wijze, Matthew H. Kramer and Ian Carter

Hillel Steiner and the Anatomy of Justice

Themes and Challenges

Edited by Stephen de Wijze, Matthew H. Kramer, and Ian Carter

Routledge
Taylor & Francis Group

New York London

First published 2009
by Routledge
711 Third Ave, New York, NY 10017

Simultaneously published in the UK
by Routledge
2 Park Square, Milton Park, Abingdon, Oxfordshire OX14 4RN

First issued in paperback 2014

Routledge is an imprint of the Taylor and Francis Group, an informa company

Typeset in Sabon by IBT Global.

Library of Congress Cataloging in Publication Data

Hillel Steiner and the anatomy of justice : themes and challenges / edited by Stephen de Wijze, Matthew H. Kramer, and Ian Carter.
p. cm.—(Routledge studies in contemporary philosophy ; 16)
Includes bibliographical references and index.
ISBN 978-0-415-99134-6
1. Justice. 2. Human rights. 3. Civil rights. 4. Libertarianism. 5. Steiner, Hillel. I. De Wijze, Stephen. II. Kramer, Matthew H., 1959– III. Carter, Ian, 1964–
JC578.H54 2009
320.1'1—dc22
2009002005

ISBN13: 978–0–415–99134–6(hbk)
ISBN13: 978-0-415-75436-1 (pbk)

Hillel Steiner

Contents

Preface

The ordering of the names of the three editors of this volume on the cover and the title page is arbitrary. Efforts and responsibilities have been divided equally among the three of us. In the course of carrying out those efforts and fulfilling those responsibilities, we have incurred debts of gratitude to a number of people. We are pleased to acknowledge those debts here.

We extend hearty thanks to the contributors (most of whom submitted their essays on time!), and we extend particular thanks to Hillel Steiner for his good-natured cooperation with the production of this festschrift. We are grateful as well to Erica Wetter and Tony Bruce at Routledge for their admirable supportiveness. The readers of the original proposal for the festschrift offered some perceptively helpful comments, which we have heeded to the benefit of this volume. We also wish to thank Michael Watters for his fine work in bringing this book through the process of publication.

Inevitably, because of constraints of space, we have been unable to request essays from some people who would have wished to contribute to a festschrift for Hillel. We apologize to those whom we could not include on the roster of contributors, but we are delighted that everyone who has been included was so eager to pay tribute to Hillel. The essays in this book, though often critical of his ideas, reinforce his own endeavors to analyze major problems of political philosophy with rigor and imaginativeness.

Introduction

Ian Carter

Hillel Steiner is widely recognized as one of the most eminent contemporary political philosophers. This volume pays tribute to his intellectual achievements with a collection of original essays on most of the principal themes in his work: liberty, rights, equality, justice, and the nature of philosophical analysis.

I shall not attempt in this introduction to present the arguments advanced by each of the authors of this volume. That task is best left to the authors themselves. Rather, my purpose is to provide an overall account of Steiner's work, so as to highlight the ways in which it is evoked or built upon or contested in the essays that follow. Viewing Steiner's work through a pair of binoculars—rather than the microscope normally preferred by analytic philosophers—will hardly do justice to the intricacies of his theory, but it should help us to draw a conceptual map on which to locate the various issues discussed in the subsequent chapters.

Steiner grew up in Toronto and studied economics at the University of Toronto before moving to England to pursue a doctoral research project in public policy at the University of Manchester. As a student in Toronto, he had been deeply involved in socialist politics and was strongly influenced by the writings of John Kenneth Galbraith and the Marxism of C.B. Macpherson, who had taught him political theory. The doctoral research project was to have been an application of their views to their prospect of an 'affluent society'. However, his growing dissatisfaction with those views, in conjunction with his growing appreciation of the importance of analytic philosophy during his early years in Manchester, led him to explore aspects of contemporary moral philosophy, economic theory and jurisprudence with a view to working out their implications for the nature of rights and justice. The eventual outcome of this philosophical investigation was a normative political theory—based on property rights and market principles combined with a measure of economic equality—that recovers and advances a pre-Marxist tradition of radical individualist thought developed by Thomas Paine, the early Herbert Spencer, Leon Walras and Henry George, among others. This kind of theory has subsequently come to be known as 'left-libertarianism' (Vallentyne and Steiner, 2000b; Otsuka, Steiner and Vallentyne 2005).

Another young philosopher working in a similar way on the concepts of property and justice (but with a more orthodox or 'right' libertarian view of economic inequality) was Robert Nozick, whose famous book *Anarchy, State and Utopia* appeared in 1974, the year in which Steiner completed his doctoral thesis. It was to take Steiner another 20 years—now as a faculty member in the University of Manchester—to produce what he at last considered a satisfactory, book-length exposition of his more heretical version of libertarianism. With hindsight, his 1994 book *An Essay on Rights* can be considered an egalitarian answer to Nozick. Like Nozick's book, it defends a conception of justice based on respect for property rights (including self-ownership), together with a classical liberal view of the limits of legitimate state intervention. But it pays far greater attention to the moral foundations and the conceptual detail of such a defence and, partly as a result of the insights produced by this deeper analysis, it includes a particular interpretation of the 'Lockean proviso'—a constraint on legitimate appropriation, explored by Nozick—that results in a number of radically egalitarian redistributive implications.

Although Steiner's work on liberty, rights, and justice represents a highly sophisticated exposition of the ideological perspective known as left-libertarianism, his writings cannot correctly be labelled as "ideological" in any pejorative sense. He would never adopt the practice, typical of a certain kind of *intellectuel engagé*, of starting out with an unquestioning endorsement of a preferred ideological position and then working backwards to embrace whatever premises are need to support it. Indeed, his own intellectual development has consisted of major, and often painful, modifications of his earlier political views. His overall vision is not painted in broad brush strokes but is instead built up slowly and meticulously, starting with the basic elements of justice (namely, rights) and working out their implications through successive layers of detailed argumentation. For Steiner, the four main analyses on which his left-libertarianism is based—that is to say, his explications of liberty, of rights, of moral reasoning and of economic reasoning, successively set out in the first four main chapters of *An Essay on Rights*—constitute independently valid foundations for a theory of justice. Were these analyses to be shown, *contra* Steiner, to yield conclusions about justice that are in fact antithetical to left-libertarianism, he would continue to think that we have good reasons for accepting them.

A political philosopher may have ideological motives in defending a particular normative stance, but such biographical facts are simply not relevant in assessing the quality of the analysis he or she succeeds in delivering. Indeed, Steiner goes further than most contemporary moral and political philosophers by additionally claiming that the validity of an analysis of any particular normative concept is itself wholly independent of any particular value perspective and rests instead only on the logical features of that concept. According to Steiner, in other words, the analysis of a normative concept can itself be value-free. The possibility of such a freestanding analysis of normative concepts is contested by some of the authors in this volume, as we shall see later on. Still, whatever their views on the methodology of Steiner's ambitious philosophical project, all of our authors agree that a measure of ideological detachment, coupled with the rigours of conceptual analysis, is a necessary means to progress in ethical and political understanding. They also agree that philosophers should resist the temptation—understandable as it may be among politicians—to perform 'unedifying gallops . . . from fragmentary moral convictions to full-blown institutional and policy prescriptions' (Steiner 1994, 3). This last thought is not itself in tension with the project of seeking reflective equilibrium, taking one's pre-theoretical moral intuitions as a starting point. However, some reflective equilibria are more superficial than others, and the latter are destined to supersede the former when we engage in detailed analysis of our normative concepts and of the philosophical assumptions we make in using them.

Ordinary language provides an important starting point in such philosophical investigations, but—for Steiner as for the original proponents of 'Oxford philosophy'—ordinary language is not the last word. (Only remember, as J. L. Austin wrote, that it *is* the *first* word). Moving beyond the analysis of ordinary language, Steiner believes that a great deal of work can be done by the requirement of logical consistency. He acknowledges that criteria for logical consistency cannot tell us which values to hold. However, because such criteria rule out many combinations of theses, he thinks that they can often filter out enough interpretations of a given set of values to leave us with only one tenable interpretation. If we are lucky enough to arrive at such an outcome, logical consistency will then force us either to endorse that interpretation or to renounce the set of values in question.

LIBERTY AND PROPERTY

Steiner's analysis of the concept of liberty[1]—one of the main building blocks in his construction of a theory of rights and justice—provides a useful illustration both of his attitude to the authority of ordinary language and of his views on the relations between normative judgements and philosophical analysis. As he notes, there is some support in ordinary language for most of the rival conceptions of liberty that have been defended by political philosophers from time to time. Steiner's own 'pure negative' conception (1975; 1994, ch. 2; 2001)—the view that a person is rendered unfree to do something if and only if some other person renders her doing that thing physically impossible—certainly has a degree of linguistic plausibility. For example, we would not normally feel inclined to say that a person was unfree to do something that she has in fact done. The mere difficulty of doing *x* or the threat of harmful consequences in the event of one's doing *x* are not sufficient to prevent one from doing *x*, for there are times when a person will succeed in doing *x* despite the difficulty of doing so, or will decide to do *x* regardless of the consequences. Such considerations support the idea that a person is unfree to do something only when that thing has been rendered physically impossible. The pure negative conception is also supported by the plausibility of saying that a person can be free or unfree to do *x* regardless of whether or not she *desires* to do *x*. Ordinary usage tells us that a prisoner who is prevented from going to the theatre is unfree to go to the theatre, even if she does not desire to go (and indeed even if she desires not to go); therefore, desiring to do *x* is not a necessary condition for being unfree to do *x*. Moreover, the rejection of any conceptual link between a person's liberty and her desires not only tells in favour of 'negative' conceptions of liberty and against 'positive' ones, but also points to the superiority of the 'pure' negative conception to other negative conceptions, for it suggests that a person's fear of the threatened consequences of doing *x* is not in itself a constraint on her doing *x* (Steiner 1994, 22–32). Threats and offers succeed in 'obstructing' particular courses of action only in the sense of inverting the agent's preferences over the options available to her (by adding certain costs or benefits to the expected consequences of those courses of action). If a person's preferences are irrelevant to her liberty, then such 'obstructions' do not remove any particular liberties.

On the other hand, ordinary language supports other conceptions of liberty that rival the pure negative conception. While ordinary language indeed supports the claim that a person who does *x* was not unfree to do *x*, it also sometimes endorses the view that liberty is distinct from 'licence'. The latter view implies that imposing obstacles to a person's performance of immoral actions does not decrease that person's liberty (it only decreases her 'licence'). Whereas Steiner's pure negative conception of liberty is an 'austere' one, which Steiner himself sees as 'value-free' (Ricciardi 1997), the distinction between liberty and licence invokes a rival conception of liberty: what T. M. Scanlon and G. A. Cohen have called a 'moralized' conception of liberty.

Other considerations must therefore be adduced in support of the pure negative conception of liberty. For Steiner, the most important of these considerations has to do with the role of rights in our normative theorizing. A theory of rights must rest on a theory of liberty, for rights themselves assign permissions to act and powers over other people's permissions to act. And if rights are to play a non-redundant role in normative theorizing (as they must do, if the concept of rights is to have any point at all), the operative conception of liberty must be an austere one—that is to say, it must follow from such a conception that the existence of a person's liberty is independent of the value of her performing one course of action rather than another. If we are to treat rights as a basic value, we cannot define them in terms of some other basic value. If, by contrast, we base our theory of rights on a moralized conception of liberty, we shall expose ourselves to Bentham's famous charge that rights are conceptually and normatively redundant (Ricciardi, 1997).

Steiner argues, moreover, that the pure negative conception of liberty lends itself particularly well to an explication of the notion of *property* rights and of their place in a theory of justice. He submits that, if one is free to the extent that others do not render one's actions physically impossible, it follows that liberty is 'the personal possession of physical objects'—that is, control over the spatio-temporal locations and material objects that constitute the 'physical components' of actions (Steiner 1975, 48; 1994, 33–41)—and this possession of physical objects is exactly what is normatively distributed by property rights. Property rights, according to Steiner, indeed consist in normative assignments of packages of pure negative liberties.

Why is it desirable to have a conception of liberty that lends itself to an explication of the notion of property rights? In Steiner's view, the reason is that property rights are the only defensible kind of rights, and the reason for holding that property rights are the only defensible kind of rights is that only property rights can be *compossible* rights.

For two rights to be compossible, there must be a possible world in which the duties correlative to those two rights are jointly fulfilled. In other words, it must be possible for both of the rights to be respected. For Steiner, the compossibility of any set of rights is a logically necessary condition for the existence of that set of rights: prescriptions of conflicting rights are logically inconsistent (1977a; 1994, ch. 3). Now, we can only ascertain whether the duties correlative to a set of rights can all be performed if we are able to specify exactly which portions of space, time and (spatiotemporally located) matter constitute the physical components of the actions that would fulfill those duties. If the (spatio-temporally specified) physical components of the duty-fulfilling actions do not overlap at all, then the duties are jointly performable and their correlative rights are compossible. In order to guarantee that no such overlapping occurs, Steiner believes, duty-bearers must not only have the normative and physical liberty to comply with their duties but must also have claims against others' making use of the physical components of the actions that would comply with those duties. Once such liberties and claims are in place—together with certain powers to waive duties in others and immunities against losing such liberties, claims and powers—one has arrived at a set of property rights. On Steiner's view, then, only a well-defined set of property rights can be a set of compossible rights, and only a set of compossible rights can be an actual set of rights.

The requirement of compossibility limits the set of possible basic rights (uncontracted rights) to what are commonly called 'negative' rights: namely, rights that others *not* do certain things. Given that most resources are scarce, basic positive rights—such as a basic right that others provide one with life-saving resources when one is in need—would generate potential duty-conflicts and therefore lead to incompossibilities. Some supporters of basic positive rights have suggested that, if the abandonment of all positive rights is really entailed by the requirement of compossibility, then perhaps the compossibility of rights imposes too high a price. Perhaps, they have said, our moral intuition favouring basic positive rights is stronger than any intuition we might have to the effect that conflicts between rights are to be avoided. Steiner's answer to this objection is that it mistakes the object of his analysis. His aim is not to convince us that compossibility is so morally weighty that it trumps other moral intuitions about rights; rather, it is to convince us that compossibility is a logically necessary feature of rights themselves: that the details of rights have been misspecified if those ostensible rights are incompossible (Steiner 1998b). Steiner's thesis is nothing less than that the notion of basic positive rights is incoherent.

EXPLOITATION, ORIGINAL RIGHTS, AND THE GLOBAL FUND

The 'left' in Steiner's left-libertarianism enters this picture at several junctures, owing to his careful analysis of liberty, of rights, and of the historical dimension of a rights-based theory of justice.

Nozick rightly called his own conception of justice an 'historical entitlement' conception. For both Nozick and Steiner, the justice of any entitlement depends on its pedigree, which in turn consists of two dimensions. The first of those dimensions is the justice of *transfers or transformations* carried out in the past. For example, my property right in my pen might depend on a shopkeeper's having voluntarily given me the pen in exchange for money, on that shopkeeper's having legitimately purchased the pen from a wholesaler, and so on, or it might depend on my having manufactured it from factors belonging to me. The second dimension of the pedigree of a sound entitlement consists in the justice of *original acquisitions* of natural resources. For instance, at some time in the past, at the beginning of the chain of transfers and transformations, someone took possession of the previously unowned raw materials needed to make my pen. As Steiner shows, the norms governing these two historical dimensions of the entitlement conception of justice (norms governing transfer/transformation and norms governing original acquisition) can be interpreted in such a way as to leave considerable space for egalitarian concerns.

Regarding the justice of transfers, Steiner goes against the libertarian orthodoxy by arguing that it is possible for exchanges to be exploitative—and thus unjust in themselves—even when they are voluntary. An exchange is exploitative where the agreed-upon price reflects a disadvantage of one of the parties that can be traced to a past injustice (either in transfer or in original acquisition). In such a situation, the past injustice has enabled the dominant party to the exchange to extract a surplus with respect to the price that would have been agreed on in the absence of that past wrong (Steiner 1987b; 2008a). The reality of exploitative market transactions has been a recurring theme in Steiner's work. Indeed, among his current research projects is an analytical and historical study of the concept of 'the just price'. Despite the socialist flavour of such a project, however, the underlying aim remains libertarian: it is to *defend* markets, by showing that the economic injustices correctly perceived by the left-wing critics of capitalism depend not on the nature of markets themselves (as those critics have often maintained), but on the injustices of the holdings with which people enter markets in the first place.

Given that the injustice of exploitation can result from injustices in original holdings, clearly the most important egalitarian move in Steiner's theory regards the interpretation of justice in original acquisition. According to Steiner, each person's liberty to acquire holdings from the world's stock of unowned resources must be constrained by a Lockean proviso to the effect that each person has certain 'original rights'. Rights over holdings do not appear out of thin air—they cannot be created simply by taking possession of spaces or matter—but must derive from an exercise of original rights. Original rights are rights that are not themselves created by the choices people make in exercising powers (such as the power to make someone a promise and the power to exchange goods with someone). They are the rights from which all other rights serially derive. And the only kind of right that can count as an original right, for Steiner, is a right to equal liberty—that is, a right to the same amount of pure negative liberty as any other person.

The notion of an original right, which itself rests on what Nozick would call a 'patterned' rather than an historical principle of justice, marks a crucial difference between 'left' and 'right' libertarians. This difference is discussed in some depth in Eric Mack's contribution to this volume. For Steiner, the historical entitlement conception of justice cannot be historical 'all the way down'. Mack, who defends a 'standard' or 'right' libertarian perspective, accepts that an historical chain of entitlements must begin at a certain point. However, from that premise he declines to conclude that the right to acquire resources must depend on an antecedent right to a certain share determined by a distributive pattern.

Assuming Steiner to be correct in deriving property rights from a universal and egalitarian original right, it might still be asked why he thinks that such an original right must be a right to *liberty*. An answer to this question can be found in his conception of rights as *choices* available to agents. In his view, rights are things that agents exercise by exercising their wills—demanding or waiving the fulfilment of the duties of others that are correlative to those rights. This 'Will Theory' of rights, which Steiner has defended at some length (1994, pp. 59–73; 1998a; 2008b) and which is discussed in the essays by Ian Carter and Cécile Fabre in this volume, contrasts with the so-called 'Interest Theory' (associated with the work of Joseph Raz, Ronald Dworkin and Matthew Kramer, among others), according to which the holder of a right correlative to a duty is someone whose situation is normatively protected by the duty in a way that is generally beneficial for a human being (or a collectivity or a non-human animal). On the Will Theory (but not on the Interest Theory), rights-bearers are necessarily moral agents with a capacity for choice, and all rights are derived either from an exercise of choice on the part of some agent (justice in transfer) or from an original right (which H.L.A. Hart called a 'natural' right) to exercise choice—that is, a right to liberty. This original right cannot be anything other than equal, in Steiner's view, for no unequal original distribution of liberty can be consistently justified (Steiner 1974; 1994, pp. 208–23).

Steiner's derivation of the fundamental or original right to equal liberty is in fact quite complex. As well as suggesting that equality can be derived by default in the above-mentioned way, Steiner claims that equality of liberty follows from the Kantian injunction to treat others as ends in themselves (1994, p. 221). This link between equal liberty and respect for persons is explored in Ian Carter's essay in the present volume. There are also times when Steiner states or implies that equality itself is a relation that has *intrinsic value* (2002b; 2003). This last thesis is subjected to critical scrutiny in Joseph Raz's essay. Raz focuses not specifically on equality of liberty but on equality more generally. Unlike Steiner, Raz is not sympathetic to the view that equality has intrinsic value. Presumably, Raz's doubts about the ascription of such value to equality entail the conclusion that Steiner is mistaken in assigning a fundamental status to the right to equal liberty, and that such a right should instead be founded on some deeper interest in wellbeing.

Whatever the way in which the original right to equal liberty is to be derived, the egalitarian implications of Steiner's theory should now be plain. Rights, in his theory, are normative distributions of pure negative liberty. Given his belief that pure negative liberty entails control over the physical components of actions and hence over resources, any just system of rights must vest every agent with an original right to an equal share of natural resources or to the value equivalent by way of compensation. With respect to the *status quo*, justice therefore requires a considerable redistribution of wealth.

Because Steiner holds that people's property rights include rights over their own bodies and labour power (as we shall see in the next section), he also believes that people are entitled to keep the fruits of their labour. If I work hard to increase the value of the resources justly at my disposal, then I am entitled to that increase in value. What I am not entitled to, however, is more than an equal share of original assets on which to expend my labour. It is important to emphasize, then, that the right-to-resources entailed by the original right to equal liberty is only a right to be left an equal share of the world's *natural* resources (Steiner 1977b; 1980; 1987a; 1994, chs. 7–8). The state is definitely not authorized by Steiner's theory to tax someone simply because she is rich. Nevertheless, some people are rich because they have appropriated more than their fair shares of natural resources. To use Steiner's terminology, these people count as 'over-appropriators' (1994, p.

268). The state is morally obligated to tax the over-appropriators and to redistribute their surplus to the under-appropriators. This implication is disputed by Mack, for whom a proper application of the Lockean proviso means leaving '*enough* and as good' for others, not '*as much* and as good'.

One of the practical redistributive measures that Steiner himself sees as a likely implication of his theory of distributive justice is that of a universal, unconditional basic endowment—a policy that has long been associated with the name of another of the contributors to this volume, Philippe Van Parijs, in whose work that basic endowment takes the form of a 'basic income'. From Steiner's point of view, one can think of the complete set of natural resources—including natural physical raw materials such as land and (as we shall see shortly) natural talents and the holdings of the deceased—as forming a 'global fund', which justice requires us to distribute equally and unconditionally to all agents in virtue of the equal original right-to-liberty held by each of them. This equal, unconditional right to a share of the global fund amounts in practice to a right to a basic endowment. In his essay in this volume, Van Parijs contrasts Steiner's account of this basic endowment with his own 'real libertarian' account, in which the sources of revenue, as well as the domain of equalization, are distinctly more extensive.

For left-libertarians, what each person chooses to do with her basic endowment is entirely her own affair so long as she does not violate the rights of others. Each person must therefore be allowed to enjoy the benefits of any wise or lucky choices she makes about how to use or invest her basic endowment, and must also be required to bear the burdens of any unwise or unlucky choices (unless others voluntarily relieve her of such burdens, as Steiner would no doubt often encourage them to do). In that respect, as Michael Otsuka observes in his contribution to this book, Steiner's left-libertarian theory bears some resemblance to the egalitarian theories that have recently come to be called 'luck-egalitarian' (Steiner 1997). According to luck-egalitarianism—some aspects of which are critically examined at length in G.A. Cohen's essay—we should legally undo only those disadvantages brought about by brute luck, while accepting as legitimate those disadvantages that people bring upon themselves as a result of their own choices. Luck-egalitarians favour equality of opportunity, in a comprehensive sense of 'opportunity', over equality of results.

Like luck-egalitarians, Steiner favours 'equal starts' in life (1987a, pp. 69–71). Indeed, he has stated explicitly that he is happy to be called a 'starting-gate libertarian', despite the fact that this phrase has mostly been used in a pejorative way (Ricciardi, 1997).[2] An important difference with luck-egalitarians, however, lies in Steiner's attempt to characterize egalitarian justice in terms of a consistent set of property rights. Luck-egalitarians do not normally pay much attention to the nature of the private property rights that equality of opportunity entails. In Steiner's view, this results in their less faithfully capturing the element of personal responsibility that they and he wish to conjoin with egalitarianism. Thus, they often ignore the fact that, while a person may be badly off through no fault of her own, the cause of her being badly off may be some harm inflicted not by nature but by some other person, in which case the cost of compensating for her disadvantage ought to be borne not by her society as a whole but by the member or members of that society who inflicted the harm (Steiner 1997).[3] The issue of who, exactly, should bear the costs of compensation for harm inflicted through rights violations, including in cases where the rights violator is less than fully responsible for such harm, forms the subject of Peter Vallenyne's contribution to this volume.

A further question that has exercised Steiner over the years concerns the distributive reach of his principles of justice and the implications of that reach for international relations (Steiner 1995a; 1996; 1999a; 2001a). Steiner rejects the idea—defended by nationalists and communitarians and to some degree by Jonathan Wolff in his essay in this volume—that national boundaries can be a legitimate factor in determining just shares of resources. For Steiner, the original right to an equal share of natural resources would ideally not be computed for and confined to each country in isolation from every other, but would instead be accorded directly to every individual considered as a citizen of the world: in referring to a global fund, Steiner really does mean a 'global' fund. In such an ideally cosmopolitan world, the inhabitants of countries that are rich in natural resources would recognize that they owe compensation to the inhabitants of countries that are poor in natural resources.

SELF-OWNERSHIP, TALENTS, AND INTERGENERATIONAL JUSTICE

Among the resources over which people can have property rights are human bodies. Left- and right-libertarians are commonly described as agreeing that every person has property in her body as a self-owner. They are said to disagree only over the distribution of external resources. (The difference between left- and right-libertarians is characterized in this way in Steiner's and Vallentyne's anthologies of left-libertarian writings; see Vallentyne and Steiner 2000a, 2000b.) Whether or not self-ownership should be understood as one of the *defining* features of left-libertarianism is a matter of debate. Certainly Steiner himself embraces the principle of universal self-ownership (1994, chap. 6). On the other hand, he regards self-ownership not as itself a bedrock principle but as a corollary of the fundamental principle of equal liberty. On Steiner's theory, self-ownership derives from the fact that moral agents come into the world inhabiting human bodies. This fact, coupled with the original right of moral agents to equal liberty, implies that 'bodies must be owner-occupied' (Steiner 1994, 232).

Since people's bodies and hence their talents are themselves resources, Steiner's Lockean proviso appears to imply that those with greater natural talents owe compensation to those with lesser natural talents. As Michael Otsuka points out in his essay, such a conclusion appears to follow from the original right to an equal share of natural resources. Steiner acknowledges, however, that such a conclusion might seem to be problematic for anyone who believes in universal self-ownership; self-ownership might appear to rule out the taxation of a person's talents. Steiner nevertheless aims to reconcile self-ownership with the taxation of natural talents. Because natural talents translate in practice into health and earning power, this reconciliation would further strengthen the egalitarian implications of his theory. The way in which Steiner squares this circle is among the most original and controversial aspects of his theory. People's bodies are not themselves purely the products of nature, but are, in great part, the fruits of the labour of their parents. Parents, however, need raw materials on which to labour in order to engage in the creation of the bodies of their offspring. Specifically, they need the germ-line genetic information which is present in their eggs and sperm and which is not itself the fruit of anyone's labour. When they produce offspring, then, parents take possession of a natural resource—germ-line genetic information—and mix their labour with that resource, so appropriating it. And where that natural resource is of greater than average value (where it has the potential to produce health and talents with greater than average earning power), such parents qualify as among the 'over-appropriators' mentioned earlier. It therefore follows that the *parents* of more talented children owe compensation to the *parents* of less talented children. (As Serena Olsaretti suggests in her contribution to this volume, we should presumably say that *a fortiori* the parents also owe such compensation to *non*-parents, who have not mixed their labour with *any* germ-line genetic information.) It is not the super-healthy or the super-talented themselves who owe compensation to those with lesser genetic endowments (a consequence that might conflict with self-ownership), but their parents who owe such compensation to other parents (and to non-parents).

Children, it should be added, do not themselves have rights under Steiner's Will Theory—not, at least, until each of them is old enough to qualify as a moral agent with a right to equal liberty and a consequent right to self-ownership and to an equal portion of the world's natural resources. Until they become moral agents, children are owned by their parents or guardians. Many commentators have found this implication morally counterintuitive. Steiner has attempted to answer these critics by pointing out that to deny rights to the unempowerable—be they children or animals or the severely mentally disabled—is not to deny that we have weighty moral duties pertaining to them. Moreover, although those duties do not correlate with rights held by the unempowerable themselves, they can correlate with rights held by agents who are actually in a position to promote the interests of the unempowerable (1998a, pp. 259–62).

The downside of owning one's children is that, apart from any compensation owed to parents in virtue of any of their offspring's having genetically-driven disabilities or inferior talents, justice requires parents to bear the full costs of their children's upbringing. Clearly procreation is not itself a matter of brute luck but is a choice for which parents can be held responsible. As Olsaretti observes, however, there is another question that Steiner's theory does not answer so clearly: whether the cost to others of the addition of new members to the world (in the form of a reduction in the equal share of resources for each person) ought to be borne by people generally—as Steiner himself appears to assume—or by the parents of those new members.

Another potentially egalitarian implication of Steiner's theory of rights is his denial of rights to the deceased. This, Steiner argues, follows directly from the Will Theory of rights, which, as we have seen, implies that one must be a moral agent in order to have rights (1994, pp. 249–61). The deceased are not moral agents (they are no longer moral agents, because they no longer exist), and they therefore have no rights over the living. Parents therefore have no right to bequeath their property to their offspring (or indeed to anyone else) after their deaths. Instead, the property (including the vital organs) of the deceased is to be construed as abandoned, and hence unowned, and hence as entering the pool of natural resources to which every existing agent has an equal entitlement. The egalitarian effects of outlawing bequests are, however, attenuated by the fact that Steiner places no limits on gifts from one living person to another, including gifts from living parents to their offspring. Parents who take the risky course of what Steiner calls the 'King Lear option', of handing over their property to their offspring before they die, do not contravene Steinerian justice. In this respect, Steiner's version of left-libertarianism appears to be less egalitarian than that of Otsuka, as Otsuka himself notes.

Still on the subject of intergenerational justice, Steiner also argues that we must deny any rights to future agents who have no element of contemporaneity with existing agents (Steiner 1991; 1994, 259–61). This conclusion is presented as yet another entailment of the Will Theory of rights. Like the deceased, members of future generations are not moral agents—in this case, they are not *yet* moral agents—and therefore they do not currently partake of the Steinerian right to equal liberty. It is possible, however, that the rights-bearing status of future generations does not itself turn on the Will-Theory versus Interest-Theory controversy. Cécile Fabre, in her contribution to this book, argues that Steiner's position on the rights of future generations should also be endorsed by Interest Theorists. If Fabre's argument is sound, then there is little scope, either way, for a coherent defence of the rights of future generations. Still, just as the denial of any rights to children does not entail the absence of any duties concerning them, the denial of rights to future generations is consistent with the claim that we are currently under weighty duties to promote the well-being of the members of those generations.

MORALITY AND METHODOLOGY

To the student of public policy, the various prescriptive implications of Steiner's theory may still appear rather abstract. From the point of view of the political philosopher, on the other hand, they are surprisingly specific—to the point of having led some to wonder 'where the rabbit was introduced into the hat'.[4] Can the analysis of a concept as general and as vague as 'justice' really produce anything as detailed as an equal right to the market value of natural resources and the basic income deriving from it, the principle of universal self-ownership, the denial of a right of bequest, the exclusion of minors and future generations from the set of rights-bearers, and a cosmopolitan stance on the international redistribution of resources? Has Steiner really succeeded in ruling out the many alternative normative claims that people often have in mind when they appeal to the notion of justice? Is not justice itself an essentially contested concept? Steiner's answer is that, if the elementary particles of justice are *rights*, his specific conclusions must indeed be drawn. The point of the various arguments sketched above is indeed to show what normative beliefs people *must* have, *if* they believe in rights and *if* their normative beliefs are logically consistent. Those who are intuitively attached to alternative views about rights and their bearers must, then, either show where the rabbit was introduced into the hat or else admit that their intuitions are faulty.

This is a bold claim on behalf of conceptual analysis, and one to which some of Steiner's critics have taken exception. Matthew Kramer's essay in this volume directly contests Steiner's claim that we can reach substantive conclusions of political morality through austere analyses that are attuned exclusively or predominantly to logical considerations. Ian Carter reaches a similar conclusion to that of Kramer, though more indirectly, through his examination of Steiner's derivation of the right to equal liberty. Also in tune with Kramer's methodological position is Stephen de Wijze, whose essay in this volume criticises Steiner's conception of evil (Steiner 1995b; 2002). According to de Wijze, Steiner's analysis of evil depends on a reductionistic foundationalist approach, which contrasts with de Wijze's preferred method of seeking moral conceptions that are acceptable in reflective equilibrium. Although Norman Geras's essay in this book does not deal with concepts of political morality, it too elaborates an understanding of conceptual analysis that is markedly different from Steiner's.

Regardless of where one stands on these methodological questions, it remains the case that Steiner's theory of rights poses a robust conceptual challenge to all those who would contest his conclusions. After all, it is one thing to deny that the soundness of a normative argument is ever wholly independent of substantive normative premises; it is quite another to embrace the lazy postmodernist view that logical consistency itself carries no more weight for us than any of our other commitments. As the essays in this volume testify, even those of us who harbour doubts about

Steiner's methodology or his substantive premises and conclusions are able to admire his extraordinary theoretical construction. His writings cannot fail to stimulate, to provoke, and at times even to convince, compelling us to improve our normative beliefs.[5]

NOTES

1. The terms 'liberty' and 'freedom' are usually used interchangeably in political and social philosophy. While endorsing such interchangeability, I use only the former term in this Introduction. I do, however, use 'free to do *x*' instead of 'at liberty to do *x*'.
2. This is not to say that Steiner interprets starting-gate libertarianism in the same way as Ronald Dworkin, who coined the term in Dworkin 1981.
3. Another important difference between Steiner and the luck-egalitarians revolves around the ways in which they respectively address the issue of unequal talents or abilities, on which point see below.
4. These words are taken from Brian Barry's endorsement of *An Essay on Rights*.
5. I am grateful to Matthew Kramer and Hillel Steiner for their helpful comments on an earlier draft of this chapter.

BIBLIOGRAPHY

Dworkin, Ronald. 1981. 'What is Equality? Part I: Equality of Welfare'. 10 *Philosophy and Public Affairs* 185–246.

Otsuka, Michael, Steiner, Hillel, and Vallentyne, Peter. 2005. 'Why Left-Libertarianism Is Not Incoherent, Indeterminate, or Irrelevant: A Reply to Fried'. 33 *Philosophy & Public Affairs* 201–215.

Ricciardi, Mario. 1997. 'Liberty, Rights and Justice: A Conversation with Hillel Steiner'. 17 *Politics* 33–38.

Steiner, Hillel. 1974. 'The Natural Right to Equal Freedom'. 83 *Mind* 194–210.

Steiner, Hillel. 1975. 'Individual Liberty'. 75 *Proceedings of the Aristotelian Society* 33–50.

Steiner, Hillel. 1977a. 'The Structure of a Set of Compossible Rights'. 74 *Journal of Philosophy* 767–75.

Steiner, Hillel. 1977b. 'The Natural Right to the Means of Production'. 27 *Philosophical Quarterly* 41–49.

Steiner, Hillel. 1980. 'Liberty and Equality'. 29 *Political Studies* 555–69.

Steiner, Hillel. 1987a. 'Capitalism, Justice and Equal Starts'. 5 *Social Philosophy & Policy* 49–71.

Steiner, Hillel. 1987b. 'Exploitation: A Liberal Theory Amended, Defended and Extended'. In Andrew Reeve (ed.), *Modern Theories of Exploitation*. London: Sage.

Steiner, Hillel. 1991. 'Markets and Law: The Case of Environmental Conservation'. In Michael Moran and Maurice Wright (eds), *The Market and the State*. London: Macmillan.

Steiner, Hillel. 1994. *An Essay on Rights*. Oxford: Blackwell.

Steiner, Hillel. 1995a. 'Liberalism and Nationalism'. 17 *Analyse & Kritik* 12–20.

Steiner, Hillel. 1995b. 'Persons of Lesser Value: Moral Argument and the "Final Solution"'. 12 *Journal of Applied Philosophy* 129–141.

Steiner, Hillel. 1996. 'Territorial Justice'. In Simon Caney, David George, and Peter Jones (eds), *National Rights, International Obligations*. Boulder: Westview Press.

Steiner, Hillel. 1997. 'Choice and Circumstance'. 10 *Ratio* 296–312.

Steiner, Hillel. 1998a. 'Working Rights'. In Matthew Kramer, Nigel Simmonds, and Hillel Steiner, *A Debate over Rights: Philosophical Enquiries*. Oxford: Oxford University Press.

Steiner, Hillel. 1998b. 'Freedom, Rights and Equality'. 6 *International Journal of Philosophical Studies*. 128–37.

Steiner, Hillel. 1999a. 'Just Taxation and International Redistribution'. In Ian Shapiro and Lea Brilmayer (eds), *Nomos XLI: Global Justice*. New York: New York University Press.

Steiner, Hillel. 1999b. 'Silver Spoons and Golden Genes: Talent Differentials and Distributive Justice'. In Justine Burley (ed.), *The Genetic Revolution and Human Rights: 1998 Oxford Amnesty Lectures*. Oxford: Oxford University Press.

Steiner, Hillel. 2001a. 'Hard Borders, Compensation and Classical Liberalism'. In David Miller and Sohail Hashmi (eds), *Boundaries and Justice: Diverse Ethical Perspectives*. Princeton: Princeton University Press.

Steiner, Hillel. 2001b. 'Freedom and Bivalence'. In Ian Carter and Mario Ricciardi (eds), *Freedom, Power and Political Morality: Essays for Felix Oppenheim*. London: Palgrave-Macmillan.

Steiner, Hillel. 2002a. 'Calibrating Evil'. 85 *Monist* 181–91.

Steiner, Hillel. 2002b. 'How Equality Matters'. 19 *Social Philosophy & Policy* 342–56.

Steiner, Hillel. 2003. 'Equality, Incommensurability and Rights'. In Lukas Meyer, Stanley Paulson, and Thomas Pogge (eds), *Rights, Culture and the Law: Essays after Joseph Raz*. Oxford: Oxford University Press.

Steiner, Hillel. 2008a. 'Exploitation Takes Time'. In Paul Samuelson and John Vint (eds), *Essays for Ian Steedman*. London: Routledge.

Steiner, Hillel. 2008b. 'Are There *Still* Any Natural Rights?' In Matthew Kramer, Claire Grant, Ben Colburn, and Antony Hatzistavrou (eds), *The Legacy of H.L.A. Hart: Legal, Political, and Moral Philosophy*. Oxford: Oxford University Press.

Vallentyne, Peter and Steiner, Hillel (eds). 2000a. *The Origins of Left-Libertarianism: An Anthology of Historical Writings*. London: Palgrave.

Vallentyne, Peter and Steiner, Hillel (eds). 2000b. *Left-Libertarianism and Its Critics: The Contemporary Debate*. London: Palgrave.

PART I
JUSTICE AND EQUALITY

1 Fairness and Legitimacy in Justice, And: Does Option Luck Ever Preserve Justice?[1]

G.A. Cohen

"What's fair ain't necessarily right." (Morrison 1987, 256)

For a long time I was preoccupied with the idea of self-ownership and, connectedly, with entitlement theories of justice. A major influence was, of course, Robert Nozick's *Anarchy, State and Utopia*. But an earlier influence in the same direction began to exercise itself on me when I met Hillel Steiner in 1968. He was visiting my then London home with his then wife whom I had known since childhood: it was through her that we first came to know each other. Hillel described the germs of an arresting point of view that was later expressed in a series of articles. I was intrigued, impressed, and resistant.

The most significant articles, in my opinion, that emerged from the germination of those years were "The Natural Right to Equal Freedom" (1974), "The Natural Right to the Means of Production" (1977), and "The Structure of a Set of Compossible Rights" (1977). The last of those three merits special admiration. The majestic project of "Structure" was to derive a complete answer to the question, what is justice? on the basis of two premisses: that people have equal fundamental rights, and that it is a condition of a coherent set of rights that all rights in the set can be exercised simultaneously, in whatever way the right-holders choose. "Structure" was the founding document, or manifesto, of what came to be known as "Left Libertarianism", a libertarianism that affirms self-ownership together with a radically egalitarian regime over worldly resources. And if "Structure" was Steiner's Manifesto, then *An Essay on Rights* was his *Capital*. (I do not say that the philosophical project of "Structure" was successful. I think it fails to prove what it sets out to prove, which is something that it has in common with Leibniz's *Monadology*, Kant's *Grundlegung*, Plato's *Republic*, and, indeed, Marx's *Capital*.)

The present paper is a set of variations on a theme to which I was introduced by Hillel.

* * * * * * * * *

It seems to me that four leading ideas that play a role in philosophical debate about just distribution are not always treated in proper distinction from one another, to the detriment of clarity in our thinking about justice. The four ideas are justice, unanimity, fairness and what I shall call "legitimacy", which is the property that something has when, to put it roughly, no one has the right to complain about its character, or, perhaps a little less roughly, when no-one has a just grievance against it.

Here is one likely locus of error. Fairness is frequently treated as necessary for justice, and unanimity is treated as sufficient for legitimacy, and therefore, in turn, for justice. But unless, what I shall deny, a distribution is legitimate only if it is fair, the stated relations among the four designated notions cannot obtain. Fairness might be necessary for one kind of justice, and legitimacy might be sufficient for another kind of justice, but one cannot say, on pain of equivocation, that fairness is necessary for justice and legitimacy is sufficient for it, since what's legitimate, to put the point with Morrisonian pungency, "ain't necessarily" fair.

In short, different kinds of justice get confused, and, so I shall argue, this may have a bearing on the question of whether option luck preserves justice.

1. NEW (I THINK) LIGHT ON THE WILT CHAMBERLAIN ARGUMENT

In 1977 I published an article called "Robert Nozick and Wilt Chamberlain: How Patterns Preserve Liberty"[2]: my subtitle was in intended contradiction of the title-message of Nozick's Wilt Chamberlain section, which is called "How Liberty Upsets Patterns" (Nozick, 1974, 160–164). But that intention, I avow below, was somewhat ill-considered.

I began the article with a quotation from the Russian Marxist George Plekhanov, because I was proud that a Marxist, a predecessor in the tradition from which I had come, had, as I then thought, so succinctly anticipated, and then replied to, a central strain in libertarian argument. I shall begin once again with the Plekhanov quote, but this time with more of it:

> . . . look at the conclusion to which the so-called *labour principle of property*, extolled by our Narodnik literature, leads. Only that belongs to me which has been created by my labour. Nothing can be more just than that. And it is no less just that I use the thing I have created at my own free discretion: I use it myself or I exchange it for something else, which for some reason I need more. It is equally just, then, that I make use of the thing I have secured by exchange—again at my free discretion—as I find pleasant, best and advantageous. Let us now suppose that I have sold the product of my own labour for money, and have used the money to hire a labourer, i.e., I have bought somebody else's labour-power. Having taken advantage of this labour-power of another, I turn out to be the owner of value which is considerably higher than the value I spent on its purchase. This, on the one hand, is very just, because it has already been recognized, after all, that I can use what I have secured by exchange as is best and most advantageous for myself: and, on the

other hand, it is very unjust, because I am exploiting the labour of *another* and thereby negating the principle which lay at the foundation of my conception of justice. The property acquired by my personal labour bears me the property created by the labour of another. *Summum jus, summa injuria*. And such *injuria* springs up by the very nature of things in the economy of almost any well-to-do handicraftsman, almost every prosperous peasant.

And so *every phenomenon, by the action of those same forces which condition its existence, sooner or later, but inevitably, is transformed into its own opposite* (Plekhanov 1956, 94–5, original emphases).

I do not agree with the "dialectical" (Plekhanov's characterization of it, a little later) generalization with which the excerpt concludes, but in this paper I do say something similar about the particular example that Plekhanov uses in the excerpt to illustrate what he thinks is dialectic. I argue that there is a deep incoherence in the idea that "whatever arises from a just situation by just steps is itself just": I claim that its apparently axiomatic status depends upon an equivocation on "just". If we purge the equivocation, what we have left is an unconvincing dialectical (or not) would-be paradox.

* * * * * * * * *

"Whatever arises" says Robert Nozick, "from a just situation by just steps is itself just" (Nozick 1974, 151). Hence, so he argues, if we assume that the initial distribution in his famous Wilt Chamberlain story is just, then, unless, implausibly, we find some injustice within or surrounding the fans' decisions to pay to watch Wilt play, we must deem the resulting distribution to be just.

Now one might think that the Wilt Chamberlain argument is intended as a paradox. For the initial distribution counts as just because it is, let us assume, egalitarian[3]: it is just under the principle that a distribution is just if and only if it is egalitarian. But the final distribution violates that very principle. In its paradox construal, the Chamberlain argument runs as follows:

(i) Whatever arises from a just situation by just steps is itself just.
(ii) The initial situation in the Chamberlain example is just according to your favourite egalitarian principle.
(iii) The payments that transform the initial situation into the final situation constitute just steps.
∴ (iv) The final situation is just.

But

(v) The final situation contradicts your favourite egalitarian principle.

∴ (vi) Your favourite egalitarian principle is self-contradictory (or some thing like that).

Yet Nozick does not conclude that the initial egalitarian principle has *no* force, that, in a certain manner, it refutes itself. He concludes, more modestly, that "it is not clear how those holding alternative conceptions of distributive justice can reject the entitlement theory of justice in holdings" (Nozick 1974, 160). He does not present his argument as a paradox.

And, indeed, whether or not one is an egalitarian, one should not readily accept that egalitarianism is paradoxical, that, together with other, supposedly undeniable premisses[4], one can derive a rejection of egalitarianism from egalitarianism itself. So there is a reason for suspecting that the justice that putatively characterizes the result of the Chamberlain transaction is not the justice that characterizes the situation that obtains before the transaction unrolls. Such a difference between kinds of justice would eliminate the appearance of paradox, even though it would not show that the argument achieves nothing, nor, in particular, that egalitarians need not countenance entitlement at all.

Before I elaborate the "different kinds of justice" proposal, let me remark that the claim that even egalitarians must acknowledge an *element* of entitlement in their view of justice is bound to be true. For Robert van der Veen and Philippe Van Parijs (1985) have shown that, although Nozick calls his theory an "entitlement theory", and thereby means to contrast it with theories that aren't entitlement theories, the truth is that all theories of just distribution have an entitlement, or historical, component *and* a non-historical component: on *any* theory of justice, one cannot tell whether a distribution is just by examining its profile alone, with no information about how that profile came to be.[5]

Consider, then, the paradox-dissolving proposal that the justice of the initial situation is not the same kind of justice as the justice of the final situation. It seems to me easy to vindicate. For, to begin with, the word "just" is clearly subject to different criteria when it is applied to initial distributions from the criteria that decide whether steps are just: whereas the initial distribution is judged just or otherwise by looking at who has what, steps are judged just or otherwise by looking at who has done what to, or with, whom. (To illustrate the difference of criteria, reflect that, to put the matter crudely, equality is completely different from voluntariness.) It follows, of course, that the final situation isn't judged just *simply* by looking at who has what. It is judged just by virtue of the just content of the initial distribution and the just character of the actions that transform the initial distribution into the final distribution.

But what sort of justice characterizes the final situation? Do we have a name for it? Not a short one, but the justice in question is the property that a situation has when no one has a right to complain against its character, when no one has a just grievance against it, and I shall call that property *legitimacy*, for short, here.[6] And it need not, in my view, be a contradiction (though, unlike me, some may think it is always false) to say: "This outcome is unjust, but nobody can complain about it". That need not be a contradiction because "unjust" need not mean "susceptible to legitimate complaint".

Let me try to vindicate that non-contradiction claim. Suppose that a democracy enacts a (not too) unjust law. I thought it was unjust when I voted against it, but I think that the state may now rightly impose it. I have been given no reason to stop believing that the law is unjust, now it's been voted for, in the sense in which I previously believed it was unjust: that belief did not entail the further belief that a majority of my fellow citizens would recognize the injustice of the proposed law. So, if I now think the law is just, which is to say, justly imposed, and I'm clear-minded, then I don't think the law is just in the sense in which I initially thought—and still think—it unjust. It is just in the quite different sense that it is legitimate.

I said that what I call "legitimacy" is the property that something has when no one has the right to complain about it. But that formulation needs further refinement. We may have a right to complain when a legitimate outcome is unfair or ugly or costly and so forth, but that does not mean that we then have a right to complain in the sense that I contemplate. Zosia Stemplowska[7] suggested that I should mean that we cannot complain if the outcome's reversal is not *enforced*. I mean that as a minimum, but more work is needed here.

Nozick asks, about people's shares: "what [were they] for except to do something with?" (Nozick 1974, 161). Well, of course the shares were given to people for them to do something with, but it does not follow that they could not, unfortunately from the point of view of the principles of the original distributors, use their shares so as to produce a result that contradicts those principles.

But why would the distributors, supposing that they had the power to forbid that use, *let* the agents use their shares in that way? Almost certainly for reasons of freedom, not justice. Contrary to what some political philosophers like to think, freedom and justice *can* conflict, and you can hold an egalitarian view of justice while giving special priority to freedom as far as legitimacy is concerned. (Such an egalitarian might not *always* put freedom before justice, for she might sometimes put (other) justice before (that special justice that is) legitimacy.)

Consider doctors who were educated at state expense and who take their services abroad. We may deplore that, but, on grounds of freedom, we may be loath to restrict their ability to do so. And we may grant that freedom consistently with thinking that the doctors behave unfairly and unjustly when they do what we believe in granting them the freedom to do. But we need not think that the doctors we educate should be free to go abroad because they have a *right* to go abroad. What we rather think is that they *should* have a right to go abroad *because* they should be free to go abroad. But the rights that they *should have* are, transparently, not rights that they (just) have, rights, that is, that are conferred by justice, rather than by (merely) the law.

Given what I permissibly meant by "liberty" in the 1977 article, I was right that, in the words of its sub-title, "Patterns Preserve Liberty": pattern-upsetting market choice can reduce people's scope of (future) choice, and therefore, and in that sense, their liberty. But it does not follow that, given what *he* permissibly meant by "liberty", namely, the freedom to do as one wishes as long as one harms no one,[8] Nozick was wrong when he said that liberty upsets patterns. I did argue for that *further* claim (one not proven by the vindication of my sub-title) in a *different* way, on the basis of considerations that were quite independent of the thought expressed in my subtitle, in the 1977 article (see Cohen 1995, 28–31). But I was wrong to think that my sub-title *itself* contradicted everything important that Nozick said.

The foregoing deconstruction of the claim that whatever arises from a just situation by just steps is itself just leaves intact a structurally similar claim. For consider. Fairness is sufficient for what I have called "legitimacy"[9] in an initial distribution, and, since the initial Chamberlain distribution is fair, it is indeed legitimate, and so are the steps that turn it into the final distribution, which is therefore *itself* legitimate, because *whatever arises from a legitimate distribution by legitimate steps is itself legitimate*. Unlike Nozick's slogan about justice, which it imitates, *that* slogan does not suffer from equivocation: the criterion of legitimacy is the same throughout.

Someone commented that the italicized substitute gives Nozick everything that he wants. But that isn't so. Nozick wants the Chamberlain example to show that egalitarianism violates all three of liberty, justice, and the Pareto Principle, even though he does not clearly distinguish those different purposes of his parable (see Cohen 2008, Chapter 4, section 7). And the claim about legitimacy that I italicized in the last paragraph vindicates none of those three theses.

The van der Veen/Van Parijs insight that I reported above runs very deep. Perhaps one may put it this way. Consider distributions that are not actually willed by the relevant parties, including, therefore, those that *could* not be willed by the parties: such distributions count as "fair", in the broadest sense of the word, when they are appropriate to everything to which a distribution ought to be appropriate (given, as it is given here, that how the parties will is not in question). And the authors' point is that there always *is* both a necessarily unwilled initial distribution to consider, *and* rules that permit agents to transform it, by appropriate "steps", that is, by exercises and executions of will. And the criteria of fairness in initial distribution, whatever they are, can be comparatively independent of the criteria for evaluating the justice of steps, and the former are therefore not identical with the criteria that qualify the final distribution as just (that is, legitimate).

2. DWORKIN ON OPTION LUCK

The foregoing reflections have implications for the question that forms the second part of my title.

According to Ronald Dworkin, justice requires some sort of initial equality of distribution, but certain inequalities are nevertheless just, some of them being those inequalities that result from option luck, or gambles, against a starting point of equality. *Option luck*, Dworkin believes, preserves justice, but *brute luck* overturns it. Dworkin distinguishes the two as follows: "Option luck is a matter of how deliberate and calculated gambles turn out—whether someone gains or loses through accepting an isolated risk he or she should have anticipated and might have declined. Brute luck [by contrast] is a matter of how risks fall out that are not in that sense deliberate gambles" (Dworkin 2000, 73).

Dworkin does not specify the "sense" in which brute luck does not count as the result of a deliberate gamble, and a large critical literature has been generated by that lacuna. It will suffice, here, to convey what brute luck is by paradigmatic illustration: brute luck is illustrated by the case of a brick that falls on your head in a not particularly dangerous place.

Now, strong arguments have been advanced for the claim that, contrary to what Dworkin says, option luck against a just background does not *always* preserve justice, but does so *at most* under rather demanding conditions.[10] I shall not explore that claim here, for the question, does option luck *always* preserve justice?, is not my question. My question is: does option luck (even) *sometimes*, or, in other words, *ever*, preserve justice? Or, more precisely, does it ever do so other than by accident, because it *happens* to replicate the pre-option luck distribution? In such a case justice indeed continues to obtain, but not *because* the outcome is a result of option luck, not because option luck has in a strong sense *preserved* justice, but simply because it happens not to have destroyed it. I shall mean "preserve" in its stronger sense throughout what follows.

In order to pursue my subtitle question, I focus on a paradigm case of putatively justice-preserving option luck. I believe that, if option luck does not preserve justice in the case upon which I shall focus, then it never does, and we can then safely return a negative answer to the question that appears in my title. To anticipate, and bearing in mind the argument of section 1, I am inclined to the view that option luck does not preserve the justice that renders the pre-gambling situation just.

Imagine, then, two people, A and B, who are relevantly identical with respect to their assets, their circumstances, their tastes, and so forth: they are, that is, identical in every respect that bears on distributive justice, and the distribution of goods between them is perfectly equal and perfectly just. Let's say that each has $100,000. Now one taste that A and B share is for gambling. And each gambles half of his assets against half of the other's, on a 50/50 toss. Dworkin would claim that the resulting distribution is entirely just, because of its origin in option luck against a background of equality, and despite the fact that one of the people emerges with $150,000, which is three times the assets that the other one comes to have, and however dire the resulting state of that other person may be.

3. THE ANTI-DWORKIN ARGUMENT

I shall shortly present an argument (the "anti-Dworkin" argument) against Dworkin's view.[11] But, before I come to the argument, we need some background. Suppose, as Dworkin does, that we regard a certain form of equality in distribution as just, *at least* provided that the people to whom the distribution applies do not will otherwise, that is, at least provided that they are either all in favour of equality or, at any rate, none of them is against it, and (this is the intended force of "*at least*") whether or not equality would remain just *even* if their wills were opposed to equality. Now suppose that the holdings of a set of people are characterized by the relevant equality, but that they *do* will otherwise, and, in particular, they unanimously will that everyone give half their assets to Sarah and Jane,[12] not because they think that is fair, but because Sarah and Jane are fair (in the other sense), and they like to bestow gifts on the fair.

Many would say, and I among them, that the upshot is unfair, and everyone must agree that it is not fair by the criteria that rendered the original distribution fair. Still, the result is legitimate, in the defined sense: no one has a right to complain about the outcome, since everyone voted for the transactions that brought the outcome about.

The result of the Sarah/Jane transfer will not be just by the criteria that endowed the unanimous choice in favour of Sarah and Jane with legitimating power, which was the justice of the initial situation. The initial just situation renders unanimity legitimating,[13] and the actual unanimity renders the outcome legitimate, but not by the criteria that made the initial situation just. Those steps indeed render the outcome in some sense(s) just, but do they render it just in any sense beyond the legitimacy sense? The legitimacy of the outcome has no tendency to remove its unfairness: instead, it ensures that nobody has the right to *complain* about that unfairness. So if unfairness (always, that is, even in *this* sort of case) implies injustice, then the upshot, though legitimate, is (in one way) unjust. And does unfairness not always imply *some* sort of injustice, even if not an injustice, all things considered?

Most would agree that, in the Sarah/Jane example, unanimity trumps *equality*, which is to say that it would be wrong for anyone (say, for example, an exogenous party) to force a return to equality from the unanimously endorsed (and therefore legitimate) unequal result. But there are two opposed understandings of what a unanimity that trumps *equality* does to *justice*. One might think either *i* or *ii*:

i The unequal outcome is not entirely just (because it is unfair) but it is legitimate. With respect to legitimacy, unanimous will trumps the justice of fairness.

ii The unequal outcome is both legitimate and entirely just. Unanimous will confers unqualified justice on an unequal outcome that would otherwise be an unjust outcome.

Dworkin holds the *ii* view. Note that the *ii* view is, at least *prima facie*, consistent both with affirming and with denying that the outcome is unfair.

Other pertinent illustrations of equality-upsetting unanimity: I wholly voluntarily enslave myself to you or agree to work for you for a wage that would not be just in the absence of that agreement. This might be because I love you, and/or because I do not care about justice. Or I accede to what I know to be, *at least* if I were *not* to accede to it, an unjust arrangement, and I accede to it simply because I refuse to demean myself by insisting on my rights in the face of my ornery opposite number, you. (I was first in line, but I allowed you to go ahead, because you're such a kvetch). As before, there are two contrasting things that we might think about what's happening in these cases. We might, once again, think (analogues of) either *i* or *ii* (the unanimity in these cases being the concordance in favour of my enslavement, or of your queue-jumping, of the wills of, in those cases, a pair of people).

Now, the anti-Dworkin argument says that the gambling case belongs with the (other) unanimity cases. It says that, as regards justice, we should say the same about both, with respect to the choice between *i* and *ii*. It presents the gambling case as one in which a concordance of wills overturns what would otherwise be a just distribution. *And* the anti-Dworkin argument *also* says, in line with the view expounded in section 1 above, that *i*, rather than *ii*, tells the truth about the unanimity cases. It follows that, if the losing gambler has no complaint, he has no complaint *not* because the outcome is just in the sense in which the initial situation was just, but because he, the loser, agreed to the procedure that produced the circumstance that has befallen him. Accordingly, option luck never preserves the justice that precedes its operation. For, as I suggested in the fifth paragraph of section 2 above, if option luck doesn't preserve justice in the entirely symmetrical two-person gamble case, then it doesn't do so anywhere.

4. A DISCRIMINATING RESPONSE TO THE ANTI-DWORKIN ARGUMENT

Let us now consider a possible response to the anti-Dworkin argument. Dworkin thinks that the outcome is just both in the unanimity cases[14] and in the gambling case. The anti-Dworkin argument of section 3 disagrees with him in both cases. But there are two logically possible, and more or less embraced (by somebody), *discriminating responses* to the Anti-Dworkin argument that merit an airing. The first defends what Dworkin says about gambling while rejecting what he says about the effect of unanimity in general, and the second, contrariwise, rejects what he says about gambling while defending what he says about unanimity in general.

According to the first discriminating response, I indeed *legitimate* an injustice when I willingly enslave myself to you, and when I let you go in line ahead of me: to that extent, Dworkin is mistaken. But, the response continues, and by contrast, *i* is not the correct description of the gambling case: there is a relevant structural difference between the two types of case, whose consequence is that unanimity does *not* confer the *same* justice property on its outcome as is conferred on their outcomes by fair and voluntary gambles. I call this response "discriminating" because it rejects what Dworkin says about unanimity in order to protect, by way of a supposed contrast, what he says about gambling.

The assimilation made by the anti-Dworkin argument of section 3 says that the claim that the result of option luck is just is simply a special case of the claim that anything that's consented to is just: the case for the justice of the relevant outcome, whatever the quality of that case may be, is the same in the two instances. But the discriminating response says that the voluntariness of a 50-50 gamble might be thought to make the gamble preserve justice in the initial sense even if that justice is not preserved by unanimous will in the (other) unanimity cases.

In the unanimity cases, everyone agrees to what would otherwise be unquestionably unjust. But what the gambler agrees to is a 50-50 chance, an equal chance, and that's certainly *not* unquestionably unjust. Crucially, for our purposes, the gambler is agreeing to a *gamble*, and, indeed, to what virtually anyone would call a *fair* gamble, and, therefore, a just procedure. The gambler is not agreeing directly, but only indirectly, to an outcome. So, this discriminating response concludes, unlike what holds in the unanimity cases, what the will directly endorses in the gambling case is *not* (at least otherwise) manifestly unjust: what the will endorses directly in the gambling case is, by contrast with the unanimity cases, something that is not otherwise unquestionably unjust, namely, a seemingly fair procedure, a procedure in which no one is at a disadvantage.

5. TWO OBJECTIONS TO THAT FIRST DISCRIMINATING RESPONSE

The first discriminating response to the anti-Dworkin argument can be construed as an argument with a premiss and a conclusion, as follows

(iii) Unlike what holds for the unanimity cases, the gamblers do not will a result that is, considered independently of their willings, unfair.
∴ (iv) Unlike what holds for the unanimity cases, the upshot of the gamble is not unfair.

The first objection questions the premiss of that discriminating argument and the second questions the inference to its conclusion.

The first objection questions the supposed independent fairness of the 50-50 gamble procedure. The objector says: if, as you think, the fact that the 50-50 gamble *is* fair[15] because 50-50, then why is voluntariness needed to *make* the gamble fair? Why isn't an *imposed* 50-50 gamble[16] *also* fair?[17] And, she might say, in the same vein, since the *outcome* of this supposedly fair gamble is supposed to be just: if the fact that the gamble is 50-50 makes the outcome of the gamble just, why is *consent* to that gamble *also* needed to make its outcome just? Why is not the outcome of an *imposed* 50-50 gamble also just?

The second objection, which is to the inference of the discriminator's argument, will be stated in section 7 below. Whereas I shall judge that the objection stated above does not succeed, the second objection strikes me as weighty. I nevertheless canvass the first objection, because it appears to me to raise some interesting issues.

6. DEFENDING THE FIRST DISCRIMINATING RESPONSE AGAINST THE FIRST OBJECTION

The first objection to the discriminating response misdescribes what the discriminator said about the 50-50 gamble, in her attempt to contrast it with the outcome that is directly willed in the unanimity cases. She did not say that a 50-50 gamble is just because fair, whether or not it is imposed. She said the weaker, yet still relevant, thing that the gamble is not, considered independently of whether it is willed, unquestionably unjust, by contrast with, for example, your occupying what should be my position in the queue.

If that sounds mysterious, an example might help. Suppose that a pound of apples are, by any standard,[18] worth precisely a dollar. Despite their being worth that, I don't like apples, and it's therefore not OK for you to take my dollar by force and saddle me with a pound of apples. For such a use of force would override (my taste or preference and consequently, here) my will. It would also not be OK for you to impose the apples and take the dollar even *if* I *did* prefer the apples to a dollar (or, *a fortiori*, even if I were indifferent between them), because those moves might *also* contradict my will: it is not an axiom that one always wills what one prefers. What's true is that *if* I want to buy apples, then one dollar per pound is the fair price. Gambling, similarly, is a matter of one's taste about risk, and, therefore, a matter where my will counts. The true parallel is not between a voluntary 50/50 gamble and the unanimity cases. Instead, a voluntary 50/50 gamble is like a decision to purchase apples at a fair price, and it is a voluntarily *unfair* gamble that resembles the unanimity cases.

You may not agree that there is such a thing as *the* fair price of an apple. But I do not need to claim that much, for the purposes of vindicating the concept exercised in the foregoing paragraph. I need only say that (at least) certain prices for apples are, by contrast with other prices, not unquestionably unjust, considered independently of whether those terms are willed: and that seems to be obviously true. In any case, enough has been said to show that the first objection to the argument against the discriminating view that what's willed in the gamble is fair fails.

The general claim suggested by the apples case is that outcomes that are not judged unjust on will-independent grounds (like the outcome in the apple purchase example, and the outcome of my will, that is, the 50-50 chance itself, in the gambling case), may be judged unjust on will-dependent grounds. The gamble is just only if the parties' wills favour gambling. Two things are required here for justice: that the outcome of my will (a dollar for a pound of apples, a gamble of 50/50) is not *independently* unjust, *and* concordant wills.

To rehearse, briefly, what has been a somewhat sinuous exposition. The anti-Dworkin argument assimilates the gamble to the fairness-upsetting unanimity cases. The first discriminating response counters that what the wills endorse, directly, in the gambling case, is a fair gamble, a gamble that could not *itself* be called unjust, by contrast with what the wills endorse in the unanimity cases. The anti-Dworkinite replies that, in that case, the 50-50 chance should be just even if it is imposed. But the discriminator responds that this doesn't follow: some things are just only if the will endorses them, but they are then undoubtedly just. So the anti-Dworkinite fails to vindicate his original assimilation. So far, then, the mooted proposal, to wit, that the voluntariness of a 50-50 gamble might be thought to make the gamble preserve justice even if justice is not preserved by voluntariness in the unanimity cases, remains on the table: it might be that some option luck preserves justice, even if unanimous willing of an unequal result doesn't do so.

7. A SECOND OBJECTION TO THE FIRST DISCRIMINATING RESPONSE

But there is a distinct objection to the discriminator's argument, which is that its inference is questionable.

True, and as the discriminating response insists, the willing gamblers, unlike the unanimous voters, don't directly will an unfairness, but why should it follow that the *upshot* of the gamble is not unfair? Why may one not say, within the assumption that fairness/unfairness is a matter of the profile of the distribution, that the gamblers' wills, if implemented, *ensure* an unfairness, one way or the other, and the difference between willing an unfairness and willing what ensures an unfairness isn't deep? In *each* case, it might be possible to say, for all that the discriminator has shown, that the result is legitimate but unfair, as the anti-Dworkinite claimed.

Michael Otsuka is a patron of the first discriminating position. He rejects the claim that unanimity preserves justice (in the sense of fairness): he accepts the force of such examples as the Sarah/Jane transfer. But Otsuka believes that, contrary to what was suggested in the paragraph above, the difference between directly willing an inequality and willing what (merely) ensures an inequality is indeed deep: he regards it as a key difference between the cases that, in the Sarah/Jane case, people vote for what all know will be a distribution that is unequal *in favour of known people*, namely Sarah and Jane. In the gambling case, the relevantly analogous proposition is false: the gamblers do know that the gamble will produce an inequality, but neither knows who will benefit from that inequality. Contrast a gamble in which one party knows how the dice will fall. The result of that gamble is not, for Otsuka, fair, precisely because now, as in the Sarah/Jane case, the full profile of the inequality is foreknown.

I hover between accepting and rejecting Otsuka's distinction.

8. AN OPPOSITE DISCRIMINATING RESPONSE TO THE ANTI-DWORKIN ARGUMENT

Nozick and Dworkin believe that the outcome is just, without qualification, both in the unanimity cases and in the willing gambling case. The anti-Dworkinite believes that the outcome is not in every respect just in either the unanimity case or the gambling case. The first discriminating response holds that the outcome is not just in the unanimity case but is just in the gambling case. An anonymous[19] luck egalitarian who affirms the Temkin/Cohen formulation of luck egalitarianism, under which an outcome is just if it shows no inequality that is nobody's fault or choice,[20] has suggested the interesting fourth view, which is a second and opposite discriminating response to the anti-Dworkin argument, that the outcome is just in the unanimity case but not in the gambling case.[21]

Anonymous reasons as follows: In the unanimity case there's a good sense in which no one is worse off than anyone else through no fault of her own, since each voted for the inequality, and it would not have obtained without her vote. In the gamble, by contrast, the inequality isn't *itself* willed, and, for Anonymous, that makes a crucial difference: it means that, in a relevant sense, someone *is* worse off through no fault of her own, but, rather, because of the way that the dice fell, and that the result is therefore *not* just. So, according to Anonymous, far from unanimous choice being a paradigm legitimating justice-subverter to which option luck might be assimilated, option luck subverts justice whereas unanimous consent does not. And note that option luck subverts justice, for Anonymous, precisely because its outcome is not directly willed: she/he makes the *opposite* contrast to the one that the first discriminating response makes.

In order to test the Anonymous view, let us move to a different example. Suppose that the initial distribution is equal, but we, all of us, have a choice whether or not to legislate in favour of permitting Pareto improvements, and it is foreknown what Pareto improvements there would be, and how people would differentially benefit from them. Then we might vote for permitting Pareto improvements wholeheartedly, or, on the other hand, we might regret that inequalities are to ensue, but nevertheless vote for permitting Pareto. But in the latter case, it is questionable *both* that we unanimously *will* the result (true, we unanimously *choose* it, but we do not *will* it, in the fullest possible sense) *and* that, even if we do, the result is just.

Now that may not be a lethal criticism, since Anonymous might enrich what she/he claims to be a sufficient condition of justice and thereby exclude the regret case. But one may nevertheless question the contrast between even an enriched version of the Anonymous claim about unanimity and the gambling case. Does it not challenge the Anonymous view that one may say to the unlucky gambler: you can't say it isn't your fault, since you willingly gambled? Something is surely my fault if my will was necessary and sufficient for it in the context (that, here, of others willing similarly) and I do so will.

And consider: if I agree to split the produce of a field 25:75 with a person who has put in equal farming time (and everything else is equal), then the share-out is just according to Anonymous, but if I agree to a 50:50 (or any other odds) gamble with him with the winner taking 75% the produce then the share-out is unjust. That claim of distinction between the cases is highly counterintuitive.

The underlying value, so Anonymous herself/himself says, is fairness, and I don't see why Anonymous's unanimous legislators cannot acknowledge that they are voting for an unfair result.

9. DOES IT MATTER?

Someone might wonder whether the *(i)*/*(ii)* distinction, which was drawn near the beginning of section 3 above, *matters*.[22] Suppose I say in line with *(i)*, that the losing gambler suffers from an injustice, about which, however, he has no complaint, then how is what I say *interesting*, given that I shall treat both winning and losing gamblers exactly as I would if I thought that losing gamblers were *not* suffering from an injustice? We can say three things here, the objection continues: first, what we might call *fairness justice* requires, to put it simply, an equal distribution, so the outcome of the gamble is not just in the fairness sense; second, what we might call *legitimacy justice* endorses the outcome of the gamble, because a voluntary gamble, against a background of justice, is a fair procedure; and, third, the right thing to do is to respect the gamble's outcome. Is there a fourth question, as to whether the outcome is just, *tout court*? Once we've said the three things that were just distinguished, isn't the *(i)*/*(ii)* distinction a distinction without a difference?

Well, whether the gambler is suffering an injustice might be thought interesting for both theoretical and, *pace* what was said above, practical reasons.

First, the distinction might be interesting for the purely theoretical reason that it's interesting to know what justice is.

Second, and rather importantly, the distinction can ground an objection to capitalism that goes beyond the transparently true claim that capitalist inequality is extensively due to brute luck. One can add that much capitalist inequality shows injustice even when it is due to option luck: the additional objection could not be made if fairness and legitimacy had not been separated as *aspects* of justice. That second reason for saying that the *(i)*/*(ii)* distinction matters is at least theoretical, but also, in some contexts, practical.

Third, the *(i)*/*(ii)* distinction possesses a certain range of practical relevance. Maybe if *(i)* is true and *(ii)* false, then, while we might be unwilling to enforce a reversal of the gamble's outcome, we might also be unwilling to enforce the outcome itself.[23] Or, with respect to rights of bequest, it might matter whether a given lump of cash was or was not acquired by gambling. If it was the fruit of a fair gamble, then you might have less right to bequeath it than if it was the product of your labour,[24] and, correspondingly, we might think that the proceeds of gambling are more legitimately taxable than some other types of income. It is simply untrue—see the second sentence of this section—that I shall treat winning and losing gamblers the same regardless of my judgments of justice here: in this and other contexts, and/or with other premisses in play, the *(i)*/*(ii)* distinction *can* make a practical difference.

Here is an example of how a view as to whether the results of a fair gamble are just or unjust (that is, not fully just) might make a difference, at the level of immediate policy. If gambling produces injustice, that is *a* reason for restricting it. If we account its results just, we lose that reason. One of the least popular policies of Tony Blair was the promotion of gambling: large casinos, of a kind new to Britain, were to be built in Manchester and elsewhere. One of the most popular early decisions of the new Prime Minister Gordon Brown was to chop the casino-promoting policy. Whether you think the results of deliberate gambles are just might affect how you evaluate that shift of policy.

10. MORE ON THE RELATIONSHIP BETWEEN THESE MATTERS AND LUCK EGALITARIANISM

This paper has defended the claim that what recommends an outcome that was achieved by just steps from a just starting point is not, in the general case, *itself* (unqualified) justice, but the different virtue of legitimacy, or, more precisely, the property that no one can legitimately complain about it.

David Miller has claimed that luck egalitarianism is inconsistent with the principal distinction that I try to draw in the paper, because luck egalitarianism says: distribute equally, compensating appropriately for luck-induced deficits, and then whatever arises from people's choices is just. If I am right in what I say in the paper, so Miller's argument goes, luck egalitarians shouldn't call whatever arises "just", but merely "legitimate" (in the technical sense of being something that no one can complain about).

When I embarked upon this paper, it was my thought that patterned and end-state theories of justice do not themselves say what just *steps* are, the latter being an intuitive matter quite separate from such theories of just distribution. But luck egalitarianism's statement, as given in the foregoing paragraph, seems to comprehend a doctrine of just steps and therefore, perhaps, to confer the title of justice itself on the outcomes that it endorses.

Can it be that plain egalitarianism doesn't define what just steps are but that luck egalitarianism does? Can it be that, unlike plain egalitarianism, luck egalitarianism *is* paradoxical,[25] because the use of shares by people is *bound* to lead to a distribution flecked by luck?

Is the following the right way to look at the matter, to wit, that luck egalitarianism is more developed than plain egalitarianism in that it answers the question about *precisely* which forms of chosen action are just steps, whereas plain egalitarianism is silent as to which steps are just? Hence, by virtue of the content of the luck-egalitarian doctrine, the status of justice proper is conferred, in an unqualified way, on the favoured upshots. Doesn't the luck egalitarian theory of, precisely, *justice*, fold the steps issue into itself?

Does luck egalitarianism therefore endorse the results of the Chamberlain transaction as not only "legitimate" but just? No, because there are caveats that affect our judgment about the voluntariness of that transaction, which are reviewed in my Chamberlain article. And there is also the deep consideration that Chamberlain benefits from the brute luck of his superior talent, a consideration that I have ignored in this paper. I did so because to have introduced the highly controversial claim that people should not benefit from endowments of special talent would have drawn attention away from the more structural issues that have occupied this paper and that are relatively independent of different views about the precise content of justice.

But what is the answer to the "flecked by luck" paradox question at the end of the paragraph three paragraphs back? Mustn't it be "yes", since one man's choice is another man's luck? Choices both to give and to buy have the property that it is accidental who is favoured by them: we both offer a commodity at £10, and it is an accident from whom a purchaser decides to buy, even in the most "perfect" of markets. And the underlying point might be that a luck egalitarian can't allow *any* transactions. Sure, she can allow transactions that preserve absence of luck in distribution, but that won't confer much choice.

Perhaps this démarche shows that we have to interrogate the initial situation/steps/resultant situation structure harder than we have done so far. It is perfectly clear in a model situation like Chamberlain, but how do we apply it to the thick of continuous transacting, that is, more generally, of continuous stepping?

So: back to the drawing board, later! I would still be there now, but *Festschrifts* have deadlines, and this one's has come. I am therefore constrained to offer Hillel, and you, an inconclusive, and also unconcluding, piece, but I hope that it raises some good questions that have received too little attention in the literature to which our honorand has contributed so substantially.

NOTES

1. I thank Chris Brooke, Dan Butt, Simon Caney, Cécile Fabre, Keith Hyams, David Miller, Mike Otsuka, Zosia Stemplowska, Larry Temkin, and Peter Vallentyne for excellent criticisms of an earlier draft of this paper, and Arnold Zuboff for stimulating the production of the paper in the first place: see footnote 11 below.
2. Cohen 1977, reprinted with revisions in Shaw and Arthur 1978, and with further revisions as Cohen 1995: see this paper's bibliography. Page references below are to Cohen 1995.
3. The assumption is merely for the sake of simplicity. The present observations are robust across all criteria for characterizing the initial distribution as just.
4. The putatively undeniable premisses are (i) and (iii) and (v). (ii), being a postulate, is neither deniable nor undeniable.
5. Van der Veen and Van Parijs acknowledge (1985, 73–74) that the entitlement component in a theory may be "strong" or "weak", but that does not prejudice the significance for my purposes of the truth that they expose. It is not clear from Nozick's words (see the quotation two paragraphs back) whether he means to conclude something stronger than the van der Veen/Van Parijs conclusion: does he mean by his words that "those holding alternative conceptions" must (comprehensively) abandon those conceptions, or merely, as the Benelux (or Bene) authors state, that they must make some *room* for entitlement within their (thus revised) conceptions?
6. Note that what I here call "legitimacy" is not legitimacy in the usual sense: "legitimacy" is simply the most (though imperfectly) suitable single word I could think of to denote what I mean. Legitimacy is, standardly, the right to exercise political power, and that is not the same thing as a universal absence of the right to complain against its exercise, or, *a fortiori*, against anything else. (The fact that there is no single word that means "universal

absence of a right to complain" has, of course, no effect on anything argued here.)

7. Private communication, December 2007.
8. Except in certain specific ways, such as by outcompeting them and thereby driving them out of business, but that qualification is beside the point here.
9. Which here, recall, is the property something has when no one has a just complaint against it. (It might be objected that fairness in an initial distribution does not suffice for legitimacy. For suppose that an unequal distribution that is strongly (or even weakly) Pareto-superior to the given fair and equal one is feasible: those who fail to obtain what they would in that Pareto-superior distribution might be thought to have a just grievance against the given fair distribution. If you agree with that objection, you can read "fairness" in the sentence in the text, and in comparable occurrences in this piece, as: fairness that is not Pareto-inferior to some other feasible initial distribution.)
10. See Lippert-Rasmussen 1999, especially 482–87; Lippert-Rasmussen 2001; Otsuka 2002; and Otsuka 2004.
11. Which was originally presented to me by Arnold Zuboff, but the elaborations of it here, are, for better or worse, mine.
12. Ironically or otherwise, the example is a modified version of Dworkin's famous Sarah example: see Dworkin 1981, 202–05.
13. Absent an initial just situation, unanimity might merely reflect unjustly differential bargaining power: the highwayman and I are unanimous that I will hand over the money.
14. Though not, perhaps, in the slavery example: being a liberal rather than a libertarian, Dworkin might seek to impugn that outcome.
15. One might question whether it suffices for a gamble to be fair that it is 50-50. Perhaps a 60-40 gamble might be considered fair when the parties to it are appropriately differentially risk-averse. But I need no doctrine of what constitutes a fair gamble here. I need just the concept of a fair gamble, and, in the given circumstances, a 50-50 gamble qualifies as fair because A and B are fully similar.
16. Or, if an "imposed gamble" is an oxymoron, an imposed 50-50 risk procedure.
17. The outcome of an imposed 50-50 gamble is (arguably, but subject to what is said in footnote 15 above) just (or as just as things can be) when the good is indivisible. But we may nevertheless regard that outcome as merely the best available second-best with regard to justice.
18. And therefore not merely by the standard of market happenstance.
19. I anonymize her/him because she/he withdrew from the claim when she/he had read a draft of this section.
20. In his article on "Inequality" (Temkin 1986) Larry Temkin wrote: "I believe egalitarians have the deep and (for them) compelling view that it is a bad thing—unjust and unfair—for some to be worse off than others through no fault of their own" (101). In my Cohen 1989 I broadened the idea, saying that inequalities are unjust when they reflect no fault or *choice* on the part of the relevant agents: "choice" is broader than fault, which is, roughly, at any rate in this context, faultful choosing. (See *ibid.*, 916 for a relevant case of choice that isn't a case of fault.) In his book on *Inequality* Temkin repeats the shorter "Inequality" formulation, but he adds a footnote in which he says that he shall mean, by "through no fault of their own", "through no fault or choice of their own" (Temkin 1993, 13).
21. A tabulation of the four logically possible views may be useful:

	Gambling Case outcome	Unanimity Case outcome
Nozick/Dworkin	Just	Just
Zuboff	Not Just	Not Just
Otsuka	Just	Not Just
Anonymous	Not Just	Just

22. Perhaps, indeed, the same someone who thinks that transforming Nozick's claims about justice into ones about legitimacy gives him everything that he wants.
23. Compare my comments on "the slavery gamble", at Cohen 1995, 47.
24. Compare Nozick's speculation about bequest in Nozick 1989, 30–31.
25. See section 1 of this paper.

BIBLIOGRAPHY

Cohen, G. A. 1977. "Robert Nozick and Wilt Chamberlain: How Patterns Preserve Liberty". 11 *Erkenntnis* 5–23. Reprinted in Shaw and Arthur 1978. Reprinted with revisions in Cohen 1995.

Cohen, G. A. 1989. "On the Currency of Egalitarian Justice". 99 *Ethics* 906–944.

Cohen, G. A. 1995. "Robert Nozick and Wilt Chamberlain: How Patterns Preserve Liberty". In *Self-Ownership, Freedom, and Equality*. Oxford: Oxford University Press.

Cohen, G. A. 2008. *Rescuing Justice and Equality*. Cambridge, MA: Harvard University Press.

Dworkin, Ronald. 1981. "Is There a Right to Pornography?" 1 *Oxford Journal of Legal Studies* 177–212.

Dworkin, Ronald. 2000. *Sovereign Virtue*. Cambridge, MA: Harvard University Press.

Lippert-Rasmussen, Kasper. 1999. "Arneson on Equality of Opportunity for Welfare". 7 *Journal of Political Philosophy* 478–487.

Lippert-Rasmussen, Kasper. 2001. "Egalitarianism, Option Luck, and Responsibility". 111 *Ethics* 548–579.

Morrison, Toni. 1987. *Beloved*. London: Picador.

Nozick, Robert. 1974. *Anarchy, State, and Utopia*. New York: Basic Books.

Nozick, Robert. 1989. *The Examined Life*. New York: Simon and Schuster.

Otsuka, Michael. 2002. "Luck, Insurance, and Equality". 113 *Ethics* 40–54.

Otsuka, Michael. 2004. "Equality, Ambition, and Insurance". *Proceedings of the Aristotelian Society, Supplementary Volume* 151–166.

Plekhanov, George. 1956. *The Development of the Monist View of History*. Moscow: Foreign Languages Publishing House.

Shaw, William and Arthur, John (eds). 1978. *Justice and Economic Distribution*. Englewood Cliffs, NJ: Prentice Hall.

Steiner, Hillel. 1974. "The Natural Right to Equal Freedom". 83 *Mind* 194–210.

Steiner, Hillel. 1977. "The Natural Right to the Means of Production". 27 *Philosophical Quarterly* 41–49.

Steiner, Hillel. 1977. "The Structure of a Set of Compossible Rights". 74 *Journal of Philosophy* 767–775.

Temkin, Larry. 1986. "Inequality". 15 *Philosophy and Public Affairs* 99–121.

Temkin, Larry. 1993. *Inequality*. Oxford: Oxford University Press.

Van der Veen, Robert and Van Parijs, Philippe. 1985. "Entitlement Theories of Justice: Nozick and Beyond." 1 *Economics and Philosophy* 69–81.

2 On the Value of Distributional Equality

Joseph Raz

Hillel Steiner's work never fails to inspire and challenge, and this is true even of those who, like me, take issue with his views. We disagree about two pillars of much political theorising: liberty and equality. Hillel affirms, and I dispute, the intrinsic value of pure negative liberty and of its equal distribution. He argued against my view and I replied briefly before.[1] The following pages deal with only one of these issues. They offer an argument against the intrinsic value of distributive equality in sections 3 and 4, to which the preceding sections serve as an introduction.

1. THE VALUE OF EQUALITY: CLARIFICATIONS

Like all aspirational[2] values and ideals which have taken root in human history and acquired a wide following, the characterisation of the value or ideal of equality, or of egalitarian principles, is fluid. This is partly because the reasons which led many to a belief in equality are diverse. And partly because as some versions of these beliefs come under criticism new versions, designed to by-pass the criticism, emerge. This process of refinement and improvement means that any hope of dealing a knock-out blow to belief in the egalitarian ideal are chimerical. No such aim is entertained for this essay. For that reason I make no attempt to provide a taxonomy of egalitarian positions, and present no arguments against each one of them. My aim is to address the core view—however crudely understood—which forms one of the two main ideals of equality, the one I refer to as distributional equality.

When arguing against the validity of an ideal with deep historical roots and considerable following one needs not only to provide reasons to reject the ideal, but also to explain why, given its invalidity, it is so popular. The hold belief in the ideal has on people suggests that there is something to it. Perhaps it is valid after all. To establish that it is not we need to understand why its validity appears plausible. We may be prone to some reasoning fallacy leading us to endorse the ideal. But more often than not the explanation lies elsewhere. Something of real value is mistaken for the invalid ideal. I will gesture towards such an explanation below. But in the main the explanation of error is not explored here. The focus is on reasons suggesting that there is no intrinsic value in equality.[3]

We need to narrow down the issue: I will consider only the non-instrumental, or, as I shall refer to it, the intrinsic, value of equality. There is no doubt that some equalities are sometimes instrumentally valuable, that they are useful for securing some valuable outcomes, or for avoiding bad ones. Often debates about the value of equality are debates about whether equality in the distribution of this or that has beneficial or adverse consequences. But no such concerns will engage us here.[4]

As mentioned this essay deals with distributive equality, that is, with the possibility that there are some things such that there is intrinsic value in distributing them equally. In the history of the political and theoretical uses of 'equality' distributive equality dominates. But there is another claim: that certain creatures (people, citizens, all animals, etc.) should be treated equally. I will not consider the value of equal treatment.

Some writers suggest that one of these principles or ideals leads to the other, for example that the value of some form of distributive equality derives from the value of, or some principle of, equality of treatment. I will not consider such claims. If distributive equality is not intrinsically valuable then it has no intrinsic value deriving from the value of equality of treatment, though it may derive some instrumental value in that way.

Any principle of distribution yields, when implemented or conformed to, some pattern or other of distributive equality. That is, any principle of distribution has as a by-product some form of equal distribution. For example, think of a distribution of food resources which leaves no one hungry (even though different people are given different kinds and quantities of food). That distribution is also one in which every person is equal to any other in being free of hunger. Or think of a distribution of educational resources and opportunities by which everyone can develop their abilities[5] and skills to their maximum potential. That distribution, though it allocates different educational resources and opportunities to different people, is also one in which every person is equal to any other person in being able to develop his or her abilities to their maximum potential.

Claims that such distributions are good or justified are sometimes expressed as statements about equality: it is valuable that everyone should be equally free from hunger, or that everyone should be equally able to develop his or her potential. At other times some such views are condemned as inegalitarian. Thus, a distribution of educational resources and opportunities by abilities is sometimes condemned as elitist. These terminological variations and their rhetorical roots are of no concern to us here. What matters is that the factor which made the distribution good or valuable was not that it was equal, but that it avoided hunger, or that it avoided the inevitability of undeveloped abilities. How do I know that? Of course, it is not my claim that there cannot be anyone who would think that equality is all that matters in these cases. Rather, I speculate that those who think that these two distributions are intrinsically good are likely to think that they are good for two different reasons (one to do with hunger, the other with being able to develop one's abilities[6]) rather than because they maximise equality.

This diagnosis of their view will be refuted or confirmed by their reaction to the following two cases: In the first case we know that at some future time Jane will be the only person alive. We can do something which will make sure that she will not be hungry. In the second case we know that at some future time both Jane and John, but no one else, will be alive. Whatever we do John will not be hungry. There is something we can do which will make sure that Jane is not hungry. In this second case we can act in order to achieve equality (in freedom from hunger), but we cannot do so in the first case, in which no distribution can be either equal or unequal. The good of avoiding hunger is achievable in both. Those who think that the reason to protect Jane from hunger in the first case is the same as the reason to protect her from hunger in the second case show in that that they take the avoidance of hunger rather than equality as the good of the distribution. So far as they are concerned the equality produced in successfully protecting people from hunger (i.e. that they are all equally protected) is neither here nor there. What matters is that they are all protected from hunger. The views of such people are of no interest to us when we explore the intrinsic value of equality. They do not endorse that value.

Egalitarians are people who believe in the intrinsic value of distributional equality of some good(s) and who take this value to be of considerable importance. Necessarily, egalitarians are value pluralists. It makes no sense to believe in the equality of what is itself of no value, say the number of stars visible from a position 10 miles to the east of one's current situation. If the distributive equality of anything is intrinsically valuable it must be something which is itself of value (or disvalue) or something necessarily related to what is intrinsically valuable. Hence egalitarians believe that there is at least one other intrinsic value besides equality. It could be liberty, well-being, resources, or whatever. Their belief in the importance of the intrinsic value of equality consists in believing that obtaining equality is worth-while even if it means a significantly lower level of realisation or instantiation of other values. There is no way of putting a precise lower limit to the importance assigned to equality by anyone who could be considered egalitarian, and no need to do so.

Needless to say egalitarianism is harder to establish and easier to refute than the thesis that some equality has intrinsic distributional value. In what follows I will argue that equality does not have intrinsic distributional value. Given that the argument falls short of being a proof it is worth bearing in mind that whatever its force against the value of equality, it is likely to have—if at all plausible—an even greater force against egalitarianism. Given that for the most part, only egalitarians believe in the intrinsic value of equality, I will refer to any believer in the intrinsic distributional value of equality as egalitarian.

2. THE LEVELLING DOWN OBJECTION

A popular argument against the value of equality, now increasingly recognised to be flawed, is known as the levelling down objection. I will consider it using a variant of the previous example:

> John & Jane: Suppose that it would be good if people were equal in their possession of some good, say food. Suppose further that there are two people, Jane and John, who are not so equal, Jane having more food than John.

There are at least two ways of establishing equality of food between them. One can deprive Jane of the amount of food she has more than John, or give John that amount of food (for present purposes I will ignore the possibility of splitting the difference between them). So far as equality goes there is nothing to choose between these two ways of securing it. Practicalities aside, they are equally good or acceptable ways of achieving equality. This symmetry appears to many to be implausible. The indifference between achieving equality by making people who are better off worse off and making people who are worse off better off appears counter-intuitive. Is not, they say, the whole point of equality to improve the lot of the deprived and the dispossessed?

Supporters of equality have, however, pointed out that the objection is invalid. It may reveal, of course, that the objectors do not really believe in the value of equality. They may simply believe in the value of alleviating poverty and deprivation. So do I, but that belief does not require commitment to the intrinsic value of distributive equality, though current political rhetoric often obscures this point. The appeal of the levelling down objection may therefore serve to separate the egalitarians from others who are sometimes confused with them. However, as an objection against the egalitarians it will not do.

Were it valid it would undermine any pluralistic view of values.[7] To see why this is so, think of any two independent intrinsic values of your choice. I will take autonomy and a sense of physical well-being as examples. I will assume that it is good to enjoy autonomy to a proper degree—it does not matter what that is. So far as the value of autonomy is concerned it does not matter if one reaches that degree by diminishing one's sense of physical well-being, or without such decline in one's sense of well-being. Similarly, in so far as one's sense of physical well-being is concerned it does not matter if one achieves it through sacrificing a degree of autonomy or without such sacrifice. These points are the precise analogues of the levelling down objection: in so far as one is concerned exclusively with achieving equality it makes no difference whether it is achieved at the expense of some other value or not. This observation is close to a tautology. However, what matters, according to all value pluralists, including egalitarians, is the instantiation or realisation of all the values there are. Egalitarians believe that equality is among them, but given that it is not alone, their overall view (the view which takes account of all the values) is asymmetric: regarding any value it is better to realise it without compromising the realisation of any other values rather than in ways which do compromise their realisation.

3. IS EQUALITY GOOD FOR PEOPLE?

The appeal of the levelling down objection may be due to failing to distinguish between it and another, more promising criticism of egalitarianism. The striking feature of egalitarianism which attracts the levelling-down objection is that according to it things are better if Jane is deprived of some of her food resources (the amount required to bring her food resources level with John's), and nothing else changes. In rebuttal it is pointed out that the premises are false. It is not true that nothing else changes. There is an additional, consequential, change, namely that equality is established. The objection fails. But, as we saw, it fails for an additional reason as well. Even if the premises were true the conclusion ('things are better . . .') does not follow from the premises (that depriving Jane of that amount of food will establish equality). The premises only show that things will be better regarding equality. It does not follow that they will be better overall.

Some of the objectors may persist and protest that things cannot be better in any respect if one person is worse off and no one is better off. This claim does not vindicate the levelling down objection in any of the forms it is commonly given. But it reveals a common assumption which is not always noticed by those who share it. At its crudest it is the assumption that values are subservient to human interests. If realising or instantiating any putative value benefits no one, then that putative value is not a value. I'll refer to that thought as the crude and simple version of the Person-affecting condition.

The objector points to the situation in which equality is established by levelling down, i.e. by adversely affecting someone without benefiting anyone, as proof that equality fails to meet the person-affecting condition and is therefore of no value. I will call this the person-affecting objection. Is it sound? Egalitarians may wish to pursue at least two avenues of reply. First, they may wish to deny that equality does not benefit people. Second, they may wish to reject the person-affecting condition.

Given its historical and political background, egalitarianism may well wish to pursue the first avenue even if the person-affecting condition is false. Even if there are values which cannot benefit people, the view that equality is among them would surprise and disappoint most egalitarians, as the ethos of egalitarianism is deeply humanist, that is concerned with the fortunes of people. Be that as it may, does equality benefit people?

The question is not whether realisation of equality is associated with other changes which benefit people. The question is whether equality itself benefits people. That is why the arguments turn on levelling down. Securing equality between Jane and John by providing the latter with more food is an example of a case in which improving the lot of a person also happens to realise equality. But it is not the equality which improves his lot. It is the extra food. And the food is not necessary for the realisation of equality. Equality can be realised by denying Jane some of the food she has and wasting it. Hence the argument that equality itself does not benefit people, that it is indifferent to their fate. It violates the person-affecting condition.

But have not the objectors been looking in the wrong place? If you consider the food benefits for people then obviously equality itself does not benefit them, only food provides a food-benefit. We need to ignore the coincidental benefits (where they exist) and ask whether equality itself is a benefit. How can it be? One line of thought is to draw an analogy with other 'environmental' benefits, as I will call benefits which consist in nothing more than living in a certain environment, e.g. in a beautiful mountainous valley. Just living there is a benefit. By and large such environmental benefits are recognised by people. Even those who prefer living in a big city with all its social and cultural amenities recognise that those who would rather live in the mountainous valley gain something which they lack. Nor is the benefit exhausted by the opportunities the mountain provides: opportunities to climb the peaks, to watch the birds, etc. Just living in those surroundings is of value.

So is life in a world in which distributional equality obtains a benefit to its inhabitants in a similar way? It may be helpful here to consider another example: Galaxy: Imagine that a state of ideal equality prevails on our planet. However, there is another planet, in a galaxy too remote for us to interact with, where there are human beings living in conditions of ideal equality with each other, but whose conditions are not equal to those of people on planet earth, not equal in the respect in which equality is a good thing. The people on either planet do not know of the existence of the other, nor can they find out (given the laws of nature). Bertie is one of those people. He lives on earth.

The question is: Would Bertie benefit if the conditions of the people on the other planet changed and became equal to the conditions of his life (and that of other people on earth)? If he would benefit then equality is not an environmental value. It is of the nature of the latter that one benefits from the valuable condition (from the instantiation of the value) only if one is aware of the facts which constitute that condition. One need not have the concepts MOUNTAIN, VALLEY, FRESH AIR, NATURAL BEAUTY and the like to benefit from living in a mountainous valley. But one has to be aware of the fact that one lives in a mountainous valley. Moreover, 'the awareness' cannot consist merely in believing, knowing or remembering that those facts obtain. It would have to be linked to perceptual and sensual awareness of the relevant valuable features of the environment. Two considerations explain these points.

First, had one benefited from living in certain conditions merely in virtue of believing them to be valuable then one could create values by believing that they exist, but that is highly implausible. We need not deny that beliefs can have a certain placebo effect, namely that (false) belief that one lives in good conditions may well make one happy, or have some other generally desirable psychological effects. Such phenomena do not, however, make one's beliefs in values self-verifying in any way.

Second, the explanation of the way we benefit from intrinsic values which are environmental in character is that they combine two features. As with other intrinsic values we benefit from them by experiencing their presence. Unlike other intrinsic values our experience of environmental values need not be through action, or activity, and need not impose on our attention. It need not impede us from engaging in any other actions, including mental acts. Sometimes we have more intensive experiences, as when contemplating the landscape, a contemplation which involves activities, absorbs our energies and attention, and precludes some other activities and experiences. But this need not be the case. The mark of environmental values is that the experience can be subliminal and leave us completely free to engage with any activities open to us.

Back to Galaxy. If Bertie benefits from the equality which came to reign in the world it is not because he experiences it. So if establishing equality benefits him that is because the value of equality can benefit people in other ways as well. I do not know of any explanation of the way equality with the remote planet can benefit people which would apply to Bertie. I will therefore assume that it does not.

It does not follow, however, that equality is not an environmental value. Think of beautiful landscapes again. There may be beautiful landscapes on some uninhabited planets. They are still beautiful even though they never did, nor ever will, benefit anyone. In general the value of anything of value does not disappear when it does not benefit anyone. *War and Peace* would remain a good novel even if people were to read it no more, and forget that it exists. The person-affecting condition does not stipulate that every instance of a value actually benefits someone or other. It merely states that:

If V is a value (a value property) then it is possible for some of its instantiations to benefit people.

One aspect of the rationale for the person-affecting condition should be noted here. Insisting on the condition implies that in some, yet to be explained, way the point of intrinsic values is that people should relate to them in appropriate ways. Values provide reasons, and, metaphorically speaking, they are unfulfilled or wasted if those reasons are not conformed to. Our current concern is that while any instantiation of a value is an instantiation of a value regardless of whether or not anyone can benefit by it, the stringency or importance of the reasons we may have to realise the value on a particular occasion, or to preserve its instances, will depend on the benefit it brings to people. Therefore, while possibly the equality of the conditions of people on Earth and on the remote planet is valuable, the person-affecting condition implies that there is little reason to bring it about or preserve it if it already exists, as this particular instantiation of equality cannot benefit anyone.

But the question remains whether under some circumstances living in conditions of equality benefits people, and I will now assume that if it does that is due to their experiences of equality, or of the egalitarian aspect of life in conditions of equality. But what is that experience? The problem with Galaxy is not merely that Bertie does not know of the remote planet, but that even if he did its existence is unlikely to yield any relevant experience of either equality or inequality. He may be pleased or displeased to know of the inequality and the subsequent equality in conditions of life between Earth and that planet, but that is not enough to establish that equality meets the person-affecting condition. Perhaps the egalitarian experience relates to the experience of living in a community in which equality prevails. I do not mean a particularly small or cohesive community. Any social environment living in which is intrinsically meaningful (for good or ill) will do.

There are two difficulties in understanding the intrinsic value of equality in this way, that is, understanding it as a value from which people who live in societies in which equality prevails benefit through experiencing the egalitarian character of these societies. First, this understanding limits the value of equality. It means that the intrinsic value of distributive equality provides very little reason, if any, to establish distributive equality among people who do not share a community. Second, it is difficult to identify any experience of living in egalitarian communities which consists in experiencing their egalitarian character (on analogy with experiencing life in the woods or the mountains).

Arguably distributional equality is a precondition of various desirable effects. Perhaps without it conflict within communities is inevitable. Perhaps without it people are unlikely to be infused with concern for all, and would not pursue the common good as they ought to. But while, if sound, arguments of this kind would establish reasons for distributional equality, they would not establish its intrinsic value. All they can do is establish its value as a precondition for achieving other things of value, a value which is a form of, or analogous with, instrumental value.

4. THE PERSON-AFFECTING CONDITION

I have no conclusive argument to show that distributional equality cannot benefit people non-instrumentally. The previous reflections indicate the difficulty in understanding how it could benefit people, except through its consequences or through being a precondition of something desirable, or as a result of people believing in its value. So perhaps it does not benefit people. Does that show that it is not intrinsically valuable? Is the person-affecting condition true?

There is a strong presumptive case for it. It is in the way we argue for or against the intrinsic value of many things. Two parallel lines of argument seem to prevail. We argue by spelling out, specifying, the value. We specify what makes a friendship good, or what makes a novel good, or a poem, or a party, or a walking holiday, and so on. At the same time, often simultaneously, we relate that value to a wider context which brings out why it has value. In that context we typically describe the way what is allegedly of value benefits people who engage with it appropriately. We describe how a good friendship enriches the life of the friends, how reading (or writing) a good novel or poem with understanding is rewarding or enriching, how enjoyable participating in a good party or going on a good walking holiday would be, and so on. Furthermore, it is difficult to make sense of the claim that values, some values, are entirely independent of the possibility of human engagement with them, independent of any potential to benefit people. Outside a religious context it is difficult to see how that can be.

Two objections stand in the way. First, there are values or putative values, other than equality, which also violate the person-affecting condition. For example, the value of retribution: meting out retribution does not benefit anyone. As with equality so with retribution, some argue that in fact meting out retribution does benefit the people who are so punished. But it is not clear how they can non-instrumentally benefit by their punishment, and I will assume that they do not. Yet the force of this counter-example is not clear. It is at least as plausible to deny the intrinsic value of retribution as to deny the intrinsic value of equality. The incompatibility of belief in the value of retribution and belief in the person-affecting condition is as likely to serve as (part of) an argument against retribution as against the person-affecting condition. Are there more secure counter-examples? Is the value of human beings a counter-example? My earlier observation that 'the point of intrinsic values is that people should relate to them in appropriate ways' seems not to apply to the value—often referred to as the 'dignity' or 'the moral worth'—of people. Their value does not depend on their existence being of possible benefit to others.

This observation is sound, but does not constitute an objection to the person-affecting condition. It is true that the value of persons does not depend on the benefit their existence or their actions or attitudes may render to others. It is often observed that the reason we have to protect a human life does not depend on the benefit the person whose life is in question renders or is likely to render to others. This may be an exaggeration. In conflict, when one has to choose whom to protect or save and it is impossible to protect all those who are at risk, the value of people to others, the benefit they render or are likely to render to them, may well determine the choice. Yet the stringency or importance of the reason to protect the life of a person does not dwindle to nothing or near nothing if the person is unlikely to benefit others. Arguably the benefit to others is relevant only when the value of people is neutralised, as when the choice is between two lives, but does not affect the stringency of reasons generated by the value of people in any other context. This fact contrasts with the reasons provided by intrinsic goods, which, as we saw when considering Galaxy, does dwindle to nothing or near nothing when they can do no good to anyone.

All that having been said, the (non-instrumental) value of persons does meet the person-affecting condition simply because human relations and interactions can be of benefit to those involved. Where my earlier statement was wrong is in overlooking the difference between two kinds of non-instrumental values (both meeting the person-affecting condition). There are the familiar intrinsic values (such as autonomy, justice, and the various valuable objects—good paintings, novels, etc.—and activities—enjoyable partying, etc.) and there is the value of creatures like persons who are valuable in themselves (who possess 'moral worth'). The person-affecting condition asserts that only what can benefit those who are of value in themselves can be of value. The condition is met by anything valuable, whether its value is instrumental or intrinsic or whether it is of value in itself. The rationale for this tripartite division, though hard to state precisely, is fairly evident. Instrumental goods are subservient, their 'point' is to secure what is of intrinsic value and of value in itself. The 'point' of what is of intrinsic value is in benefiting persons, or other creatures of value in themselves. We say of people and certain other animals that they are of value in themselves precisely because their existence is of value independently of any service to anything else, even though people and other animals can also benefit from interacting with one another, can also be of benefit to others.

This leads to the second objection. The person-affecting condition stipulates that what is of value must be capable of benefiting people. The previous paragraphs show that rather than referring to people it should refer to anyone and anything that is valuable in itself. Let us accept this emendation. More problematic is the reliance on the idea of benefiting people. It suggests that what is good for people is independent of values, and intrinsic values are values because they are of benefit for people in that value-independent sense. That seems to be an incoherent view. Roughly speaking, we benefit from an event or an action when it facilitates acting as we have sufficient reason to act, or when we do so act, provided the action does not disrupt our long term plans and commitments.

This, says the objection, means that the person-affecting condition does not rule out any putative value. If something is of value then people have reasons to engage with it (read it if it is a novel, go to it if it is a party, etc.), and to protect its existence. And if it provides reasons then it is plausible that some conditions could exist in which conforming to those reasons will not disrupt some people's long term plans and commitments. Therefore so far as the person-affecting condition goes any claim that something is of value is self-verifying. The objection fails for it misconstrues the person-affecting condition. If possessing a certain property makes its possessor valuable to some degree there must be an explanation of why it is so, how possessing the property makes its possessor valuable. The person-affecting condition stipulates that that explanation must include an explanation of how what possesses that property could benefit people. A proposed explanation of the value of anything which does not explain how it could benefit people (or others of value in themselves) fails.

Applied to equality the condition says that equality is of intrinsic value only if it can benefit people, and that condition is not toothless. In fact, the previous section has established that equality fails this test, and can therefore have no intrinsic value.

NOTES

1. Steiner 2003, 119. For a brief reply see Raz 2003, 264–5.
2. I use 'aspirational' to indicate that people have taken them to be values or ideals and aspired to see them realised, without committing on whether or not they truly were values or ideals.
3. For more by way of explanation of the error see Raz 1986, chapter 9. Various writings sympathetic to the ideal of equality also constitute explanations of what may motivate belief in the intrinsic value of distributive equality, without justifying such beliefs. See Marmor 2003, 127.
4. The instrumental will be understood broadly, to include not only the causes, but also necessary conditions for a result, in the way that the existence of gravity on our planet is a precondition for the existence of life on it.
5. The statement applies non-vacuously only to those abilities which can develop, and whose development can be affected by educational opportunities and resources.
6. This need not deny that the same people will think that the two intrinsic goods are constituents of one more general good, such as happiness.
7. Egalitarians are by necessity pluralists about value. According to them there is value only in the distribution of something which is in itself of (some) intrinsic value, that is something whose value is independent of equality. The full proof of this is somewhat complex and tiresome. The beginning of the proof is to note that there is no value in the equal distribution of something which is itself neither good nor bad, like the number of hairs to be found on one's shirt at any given time. To be plausible at all the value of equality must relate to the distribution of items like food, opportunities for valuable activities, freedom, and other things of value independently of their distribution.

BIBLIOGRAPHY

Marmor, A. 2003. 'The Intrinsic Value of Economic Equality'. In L.H. Meyer, S.L. Paulson, T.W. Pogge (eds.), *Rights, Culture & the Law*, Oxford: Oxford University Press.

Raz, J. 2003. 'Comments and Responses'. In L.H. Meyer, S.L. Paulson, T.W. Pogge (eds.), *Rights, Culture & the Law*, Oxford: Oxford University Press.
Raz, J. 1986. *The Morality of Freedom*. Oxford: Oxford University Press.
Steiner, H. 2003. 'Equality, Incommensurability, and Rights'. In L.H. Meyer, S.L. Paulson, T.W. Pogge (eds.), *Rights, Culture & the Law*, Oxford: Oxford University Press.

3 Global Justice and Norms of Co-Operation

The 'Layers of Justice' View

Jonathan Wolff

Theorists of global justice confront an apparent dilemma. If citizens in the developed world have duties of (socio-economic) justice to those elsewhere on the globe, then it is supposed that the duties must be very extensive indeed, requiring the same concern to be shown for everyone on earth. Those who deny that global obligations are as extensive as domestic obligations seem therefore to have to concede that any obligations beyond borders must be based on charity, rather than justice. The assumption on which this dilemma is based is that 'justice is uniform'. In this paper I argue that such an assumption should be rejected in favour of the view that justice is relative to norms of co-operation. Consequently it is possible to develop a view of 'justice but not the same justice': the 'layers of justice' view.

1. THE DILEMMA OF GLOBAL JUSTICE

Do citizens of wealthy, developed, nations have duties to provide assistance in some form to impoverished citizens of poor countries? If so, what is the source of those duties, and what is their extent? Broadly, contributions to this debate are coloured by what they take to be, or at least treat as, their ground level assumption. At one end are those—often called cosmopolitans—who argue that we must start from assumptions about the universal moral equality of all individuals. It has sometimes seemed that an irresistible consequence of such an assumption is that, in principle, one's duties to all other human beings have the same basis, and as a consequence all duties of justice are as extensive as duties to our fellow citizens. Consequently, whatever principles society adopts for 'domestic justice' must also apply across the globe. So, for example, those who argue for the Difference Principle—that society should be so arranged as to maximise the wealth and income of the least advantaged—must, in consistency, apply it on a global scale, which entails a very radical redistribution indeed.

Some cosmopolitan theorists find this an acceptable, perhaps even welcome, consequence of their view (see, for example, Steiner 2005). Other political philosophers, however, find the idea of global distributive justice, modelled on their preferred theory of domestic justice, unacceptable (Rawls 1999, Nagel 2005). There are various reasons why this might be. There are, for example, technical questions such as whether a global principle of equality is meaningful: is there a suitable international metric of wealth and income, for example? But much more commonly the theory of global equality has been thought to be unacceptably demanding. This unacceptability could have numerous different sources. One is pragmatic. Some might feel that advocacy of global equality would be naïvely counterproductive (even if morally it is the correct view), for it is already hard enough to get people to take seriously claims of domestic distributive equality. Extending economic equality to the globe could be treated as a reductio ad aburdum, and hence, in order not to discredit one's arguments concerning domestic justice, it is necessary to find some way of resisting the spread of those principles to the global context. Alternatively, one could simply find it impossible to convince oneself that there are such extensive duties of justice, whether for reasons of justice or of feasibility. A further worry is that a programme of global redistribution to achieve equality is in some way patronising and paternalistic. Granted, there may be strong reasons for redistribution, but applying the same principles to the globe as one applies to one's own society undercuts the local autonomy and self-determination of peoples (see, for example, Bertram 2005).[1] Accordingly some theorists would wish to adjust their fundamental principles in ways that differentiate local and global duties.

One popular way of pursuing this more minimalist line is to argue that duties of justice only arise in a certain context, and that context is met in the domestic case but not in the global case. Strictly speaking, such theorists have argued, economic and social duties to those in other countries are not duties of justice. Perhaps they are duties of charity, or of humanity. This 'political' or 'nationalist' position allows the theorist to insist on stringent domestic duties of redistribution, but without also being committed to equally extensive duties of global redistribution (Rawls 1999, Nagel 2005).

Neither the cosmopolitan nor the political view seems particularly comfortable or attractive. Neither accords with what I take to be 'common sense global justice theory': that there are global duties of redistribution, based on principles of justice, not charity, but such duties are not as extensive as those of domestic justice. The question is whether such a view can be made out coherently. Both cosmopolitans and nationalists will presumably argue that such a view must be mistaken: cosmopolitans on the grounds that the duties of justice must be as extensive as domestic duties; nationalists on the grounds that the duties of redistribution cannot be duties of justice. Most likely, the central reason for objecting to the common sense middle view is that it conflicts with what we could call the assumption of 'the uniformity of justice'. This is the principle that the duties of justice are uniform, in the sense that they are equally demanding in respect of everyone to whom they apply. My duties of justice to my neighbour must, on this view, be the same as any such duties that are owed to someone over the other side of the globe. The cosmopolitan view accepts the assumption of the uniformity of justice and is thereby committed to extensive global duties. The nationalist also accepts the assumption of the uniformity of justice and consequently denies that one's obligations to distant peoples are obligations of justice. Hence the cosmopolitan and the nationalist must reject the 'differential global justice' view, if their own positions implicitly or explicitly are based on the assumption of the uniformity of justice. But could it be that we should instead reject the uniformity of justice?

In fact, there are at least two ways of making out a differential global justice view. One is to argue that while principles of justice are uniform, their consequences vary from situation to situation. It could, for example, be argued that justice requires sufficiency, but what counts as 'enough' varies from place to place (Bertram 2005). This is a cosmopolitan view, but we could call it 'weak cosmopolitanism, in contrast with 'strong cosmopolitanism' which suggests that duties are uniform as well as principles. Another way of rejecting uniformity of duties is theoretically more radical, arguing that principles of justice, as well as duties, are variable. This is the view I shall explore here: the 'layers of justice' view. (Mollendorf 2005 has defended a view of this type.)

In passing, it is worth noting that the substantive thesis that duties are variable has been implicitly accepted even by some thought to be in the cosmopolitan camp. Thomas Pogge quotes Rorty's attempt to impress on us how extensive the demands of global distributive equality would be, where Rorty argues that such redistribution would impoverish citizens of the currently wealthy nations to a point where they would no longer 'recognise themselves' or find their lives worth living. Pogge's answer is that it would only take a transfer of 1.2% of the gross national income of the wealthy nations to eradicate severe poverty worldwide (Pogge 2002, 7–8). This is a remarkable claim, and one that might even shame some people to action, but it hardly answers Rorty's argument, unless one thinks that the only duty of egalitarian distributive justice is to eradicate severe poverty. Rorty's point remains; achieving world equality would be almost unimaginably demanding for the rich. But if Pogge thinks he has answered Rorty, then it appears that he is assuming that the duties of global justice are less extensive than those of domestic justice. Hence he appears to adopt a 'layers of justice' view even if he is normally represented as a cosmopolitan. It is, of course, also possible that he is a weak cosmopolitan, asserting a single set of principles that are variable in their implications, but it is not the task of this paper to settle that question.

Before looking at the arguments for and against the uniformity of justice it would be helpful to consider some aspects of the scope of the question. We can distinguish at least three contexts in which questions of global justice arise. The first looks to past history; many of the world's poorest countries have in common that they were once colonial possessions of now much wealthier countries. Commonly, indigenous peoples were slaughtered on a mass scale, the best land was appropriated for settlers, and natural resources claimed and taken without payment.[2] This raises the 'backward looking' question of reparation or compensation (Lyons 1982).

A second domain in which questions of global justice emerge looks to the present rather than the past, that of what we can call 'transactional justice': justice in trade. Such a topic is an intense matter of international debate, involving questions of protectionism, dumping, loan terms, and other such matters. Here the point in question is whether international transactions are currently being conducted on fair terms, and if not, what is needed to rectify the situation (Risse 2007; Kurjanska and Risse 2008).

Finally, there is what we might think of the question of pure distributive justice. Imagine that there had been no historical injustice calling for possible compensation, and that no questions of fairness of transactions arise. Nevertheless, could it not be that questions of what we might think of as pure distributive justice still arise? This, to contrast with the past-looking perspective of compensation, and the present-looking perspective of fair trade, might be thought of as a future- looking perspective of pure distributive justice. Hence there could be a topic of distributive justice which is not at all corrective for past and present acts of injustice. However, given the history of the world, and its current practices, the three perspectives are entangled, in that facts about the past and present must strongly influence our thinking about a just future.

2. QUESTIONING THE 'UNIFORMITY OF JUSTICE'

As suggested above, the stark choice between strong cosmopolitanism and the political view of 'justice in one country' is a consequence of the assumption of the uniformity of justice. In its simple formulation, the assumption of the uniformity of justice runs up against an obvious counter-example. Consider discussion about redistribution within the European Union. Some states give more than they receive back, and arguments concerning the justice and injustice of various arrangements—the common agricultural policy, the U.K.'s rebate, the distribution of the 'social fund'—fly backwards and forwards. Yet the argument that if these discussions concern relations of justice then any principles to which appeal is made must be uniform with the conceptions of justice operating in each member state would seem highly implausible, and in any case, given that different norms of justice operate in different member states, would be impossible. Hence, it appears, these duties are not uniform, and it would be very implausible to suggest that they are duties of charity rather than justice.[3]

In response it could be said that duties of redistribution within the EU are not duties of justice, but rather the consequence of a pact for mutual advantage. Such a reply can be taken in more than one way. On one reading the operative concept in this response is *pact*; in the other it is *mutual advantage*. To take the latter first, such a response, even if based on a correct analysis, assumes that mutual advantage cannot be a source of norms of justice. This is an issue to which we shall return, and so I will suspend discussion of it. The 'pact' response assumes that duties between member states are essentially treaty obligations, and so the operative notion of justice is legal, rather than socio-economic. While reasonable in some circumstances, it appears that this analysis cannot explain the apparent application of questions of justice when the terms of membership of new states are under discussion. Furthermore, when considering the existence of long-established federal structures, as, for instance, the USA, it seems less plausible that questions of economic justice, and the redistribution of federal funds, insofar as that takes place, is the result of the interpretation of treaty obligations.

The example of federalism can, no doubt, be made consistent with both cosmopolitan and nationalist views.[4] Nevertheless it also appears consistent with the idea that there can be 'levels' of justice, and therefore, gives us reason not to dismiss such a possibility.

3. JUSTICE AND BACKGROUND NORMS

What sense, however, can we make of the idea of levels of justice? We can imagine easily enough how this would work on an institutional level. As Nagel illustrates the point, as a prelude to dismissing it:

> [E]ven if economic globalization does not trigger the full standards of social justice, it entails them in a modified form. In fact . . . there is a sliding scale of degrees of co-membership in a nested or sometimes overlapping set of governing institutions, of which the state is only the most salient . . . [W]e should conclude that there is a . . . spectrum of degrees of egalitarian justice that we owe to our fellow participants in these collective structures in proportion to our degrees of joint responsibility for and subjection to their authority. My relation of co-membership in the system of international trade with the Brazilian who grows my coffee or the Philippine worker who assembles my computer is weaker than my relation of co-membership in U.S. society with the Californian who picks my lettuce or the New Yorker who irons my shirts . . . One may even see an appeal to such a value in the call for standards of minimum compensation, fair labor practices, and protection of worker health and safety as conditions on international trade agreements—even if the real motivation behind it is protectionism against cheap third world labor. Perhaps such a theory of justice as a "continuous" function of degrees of collective responsibility could be worked out. It is in fact a natural suggestion, in light of the general theory that morality is multilayered.

Now, many, I think, will be attracted to this picture, yet it is a picture that Nagel himself rejects. His objection is:

> But I doubt that the rules of international trade rise to the level of collective action needed to trigger demands for justice, even in diluted form. The relation remains essentially one of bargaining, until a leap has been made to the creation of collectively authorized sovereign authority (Nagel 2005, 140–41).

His argument is that where the state, or a similar institution, does not exist, there is not justice, but simply bargaining. We do not ascend to 'real justice' until global sovereign authority exists. One can read this objection either as an intuitively plausible analysis which lends support to Nagel's position, or as tending towards the question-begging, assuming, first of all that bargaining for mutual advantage has nothing to do with justice, and second that until sovereignty exists there is no justice, which is Nagel's main thesis.

However, one can agree with Nagel that justice is relative to some background conditions without agreeing with the particular way in which he fleshes this out. It has become common to make a distinction between the thesis that justice is relative to institutions—Nagel's thesis—and that justice is relative to interaction. The official Rawlsian story, in fact, is that justice is relative to co-operation, which sounds like the interactional view, although, Nagel's version of Rawls somewhat incongruously presents him more like Hobbes in assuming that institutions of a particular type are necessary; states that can secure the conditions of background justice. While this is a plausible reading of Rawls, space is also open for alternative views. Nagel asserts several times that interaction without shared sovereignty is not sufficient to generate norms and duties of justice. Yet the argument seems hampered by a refusal to take seriously what seemed so plausible in the view that he wished to reject: that justice is somehow layered, and so we have duties of different 'thickness' to our fellow citizens and to the citizens of our trading partners.

Nagel's main argument, in fact appears to echo Rawls' response to libertarianism: justice requires a basic structure, especially to co-ordinate action and enforce rules, and only a state or similar sovereign institution can do this (Rawls, 1993 262–5). It is highly plausible that Rawlsian principles of justice do need a sovereign institution, for the actions of uncoordinated individuals are extremely unlikely to bring about distributions sanctioned by the difference principle, however good-willed individuals are. But if duties of global justice are less extensive than those of domestic justice, then it is less obvious that a basic structure co-ordinated by a state is necessary to achieve global justice. That is, if the Rawlsian argument is a practical one, rather than a conceptual one, everything depends on the content of the appropriate theory of justice. A more minimal theory possibly will not confront such serious problems of coordination.

4. JUSTICE AND NORMS OF CO-OPERATION

The idea that justice emerges under condition of interaction needs further exploration. Interaction is not a simple idea, and it comes in different forms. Elsewhere I have discussed this in terms of the thesis that justice is relative to norms of co-operation, and that just as norms of co-operation can differ, so too will norms of justice. My first attempt to consider this issue was in terms of an analysis of the principles of justice appropriate for the European Union,[5] and it is worth briefly revisiting this issue, as a way of approaching the issue of global justice.

In addressing the question of what principles of justice are appropriate for the European Union it seemed to me first of all we need a conception of the nature of the basis of the union; why have the countries of Europe decided to form themselves into a Union? Is Europe a collection of small and medium-size nations huddling together to protect themselves against a world then dominated by two 'super-powers', one to the east and one to the west? Or is the goal of an 'ever-closer union' genuinely part of the ideal, rather than mere ideology? It seemed plausible that the principles of justice appropriate for the European Union must depend first on how its members conceive its nature. It may also seem that if there is dispute about what type of entity the European Union is, then there is little surprise that there is also dispute about its appropriate norms of justice.

Putting the European Union to one side, let us consider a number of possible models of co-operation, and their associated norms of justice. Perhaps the weakest notion of co-operation is what is now known as the 'stag-hunt' game, after an example from Rousseau:

> Taught by experience that the love of well-being is the sole motive of human actions, [the savage] found himself in a position to distinguish the few cases, in which mutual interest might justify him in relying upon the assistance of his fellows . . . [and] joined in the same herd with them, or at most in some kind of loose association, that laid no restraint on its members, and lasted no longer than the transitory occasion that formed it . . .
>
> In this manner, men may have insensibly acquired some gross ideas of mutual undertakings, and of the advantages of fulfilling them: that is, just so far as their present and apparent interest was concerned: for they were perfect strangers to foresight, and were so far from troubling themselves about the distant future, that they hardly thought of the morrow. If a deer was to be taken, every one saw that, in order to succeed, he must abide faithfully by his post: but if a hare happened to come within the reach of any one of them, it is not to be doubted that he pursued it without scruple, and, having seized his prey, cared very little, if by so doing he caused his companions to miss theirs (Rousseau, 1973 86–7).

There is a clear question of whether this 'loose association' generates any principles of justice at all. Each person is free to come and go as they please, and co-operation lasts only for as long as each individual is prepared to co-operate. As soon as they see a prospect they prefer they can, and do, leave. Here they treat others as purely instrumental to their ends. Repeated interactions of this sort may lead to the develop of conventions concerning the division of the spoils, or how one should conduct oneself when on the hunt. But the key feature in Rousseau's example seems to be that the participants are not committed to each other in any way. Any savage who leaves to chase a rabbit has not violated obligations to others.

Over time, though, more committed models of co-operation are very likely to develop. Those who too readily chase a passing rabbit will find themselves not invited to future stag hunts. Hence those with the self-discipline to accept a short-term loss for the sake of a longer-term gain will be rewarded. This generates the next model; co-operation for enlightened self-interest, or justice as mutual advantage. If everyone went their separate ways, they would achieve modest benefits. However with the continued co-operation of others, they can each do better. A surplus is possible, compared to independent action. Justice then is a matter of working out rules for the division of the benefit provided by co-operation.

This is the idea of justice as a mutual advantage; a type of bargain, in which those with the greatest bargaining power will, as a matter of justice (according to this theory), receive most. Note that bargaining power is determined by how much one—or rather one's agreement—is needed by others, and not the extent of one's contribution. This we see, rather chillingly, illustrated in Hume's own application of his theory, worth quoting at length:

> Were there a species of creatures intermingled with men, which, though rational, were possessed of such inferior strength, both of body and mind, that they were incapable of all resistance, and could never, upon the highest provocation, make us feel the effects of their resentment; the necessary consequence, I think, is that we should be bound by the laws of humanity to give gentle usage to these creatures, but should not, properly speaking, lie under any restraint of justice with regard to them, nor could they possess any right or property, exclusive of such arbitrary lords. Our intercourse with them could not be called society, which supposes a degree of equality; but absolute command on the one side, and servile obedience on the other. Whatever we covet, they must instantly resign: Our permission is the only tenure, by which they hold their possessions: Our compassion and kindness the only check, by which they curb our lawless will: And as no inconvenience ever results from the exercise of a power, so firmly established in nature, the restraints of justice and property, being totally USELESS, would never have place in so unequal a confederacy.

> This is plainly the situation of men, with regard to animals; and how far these may be said to possess reason, I leave it to others to determine. The great superiority of civilized Europeans above barbarous Indians, tempted us to imagine ourselves on the same footing with regard to them, and made us throw off all restraints of justice, and even of humanity, in our treatment of them. In many nations, the female sex are reduced to like slavery, and are rendered incapable of all property, in opposition to their lordly masters. But though the males, when united, have in all countries bodily force sufficient to maintain this severe tyranny, yet such are the insinuation, address, and charms of their fair companions, that women are commonly able to break the confederacy, and share with the other sex in all the rights and privileges of society (Hume 1975, 190–91).

The logic of Hume's position is that if others have nothing to offer us, or what they have we can take from them independently of what they decide or want, then we have no duties of justice, strictly speaking, towards them. If there is no point to making a bargain, or no need to do so, then there is no justice. Hume can allow that we have moral duties of humanity in such cases, but not of justice.

Hume's argument appears to be, then, that if the stronger party can get what it wants from others, without their co-operation, then there are no norms of justice by which the stronger party's behaviour can be criticized. As Hume himself implies, this sounds more like colonialism than like global justice. Yet on the basis of the theory of mutual advantage such things as colonialism can be criticised in the following terms: if one of the parties is made worse off by interaction than they would have been without it, then it has not even reached the level of mutual advantage and must be an example of fraud, theft or force.[6]

The obvious problem with the idea of justice as mutual advantage is that it does not rule out the possibility of the stronger party using their bargaining advantage to reap virtually the entire surplus. There are, of course, many historical examples of such arrangements: such as the wage rates of workers in early capitalism, and international trade between rich and poor nations. Somehow, to achieve a more appropriate understanding of justice, the idea of 'proper reward' needs to be introduced, which generates the theory of justice known as 'justice as reciprocity' or 'justice as fair exchange'. On this view justice requires not so much bargaining as proportionality: those who make the greatest contribution should, in justice, receive the greatest return. It is easy to see that ideas of desert naturally fit into this picture, although as soon as this is said it will also be seen that there are many ways of fleshing this out. Does desert attach to effort? Or to achievement? Or to some hybrid of the two? Many theories are possible, but the general notion of justice as fair exchange has great popular resonance, underlying slogans such as 'a fair day's pay for a fair day's work'. It is this notion which makes the biblical 'parable of the workers in the field' so troubling (where the workers engaged near the end of the day were paid the same as those who had worked since the early morning), and in the international arena ideas of 'fair trade' so appealing.

Justice as reciprocity is an intuitively powerful theory of justice. Yet it shares a problem with justice as mutual advantage. Both leave out of account those who may have nothing to contribute or exchange. Consider those people who are so severely disabled that they are unable to make any productive contribution, or those living in under-developed countries who produce nothing that those in the developed world wish to purchase, and are now suffering in a famine. On the two views of justice discussed so far there is no obvious way of generating duties of justice in such cases. If under these circumstances such people are nevertheless owed assistance from those who are in a better position, then according to justice as mutual advantage and justice as impartiality these duties would have to be of charity rather than of justice. But to many this conclusion will seem wrong. If we want to maintain that others have a duty of justice to help those who cannot help themselves or offer anything in exchange for help, we shall need a different theory of justice.

The most prominent candidate is 'justice as impartiality', where justice requires taking everyone's situation and interests into account in determining what is to count as a just outcome. Here mechanisms for determining just outcomes take as their inspiration the thought 'how would you like it if you were in that situation?' So, for example, Adam Smith's device of the 'impartial spectator' (Smith 2002, Part 3, Ch. 3), or John Rawls's 'veil of ignorance' (Rawls 1971) require the decision-maker to take on the perspective of every individual involved or affected. To apply Rawls' model to the problems of international justice (something Rawls himself does not do, of course) would be to ask the question: 'what provisions for poor members of less-developed nations would you wish to see if you didn't know whether or not you were rich or poor?' Here a balance needs to be struck between the interests of those who are from poor countries and the interests of those who will have to work to provide things such people cannot provide for themselves. Some have argued that a global difference principle would be the result, or, perhaps, a theory of global sufficiency. Indeed it is this conclusion that takes us back to our starting point: once we recognize that the 'correct' theory of justice is justice as impartiality, then global justice becomes hugely demanding; so demanding as to be off-putting for all except the most enthusiastic cosmopolitans.

Can we draw back from this conclusion? We have, after all, introduced three different models of justice: mutual advantage, reciprocity and impartiality. Why should it be that we have to accept justice as impartiality? One answer is that both mutual advantage and reciprocity allow significant injustice, and therefore are flawed as theories of justice. Accordingly justice as impartiality is the best theory, and so, it may be argued, is the only one that should be applied. (This is the conclusion drawn in Barry 1995.) However it is not so clear that this is the right conclusion to draw. The lesson so far seems to be that theories of justice are relative to norms of co-operation, and as norms of co-operation vary so will appropriate theories of justice. Within a very close-knit society, in which each person feels the weight of mutual responsibility, the type of collective sharing of fate required by justice as impartiality might seem an appropriate demand of justice, meaning, for example, that those who cannot look after themselves have the right to very substantial assistance from others. But where co-operation is much more fleeting and instrumental, substantial demands, as a matter of justice, may seem very implausible.

We can see, therefore, that if principles of justice are relative to norms of co-operation, and norms of co-operation differ in the contexts of domestic and global justice, then some version of the layers of justice view follows quite naturally. It is, surely, not implausible that norms of co-operation do differ in these contexts, and I will say a little more about this shortly. I have also claimed that principles of justice are relative in this way, and illustrated such a thesis, although perhaps not yet explained it, which will be our next task, in attempting to establish the layers of justice view.

To get started, let us consider a simple case to illustrate the different norms of co-operation and their relative principles of justice. Consider a wealthy farmer who employs a farmhand. At first, the farmer might pay the lowest possible wage, perhaps a subsistence level. In this way the farmer is trying to exert the maximum possible personal benefit, consistent with the recognition that the other is a human being with some rights, and cannot, for example, be legitimately enslaved. Here, then, we have an arrangement based on bargaining and mutual advantage. The farmer might defend his wage policy by saying that the worker has agreed to it; that it is better for the worker to work at this wage than to be unemployed; and that he owes nothing to this particular worker except to abide by the terms of their contract.

As time goes on, however, the farmer might start to appreciate the productive benefit this particular worker brings, and raise her wages to reflect her contribution. This could be a purely self-interested market move, to prevent the worker leaving. Or, more interestingly, it could be that the farmer has understood that their relationship has moved on to a new level, where each must pay attention to the other's contribution and desert, and start to apply at least some norms of reciprocity. Now suppose they grow old together, and there comes a point where the worker is no longer productive, and in fact presents a net loss to the farmer. Nevertheless, the farmer may continue to employ the worker, at a loss, or offer her a pension, even if that was never part of the contractual relationship. One reason for this could be pure self-interest; to gain a reputation as a good employer. Or it could be pure sentimentality, an act of charity, or a feeling of desert: she has been a loyal and productive worker and deserves to be taken care of in her old age. But to move us on to new ground it could be that, after having known his worker for so long, the farmer may have come to the belief that there is no particular reason in justice that he is rich and she is poor, and that their fates could easily have been reversed. Hence, it is only just that he should make a sacrifice now to help her—not as an act of charity but out of a sense of justice. This would be to see their relationship as having generated norms that justify impartial principles of justice.

Yet in saying that norms of justice are relative to practices of co-operation I have not yet said very much about the nature of norms of co-operation, and, indeed, how they generate principles of justice. This is a highly complex question, but, to get started, we can see from the various examples given that a number of issues seem to be highly salient. Let me consider, in the first instance, two issues: First, to what degree is there a belief or expectation that the relationship will be continuing for some time? Second, to what degree does it generate dependency, perhaps by requiring at least one of the parties to decline other opportunities, or put themselves in a position where they are less able to take advantage of such opportunities?

Although it would be too much to hope for a deductive argument here, it seems plausible that a short-term arrangement that does not generate dependency will generate weaker norms of justice than a long-term relationship creating dependency. However, if the parties have equal bargaining strength—for example they operate in a genuinely free market on both sides—then agreements will generally approximate towards reward to productive contribution, which is to say that justice as mutual advantage will yield justice as reciprocity. The more difficult case is where a long-term arrangement (whether or not it creates dependency) is made between two parties with differential bargaining strength. Under such circumstances the weak party is ripe for exploitation, which consists in the use of the stronger party's superior bargaining power to obtain an agreement that is unfair to the weaker party. It seems that the appropriate norms in this context are norms of reciprocity. One test could be the restricted veil of ignorance: imagine you knew everything about the transaction, except which party you were to it. Would you be equally happy from each hypothetical side? If not, it seems that it fails the reciprocity test.

There are many examples of trade between two groups where the wealthier group has managed to create a dependency in the weaker group and, in a relationship continuing for many years, has been able to extract virtually all the benefits of trade for itself. A museum in Bergen, for instance, shows a video recounting the trade between Norwegian cod fisherman and the German Hanseatic League. The fisherman had become utterly dependent on selling their annual catch to the Hanseatic League, and according to the story, the Hanseatic League would pay them each year at subsistence level, to keep the Norwegians fishing for another year, while always holding out the hope of a better deal next time round. Here it is tempting to say that perhaps in the first year or two whatever the parties agreed to was fair, or at least 'fair enough'. After a while, though, the Norwegians had adjusted their behaviour so as to be in a position to trade with the Hanseatic League, which in turn made it more difficult to trade with others; the continuing nature of this transaction, and the accompanying dependency, made reciprocity appropriate. However, the Hanseatic League continued to exploit their superior bargaining strength, for they could have survived perfectly well even without a contract to purchase the catch for a year or two—whereas no sale would have been a disaster for the Norwegians. Principles of reciprocity were called for, but were ignored by the Hanseatic League, which, in the circumstances as described made their behaviour exploitative and unjust.

Reciprocity evolves out of mutual advantage, under the right conditions. The next step, to impartiality, does not seem to be part of a natural evolution. It requires norms of justice, and redistribution, even when there is no existing co-operation or interaction. In this way, then, it is quite different from the other models. What then brings it into existence? One possible example to consider is provision within the welfare state, most notably unemployment benefit. Now it was considered a major advance to accept that states had a duty of justice, rather than charity, to provide for those who could not support themselves at an appropriate level. Reflecting on why it is we accept that the welfare state generates rights even for those who are not co-operating, and not even, in some cases, capable of co-operating, could help us gain insight into when justice as impartiality becomes appropriate.

A first view is that the welfare state is not, genuinely, a realm of justice as impartiality. For example, it could be said that it is simply the price that the better off pay for social order, and hence is a matter of enlightened self-interest rather than impartiality. A similar conclusion follows from the thought that the reason why the wealthier are happy enough to support the welfare state is that they realise that they, or their friends or family, might need it themselves. Hence it is a form of compulsory insurance, and, once more a matter of enlightened self-interest.

It is, therefore, possible to support the welfare state without endorsing justice as impartiality. Justice as impartiality requires in addition the thought that others have a right to my help, not because they pose a potential threat or occupy a position that I might one day occupy, but because it is morally arbitrary that I occupy a position of relative wealth and they of relative poverty. 'There for the grace of God go I', as distinct from 'who knows, one day go I'. This level of fellow-feeling generates norms of impartial justice, and is a fine aspiration. How widely it is achieved in the real world is another question.

Applying the Layers of Justice View

I hope I have made it plausible that principles of justice are relative to norms of co-operation. I have also implied that the norms of co-operation that apply to any situation are an empirical matter, but one that has powerful normative consequences: the norms of co-operation can generate principles which are out of step with the way the parties act. Discrepancies between those norms and those principles often consist in exploitation, as discussed above. However we need to explore how this view can be applied to the international, and to the domestic, cases.

Insofar as international global justice is concerned, it is arguable that the world has largely achieved a transition from something approaching theft to mutual advantage, and is, at least in part, going through a slow transition from mutual advantage to reciprocity. We have, officially at least, moved from a set of relationships outside justice, as described by Hume, where Europeans simply felt that the world was theirs for the taking. This was initially replaced by an ideology of trade in which notions of fairness, beyond respect for property rights, had no place, and whatever was agreed to was just. In such a world, as we saw, the rewards go to those with the greater bargaining strength, which, roughly, is the party better able to deal with non-agreement and therefore to hold out for longer. This is a world in which rich countries can simply trade as they like, in respect to poor countries, and thereby cream off most of the gains of trade. However, we can see the fair trade movement, and trade-round talks, as evidence that the relationships between the trading parties have reached a level where reciprocity is appropriate, but the gains of the wealthy parties are disproportionate and do not meet norms of reciprocity. Underlying such a criticism is the assumption that principles of reciprocity should now be governing interaction, which in turn, at least according to the analysis here, implies that the norms of cooperation we now have in place—that is the depth of forms of interaction between the peoples of the world—can in many cases make mutual advantage no longer appropriate. This is, of course, a struggle. And the world is nowhere near generating the norms of solidarity and fellow-feeling that make the theory of justice as impartiality appropriate on a global scale. This is why strong cosmopolitan views appear so implausible: we do not (yet?) have the norms that would give justice as impartiality a motivational hook into individuals.

Indeed, as a matter of description of our practices, we can see that even in the case of domestic justice it is far from clear that we are 'ready' for justice as impartiality as a complete and single account of justice, at least in many societies. Perhaps the Nordic countries, with small, relatively stable populations have been able to develop the level of fellow-feeling and respect among all that gives justice as impartiality sufficiently strong roots to have motivational force. Yet elsewhere, especially taking the USA and UK as examples, domestic justice is shot through with a mix of principles of justice. Minimum wage legislation is partly guided by weak norms of justice as reciprocity; the provision of the welfare state has elements of mutual advantage and impartiality mixed in. Trade often combines mutual advantage and reciprocity to some degree, and only very rarely any element of impartiality. Roughly, the greater the weight given to impartiality, the greater the redistribution there will be. It appears, however, that in virtually all societies there is a cocktail of norms of co-operation and accompanying principles of justice, often in some tension. In domestic justice there is what we might think of a 'thicker mix' including some emphasis on impartiality.

When we turn to global justice, it is not at all uncommon to think in terms of rights and justice, but normally in relation to trade, which is the home of justice as mutual advantage and reciprocity. Of course a great deal of famine, emergency, and health aid is offered, but this is generally regarded as a matter of charity rather than justice, which is to say that principles of justice as impartiality do not extend very far into the global sphere. Nevertheless it can be argued that extreme poverty gives rise to duties of justice. How, though, can one argue for this without the full force of a global principle of equality coming in its train?

The answer is that appealing to justice as impartiality does not automatically rule out appealing to other principles of justice. Consider how different principles can be used to modify each other. Let us assume that an impartiality principle alone generates something like the difference principle.[7] However, as we have noted, few if any societies have such a generous social structure as to guarantee that the worst off will be as well off as possible. One possible explanation for this is that such societies also contain norms of mutual advantage and reciprocity. From these it would follow that those people who are not contributing (very much) to the social product should receive less than those who are. Hence if reciprocity, in the sense in which it has been used in this paper, has any role to play, unemployment benefit, for example, should be significantly below the average wage, perhaps even below the minimum wage.

Now, the situation is dynamic and the fact that certain norms are in play does not mean that they must remain so for ever. Those who are convinced that human beings should rise to high levels of solidarity, and with it norms of impartiality, should see their primary task not so much as arguing for the best theory of impartial justice, but to argue why it is no longer appropriate to 'cut' the principle with a mixture of mutual advantage and reciprocity. In the global sphere we can see the right to be relieved from the most extreme poverty as the residue of a theory of justice as impartiality which is not drowned out by mutual advantage and reciprocity: that is, there are situations which are so extreme as to render irrelevant the fact that no profitable interaction is currently taking place. And again the argumentative task of cosmopolitans is to explain why human beings should have the level of global solidarity, unmixed with norms of mutual advantage and reciprocity, that would justify something like a global difference principle.

I hope I have said enough to at least cast grave doubt on the thesis of the uniformity of justice, and thereby make room for the layers of justice view. Now, it will be said that, even if I am right, all I have done is to provide a sort of moral sociology; that in the domestic sphere our ties with each other are much closer than they are in the global sphere, and as a result we tend to treat those closer to us as having more rights against us than those who are further away. However if I have done this much—if what I have said really counts as an explanation—then I have at least explained how the layers of justice view is possible. If there are different norms of justice, and different norms in play in different spheres, then it is not difficult to see how my obligations of justice to the members of my own society are stronger than my obligations of justice to those who live elsewhere, but remain, nevertheless norms of justice rather than charity. Much more, of course, needs to be done to work out the details of a 'layers of justice' view, but the prior task—my task in this paper—is to create the conceptual space for it.

NOTES

1. It is striking that the perspective of those who would be the beneficiaries of international redistribution has rarely been discussed at length in this debate. Relatively little has been said about their needs, desires or preferences. Indeed, to take this thought further, the potential intellectual contribution of recipient nations has also been largely ignored. The terms of the debate have been set by western political philosophy with little, if any reference, to the conceptions of justice that might be found in Africa, Asia or other recipient countries. Here I can do no more than note this gap, and express the hope to make some steps towards addressing it in future work.
2. For one example, the case of Namibia, see Okupa 2006.
3. I owe to Mike Otsuka the observation that duties within the European Union cannot plausibly be thought of as duties of charity.
4. Nagel mentions the possibility of a federal system with differing obligations at the state level and the federal level, which are different again to the obligations to non-members. Here, however, he seems to give priority to the federal level, which regulates the affairs of each member state. "Cosmopolitan justice could be realized in a federal system, in which the members of individual nation-states had special responsibilities toward one another that they did not have for everyone in the world. But that would be legitimate only against the background of a global system that prevented such special responsibilities from generating injustice on a larger scale. This would be analogous to the requirement that within a state, the institutions of private property, which allow people to pursue their private ends without constantly taking into account the aims of justice, should nevertheless be arranged so that societal injustice is not their indirect consequence" (Nagel 2005, 120). Nagel does not seem, in this passage, to consider the possibility that there is a degree of independence between the two levels.
5. Wolff 1996a. See also Wolff 1996b. Both of those articles draw on Barry 1995.
6. This needs to be made out somewhat more carefully, as a party might enter a transaction making a calculated risk that fails to pay off. Hence the criterion should be formulated in terms of 'expected benefits' but I will leave this complication aside.
7. I say 'something like' because the metric of primary goods, and especially the difference principle's concentration on income and wealth, is clearly inadequate when Rawls's simplifying assumptions are dropped. For an attempt to show how something like the difference principle can be recovered on a more pluralistic view of well-being see Wolff and de-Shalit 2007.

BIBLIOGRAPHY

Barry, Brian. 1995. *Justice as Impartiality*. Oxford: Oxford University Press.

Bertram, Christopher. 2005. 'Global Justice, Moral Development, and Democracy'. In Brock and Brighouse 2005.

Brock, Gillian and Brighouse, Harry (eds). 2005. *The Political Philosophy of Cosmopolitanism*. Cambridge: Cambridge University Press.

Hume, David. 1975. *Enquiries concerning Human Understanding and concerning the Principles of Morals*. Edited by L.A. Selby-Bigge and Peter Nidditch. Third Edition. Oxford: Oxford University Press.

Kurjanska, Malgorzata and Risse, Mathias. 2008. 'Fairness in Trade II: Export Subsidies and the Fair Trade Movement'. 7 *Philosophy, Politics and Economics* 29–56.

Mollendorf, Darrel. 2005. 'Person's Interests, State's Duties and Global Governance'. In Brock and Brighouse 2005.

Lyons, David. 1982. 'The New Indian Claims and Original Rights to Land'. In Jeffrey Paul (ed.), *Reading Nozick*. Oxford: Blackwell.

Nagel, Thomas. 2005. 'The Problem of Global Justice'. 33 *Philosophy and Public Affairs* 113–47.

Okupa, Effa. 2006. *Carrying the Sun on Our Backs*. Berlin: LIT.

Pogge, Thomas. 2002. *World Poverty and Human Rights*. Cambridge: Polity Press.

John Rawls. 1971. *A Theory of Justice*. Oxford: Oxford University Press.

Rawls, John. 1993. *Political Liberalism*. New York: Columbia University Press.

Rawls, John. 1999. *The Law of Peoples*. Cambridge MA: Harvard University Press.

Risse, Mathias. 2007. 'Fairness in Trade I: The Pauper-Labor Argument'. 6 *Philosophy, Politics and Economics* 355–77.

Rousseau, Jean-Jacques. 1973. *Discourse on the Origins of Inequality*. In *The Social Contract, and Discourses*. Edited by G.D.H. Cole. London: Dent.

Smith, Adam. 2002. *Theory of the Moral Sentiments*. Edited by Knut Haakonssen. Cambridge: Cambridge University Press.

Steiner, Hillel. 2005. 'Territorial Justice and Global Redistribution'. In Brock and Brighouse 2005.

Wolff, Jonathan. 1996a. 'Integration, Justice and Exclusion'. In Ulf Bernitz and Par Hallstrom (eds), *Principles of Justice and the European Union*. Stockholm: Juristforlaget.

Wolff, Jonathan. 1996b. 'Rational, Fair and Reasonable'. 8 *Utilitas* 263–71.

Wolff, Jonathan and de-Shalit, Avner. 2007. *Disadvantage*. Oxford: Oxford University Press.

PART II
RIGHTS

4 Preconception Rights*

Cécile Fabre

1. INTRODUCTION

Hillel Steiner needs no introduction as a leading proponent of the so-called Will Theory of rights. According to the Will Theory, X has a right against Y that Y ϕ if, and only if, X is able to demand that Y fulfil his duty to ϕ, and to ask for remedies should Y desist—in other words, if, and only if, X is able to exercise his will with respect to Y's conduct. According to the Will Theory, then, one can be a right-holder if, and only if, one is able to act according to one's will (Hart 1955; Simmonds 1998, Steiner 1994; Sumner 1987; Wellman 1985, 1995.) By contrast, on the Interest Theory of rights, whereby X has a right against Y that Y ϕ if, and only if, Y's ϕ-ing furthers some interest(s) of X, X need not be able to control Y's performance of his duty in order to count as a right-holder (Raz 1986; MacCormick 1977; Kramer 1998, 2001).

That issue—of who can hold rights—is one of the main points of disagreement between the two theories. Thus, Will Theorists claim that children, the comatose, the dead, and future generations cannot, by definition, have rights. Interest Theorists tend to disagree, and to regard the failure of the Will Theory to confer the status of a right-holder to such beings as a decisive reason to reject it.

In this paper, I shall focus on preconception rights, to wit, on rights which X has that Y ϕ, where Y must ϕ before X's conception. As we shall see later, the notion of preconception rights needs disambiguating. For now, it suffices to note that preconception rights are often thought to include, typically, a right as held by future generations that we, here and now, stop wasting finite natural resources, or avoid leaving them with unmanageable levels of public debt; or a right as held by an as-yet unconceived individual that his parents, who are both carriers for the gene of Tay-Sachs disease, take all reasonable steps not to bring him into existence; and so on.[1]

I shall first describe Will Theorists' reasons for rejecting the view that one can have preconception rights, by focusing on the works of H.L.A. Hart and Hillel Steiner (section 2). I shall then argue, more controversially, that there cannot be such a thing as an interest-based preconception right except in very few, morally non-significant cases (section 3). Thus, on my account, even if Interest Theorists are correct in regarding the dead or the comatose as possible rights-holders, they err when conferring such a status on future generations. In other words, Steiner does indeed have a point against Interest Theorists.[2]

Before I begin, I should make it clear, first, that my concern is with moral, rather than legal, rights. Moreover, my aim is not to assess, normatively, whether we have preconception rights; rather, my aim is to explore reasons for rejecting the conceptual point that there can be such a thing as a preconception right. Thus, even if I am wrong on that score, one might still be able to show that, although one can have preconception rights, one does not in fact have them (for example, because the interests they protect are not important enough to hold Y under the relevant duty, etc.)

2. THE WILL THEORY AND PRECONCEPTION RIGHTS

As Hart—another leading proponent of the Will Theory—puts it in his classic 'Are There Any Natural Rights?', 'to have a right entails having a moral justification for limiting the freedom of another person and for determining how he should act' (Hart 1955, 183). Likewise, in Steiner's words, 'rights are claims or immunities to which are attached powers of waiver and enforcement over their correlative constraints' (Steiner 1994, 73). According to the Will Theory, thus, rights serve to give their holders some degree of control over the actions of third parties. Put more technically, a right-holder has both a claim that others act or desist from acting in certain ways, and the power to waive, or demand, their performance of the relevant duties. This, in turn, presupposes that being able to exercise such control—and thus, having some capacities for rational and moral agency—is a necessary and sufficient condition for being a right-holder.

Now, before assessing whether the Will Theory can allow for pre-conception rights, we must disambiguate that term itself. More precisely, we must draw two distinctions. First, we must distinguish between the case where a future generation (G_2) will, at some point, overlap with G_1, from the case (that of, say, G_6) where it will never overlap with G_1. Second, we must also distinguish the claim that a future generation (G_6), which does not yet exist, now has a right against an existing generation (G1) that it ϕ, from the claim that existing generations now have rights against their predecessors that they should have ϕ-ed. Thus, the claim that G_6 now has a right, at time t_1, that G_1 not pollute, is not the same as the claim that G_6 has a right at t_6 that G_1 should have acted at t_1 so as not to pollute. Both kinds of rights qualify as *preconception* rights, since they both correlate with a duty to act in certain ways before their holders are conceived. They differ, however, with respect to the location in time of the right-holding and of the duty-holding respectively. On the first interpretation of preconception rights, the right-holding and the duty-bearing are contemporaneous, even though the right-holders and the duty-bearers are not. In the second interpretation, the right-holding and the duty holding are not contemporaneous.

As those two distinctions cut across each other, the phrase 'preconception rights' can refer to any of the following four rights (for ease of exposition, and by way of example, I shall mean, by ϕ, a duty not to pollute):

(1) G_2 has a right at t_1 that G_1 not pollute at t_1
(2) G_6 has a right at t_1 that G_1 not pollute at t_1
(3) G_2 has a right at t_2 that G_1 should not have polluted at t_1
(4) G_6 has a right at t_6 that G_1 should not have polluted at t_1.

Now, it should be immediately obvious that, if the Will Theory is correct, future generations cannot have rights, but the reasons why that is so differ depending on what is meant by preconception rights. In (1) and (2), future generations do not exist at the point at which they are alleged to have a right against G_1. In so far as they do not exist at that point, they are unable to exercise control over G_1's performance of its duty, and they therefore cannot have a right that G_1 not pollute. In (3) and (4), by contrast, G_2 and G_6 do exist at the point at which they are alleged to have a right, and therefore are in a position generally to exercise control over third parties' conduct (provided of course that they also have the capacities for moral and rational agency). However, the Will Theorist is likely to insist that G_2 and G_6 lack the stated rights. For a start, in G_6's case, the duty-bearer, G_1, no longer exists, and therefore is not liable to G_6's power of enforcement. Moreover, and more importantly, in both cases, the time at which G_1 was supposed not to pollute has passed, so that neither G_6 nor G_2 (although the latter is contemporaneous with G_1) is in a position to control G_1's conduct.

The foregoing discussion suggests that there are three kinds of obstacles, in the Will Theory, to the acceptability of preconception rights: first, their putative holders do not exist, and are therefore unable to exercise the relevant control, at the moment at which they are said to have rights; second, their putative holders do exist at that moment, but the putative duty-bearers do not and are therefore beyond their reach; third, the putative right-holders and the putative duty-bearers both exist at that point, but the former acquire the right after the moment at which the duty was supposed to be performed, which puts the performance of the duty beyond their reach. Accordingly, whichever understanding of preconception rights is at issue, future generations cannot have a right that the current generation not deplete finite natural resources or burden them with an unmanageable level of public debt; an individual cannot have a right that his procreative parents not create him if he would thereby suffer from a irredeemably severe disability; etc.

For the Will Theorist, then, the problem with preconception rights, in either interpretation of the term, is that its holders are unable (in the aforementioned three senses) to exercise control over the conduct of existing generations. However, the Will Theory's commitment to locating enforcement powers in the right-holder as a necessary condition for having rights has elicited unease—not merely amongst opponents of the theory, but, in fact, in Hart himself. In his article 'Legal Rights', Hart attempts to block the claim that the Will Theory implausibly denies rights to children, the severely disabled or the temporarily comatose. In the remainder of this section, I argue that Hart's suggestion does not rescue preconception rights, and that Steiner is correct to insist that, on the Will Theory, such rights are incoherent.

Hart's argument in favour of conferring the status of right-holder on children, the severely disabled and the temporarily comatose goes as follows:

> Where infants or other persons not *sui juris* have rights, such powers and the correlative obligations are exercised on their behalf by appointed representatives and their exercise may be subject to approval by a court. But since (a) what such representatives can and cannot do by way of exercise of such powers is determined by what those whom they represent could have done if *sui juris* and (b) when the latter become *sui juris* they can exercise these powers without any transfer or fresh assignment; the powers are regarded as belonging throughout to them and not to their representatives, though they are only exercisable by the latter during the period of disability (Hart 1982, 184).[3]

On the Hartean view mooted here, future generations would have the power, which they would be unable to exercise, to waive or demand the performance of their predecessors' duties towards them. At the point at which they would come into existence (and in fact, acquire the relevant capacities for moral and rational agency), they would 'exercise those powers without any fresh transfer or assignment'—further indication, according to the Hartean view, that the powers vest in them, rather than in their predecessors.

But this will not do, for reasons which are deployed by MacCormick in the case of children and the disabled, and which apply, *mutatis mutandis*, to preconception rights (in either of the two senses of the term.) For consider. The person who is the most likely to act as the child's or the disabled person's representative is also he who is under obligations towards her, to wit, her legal guardian or parent: clearly, though, it is not acceptable to authorise a parent to waive his own duty to, for example, feed his child (MacCormick, 1982).[4] Likewise, those who are in a position to act, at t_1, as future generations' representatives, are also most likely to be those who are under the relevant duty.

To be sure, a defender of Hart might be tempted to claim that, in some cases, third parties other than parents enforce the latter's duties to their children. As applied to future generations, the move, if it works at all, would do so only in cases where it is possible to draw such a distinction—and thus in cases involving parents' procreative choices (where the third party would be the state), but not in cases involving collective decisions to, for example, needlessly deplete finite natural resources. In any event, the difficulty with this suggestion, as MacCormick remarks, is that those third parties, typically state officials, do not have in these matters the kind of discretion which is at the heart of the Will Theory (MacCormick 1982, 137–38).[5] Thus, if a child is said to have a right against his parents that the latter feed him, a state official cannot allow the parents to let him starve. Invoking what those individuals could have done had they been *sui juris* will not broaden the state official's discretionary powers. For even if, when faced with a child whose parents are neglecting her, one can plausibly imagine her as a suicidal adult who would, if *sui juris*, release her parents from their duty of care, this cannot plausibly serve as a justification for allowing the state official to do so, here and now, while she is still a child. In a similar vein, if a (temporarily) comatose patient has a right against the hospital trust to receive appropriate care, the state official cannot release the latter from its duty to do just that, even though one might imagine that, were the patient *sui juris* he could plausibly ask not to be kept alive.[6] Likewise, if an individual as a child has a right against his parents that the latter not bring him into existence if he would suffer from Tay-Sachs disease, the state official cannot release them from the corresponding duty.

Finally, Hart's move succeeds only if it does make sense to distinguish between having a power and exercising it. For if the Will Theorist is to concede that children or future generations can have rights without altogether abandoning the Will Theory, he must maintain that they have powers (although they cannot exercise them): that is, he must maintain that the power to control the performance of the duty imposed by the right vests in the right-holder, since, as we saw, this is a defining feature of the theory. And yet, to say that someone has a power which he is not authorised or competent to exercise seems odd. Suppose that Blue, aged 16, is not competent or authorized to sell a painting which is held in trust for her until she turns 18. Should she sell the painting to Green for 10,000 pounds, that particular transaction would be regarded as null and void: Blue would not, in fact, be deemed to have transferred to Green the rights, liabilities, duties and powers afferent to that painting, and Green would not, in fact, be deemed to have transferred to Blue the rights, liabilities and powers afferent to that sum of money. It is not the case, here, that Blue has a power which she cannot exercise: rather, she lacks the power in the first instance.

As we have just seen, a Will Theorist could use Hart's (more recent) view on the rights of children and the disabled as a basis for preconception rights only at the cost of implausibly maintaining that one can have powers which one cannot exercise (assuming of course that it can block the aforementioned objections.) Interestingly, Steiner would undoubtedly reject the Hartean view outright. True, it does seem, at first blush, that he allows for preconception rights: for contrary to what I have just suggested, X can have a right to Y's ϕ-ing—Steiner claims—even if he is not 'actually able to exercise such powers' (Steiner 1994, 260). However (and here it is worth quoting him in full):

> It's perhaps worth emphasizing that such powers can be conferred—their exercise by others can be authorized—only by the right-holder himself. For White's waiving or enforcing Red's duty to do A to count as an exercise of the powers entailed by Blue's right that Red do A, it must be the case that Blue has conferred those powers upon White. If White's possession of those powers did not presuppose Blue's authorization, there would be no reason why anybody else might not equally claim to be possessed of those powers and hence authorized to decide whether to enforce or waive Red's compliance with his duty to do A. In short, to be possessed of the power to uphold a right is either to be, or to be authorised, by that right-holder (Steiner 1994, 260–61).

If, by a preconception right, one means a right held by G_6 at t_6 that G_1 not pollute at t_1, then G_6 cannot have it, since, the time at which G_1 should have acted having long passed, G_6 is no longer in a position to authorise a third party to act on its behalf at t_1. To be sure, G_6 is in a position to demand remedies if G_1 has failed to fulfil its duty. G_1 being long gone, however, G_6's ability in that regard is rather meaningless—unlike that of G_2, since the latter overlaps with G_1. However, although G_2 is in a position to extract remedies from G_1, as we saw, it cannot exercise control over the performance of the duty itself. In so far as, according to the Will Theory, being able to exercise such control (or, on Steiner's view, being able to authorise someone to do so on one's behalf) is a necessary condition for being a right-holder, there cannot be such a thing as a preconception right in that sense.

If, by preconception right, one means a right held by G_6 at time t_1 that G_1 not pollute at t_1, then G_6 cannot have it either, since, as it does not exist at t_1, it cannot authorise anyone to act on its behalf. On Steiner's view, the issue really could not be more straightforward: there can be no such thing as preconception rights, period (Steiner 1983). Interest Theorists tend to disagree. They believe that their preferred account of rights allows for conferring on future generations the right that their predecessors take greater care of the environment; they also believe that it allows for conferring on the unconceived a range of rights against their parents. The Interest Theory's greater generosity, as it were, to our successors is a good reason, or so its proponents often claim, to reject the Will Theory in its favour. As we shall now see, they are somewhat optimistic in their assessment of the relative merits, in this particular respect, of the Interest Theory over the Will Theory.

3. THE INTEREST THEORY AND PRECONCEPTION RIGHTS

According to the Interest Theory, you recall, X has a right against Y that Y ϕ if, and only if, Y's ϕ-ing furthers some of interest(s) of X's. By implication, X need not be able to control Y's performance of his duty in order to count as a right-holder. But although the Interest Theory does not rule out the possibility of conferring on X the status of a right-holder, even if he lacks the requisite control over Y's conduct, it is not definitionally committed to doing either. Put differently, the Interest Theory, as an account of what it means to have a right, is compatible both with the view that someone who lacks such control can, and the view that he cannot, have rights. Which of these views the theory endorses will depend on the account of interests and, by implication, of harm, on which it rests. Let me explain. The theory holds that X has a right against Y that Y ϕ if, and only if, Y's ϕ-ing furthers some interest of X's; conversely, it holds that, to the extent that Y's not ϕ-ing would harm that interest, then Y is under a duty to X to ϕ, which implies that X has a right that Y ϕ. Thus, the Interest Theory can confer the status of right-holders only on entities of which it makes sense to say that they can be harmed, or benefited, by Y.

As I argue elsewhere, X is harmed at time t by some event E if, and only if, E makes a difference to X's experience at t (Fabre 2008). Contrast two scenarios, one in which White slashes up a painting, and one in which he slashes up a (conscious, un-anaesthetised) dog. Even if one allows that it is in the interest of the painting not to be damaged, one cannot plausibly say that White harms the painting, whereas it is uncontroversially true that he harms the dog. (Whether or not he wrongs the dog is a different matter which I need not settle here.) And the reason for reaching that judgement is that White's action makes a difference to the dog's experience (the dog moves from a pain-free state to pain-filled state), but does not adversely affect the painting's experience since a painting, inanimate object as it is, is not a subject of experience. The dead, I argued there, are in that respect like the painting, and cannot be harmed (nor, in fact, can the living be harmed posthumously.)

Now, with that experiential account of harm in hand, let us look at preconception rights. As we have seen throughout, we must distinguish, and thus address separately, the claim that future generations, which do not yet exist, now have rights that a given state of affairs, S, obtain now, and the claim that existing people now have rights that their predecessors should have acted in the past so as to bring S about.

Neither claim does particularly well on the Interest Theory. Consider first the claim that G_6 has a preconception right, at time t_1, that G_1 not pollute at t_1. At first sight, it is bedevilled by the so-called problem of the subject, which is most often raised in discussions of posthumous rights, and which is worth examining, somewhat digressingly, in that context.[7] Just as the term 'preconception rights' ought to be disambiguated along the aforementioned line, so must the term 'posthumous rights'. That is, to claim that P can have a right once dead that a posthumous state of affairs, S, obtain is not the same as to claim that P, while alive, can have a claim that S obtain once he is dead. In so far as we are concerned with the thesis that G_6 can have a right at t_1 that G_1 not pollute at t_1, we must turn our attention to the claim that P can have a right once dead that S obtain. Now, for P to be in a position, once he is dead, to have a right that S obtain requires that he can, once dead, have an interest in S and be harmed by the duty-bearers' failure to comply. This, in turn, presupposes that we can give a coherent account of the subject of the harm. And this is precisely where the problem is. For the subject of the harm can be neither P's corpse nor his ashes, since neither has any kind of experience which can be affected by the duty-bearer's conduct. In so far as no coherent account can be given of P as subjected to posthumous harm, no such account can be given of him as a holder of posthumous rights.

The foregoing reasoning can be applied, step by step, to G_6, as follows. For the members of G_6 to be in a position, before conception, to have a right that S obtain, requires that they can, before conception, have an interest in S and be harmed by G_1's failure to bring it about. This, in turn, supposes that one can give a coherent account of the subject of the preconception harm. Quite obviously, it cannot be the gametes which will make G_6 since gametes have no capacity for experience. In so far as no coherent account can be given of the members of G_6 as subjects of pre-conception harms, no such account can be given of them as holders of pre-conception rights (so understood).

Consider now the claim that G_6 can have a right at t_6 that G_1 should not have polluted at t_1, together with its posthumous counterpart, namely the claim that P can have a right, whilst alive, that S obtain once he is dead. That latter claim implies that P can be harmed once dead, since it is only *once P is dead* that duty-bearers will be called upon to perform their duty to him, and that the question of whether P will be harmed or not by their conduct will arise. Likewise, to claim that G_6 can have a right at t_6 against G_1 that G_1 not pollute at t_1 supposes that the members of G_6 can be harmed before conception, since it is *before* they are conceived that G_1 is called upon to fulfil its duty, and that the question of whether they can be harmed by G_1's conduct arises. As we have just seen, however, neither the dead, nor the unconceived, can be harmed at that crucial point (after death and before conception respectively), since at that point—the point at which the duty-bearer is called upon to act—we cannot say of them that their experience is adversely affected by the duty-bearer's conduct.

In the remainder of this section, I discuss two arguments in favour of conferring on individuals rights relative to preconception states of affairs. I shall claim that the first argument fails, and that the second works only in those cases where G_1 would not change the identity of members of G_6 by acting as required by its putative obligations to it.

The first argument is deployed by Matthew Kramer in support of preconception rights of the kind 'G_6 has a right at t_1 that G_1 not pollute at t_1' (Kramer 2001, 52–57). According to him, future generations are present in the lives of the living, in that the latter adjust their expectations and make a whole range of decisions in the anticipation of the fact that the former will, at some point, come into existence. This, according to Kramer, is enough to assimilate them to competent live adults, whose status as rights-holders is beyond question.

I remain unconvinced. For although a person as yet unconceived can already be present in the lives of his predecessors in those ways, it is hard to see why that is enough to make him a right-holder: in addition, one must be able to account for him as an interest-bearer susceptible to be harmed, or benefited, by Y's conduct. Pre-conception, I have argued, individuals cannot be accounted for as such subjects. Thus, notwithstanding the undeniable presence of our successors in our lives, the problem of the subject still looms large.

Kramer's defence of preconception rights runs aground on the difficulties posed by the necessity of identifying plausible bearers of preconception interests. Another defence, as found in recent work by Buchanan *et alii*, as well as Gosseries, seeks to solve those difficulties (Buchanan et al 2000; Gosseries 1998, 2004, 2008).[8] Unlike Kramer's, it insists, not that future generations can have a right now that the present generation not pollute, but, rather, that the present generation can have a right now that its predecessors should have desisted from polluting. And the reason why that is so, they claim, is this: although compliance failure at time t on the part of duty-bearers will not affect the experience, at t, of those to whom the obligation is owed, the consequences of that failure will be felt by the latter once they are conceived—at a time, then, when they can have interests. Thus, whereas Kramer claims that right-holding and duty-holding can be contemporaneous even though right-holders and duty-holders are not, the view under consideration sees no difficulty in the claim that rights and their correlative duties need not be coeval.

The point that right-holding and duty-holding need not be contemporaneous was raised in section 2. There, we saw that non-contemporaneity blocks the Will Theory from allowing for the possibility that individuals might have preconception rights. But even if the Interest Theory can cope with non-contemporaneity, it is important to note that this second argument in favour of preconception rights does suppose that there will be a right, at some point, as held by as yet unconceived individuals. Even if the duty to ϕ, owed to X by Y, need not be performed at the time at which X acquires a right that Y ϕ, it must be the case that X will, at some point, acquire that right. This will prove unproblematic in a range of cases. Imagine, for example, that a manufacturer of powdered milk for babies realizes that a vast number of tins destined for exports have been contaminated with some lethal agent. Suppose that some of those tins will be bought and used, in 11 months from thence and in a different country, by parents whose children are not yet conceived (Gosseries 2004, 83). The claim that the manufacturer is under a duty to those as-yet non-existing infants to recall the tins survives the challenge raised by problem of the subject, in so far as the infants will exist, will thus be subjects of experiences, and will be adversely affected by drinking the milk.

In some cases, though, the Buchanan/Gosseries strategy will not work. For a start, as Gosseries himself notes, sometimes the only way for Y to fulfil his obligation to X will be to ensure that X does not exist (Gosseries 2004, 94; Elliott 1989, 136). Thus, suppose that Y and his partner Z are told that they both carry the gene for Tay-Sachs disease, so that any one of their offspring has a 25% chance of suffering from it. In the light of the gravity of this particular condition, it is plausible to surmise that its sufferers do not lead lives which are worth living. To say, as some undoubtedly will, that Y and Z are under a duty to that child not to bring it into the world falls foul of the requirement that there should be a right as held by him since, if they fulfil their obligation, Y and Z will make it impossible for that child to exist, and thus for his or her right to exist.

In other scenarios, Y's fulfilment of his obligation to X will result, non-intentionally, in X's non-existence *and* in the creation of a different individual (Parfit 1984, iv). Suppose that G_1 its under a duty at t_1 to G_6 not to pollute the environment. If G_1 fulfils its duty, and thus builds very few factories, restricts opportunities for travel by levying high taxes on aviation fuel, and develops alternative sources of energy, it will create a state of affairs in which some individuals will meet and procreate with one another and thus create distant successors G_{6a}. If, however, G_1 desists, it will bring about a state of affairs in which individuals' lives will be rather different—more opportunities for travel, different job opportunities, etc.—so that they will meet and procreate with different individuals at different times, and thus create different distant successors G_{6b}. In so far as G_{6b} would not have existed if G_1 had conducted a non-pollution policy, the rights which correspond to those duties would not have existed either—and this putative defence of preconception rights therefore fails.

To this—the so-called and well-known non-identity problem—the following solution is sometimes offered. Rather than focusing on the identity of the individuals which make up G_6, it is said, we ought to say that we have an obligation not to act in such a way as to harm our successors, whoever those successors are. For although we know for sure that some future individuals, I_{6b}, will not exist if we act as stipulated by the duty at issue, we do know for sure (barring some major disaster like a world-wide nuclear war or a collision with a sufficiently large meteorite) that there will be some people at t_6, be they I_{6a} or I_{6b} or I_{6c}, and so on, and it is those people's welfare, whoever they are, which matters to us (Beckerman and Pasek 2001).

Now, it may well be true that we should not care about our successors' identity. However, the move will not rescue preconception *rights*, for the latter are tied to the existence of their (specific) individual holders. According to the argument under consideration here, future individuals, whoever they are (say, I_{6a} or I_{6b}) acquire at t_6 a right against G_1 that the latter act at t_1 in such a way as to ensure that I_{6a} or, as the case may be, I_{6b}, do not incur harm at t_6. The problem, of course, is that if G_1 acts as required by its duty to G_6, it will bring about a state of affairs in which (say) I_{6a} will exist, rather than I_{6b}. Given that the latter will not exist if G_1 so acts, they cannot possibly acquire a right (at t_6) that G_1 does so. (Remember that the view under consideration supposes that, although the duty-bearing and the right-holding need not be coeval, the right will be acquired at some point by the individuals to whom the duty is owed.)

Note, incidentally, that this particular objection is compatible with the claim that G_1 is under a duty to G_6, but at a cost which Interest Theorists are likely to find unacceptable. The cost consists in accepting that rights and obligations need not correlate with one another. On that view, G_1 can be under an obligation to their successors, even though the latter, precisely because they would not exist if G_1 so acted, could never acquire a right against G_1. However, in so far as Interest Theorists believe that Y's having an obligation to X to ϕ correlates with X's having a right against Y that Y ϕ, and vice-versa, they could not accept that solution without modifying the theory in ways which (according to some of them at least[9]) would in fact amount to jettisoning it. I lack the space, in this paper, to undertake a full assessment of the connections between the Interest Theory of rights and the correlativity thesis. Accordingly, in the remainder of this section, I will assess another possible (and less standard) solution to the problem, which does not require abandoning the thesis.

As we have just seen, solving the non-identity problem by divorcing the conferral of rights from the precise identity of their holders will not help us rescue preconception rights (at least, not if we want to uphold the correlativity thesis, as Interests Theorists on the whole seek to do.) A perhaps more fruitful route might come in the form of group rights. For consider. Although we do not know who will exist at t_6 and thus who will constitute G_6, we do know that G_6, as a group, will exist at t_6. Moreover, as a group, G_6 can have, indeed does have, interests. Might these two points allow us to claim that G_1 is under a duty to G_6 to further those interests, even if it thereby modifies the genetic identity of G_6's members, and that G_6, as a group, has a right that G_1 do so? (Kramer 2001, 56; Page 1999).

Whether or not groups can have interests, and therefore rights, is yet another thorny issue in the debate over rights. Interestingly, whereas most (book-length) accounts of rights treat both the issue of the rights of non-existing people and the issue of the rights of groups, they do so separately.

However, in the light of the aforementioned standard solution to the non-identity problem, it pays to explore whether the notion of an interest-based group rights might help rescue preconception rights, in cases where Y's performance of his duty affects the existence of individual group members.

As should be clear, the proposal under consideration will not protect preconception rights from the non-identity objection in cases where the duty, if it is owed to anyone at all, is unquestionably owed to an individual. The aforementioned example of parents whose (as yet unconceived) children run a 25% of being affected by Tay-Sachs disease is a case in point. Moreover, for similar reasons, the proposal will leave a number of preconception rights as held (allegedly) by future generations vulnerable—those rights, that is, which are commonly described in such a way that they appear to be group rights, but in fact are not group rights. Take, for example, the claim that G_6, as a group, has a right to live in a clean environment, or to breathe clean air. Notwithstanding appearances to the contrary, this is not a group right at all, but, rather, a right which each member of G_6 holds severally, and which protects an interest which they each have, as individuals, irrespective of the fact that they belong to G_6 (Jones 1999, 359; Réaume 1988).

The foregoing remarks suggest that, for a right to count as a group right, it must protect an interest which group members have qua group members—in other words, one which they would not have unless they belonged to that group. Rights to national self-determination are a good example. A citizen of a given nation, N, has a right that N be self-determining, and thus that N's citizens together be able to shape N's future, precisely in so far as he is one such member: if he belonged to some other nation M, he would not have a right, as a citizen, that N-members shape their nation's future (Fabre 2007, 79; Jones 1999).

That, however, is not enough to get a sense of what a group right is. For the requirement that the interest it protects be borne by the group members *qua* group members may yield two very different kinds of rights, to wit, corporate and collective rights (Jones 1999).[10] On the corporate conception, a group right is held by the group as a group, and the justification for its conferral lies in the importance for the group, as a group, of furthering the interest in question. On that view, the group has moral standing independently of the moral standing of its individual members. On the collective conception, a group right is held by individual members as group members, and the justification for its conferral lies in the importance, for those individuals, of protecting the interest in question. On that view, the group's moral standing is reducible to that of its individual members (Waldron 1993).

Although both corporate and collective rights are easily accommodated by the Interest Theory (in the sense that one can ascribe interests to entities on both corporate and collective models), neither offers a plausible framework for rescuing preconception rights from the non-identity problem. Suppose, for example, that G_6, as a political community, has a group interest in being able collectively to determine its own future as it sees fit, and suppose further than this interest is entirely reducible to the interest which each individual member of G_6, *qua* such member, has in the self-determination of his community (for example, for his individual well-being). In so far as the individuals who constitute G_6 would not have that specific interest if they were not members of that particular group, their right is properly regarded as a group right, albeit a collective, rather than corporate, right. Suppose, further, that this right holds G_1 under a duty not to burden G_6 with unmanageable levels of public debt. One might think that G_1 can have that duty irrespective of the genetic identity of G_6's members; one might also say that G_1 can be sure that G_6, whoever its members are, will exist. In combination, those two thoughts might seem to deliver the conclusion that G_6, once it exists, can have a right that G_1 not incur such a debt, even though G_1 would thereby modify G_6's composition.

The problem, however, is that in so far as the justification for holding G_1 under that duty lies in the interest(s) of individual members of G_6, to hold G_1 under such a duty is to say that were it to default, it would thereby harm the *individuals* which make up G_6. To be sure, it would harm them in their capacity as members of that group; but it would harm them to the extent that having to service, as a political community, a crippling level of debt would be detrimental to their flourishing as individuals. Were G_1 to fulfil its duty, it would bring about a state of affairs where different individuals would exist, and one, thus, where the rights correlative to the duty would not exist.

At first sight, one might think that the corporate conception of group rights is not vulnerable to this particular problem, since it locates the justification for the right, not in the interests of individual group members, but in the interests of the group as such. Suppose, then, that G_6, as a political community, has a moral standing which is not reducible to that of its members, and that, as such, it has an interest in not having to service a crippling level of public debt. It is precisely because *it*, and not its members, would be harmed by G_1's profligate borrowing that—or so one might suppose—the latter is under a duty not to overspend. And if that is so, then the fact that G_6's individual members would not exist if G_1 fulfilled its obligation is irrelevant.

But this will not do. For although, on this conception of group rights, the group's standing and interests are not reducible to those of its members, they cannot but be explained by reference to it.[11] If crippling levels of public debt made no difference at all to the well-being of the group's *individual members*, it would be hard to understand why the *group as such* would have such an interest in the first instance. Furthermore, and crucially for our purpose here, it would also be hard to see what justification there would be for holding G_1 under a duty not to overspend. If that is correct, then the corporate conception of group rights fails to rescue preconception rights for reasons similar to those adduced against collective rights.

It seems, in fact, that the only way to allow for preconception rights in non-identity cases is to confer on G_6 group rights which are held by the group as a group, and which protect an interest of the group as a group, with *no* reference to the interests of individual group members. However, this is not a defensible view of rights, at least not within a liberal, individualistic and humanistic framework, in which individuals are the fundamental units of moral concern, and in which groups' acts and interests are explainable by reference to their members' acts and interests, even though they are not reducible to them. In so far as Interest Theorists locate their account of rights within precisely such a framework, they cannot but renounce preconception rights, at least in those cases where the performance of the correlative duties would affect the existence of putative right-holders.[12]

4. CONCLUSION

In this paper, I have shown why the Will Theory of rights is committed to ruling out preconception rights. Hart's attempt to show that the theory can accommodate children's rights, as well as rights for the comatose and severely disabled, does not work, or so I have argued, for reasons which apply, *mutatis mutandis*, to future people. In that sense, Steiner is absolutely right to maintain that there cannot be such a thing as a will-based preconception right. But in rejecting the Will Theory on those grounds, Interest Theorists fail to see that their preferred account of rights is not as friendly to such rights as it seems—at least on what I take to be a plausible, experiential account of harm. To be sure, as we saw, the notion of interest-based preconception rights is sometimes coherent—in those cases where the existence of putative right-holders is unaffected by the duty-bearers' conduct. However, our existence is so contingent on the myriads of actions which take place before our conception, that there are very few of those cases; accordingly, it is unclear that the fact that the Interest Theory does allow for them confers on it a decisive advantage over the Will Theory.

Of course, nothing I have said here precludes imposing on the living obligations with respect to future generations. Consider, by analogy, the case of the dead, and suppose that they cannot have rights either. That claim is compatible with the view that the living are under an obligation to some other living person (for example, relatives of the deceased) to act in certain ways regarding the dead. Likewise, the claim that future generations cannot have rights, once they exist, that their predecessors should have acted in certain ways, is compatible with the view that the latter were under an obligation to some of their contemporaries to act in certain ways vis-à-vis those generations. Moreover, that claim is also compatible with the view that we have an impersonal obligation vis-à-vis our successors to minimise harms which may accrue to them once they come into existence. Will Theorists in general, and Hillel Steiner in particular, will have no difficulty accepting those views. Whether or not Interest Theorists who subscribe to the correlativity thesis can do so as well must await another occasion. So must a full treatment of the similarities and differences between preconception and posthumous rights.

NOTES

*An earlier version of this paper was presented at the Edinburgh Legal Theory Workshop. I am grateful to all participants for a very stimulating discussion, as well as to Ian Carter, Rowan Cruft, Axel Gosseries, Matthew Kramer and Leif Wenar for their comments on an earlier draft.

1. Tay-Sachs disease is characterized by a progressive and severe deterioration of physical and mental functionings in early infancy, paralysis of respiratory and feeding functions, and early death—usually before the age of 5.
2. In fact, in a separate paper, I argue that there cannot be such a thing as interest-based posthumous rights (Fabre 2008).
3. Note that in virtue of (b), Hart's rescue attempt does not apply to the permanently comatose. I should add that Hart himself does not examine the cases of non-existing people in this particular piece. Thus, what follows is an interpretative attempt to assess whether his comments on the rights of children and the disabled are applicable to future people. Incidentally, Hart's suggestion cannot possibly work for posthumous rights, for the dead will never be in a position of exercising the rights which, as they are dead, they are said to have but are unable to exercise. Even if, on principle, one can have a power which one cannot exercise, to confer on someone a power which she will *never* exercise is not in the spirit of the Will Theory. For if the role of rights is to give right-holders some degree of control over third parties' conduct, and if that is the rationale for insisting that the powers through which such control is exerted vest in the right-holders themselves, then it is hard to see what reasons one would have to confer on the dead powers which they will never be able to exercise.
4. My argument in this paragraph and the next essentially follows his own.
5. Moreover, a defender of Hart, on this point, could not claim that parents are empowered to relinquish their duties to their children, for example by putting them up for adoption: for transferring one's duty to feed one's child to someone else is not the same as not feeding one's child. As long as the transfer has not taken place, one is under a duty to feed her.
6. The case of a temporarily comatose patient who has signed a DNR order is interesting. In having signed the DNR order, the patient has released doctors from their duty of care: it seems that no third party is needed here to exercise the power to control doctors' conduct. However, third parties would be needed to demand, or waive, remedies should doctors attempt to resuscitate the patient.
7. See Fabre 2008 for a longer argument to that effect.
8. This defence of preconception rights will not work for posthumous rights, for it claims that the right is acquired when its holder will be in a position to be harmed by the duty-bearer's failure to comply. In the case of preconception rights, the right-holder—G_6—acquires the right at t_6, when it is harmed by G_1's failure to act at t_1. In the case of posthumous rights, however, the defence would suppose that the right is acquired at the point at which its holder is harmed, which, according to my experiential account of harm, could only be when he is alive, say at t_1; at t_1, however, the duty-bearer will not have yet failed to comply (and the alleged right-holder therefore will not have been harmed), since he can exercise his duty only once the alleged right-holder is dead (one cannot break, or indeed respect, a will, until its author has died; one cannot desecrate someone's body until that person has died, etc.).

9. For example, Matthew Kramer, who argues that the Interest Theory is committed to the correlativity thesis (Kramer 1998). For a discussion of this possible solution, see, e.g., Alex Gosseries 2008.
10. For important discussions of group rights in the Interest Theory, see Kramer 1998, 49–58 and Raz 1986, chs. 8 and 10.
11. As Kramer, who does seem to hold that view of group rights, himself notes (Kramer 1998).
12. As Axel Gosseries pointed out to me in private correspondence, the notion of a group right is itself vulnerable to the non-identity problem. For consider. To say that a group G has a right to X is to say, generally, that it has that right now, and at future times—as new generations of group members come into existence. Suppose, for example, that a political community C has a group right against Y that the latter let it determine its own future. On that view, Y is under a duty now, but also in five, ten, twenty years from now, for as long as that community exists (and does not forfeit its right) not to interfere in its internal affairs. If Y fulfils its duty to C, some individuals C_1 will come into existence. If, by contrast, Y defaults on its duty, other individuals C_2 will come into existence. According to the non-identity objection, *in that latter case*, C-members cannot claim to have been wronged, as a group, because they would not have existed as a group had Y fulfilled its duty. If that is correct, then it does not make sense to confer on C a right to shape its own future. In order to rescue the notion of a group right, one must either defend an identity-independent conception of harm (which would enable us to conceive groups as irreducible to the precise identity of their members at any point in time), or deploy an account of group rights, and more widely of the ontological and moral status of groups, whereby groups cannot be thought of independently of the precise identity of their members (which would enable us to retain the identity-dependent conception of harm on which much of our moral thinking rests.) I lack the space to address this issue here.

BIBLIOGRAPHY

Beckerman, Wilfried, and Pasek, Joanna. 2001. *Justice, Posterity and the Environment.* Oxford: Oxford University Press.

Buchanan, Allan, Brock, Dan, Daniels, Norman and Wikler, Dan. 2000. *From Chance to Choice; Genetics and Justice.* Cambridge: Cambridge University Press.

Cruft, Rowan. 2004. “Rights: Beyond Interest Theory and Will Theory”. 23 *Law and Philosophy*, 347–97.

Elliot, Robert. 1989. “The Rights of Future People”. 6 *Journal of Applied Philosophy* 159–69.

Fabre, Cécile. 2007. *Justice in a Changing World.* Cambridge: Polity Press.

Fabre, Cécile. 2008. “Posthumous Rights”. In Clare Grant, Matthew H. Kramer, and Ben Colburn (eds.) *The Legacy of H.L.A. Hart.* Oxford: Oxford University Press.

Feinberg, Joel. 1989. “Is There a Right to be Born?”. In Joel Feinberg, *Rights, Justice and the Bounds of Liberty.* Princeton: Princeton University Press.

Gosseries, Alex. 1998. “L’ethique environnementale aujourd’hui”. 96 *Revue Philosophique de Louvain*, 395–426.

Gosseries, Axel. 2004. *Penser la Justice entre les Générations.* Paris: Aubier.

Gosseries, Axel. 2008. “On Future Generations’ Future Rights”. 16 *Journal of Political Philosophy* 446–74.

Hart, H. L. A. 1955. "Are There Any Natural Rights?" 64 *The Philosophical Review* 175–91.
Hart, H. L. A. 1982. "Legal Rights". In H. L. A. HART, *Essays on Bentham: Studies in Jurisprudence and Legal Theory*. Oxford: Clarendon Press.
Jones, Peter. 1999. "Group Rights and Group Oppression", 7 *Journal of Political Philosophy*, 353–77.
Kramer, Matthew H. 1998. "Rights Without Trimmings". In Matthew H. Kramer, N.E. Simmonds, and Hillel Steiner, *A Debate over Rights*. Oxford: Oxford University Press.
Kramer, Matthew H. 1998. "Getting Rights Right". In Matthew H. Kramer (ed.), *Rights, Wrongs, and Responsibilities*. Basingstoke: Palgrave.
Kramer, Matthew H. and Steiner, Hillel. 2007. "Theories of Rights: Is There a Third Way?", 27 *Oxford Journal of Legal Studies* 281–310.
MacCormick, Neil. 1977. "Rights in Legislation". In Hacker, P. M. S. (ed.), *Law, Morality and Society*. Oxford: Clarendon Press.
MacCormick, Neil. 1982. "Children's Rights: A Test-Case of Theories of Rights". In Neil MacCormick, *Legal Rights and Social Democracy. Essays in Legal and Political Philosophy*. Oxford: Clarendon Press.
Page, Edward. 1999. "Intergenerational Justice and Climate Change". 53 *Political Studies* 47–66.
Parfit, Derek. 1984. *Reasons and Persons*. Oxford: Clarendon Press.
Raz, Joseph. 1986. *The Morality of Freedom*. Oxford: Clarendon Press.
Réaume, Denise. 1988. "Individuals, Groups, and Rights to Public Goods". 38 *Toronto Law Journal* 1–27.
Simmonds, N. E. 1998. "Rights at the Cutting Edge". In Matthew H. Kramer, N.E. Simmonds, and Hillel Steiner, *A Debate over Rights*. Oxford: Oxford University Press.
Sreevenisan, Gopal. 2005. "A Hybrid Theory of Claim-Rights". 25 *Oxford Journal of Legal Studies* 257–74.
Steiner, Hillel. 1983. "The Rights of Future Generations." In Peter G. Brown and Douglas MacLean (eds.), *Energy and the Future*. Totowa: Rowman and Littlefield.
Steiner, Hillel. 1994. *An Essay on Rights*. Oxford: Blackwell.
Sumner, L. W. 1987. *The Moral Foundation of Rights*. Oxford: Clarendon Press.
Waldron, Jeremy. 1993. "Can Communal Goods be Human Rights?". In Jeremy Waldron, *Liberal Rights*. Cambridge: Cambridge University Press.
Wellman, Carl. 1985. *A Theory of Rights*. Totowa: Rowman and Littlefield.
Wellman, Carl. 1995. *Real Rights*. Oxford, Oxford University Press.
Wenar, Leif. 2005. "The Nature of Rights". 33 *Philosophy and Public Affairs* 223–52.

5 Choice, Circumstance and the Costs of Children

Serena Olsaretti

1. INTRODUCTION

The creation of new persons involves substantial costs. Children are expensive to raise—some more so than others—both in terms of the labour time that is required to satisfy their various needs and the resources they consume in the process of growing up.[1] (Call these the *costs of care.*) And once they reach adulthoods, new persons join the ranks of pre-existing members as fellow claimant of just shares, thereby possibly decreasing the size of those shares.[2] (Call these the *costs of added members.*) While we assume that justice requires that both types of costs of children be borne by someone, we may ask who that someone is. Does justice require that the costs of children be shared by all members of society equally? Or should some or all of those costs be borne by parents alone, in virtue of either the fact that they are special beneficiaries of having children, or the fact that they are responsible for having them?

Any theory of distributive justice should provide an answer to this question, since it is a question about the fair distribution of burdens among individuals. And Hillel Steiner's theory, in particular, seems especially well-equipped to shed light on it, both because it discusses explicitly some of the implications of the fact that people beget children, and because it underscores the importance of the question of who should bear the costs of satisfying others' claims. In this paper I examine Steiner's position on who should bear the costs of children. I suggest that that position seems unstable as a result of a tension between Steiner's avowed views on just taxes—which support not holding parents responsible for all the costs of children—and his views about responsibility—which do seem to support holding parents responsible for all of them. I then ask how Steiner could respond to this problem, and argue that, rather than solving that tension by forgoing either the commitment to responsibility or that to expecting that some of the costs of children be shared, he could show that that tension is only apparent.

2. STEINER ON THE COSTS OF CHILDREN

Steiner does not himself address the question I have raised here, of who should bear the costs of children, but we can reconstruct his position on this question by looking at two parts of his account: his views about just taxes and his views about responsibility.[3]

Steiner's views about just taxes are, of course, the upshot of his theory of justice as a whole, and a full exposition of them would take us too far afield. For our purposes here, what matters is that according to Steiner's historical entitlement theory, all persons have only two original rights, the right to self-ownership and the right to an equal share of natural resources, with the latter being the only right that has redistributive implications.[4] Those implications, in a nutshell, are as follows. Given that persons come into the world at different times (which, from the point of view of their having a right to an equal share of natural resources, is a morally arbitrary fact), and arrive into a world in which natural resources are already fully appropriated, they are best seen as having a right to an equal share of the *value* of natural resources (Steiner 1998, 99). Respecting this right will require holding every person who owns resources (and regardless of whether or not she uses them (Steiner 1999, 180–85)) liable to a tax in proportion to those resources' competitive value, which tax goes into a social fund that subsidises a universal basic income (Steiner 2002, 189; Steiner 2002, 193, note 11; Steiner 1998, 99).[5]

An ancillary fact that is also relevant here is that, according to Steiner, genetic information counts as a natural resource, so that, by begetting children, parents can be characterised as appropriating a natural resource (Steiner 1992, 87–8; Steiner 1994, 247; Steiner 1998, 100; Steiner 2002, 189;).[6] As a result, they are potentially liable to paying more than non-parents to the fund, depending on the value of the genetic information they appropriate, where that value is determined in accordance with how much input, by way of gestational and post-natal care, is required to obtain a certain output, that is, a certain ability level (Steiner 2002, 186). (But note that if some parents appropriate some not very valuable genetic information, they, as well as non-parents, are entitled to some compensation from parents who appropriate very valuable genetic information.[7])

From this very succinct summary of Steiner's views on just taxes, it emerges that they seem to support the following two-pronged position about transfers between parents and non-parents. On the one hand, parents, just like non-parents, are only entitled to the universal basic income that is ultimately justified by everyone's right to an equal share of natural resources. They do not have any further rights to receiving resources, and therefore no rights to assistance for covering the costs of care, although some of them will be entitled to some compensation for appropriating less valuable genetic information than other parents. This further right, however, is not a right that parents have to sharing the costs of care with non-parents, for three reasons: not every parent has it; other parents, rather than non-parents, have the correlative obligation; and in any event, this right is not grounded in the fact that parents incur costs of care, but in their right to an equal share of natural resources, so it results in (some) parents' being relieved of some costs of care only contingently.[8]

On the other hand, while parents are not entitled to assistance for bearing the costs of care, they *are*, on Steiner's view of just taxes, entitled to sharing the costs of added members, since, when it comes to taxation for the appropriation of natural resources (other than genetic information), non-parents and parents are equal contributors to, and equal beneficiaries of, the fund that provides for everyone's universal basic income.[9] Parents are not asked to internalise the costs of added members by having to forgo their basic income, wholly or in part, in order to subsidise their children's.

This second prong of Steiner's position on who should bear the costs of children, however, may be said to jar with Steiner's own stance about responsibility. That stance is most fully elaborated in a discussion of how the historical entitlement theory Steiner defends compares with some recent egalitarian thinking that accommodates a principle of responsibility.[10] According to this now very familiar type of egalitarianism, equality requires reducing or eliminating inequalities in people's *circumstances*, but not inequalities that reflect people's *choices*. Steiner endorses this commitment to holding people responsible for the consequences of their choices.[11] Indeed, he suggests that he takes it a step further than responsibility-sensitive egalitarians. For responsibility-sensitive egalitarians, Steiner claims, have a tendency to overlook that in some cases someone's circumstance is someone else's choice, so that compensation for that circumstance is not to be shared equally among all, but is the responsibility of a particular person. In other words, when someone suffers a disadvantage through no fault of hers, so that she is not responsible for it and is owed compensation, we should raise the further question of who owes her compensation, since there may be someone else who is responsible for her predicament and is liable to pick up the tab.

To keep the question of who owes compensation in focus, Steiner suggests that we adopt a threefold distinction between the acts of an agent, the acts of nature, and the acts of others. Accordingly, he distinguishes between a world in which the only source of disadvantage is nature (people are both benevolent and prudent); a world in which the only source of disadvantage is the non-benevolent, harmful behaviour of others (people are prudent and nature is kind); and a world in which the only source of disadvantage is imprudence: people suffer adversity because they harm themselves (others are benevolent and nature is kind). In the first world, disadvantage is a matter of luck for everyone, and everyone should share the costs of eliminating or reducing it; in the second, disadvantage is a matter of luck for those who suffer it, but not for those who, through their non-benevolent conduct, cause it: the latter are to be held responsible for the costs of eliminating or reducing disadvantage. Finally, in the third world, disadvantage is not a matter of luck for those who suffer it, as they bring it upon themselves and may, as far as justice is concerned, be left to suffer it.[12]

To return to the issue of the costs of children, it seems that Steiner's commitment to asking whether there is someone who is responsible for someone else's circumstances should lead him to ask parents to internalise all the costs of children. Since (most) parents have the option to not have children and choose to have them freely, they alone, it seems, should bear the consequences of producing children, both in terms of bearing the burden of providing for their children's needs while they are growing up, and, later on, in terms of paying for the costs of securing their children's just shares, insofar as this is feasible. Indeed, it seems that, in the absence of an argument to the contrary, the endorsement of responsibility, which underlies Steiner's view (as I am reconstructing it) that parents bear the costs of care, would also commit him to holding parents responsible for the costs of added members.

Strangely, however, Steiner never considers this possibility, even when he asks explicitly what the consequences are of the fact that people beget people (Steiner 1994, 242), and that 'later choosers are the products of earlier ones' (Steiner 1998, 100). Indeed, in one place Steiner quotes Eric Rakowski, who is one of the responsibility-sensitive egalitarians who stands out for having explicitly argued that parents should pay for the costs of added members. Rakowski writes:

> . . . babies are not brought by storks whose whims are beyond our control. Specific individuals are responsible for their existence. It is therefore unjust to declare . . . that because two people decide to have a child, or through carelessness find themselves with one, *everyone* is required to share their resources with the new arrival, and to the same extent as its parents. With what right can two people force all the rest, through deliberate behavior rather than bad brute luck, to settle for less than their fair shares after resources have been divided justly?[13]

Yet Steiner does not adopt Rakowksi's view, and what he takes out of the passage just quoted is not Rakowski's commitment to holding parents responsible for the costs of children, but the altogether different point that, since children and their ability levels are not in the main the result of luck (a point Rakowski does make), but the product of parents' labour *and* the use of natural resources, the right to an equal share of natural resources has the implication, which I mentioned earlier, that parents may either owe or be owed compensation, depending on the value of the genetic information they appropriate.

There seems to be a tension, then, in Steiner's position on the costs of children. This tension could be resolved, quite straightforwardly, in one of two ways. First, Steiner could forgo the commitment to responsibility and insist that non-parents should indeed subsidise parents' choices to have children by sharing all the costs children create; second, he could stick to the responsibility principle and revise his view about just taxes, so that they reflect parents' obligations to pay for all the costs of children. Parents would then be asked to forgo their basic income to subsidise their children's rights to an equal share of natural resources, insofar as this is feasible.[14] However, neither of these strategies is wholly attractive. Both would require substantial revision of Steiner's views, and would conflict with some deep-seated convictions we have about justice. We believe responsibility should play some role in determining people's just shares, but at the same time, while most people are ready to consider an imprudent motorcyclist liable for the medical costs of his dangerous hobby—to take a familiar example of an activity for which it seems justified to hold someone responsible—few find the choice of parenting a justification for thinking that parents should pick up all the bills arising from their children's claims to get their just due.

Moreover, it is worth noticing that acceptance of the view that parents must internalise the costs of added members implies not only that non-parents have no obligation of justice (towards parents, that is) to share resources with the next generation, but also, more surprisingly, that non-parents have *no claim* of justice to receiving resources from anyone but their own parents. If the adoption of the principle of responsibility did require holding parents responsible for all the costs of children, then, applied consistently, it would condemn transfers from children to non-parents as much as transfers from non-parents to parents. It would require, ultimately, the abolition of a social fund, and the establishment, in its place, of what we could call *pure parental provision* of the claims of justice. This fact alone may be taken to constitute a *reductio ad absurdum* of the argument that parents are responsible for all the costs of children.

While I think this is the case, here I do not pursue this point. All I claim is that it would be fruitful for Steiner if he could avoid the radical revisions this argument would support, by showing that the tension in his position is only apparent. It is therefore worthwhile to ask whether he could indeed claim that the endorsement of a principle of responsibility can in fact be reconciled with a commitment to sharing some of the costs of children. In the remainder of this paper I examine this possibility and argue in its favour, in two steps. The first, negative step, establishes that, first appearances notwithstanding, adoption of the principle of responsibility does not, by itself, necessarily support the conclusion that parents should be held responsible for *all* the costs of children; the second, more positive step consists in identifying what line of argument is available to Steiner in support of the claim that the costs of added members should in fact be shared.

3. WHAT THE PRINCIPLE OF RESPONSIBILITY DOES NOT COMMIT US TO

As a preliminary for the first, negative step of the argument I am constructing, it is helpful to note that even those responsibility-sensitive egalitarians who have explicitly addressed the issue at hand, and highlighted that parents should be liable for the costs of children, are not unanimous in thinking that they should bear *all* of those costs. For example, Rakowski, whose passage on parents' responsibility is quoted by Steiner and I reported earlier, holds that parents should indeed bear *some* of the costs of added members, but not all of them: parents must provide their children with a basic bundle of resources, that to which all members of all generations are entitled to; but parents are not responsible for the costs of compensating for their children's bad luck.[15] Peter Vallentyne's position is more demanding of parents. On his view, parents are responsible not only for all of the costs of added members, but also for the damages those children, as adults, inflict upon others.[16]

The question arises, then, why there are such differences in the positions which the endorsement of responsibility seems to underpin, and which of these, if any, we are committed to if we endorse the responsibility principle. In this section I suggest that the differences in the positions of responsibility-sensitive egalitarians reflect differences in that part of a theory of responsibility that determines what the stakes or consequences of choice should be. This part of a theory of responsibility, which I refer to as *an account of stakes*, is, so I claim, an integral but not much discussed component of a theory of responsibility. Since different accounts of stakes can be defended, with varying implications for just what the consequences of choices should be, it is wrong to believe that an endorsement of the principle of responsibility *in itself* necessarily commits us to a particular conclusion about what people are responsible for. So, the possibility is at least in principle open, to a responsibility-sensitive theorist of justice, of defending a principle of stakes that does *not* support holding parents responsible for all the costs of children.

A theory of responsibility that can generate determinate judgments of responsibility must include both what I call a principle of attribution and a principle of stakes. A principle of attribution answers a question about the grounds of responsibility: 'What factors determine whether actions or choices are attributable to individuals in a way that justifies making them internalise the costs of their actions or choices?'. A principle of stakes, by contrast, answers a question about the consequences of choice: 'Assuming that individuals are responsible for their actions or conduct in a sense that justifies, other things being equal, making them pick up some costs, just what costs should they bear?'. Now, while virtually all discussions of justice and responsibility focus on formulating and defending an answer to the first question, few raise and explicitly address the question of stakes at all.[17] We are all too familiar with debates over whether, for example, having equal freedom, making a genuine or voluntary choice, or identifying with the preference that leads one to act in a certain way are either necessary or sufficient conditions for agents to be responsible for their actions.[18] But hardly any defence is ever offered of why, when the conditions for holding people responsible for their actions or choices are met, they should be held responsible for some rather than other consequences that those actions or choices could generate.

To see that there are various possible answers to the question of stakes, consider a paradigmatic case of imprudent conduct for which it seems plausible to hold individuals responsible, that of a person who ends up poorly off as a result of deliberately taking a risk of harm by driving a motorbike at high speed without wearing a helmet.[19] Just what should the consequences of the motorcyclist's actions be? Do they include being left to the side of the road, even if this means that she might die there, and even if there is a hospital right around the corner? Or are they that she should be taken to a hospital and pay for treatment of all her injuries, or only those injuries which resulted from the accident itself, rather than from the unforeseeable effect of the accident on her hitherto unknown predispositions to certain illnesses? And at what price should the treatment be charged, so that that price may also be deemed 'a consequence of her actions'? (If a hospital has a policy of charging motorcyclists more than others, is the additional expense also a cost the motorcyclist should be held responsible for?) Are the consequences of her action also that passers-by may appropriate her motorbike from the side of the road? Does the fact that she may lose her job if, once she has recovered from her accident, her limpness makes her a less attractive employee?

So, when we endorse the principle of responsibility, it is not enough to hold that a person who is responsible for her actions should bear the consequences of her actions: we need to ask what those consequences justifiably include, and why. There is no answer to this question that is privileged, in the sense that it is self-evidently the right one *given* our commitment to the principle of responsibility. We may at first think otherwise because we may assume a contextualist account of stakes, on which people are responsible for whatever the consequences of their actions are in the context in which they act. But on second thought this account is implausible: there are clearly cases in which we do not think that people should bear the consequences which their actions happen to have in the context in which they are carried out. For example, suppose that employers refused to employ parents of young children, on the grounds that children thrive best under parental care than under alternative day care arrangements.[20] People who choose to have children in this context face unemployment for several years and the prospect of serious financial hardship. I submit that it would be implausible to say, of the people who do choose to have children, that their resulting economic disadvantage is just, simply because it is the result of their choices, even if it were made clear to them in advance of having children that their making this choice would have this consequence.

Since a principle of responsibility, in order to yield determinate judgments of who should bear what costs, must include an account of stakes, and since it is possible to defend different accounts of stakes, to accept that justice should be responsibility-sensitive does not by itself necessarily commit us to a particular view of what costs people should bear. This is not to say that all accounts of stakes are equally plausible, but only that we would be wrong to assume that Steiner, and indeed all defenders of responsibility-sensitive theories of justice, are being inconsistent if they require that some of the costs of children be shared by non-parents and parents alike. Whether or not they are depends on their account of stakes. In Steiner's case, that account is given by his view of what rights people have. So, the next question is whether it would be wrong to come to the conclusion that responsibility and sharing the costs of children are compatible after examining what considerations Steiner could invoke for why the stakes of the choice of having children do not include the costs of added members.

4. RECONCILING RESPONSIBILITY AND SHARING THE COSTS OF CHILDREN

The grounds we could appeal to for sharing the costs of children are diverse. Some that immediately spring to mind are forward-looking or incentive considerations of the kind that arguably motivate most country's policies of subsidising parenting (we need to support parents if we want to maintain a birth-rate that is high enough to sustain a healthy economy and welfare policies put under strain by our increased longevity)[21], and considerations of gender equality (supporting parents amounts to doing justice to women, as they currently do the lion's share of child-rearing in the context of norms and institutions that are gender-biased, and which render them economically vulnerable and lacking in recognition compared to their male counterparts). There are also arguments that press a case for the justice-based claims of parents as such (as opposed to incentive-based ones, or the justice-based claims of women). The most prominent of these is the public goods argument, which points to the fact that parents produce positive externalities by producing children (their children will become tomorrow's workforce and help pay for non-parents' pensions) and that, by accepting these benefits, non-parents incur an obligation of fairness to help bear the costs incurred in producing them.[22]

While some of these lines of argument are, in my view, promising, I do not examine them here, since my concern is not with the general question of whether a convincing case for the sharing of the costs of children can be made but with the more specific one of whether Steiner can be justified in thinking that on his historical entitlement theory non-parents are required to share some of these costs, those of added members. The arguments I have mentioned so far would not help answer that question. Incentive considerations could not, on Steiner's view, ground enforceable obligations. And while Steiner may be sympathetic to considerations of gender equality, the gender-based argument is not one that would necessarily require transfers from non-parents to parents, and would in any event point to a demand of non-ideal justice for why (female) carers should be assisted. Nor would Steiner support the public goods argument. That argument supports too extensive a range of enforceable obligations, and, by holding that someone can incur an enforceable obligation as a result of someone else's choice, it violates a principle which Steiner says his view of responsibility respects. That principle, formulated by Alan Gibbard, states that '[m]oral rules should be so constructed that, if the rules are obeyed, the acts of each person benefit or harm only himself, except as he himself chooses to confer or exchange the benefits of his acts' (Gibbard 1976).

So, just what grounds are available to Steiner for showing that his endorsement of responsibility is not in tension with his view about just taxes, which support the sharing of the costs of added members? I suggest that Steiner could claim that the principle of responsibility he supports is qualified, so that it requires that the only other-affecting form of behaviour that individuals should be held responsible for is harmful interference, where this is understood as rights-violating interference; and hold that parents' choice to have children and externalise the costs of added members is not rights-violating.

The qualification of the principle of responsibility I have in mind is suggested by Steiner's own discussion of responsibility. On this view, we should hold people responsible only for *harmful* other-affecting behaviour, where harmful behaviour is rights-curtailing behaviour. This suggestion can be extracted from Steiner's discussion of the three-world story I mentioned earlier. Recall that Steiner distinguishes between a world in which the only source of disadvantage is nature, a world in which the only source of disadvantage is the non-benevolent behaviour of others, and a world in which the only source of adversity is imprudence. In order to ask parents to internalise the costs of having children within this framework, we would have to show that their choice amounts to a failure of benevolence of the sort that arises in the second world, where '. . . on any view of personal responsibility, the sort of regime required to eliminate adversity [. . .] must be one based on *redress*: one that compels harmers alone to bear the full costs of compensation' (Steiner 1998, 103).

Should we consider parents as harmers who owe redress to non-parents? The answer is negative. While it is true that parents' choice to have children (may) negatively affect others, by diminishing the share of resources available to them, this does not, on the view at hand, suffice to establish their liability. Parents' choices to have children do not, arguably, fit the bill, for it is plausible to understand the benevolence baseline, departures from which people are held responsible for, as requiring only that people do not *harm* others, where this is not coextensive with the more demanding requirement that they do not affect others' interests negatively. And one possible way of drawing the distinction between negatively affecting others' interests and harming them is by adopting a rights-based definition of harm.[23] Someone is harmed only when her rights are violated; if others, by contrast, impose on someone costs while acting within their rights, that does not constitute harm in the relevant sense—not in the sense, that is, that justifies asking that person to internalise those costs, or asking her for redress.

Someone might object that even if we accepted, for the sake of argument, the restriction on the principle of responsibility I have just mentioned, it still would not follow that parents are not liable for the costs of added members. This is because, according to the objection I am considering, we should reject one of the premises of this argument, namely, that parents are not violating non-parents' rights (even on Steiner's view of what rights people have) by having children and creating costs of added members which non-parents are required to internalise. After all, isn't what is at issue, in the argument from responsibility, precisely whether non-parents' rights would be violated by the externalisation of the costs of added members? The objection at hand insists that those rights would indeed be violated. More precisely, people's right to an equal share of natural resources is violated by a demand that they forgo some of those resources in order to ensure that new persons' rights to an equal share of natural resources are met.

In reply, Steiner could argue as follows. The claim that non-parents' rights would be violated by a requirement to internalise the costs of added members, where the latter is expressed in Steiner's commitment to viewing those rights as encumbered, would, if applied consistently, lead to an implausible interpretation of those rights. If we thought that non-parents' rights to an equal share of natural resources were violated by the externalization of the costs of added members, then it would seem to follow that everyone would each have a right to *all* the natural resources. This is because, if we apply the principle that underlies the objection consistently—namely, that our right to a share of natural resources is violated whenever the share of resources at our disposal is diminished by new members for whose existence someone else is responsible—then non-parents' rights to a share of natural resources would be violated not only by having to share resources with the children of their cohorts, but also by having to share resources with their cohorts, who are the children of parents of the previous generation, and whose share of resources should therefore be the responsibility of those parents. And that right would also be violated by having to share resources with their cohorts' parents, who in turn are the responsibility of their own parents. Since everyone is someone's child, there is no one whose claim to an equal share of resources would not, on the view in question, count as a rights-violation; each non-parent would then claim to have a right to all the natural resources. But this would obviously amount to a set of incompossible rights, or rights which are not mutually consistent, and would be unacceptable by Steiner's lights.[24]

So, it is wrong to assume that non-parents' rights to a share of natural resources is a right to a determinate share of natural resources, that equal share of natural resources they have at their disposal prior to new children's arrivals. A plausible interpretation of those rights is one on which the share of natural resources which everyone is entitled to varies depending on how many other persons, in previous and subsequent generations as well as in one's own generation, are fellow claimants of just shares.

5. CONCLUSION

Steiner can defend himself against the charge that his views on responsibility and his views on just taxes are inconsistent. While parents can legitimately be held responsible for the costs of care of their children, they may externalise the costs of added members they create by creating new persons. To suggest as much does not indicate a failure to take the principle of responsibility seriously. Adoption of that principle by itself does not, I have argued, necessarily commit us to the view that parents are responsible for *all* the costs of children, and Steiner can adduce considerations for why they should not bear the costs of added members which are consistent with his views on rights and on responsibility.

Those who, unlike Steiner, contest the rights-based definition of harm which I have suggested Steiner could adopt in his argument, and, or, reject the Gibbard rule, would not support Steiner's conclusion. They could argue that the principle of responsibility for other-affecting behaviour as Steiner understands it is too restrictive, that the adversity of a person can be another's responsibility even when she has not infringed the former's rights, and that parents are responsible for the costs of added members, as well as the costs of care. Some of the points I have raised in my discussion of Steiner, such as that concerning the role of the principle of stakes in any conclusion about what people are responsible for, could be deployed in a reply to these arguments. Moreover, that reply could also import considerations such as the idea that the creation of children produces benefits as well as costs, which are barred to Steiner and which I have not examined here. What an examination of these further arguments reveals—and this is a point that should be of interest to Steiner as well as to responsibility-sensitive egalitarians—is that there is a greater difference than Steiner thinks between various responsibility-sensitive egalitarian views and Steiner's own view on the costs of children, since adoption of the principle of responsibility can be argued to be compatible with a range of very different positions on sharing the costs of children.

NOTES

1. In the UK the average cost of raising a child to the age of 21 was estimated, in 2004, to be the highest in Europe at £153, 620; in 2007 this figure had risen to £186,000, with the largest expenditure being on childcare and education. See http://www.guardian.co.uk/money/2004/nov/26/business.childtrustfunds, and http://www.lv.com/media_centre/press_releases/cost.
2. As working adults, (most) new persons also help sustain those shares, whether or not their contribution is less than their withdrawal of resources. This may affect our appraisal of parents' choices to produce new persons. Notice that on some views of children's rights and of justice, the distinction between the costs of care and the costs of added members is somewhat blurred, as children may have claims of justice to receiving a certain level of care, and what they receive while they are children is part of their just lifetime share.
3. The notion of responsibility that is relevant here is that which has been referred to as 'consequential responsibility', 'substantive responsibility', 'accountability', or 'liability'. To attribute responsibility to someone is to claim that that person can justifiably be made to pick up or internalise some costs of her conduct, and that others are justified in treating her in a certain way (letting her bear the consequences of her actions, enforcing an obligation she has undertaken, exacting compensation from her, and so on). See Scanlon 1998, Roemer 1998, Dworkin 2000. In what follows, I talk interchangeably of someone being responsible and of someone being held responsible to refer to this sense of responsibility.
4. Our right of self-ownership, that is, the right to control, use and exchange one's mental and physical abilities and the products of those, would be violated by redistributive taxation. Steiner writes: 'Self-owners are each responsible for their own choices and cannot justly compel one another to undo the distributive consequences of those choices (Steiner 2002, 185). According to Steiner, both the right of self-ownership and the right to an equal share of natural resources are grounded in a right to equal freedom.
5. Steiner leaves it open whether he supports an unconditional basic *income* or an unconditional basic *initial endowment.*
6. There seem to be two puzzles surrounding Steiner's position on genetic information being a natural resource: First, can genetic information really be thought to be a natural resource for which people are liable to taxation? Second, why are only parents liable to taxation? Concerning the first point, Steiner writes that 'Natural resources are taxable because, since they are initially unowned, all self-owners are at liberty to use them' (Steiner 1992, 82). But since the genetic information parents appropriate is carried by parts of their bodies, it is not clear that Steiner can say that it is a resource anyone is at liberty to appropriate: to appropriate it would *necessarily* involve violating the self-ownership rights of those who carry that information. A way out of this conundrum may be this: parents could be seen as (involuntary!) appropriators of genetic information *just in virtue of their carrying it* in particular body cells. But then this raises a second puzzle: why are only parents, rather than *all persons*, liable to this tax? Since Steiner believes that natural resource ownership, rather than use, grounds tax liability, and since all persons can be seen to appropriate this resource, it seems unjustified to tax parents alone.
7. Steiner states that, through the fund, we redistribute wealth from 'those adults who own children with superior genetic endowments to *those who don't*' (Steiner 1994, 277). I assume that 'those who don't' refers to *both* those who appropriate genetic information that is not very valuable (i.e. par-

ents of children with less golden genes, as Steiner would put it) and those who do not appropriate genetic information at all (i.e. non-parents).

8. It is true that the fact that (some parents) incur *greater* costs of care than others may affect what compensation they are owed: if they incur greater costs, this may mean that the resources they have appropriated are less valuable than others', and will be owed compensation to offset this. But that fact does not figure in the justification of their right to compensation. Notice, moreover, that it is arguably not the case that parents *must actually* incur those greater costs. While parents are owed compensation because the resources they appropriate are less valuable than others', why should they use the compensation they receive to make those resources more valuable, by offering more or better care for their children, rather than to improve their stock of resources in some other ways? According to Steiner, parents must secure only a *minimum*, not an *equal* amount of inputs. See Steiner 1998, 105–6; Steiner 2002, 187.
9. We may think that parents are internalising some costs of added members by having to pay a tax on valuable genetic information. But when children, as adults, come to claim rights, *all* adults (non-parents as well as parents) contribute equally to securing those rights. Although Steiner requires that the costs of added members be shared, he does hold parents liable for *some* costs, i.e. *the costs of damages*, until adulthood. See Steiner 2002, 187.
10. Steiner 1998. In this paper Steiner concentrates on John Roemer's egalitarian view. Since Steiner's contribution, this type of egalitarianism, which is now often referred to as 'luck egalitarianism', has received extensive discussion and elaboration. See, for example, Anderson 1999.
11. Steiner 1998, 97. He states that '. . . the set of entitlements should reflect the requirements that persons be held *responsible* for the adverse consequences of their own actions'.
12. Steiner says that the difference he identifies between his account of responsibility and the view of responsibility-sensitive egalitarians is somewhat overdrawn. In fact, responsibility-sensitive egalitarians may argue that there is really no difference between them at all, in terms of the kind of judgments of responsibility they recommend. The choice-circumstance distinction can do all the requisite work: we only need to ask who—whether a particular agent who suffers a disadvantage or someone else—is responsible for that disadvantage. And, once we have set up the background against which make choices, and therefore, the consequences of their choices, in a certain way, we can always redescribe people's non-benevolent behaviour as imprudent. If we set up institutions that penalise the choice to act in ways that negatively affect others, we can describe the choice to do so an imprudent one, as the person who acts non-benevolently will end up disadvantaged as a result. So, responsibility-sensitive egalitarians can, and do, say that someone's circumstance can be the result of someone else's (imprudent) choice. However, in my view Steiner's distinctive way of mapping out the territory highlights something important. By emphasising the distinction between a world in which someone ends up worse off than others as a result of his own actions and a world in which someone ends up worse off than others as a result of others' actions, Steiner draws attention to that fact that when we ascribe responsibility, we invoke both a standard of prudence and a standard of other-affecting behaviour as standards (chosen) departures from which warrant departures from equality. Egalitarian philosophers have often drawn attention only to the former, by observing that a responsibility-sensitive egalitarian view requires that institutions be so set up that, if people behave prudently, they end up no worse off than others; but they may end up worse off than oth-

ers if they make imprudent choices. See, for example, Arneson, 1989. That we must also assume a standard of other-affecting (as well as self-affecting) behaviour we expect from people (so that, if they comply with it, they end up equally well off as others) is overlooked if we subsume all responsibility judgements under the category of 'imprudent behaviour'.

13. Rakowski 1991, 153. Cited in Steiner 1994, 278–9. The last sentence here is unhelpful: whether resources have in fact been divided justly is precisely what is in question; so Rakowski shouldn't assume that. Note also that Rakowski continues: 'If the cultivation of expensive tastes, or silly gambles, or any other intentional action cannot give rise to redistributive claims, how can procreation?'.
14. I assume that, on this view, it is mandatory that children's rights be met, so that, if parents cannot meet them, the costs of meeting them will have to be shared. It is then a further question what sorts of action are legitimate against parents who choose to have children when they cannot fully bear the costs. One view would be that parents have an obligation not to have children under those circumstances, and/or that they can be penalised in various ways if they nonetheless choose to have them. See Vallentyne 2002b. Steiner seems to support a different view. See Steiner 1998, 103, note 22.
15. Rakowski 1991, 154. Rakowski does not offer a reason for discriminating in this way between the costs that parents should and those they should not be liable for.
16. Vallentyne 2002b.
17. Some exceptions are Fleurbaey 1998; Vallentyne 2002a; Ripstein 1994; Ripstein 1999; Ripstein 2004; Arneson 2001. For a recent discussion see Stemplowska.
18. See, for example, Cohen 1989; Cohen 2004; Dworkin 2000; Dworkin 2004.
19. For this example, see Fleurbaey 1995.
20. I stipulate this so that we do not think that a minimally plausible interpretation of equality of opportunity would clearly condemn the employers' initiative.
21. The moral status of these incentive-based case is dubious in light of the fact that population growth could be achieved by allowing for immigration, which the same countries that offer subsidies to parents set strict limits to. For a discussion see George 1993 and Casal 1999.
22. For a defence of the public goods argument, see George 1993; for critiques, see Casal 1999; Casal and Williams 2004; Rakowski 1991. Other arguments appeal to the objective good of parenting, and claims of parental autonomy. See, for example, Alstott 2004.
23. Steiner does not himself discuss a rights-definition of harm. I discuss the rights-definition of harm and the use Robert Nozick makes of it in Olsaretti 2004.
24. On the requirement of compossibility, see Steiner 1994, 2–3.

BIBLIOGRAPHY

Alstott, A.L. 2004. *No Exit: What Parents Owe Their Children and What Society Owes Parents*. Oxford: Oxford University Press.

Anderson, E. 1999. 'What is the Point of Equality?' 109 *Ethics* 287–337.

Arneson, R. 1989. 'Equality and Equality of Opportunity for Welfare.' 56 *Philosophical Studies* 77–93.

Arneson, R. 2001. 'Luck and Equality.' 10 *Proceedings of the Aristotelian Society* 73–90.
Casal, P. 1999. 'Environmentalism, Procration, and the Principle of Fairness.' 13 *Public Affairs Quarterly* 363–76.
Cohen, G.A. 1989. 'On the Currency of Egalitarian Justice.' 99 *Ethics* 906–44.
Cohen, G.A. 2004. 'Expensive Tastes Ride Again.' In J. Burley (ed.), *Dworkin and His Critics*, Oxford: Blackwell.
Dworkin, R. 2000. *Sovereign Virtue*. Cambridge, Mass.: Harvard University Press.
Dworkin R. 2004. 'Ronald Dworkin Replies'. In J. Burley (ed.), *Dworkin and His Critics*, Oxford: Blackwell.
Fleurbaey, M. 1995. 'Equal Opportunity or Equal Social Outcome?' 11 *Economics and Philosophy* 25–55.
Fleurbaey M. 1998. 'Equality among responsible individuals.' In J. F. Laslier, M. Fleurbaey, N. Gravel, A. Trannoy (eds), *Freedom in Economics: New Perspectives in Normative Analysis*. Routledge.
George, R. 1993. 'On the External Benefits of Children.' In D.T. Meyers, K. Kipnis, C.F. Murphy (eds), *Kindred Matters: Rethinking the Philosophy of the Family*, Ithaca and London: Cornell University Press.
Gibbard, A. 1976. 'Natural Property Rights.' 10 *Nous* 77–88.
Olsaretti, S. 2004. *Liberty, Desert and the Market: A Philosophical Study*. Cambridge: Cambridge University Press.
Ripstein, A., 1994. 'Equality, Luck, and Responsibility.' 23 *Philosophy and Public Affairs* 3–23.
Ripstein, A. 1999. *Equality, Responsibility, and the Law*. Cambridge: Cambridge University Press.
Ripstein, A. 2004. 'Justice and Responsibility.' 17 *Canadian Journal of Law and Jurisprudence* 361–86.
Roemer, J. 1998. *Equality of Opportunity*. Cambridge, Mass.: Harvard University Press.
Scanlon, T.M., 1998. *What We Owe To Each Other*. Cambridge, Mass.: Harvard University Press.
Steiner, H. 1992. 'Three Just Taxes.' In P. Van Parijs (ed.), *Arguing for Basic Income*. London and New York: Verso.
Steiner, H. 1994. *An Essay on Rights*. Oxford: Blackwell.
Steiner, H. 1998. 'Choice and Circumstance.' In A. Mason (ed.), *Ideals of Equality*. Oxford: Blackwell.
Steiner, H. 1999. 'Just Taxation and International Redistribution.' In I. Shapiro & L. Brilmayer (eds), *Nomos XLI: Global Justice*. New York: New York University Press.
Steiner, H. 2002, 'Silver Spoons and Golden Genes: Talent Differentials and Distributive Justice.' In D. Archard and C.M. McLeod (eds), *The Moral and Political Status of Children*. Oxford: Oxford University Press.
Stemplowska, Z. 2008. 'Making Justice Sensitive to Responsibility.' Forthcoming in *Political Studies*.
Vallentyne, P. 2002a. 'Brute luck, Option Luck, and Equality of Initial Opportunities.' 112 *Ethics* 529–557.
Vallentyne, P. 2002b. 'Equality and the Duties of Procreators'. In D. Archard and C.M. McLeod (eds), *The Moral and Political Status of Children*. Oxford: Oxford University Press.

6 Responsibility and Compensation Rights

Peter Vallentyne

I address an issue that arises for rights theories that recognize rights to compensation for rights-intrusions. Do individuals who never pose any risk of harm to others have a right, against a rights-intruder, to full compensation for any resulting intrusion-harm, or is the right limited in some way by the extent to which the intruder was agent-responsible for the intrusion-harm (e.g., the extent to which the harm was a foreseeable result of her autonomous choices)? Although this general issue of strict liability vs. fault liability has been much analyzed and debated, there is a promising position that, to the best of my knowledge, has not been much discussed. This is the view that (1) when the intruder is agent-responsible for violating the rights (e.g., does so knowingly), she owes the intrudee compensation for the entire intrusion-harm, but (2) when the intruder is not agent-responsible for wrongly intruding upon the rights (because the intrusion was not wrong or because the intruder could not reasonably have known it was wrong), then she owes the intrudee compensation only for the intrusion-harm for which she is agent-responsible (and not, for example, harm that she could not have reasonably foreseen). I shall develop and motivate this position without attempting a full defense. Throughout, I focus on the rights of the intrudee, against the intruder, to compensation and the correlative duty of the intruder to the intrudee.

I'm pleased and honored to have this paper included in this collection in honor of Hillel Steiner. Much of what I know about rights and libertarianism I learned from him—both from his written works and from his very helpful correspondence over the years. Moreover, his intellectual rigor, honesty, and modesty have been a source of inspiration. Although Hillel has not written extensively on compensation for intrusion-harms, it is a topic central to his view of justice, as it is to mine.[1]

1. BACKGROUND

We shall focus on theories that recognize certain basic rights (such as the right not to be killed or assaulted), where these include rights to compensation (and associated enforcement rights) for a rights-intrusion. Such theories hold that, at least under certain conditions, agents owe compensation for the *intrusion-harm* (i.e., harm from a rights-intrusion) that they impose on others.

A person's rights define certain boundaries, which, if crossed, raise the question of whether the right has been intruded upon (as opposed to merely crossed). If rights are understood as protecting *choices*, then crossing the boundary of a right does *not* intrude upon the right, if the crossing is with the valid *permission* of the right-holder.[2] Rights can, however, be understood as protecting *interests*—with boundary crossings being intrusions, for example, when they are against the interests of the right-holder.[3] There is also the possibility (which I favor) that rights that protect *both* choices and interests, with the protection of choices taking priority. In general, however, I here remain neutral on this issue. For simplicity of presentation, I shall focus on the choice-protecting account.

We shall be asking what compensation rights individuals have in virtue of their rights being intruded upon, where intrusion is understood as follows (assuming a choice-protecting conception of rights for simplicity). If the boundary is crossed with the permission of the holder, then the right is *not intruded upon*. If the boundary is crossed without the right-holder's permission, then her right is *intruded upon*. A rights intrusion does not, however, establish that the intrusion was impermissible. If the intrusion was not the result of an autonomous choice of the intruder (e.g., the wind unexpectedly blew her against you or she attacked you while insane), then the right is *not infringed* and the intrusion is neither permissible nor impermissible (because not the result of an autonomous choice).[4] If, however, the intrusion is the result of an autonomous choice of the intruder, then the right is *infringed*.[5] Because rights need not be absolute, the infringement of a right need not be impermissible.[6] Sometimes, there may be special justifying conditions that specify that the right may be permissibly overridden under certain conditions (e.g., avoiding social catastrophe).[7] If, however, the infringement is not justified by such considerations, then the right is *violated* and the intrusion is impermissible.

We shall be addressing what compensation is owed for each of the following ways of intruding upon a right:

Intrusion: Borders defined by rights were crossed by the intruder without permission of the right-holder.
Non-autonomous intrusion: The intrusion is not the result of an autonomous choice of the intruder and thus neither permissible nor impermissible.
Infringement: The intrusion is the result of an autonomous choice of the intruder and is thus either permissible or impermissible.
Mere infringement: Justificatory conditions hold for the infringement of the right. The action is not wrong in virtue of the infringement (but may be for other reasons; see below).

Violation: Justificatory conditions do not hold for the infringement of the right. The action is wrong in virtue of the infringement.

It's worth noting that, although a rights-violation entails that an infringement is impermissible, the reverse entailment does not hold. An infringement of a given right can be impermissible without being a violation. Justificatory conditions for the infringement of the given right might hold (and thus the right is not violated), but the infringement might be wrong for some other reason. It might violate an impersonal constraint or might violate some other right (perhaps of someone else). Thus, an infringement of a right can be wrong (impermissible) without violating that right.[8] We shall return to this below.

Throughout, I shall focus on the case where the intrudee is strictly harmless in the sense of not having ever imposed an intrusion-harm on anyone and with no chance of doing so in the future. Although few, if any, people are strictly harmless in this sense, this is the core case. Intrudees who are not strictly harmless may be owed significantly less than full compensation (e.g., compensation only for the harm from excess force used to stop them from imposing intrusion-harm). That, however, is a topic for another time. Here I focus exclusively on intrudees who are strictly harmless.

I shall focus on the question of what an intruder owes an intrudee. I shall not address the question of what happens if the intrudee dies before fully compensated—either because the intruder killed her or because she died for unrelated reasons. It's clear that the debt-claim cannot simply disappear, and merely transferring the debt to the intrudee's heirs fails to reflect the fact that compensation was never fully provided to the intrudee. This is a difficult and important question that I will set aside in this paper.

There are two main views about the duty to compensate for one's intrusion-harms. On the *strict-liability* view, intruding agents have a duty to compensate for the intrusion-harm for which they are *causally* responsible.[9] By contrast, on the less demanding *agent-responsibility* (or fault) view, intruding agents have a duty to compensate for the intrusion-harm for which they are *agent-responsible* ("outcome-responsible", "morally responsible").[10] To be agent-responsible for an outcome, the agent must be causally responsible for the outcome and the outcome must be "suitably reflective" of the agent's autonomous agency. There is much debate about what exactly determines when an individual is agent-responsible for something,[11] but it's clear that one can be causally responsible for harm without being agent-responsible for it. This is arguably so when: (1) the intruder's *agency* was not involved at all (e.g., because an unforeseeable gust of wind blew her against the right-holder), (2) the intruder's agency was involved but her *autonomy* was radically impaired (e.g., the actions of psychotics or of someone in an extreme panic), or (3) the intruder's autonomous agency was involved but the intruder *could not have reasonably known* that her choice would have the specified result (e.g., she could not have known that the terrorist had rigged the light switch to set off the bomb).

Agent-responsibility, it should be stressed, is relative to a specified outcome. One can be agent-responsible for some outcomes (e.g., the foreseeable results within one's control) but not for others (e.g., those results that could not have been foreseen). Suppose, for example, that an agent intentionally shoots another in the leg because she reasonably but falsely believes that the other is a terrorist about to set off a bomb. She is agent-responsible for the foreseeable harm but not for violating the innocent person's rights (even though she does violate his rights). It should also be noted that agent-responsibility for harming a person entails nothing about whether the harming was morally permissible. One can be agent-responsible for morally permissible harms (e.g., against a terrorist to stop her attack) and for morally impermissible harms (e.g., against innocents with no valid justification). Agent-responsibility for an outcome merely establishes that the outcome is suitably attributable to one's autonomous agency.

I shall suggest below that the duty to compensate depends in part on issues of agent-responsibility, and hence on what the agent knew or reasonably should have known. It's important to note that the appeal to agent-responsibility is for determining the extent of the *duty to compensate*. I do not claim—indeed, I would deny—that whether an intrusion, infringement, or violation takes place depends on agent-responsibility or what the agent knew or should have known.[12] The only claim is that the duty to compensate for damages from an intrusion so depends. Whether an intrusion took place is one question; the extent to which the intruder is liable for the resulting harm is another.

When an intruder owes compensation for an intrusion-harm, what is the currency of the debt? It is often assumed that some kind of cash-value payment (in cash or resources) is owed, and this may make sense for legal duties to compensate. For morality, however, it seems mistaken. The relevant harm imposed was a loss in life prospects for wellbeing and it seems more plausible that an offsetting increase in such prospects is what is owed. Obviously, there are many possible conceptions of wellbeing and of prospects that might be invoked here, but I shall leave this aspect of the position open. The important point is that, although a cash payment (or equivalent) may often discharge a duty to compensate, when it does, it is the means and not the end. Suppose, for example, that I owe you compensation for a 10-unit loss of wellbeing and, before I discharge this debt, the cost of providing this increase in wellbeing increases from $100 to $1000 (e.g., because you have an accident that limits your ability for gains in wellbeing). I still owe you 10-units of wellbeing, no matter what the cost (as opposed to only owing you only $100 plus interest). The currency of compensation is life prospects (for wellbeing), not cash value.[13]

Although I believe that the only reparation duties agents have in virtue of a rights-intrusion are duties to compensate, I do not assume that here.

I leave open, for example, whether there are duties to apologize or submit to punishment. My only claim is that the duty to compensate is a duty to provide an offsetting increase in life prospects. Thus, if an intrusion *benefits* the right-holder (e.g., accidentally or because done paternalistically), no compensation is owed.

I shall now suggest that the duty to compensate for an intrusion-harm depends on whether the intruder was agent-responsible for violating the right (e.g., knew that she was violating the right). Strict liability, I suggest, holds if she is so agent-responsible but not if she is not agent-responsible for acting wrongly (e.g., was not acting wrongly at all or could not have known that she was acting wrongly). As far as I know, the idea of making the duty to compensate depend on agent-responsibility for a rights violation (or perhaps, more generally, acting wrongly) has not been systematically developed. Below, I shall take a first step in articulating and motivating such a position. I will not, however, attempt a full defense.

2. WHERE THE INTRUDER IS NOT AGENT-RESPONSIBLE FOR WRONGLY INTRUDING UPON THE RIGHT

To start, we shall consider the case where an intruder is not agent-responsible for wrongly intruding upon the right ("non-culpable" intrusion). This is compatible with the intruder being agent-responsible for some intrusion-harm, since the agent may have intended the harm reasonably believing that she was acting permissibly. (Keep in mind that agent-responsibility is relative to some specified outcome.) In such cases, the intruder's duty of compensation is limited, I suggest, to compensating for the intrusion-harm, if any, for which she is agent-responsible (and not for intrusion-harms that were not the result of her autonomous choices or that were reasonably unforeseeable).

There are three relevant kinds of case where the intruder is not agent-responsible for wrongly intruding upon the right. In one, the agent intruded upon the right, but did not do so as the result of an autonomous choice (e.g., the wind blew her against the intrudee, or she struck at him while insane or in an extreme panic). In such cases, the intruder does not act wrongly (since her autonomous agency was not involved; it was a mere bodily movement), and hence she is not agent-responsible for wrongly intruding upon the right. My general claim is that intruders who are not agent-responsible for wrongly intruding owe compensation only for any intrusion-harm for which they are agent-responsible. In the case where there is no autonomous agency involved, the intruder is not agent-responsible for anything and hence owes *no compensation* for the intrusion-harm imposed. This seems correct. Although the agent's body is causally connected with the intrusion-harm, her agency is not. There is therefore little reason for her, rather than someone else, to have a duty to compensate for that harm.[14]

This does not mean that the intrudee has no right to compensation for the intrusion-harm. It merely means that he has no *special* right *against the intruder*. If, as I believe, individuals have a (perhaps limited) right, *against others in general*, to be compensated for below-average brute-luck wellbeing (i.e., wellbeing for which they are not agent-responsible), then the intrudee may well be eligible for at least partial compensation for the intrusion-harm. There is, however, little reason to hold the non-autonomous intruder accountable for such compensation.

A second case where the intruder is not agent-responsible for wrongly intruding upon the right is one where she autonomously intruded upon (i.e., infringed) the right but *did not violate* the right because the right was not absolute and was justifiably overridden (e.g., to avoid social catastrophe). Here, we further suppose that she did not violate anyone else's rights or any impersonal constraint. (We'll return to those issues below.) Thus, the intrusion was permissible. Perhaps pushing a harmless innocent person on top of a terrorist to prevent the latter from setting off a bomb is such a case. What compensation is owed for such permissible intrusions? Some might argue that compensation is owed only for *violations* of rights and not for permissible infringements. It seems more plausible, however, to hold that compensation of some sort is owed even in the latter cases. Although it may be permissible to infringe rights in special cases, there is little reason to hold that the right to compensation would be eliminated in such cases.[15] In any case, my main claim here is that, if compensation is owed to the intrudee in such cases, it is limited—given that the intruder was acting permissibly—to the intrusion-harm for which the intruder was agent-responsible. She owes the intrudee no compensation for intrusion-harms that she did not foresee and could not have foreseen.

Suppose, for example, that an agent takes the initiative to gently push a harmless innocent to stop a terrorist from bombing. Suppose that the agent could not have foreseen the result that the innocent person suffers a freak devastating injury from the gentle push. Nor could she have foreseen that several bystanders would also be injured by the act. It seems unreasonable to hold that the agent must fully compensate these innocents for the harm imposed, as opposed to the reasonably foreseeable harm (for which she is agent-responsible). As noted above, this does not entail that the innocents are not owed compensation by others in general.

It might be objected that, where an agent permissibly infringes someone's rights to prevent harm to others, others have a duty to share in the compensation owed to the infringee. The duty to compensate for infringement-harms for which the infringer is agent-responsible does not, it is suggested, fall entirely on the infringer in such a case. I do not here rule out the possibility that, in such cases, others *owe the infringer* their fair share of the compensation cost that she incurs towards the infringee. I merely claim that the infringer owes full compensation to the infringer for the intrusion-harms for which she is agent-responsible. She is agent-responsible for the infringement-harm in question, and she owes a duty to the infringee to provide such compensation. She may also have a right to collect from others, but that is a separate issue. The failure of others, for example, to provide their fair share of the owed compensation does not affect the duty the infringer owes the infringee.

A third and final case where the intruder is not agent-responsible for wrongly intruding upon the right is one where she (wrongly) *violates* the right but could not have reasonably known that she was doing so (e.g., all the evidence strongly supported the mistaken view that the intrudee was a terrorist about to set off a bomb).[16] My claim is that the duty to compensate in this case is no different from that of the previous case where the intruder permissibly infringed the right. Admittedly, in this case, the action is wrong and in the above case, it is not. In neither case, however, does the agent bear any responsibility for acting wrongly, since she could not reasonably have known that she was acting wrongly in this third case. It thus seems plausible that, in this third case (like the second), the intruder must compensate the intrudee only for the intrusion-harm for which she is agent-responsible.[17]

3. WHERE THE INTRUDER IS AGENT-RESPONSIBLE FOR VIOLATING THE RIGHT

Where an intruder is not agent-responsible for wrongly intruding upon the right, she owes the intrudee, I have claimed, compensation only for the intrusion-harm for which she is agent-responsible. In such cases, strict liability for all intrusion-harm is excessive, given that the intruder had no reason to believe that she was acting wrongly. Things are different, I suggest, where the agent is agent-responsible for (wrongly) violating the right. In such cases, the agent has, or should have, "a guilty mind". She knows, or should reasonably know, that she is violating the right, and it seems reasonable that she should be morally accountable for the full intrusion-harm even if greater than she reasonably believed it to be (strict liability).

A weak version of my claim is simply that the duties of compensation are *more* onerous when one is responsible for violating the right (e.g., when one does so knowingly) than when one is not responsible for wrongly intruding (e.g., when one does not act wrongly or when one does so but could not have known that one was doing so). The key claim here is that the culpability of the intruder (in the sense of being agent-responsible for the violation) is relevant to the duty of compensation, just as many think it is for liability to punishment. I have no argument here. I just can't see why this wouldn't be so. Those who knowingly violate a right are subject to higher standards of compensation than those who are not responsible for wrongly intruding.

My key claim, of course, is the much stronger claim that the intruder in such cases is liable for the entire intrusion-harm and not merely the portion for which she is agent-responsible. The main objection to this position is that it is too severe. Suppose that I knowingly violate your rights by flicking your ear, and I reasonably expect that this will cause you only minor harm. Suppose further that I could not have foreseen the fact that you have a special condition (physiological or psychological) that ensures that you suffer great harm from my intrusion. Do I really owe you a large increase in life prospects, given that I could not have known that you would suffer such great harm? My claim is that I do. One can avoid the risk of being so liable by avoiding being agent-responsible for acting wrongly. One can do that simply by not acting in ways that one knows, or should reasonably know, are wrong. Although severe, this is much weaker than the general strict liability view (which holds agents strictly liable even if they are not agent-responsible for acting wrongly).

This is not to say that intruders held strictly liable must bear the full cost of providing the required compensation. Often, they could not have reasonably expected that they would have to bear these costs (as in the above example). Perhaps they reasonably believed that the intrusion-harm would be less. To the extent that they are forced to bear costs that they could not have reasonably anticipated, they suffer bad brute luck (prudentially undesirable outcomes for which they are not agent-responsible). To the extent that everyone has a duty to pay her fair share of perhaps partial compensation to the victims of bad brute luck (a controversial view that I accept), such intruders may be eligible for compensation. The point here is that, intruders who are agent-responsible for violating rights owe full compensation to those who suffer intrusion-harm, but they, in turn, *may* be eligible (depending on brute luck equalization issues that I here leave open) for compensation from others, if the compensation costs are a matter of bad brute luck for them.[18] If the compensation from others is not full, then the intruders, rather than the victims, must bear the shortfall.

Before turning to our final category (agent-responsible for acting wrongly but not for violating the right), I shall briefly comment on an aspect of compensation that has not yet been addressed. We have been focusing on compensation owed to the intrudee. Often, of course, an intrusion harms non-intrudees as well. For example, if someone beats me up, my wife will suffer as well. Is she owed compensation by the intruder? A common view is that one has rights to compensation only for intrusion-harms suffered from intrusions upon one's own rights. On this view, my wife has no right to compensation, since her rights were not intruded upon.[19] This seems correct when the intruder is not agent-responsible for acting wrongly (e.g., acted permissibly, or reasonably believed she was so acting). When she is agent-responsible for violating someone's rights (e.g., does so knowingly), however, it seems very plausible to me that the intruder should be liable for *all* the intrusion-harm for which she is responsible—both the direct intrusion-harm to the intrudee and the indirect intrusion-harm to third parties. In such cases, the intruder knew (or should have known) that she was violating someone's rights. If she also knew that this would harm others, it seems entirely appropriate for her to owe them a duty of compensation for their harm that she foresaw from the intrusion. (Yes, as Ian Carter objected, this means that you owe compensation to a lot of people, if you beat up a beloved national figure, knowing that you were violating her rights and also causing others to thereby suffer. This seems right to me. Why should anyone else have to bear the cost?) Indeed, one might even argue that intruders who are agent-responsible for violating someone's rights owe *full* compensation—not only to the intrudee, but also—to third parties harmed by the intrusion (even if the intruder could not reasonably foresee that harm). Obviously, that is a big issue, and I raise it here merely to flag it for further consideration.[20]

4. WHERE THE INTRUDER IS AGENT-RESPONSIBLE FOR WRONGLY INTRUDING UPON BUT NOT FOR VIOLATING THE RIGHT

I shall now briefly address a case of which I am less sure. It is where the intruder is not agent-responsible for *violating* the right but is agent-responsible for *wrongly intruding upon* the right. This can arise because not all impermissible intrusions of a person's right are violations of that right. There may be no violation of that right because justificatory conditions hold for that intrusion (e.g., the intrusion is necessary to avoid social catastrophe), but the intrusion may still be impermissible (wrong) for other reasons. It may violate an impersonal constraint[21] or it may violate *someone else's* rights. (The justificatory condition for the given right may not justify violating the impersonal constraint or someone else's right.) Thus, an agent may know that she is wrongly intruding upon a person's right without believing that she is violating that right.

Above I claimed that one is strictly liable for intrusion-harm when one is agent-responsible for *violating* the right. Is this also true when one is agent-responsible for *wrongly intruding upon* the right but not for violating it? I am not sure, but I shall briefly comment on this issue.

There are four possible cases based on the following two dimensions: (1) Is the intruder not agent-responsible for violating the right because she does not violate the right at all, or because she violates the right but could not have reasonably known that she was? (2) Is the intruder agent-responsible for acting wrongly because she violates an impersonal (non-rights-based) constraint or because she violates someone else's rights? Here is an example of the easiest case to justify strict liability: where the intruder *violates* (as opposed to merely infringes) the intrudee's rights but could not have known that she was doing so (and thus is not agent-responsible for doing so) and she is *agent-responsible for violating someone else's rights.* Suppose that I knowingly push A onto B in order to knock over B. I do this because I reasonably, but falsely, believe that B is a terrorist and that knocking him over is the only way to stop the bomb from going off. In fact, B is perfectly innocent. Thus, I violate the rights of both A and B. I am not, however, agent-responsible for violating B's rights, because I could not have reasonably known that I was doing so (since I reasonably believed that justificatory conditions held). Suppose further that I knew that it was not necessary to push A in order to knock over B. I knew that I could just as easily and effectively have pushed B directly. Out of negligence or malice, I nonetheless pushed A. I thus am agent-responsible for violating A's rights. The suggestion of the previous section entails that I am strictly liable for the intrusion-harm that I imposed on A (since I am agent-responsible for violating his rights). Here, our question concerns what I owe B. I am agent-responsible for wrongly intruding against him (because I knowingly intrude upon B's rights in pushing A onto to him and I know that this is wrong because I know it violates A's rights). I am not, however, responsible for violating B's rights. What do I owe B?

My inclination is to think that I owe full compensation for the intrusion-harm that I impose on here. More generally, the intruder is strictly liable to all intrudees in all four cases above. This is because it seems to me (very tentatively!) that what matters is that the intruder is agent-responsible for wrongly intruding. She knows, or should reasonably know, that she is acting wrongly. It doesn't matter whether she is agent-responsible for violating an impersonal constraint, someone else's rights, or the rights of the intrudee in question.[22] In all cases, she has, or should have, a "guilty mind".[23] That, it seems to me, is enough to put her on the hook for strict liability, at least where she is violating the intrudee's rights (without knowing she is). Moreover, it seems to me that the strict liability does not depend on whether she is permissibly infringing the right or violating it, since in both cases she could not reasonably have known that she was wrongly intruding.

These are, however, mere speculations. My purpose here is to draw attention to the case, not to resolve it.

5. CONCLUSION

I have suggested, without compelling argument, that those who are agent-responsible for violating rights—and perhaps also those who are agent-responsible for wrongly intruding upon rights—owe the intrudee compensation for the entire intrusion-harm whereas those who are *not* agent-responsible for wrongly intruding upon rights are only liable for compensating the intrusion-harm for which they are responsible (e.g., could reasonably have foreseen). If this is right, then strict liability is correct for those who are agent-responsible for violating rights and fault liability is correct for those who are not agent responsible for wrongly intruding upon rights. Culpability (agent-responsibility for acting wrongly) thus seems relevant not only for liability to punishment but also for duties to compensate. My goal has been to articulate a promising position and provide enough motivation for it to be taken seriously. Further work is needed to refine the position and to see whether it is genuinely promising.[24]

NOTES

1. See, for example, his article "Choice and Circumstance" (Steiner 1997), in which he argues that compensation for intrusion-harms is an important, if neglected, issue for luck-egalitarians.
2. Throughout, I understand rights as durable rights, as opposed to effective rights in a context. Thus, when I grant revocable permission for you to use my car, I maintain the durable right, against you, not to use my car (without my consent)—even though in that context, I have no effective right, against you, that you not use it. The fact that I can revoke my permission shows that I still have the durable right. By contrast, if I sell you my car, then I transfer my rights over the car to you and no longer have the durable right.
3. For superb discussion of the debate between choice-protecting and interest-protecting conceptions of rights, see Kramer, Simmons, and Steiner 1998.
4. This terminology departs from that used by Thomson (1990, 366–69; 1991, 300–02), who lumps non-autonomous intrusions along with infringements and allows that they can be violations. Otsuka (1994), however, successfully argues that such non-autonomous intrusions cannot be violations (e.g., because rocks and bears can intrude upon rights but cannot act wrongly). It follows, I believe, that they cannot even be infringements, since such intrusions are not wrong even in the absence of special justificatory conditions. Hence, we need the more general notion of intrusion to cover non-autonomous intrusions.
5. I use "infringe" in the sense given by Thomson (e.g., 1990, 122) according to which violations are an impermissible kind of infringement. Others reserve "infringe" for cases of permissible infringement. See, for example, McMahan (2005, 388) and Coleman (1994, 129).
6. Actually, I believe that, fully specified (in perhaps highly conditional ways), all rights are absolute, but I here waive that concern.
7. The justifying conditions can (and typically do) appeal to the objective facts about the situation, and not merely to the evidence that the agent has, or should have had.
8. In places, Thomson (e.g., 1976, 40; 1977, 51) seems to define violations as any impermissible infringement. In Thomson 1990, however, she more cautiously states that an infringement is a violation only if it is impermissible (leaving open when further conditions are necessary for an infringement to be a violation). My definition of a violation requires that the infringement of the right be impermissible *because* there are no justificatory conditions for the infringement of that right—and not for other reasons (impersonal wrongs, violations of other people's rights). I suspect that this is what Thomson had in mind all along.
9. See, for example, Epstein 1973.
10. See, for example, Coleman 1992, chs. 16–18; 1994; and Perry 1992. For discussion and criticism of these views, see Zipursky 1998. The view that I propose is a kind of responsibility account, but the role played by agent-responsibility *for violating rights* (i.e., culpability) is, I believe, not present in the work of Coleman or Perry.

11. See, for example, Fischer and Ravizza 1999, Vallentyne 2008, and the many references in each. For simplicity in the present paper, I assume that agents are fully agent-responsible for the foreseen or reasonably foreseeable results of their autonomous choices. In Vallentyne 2008, however, I defend the view that agents are agent-responsible only for the (foreseeable) *probability shift* that their autonomous choices induce. This is a more limited conception of agent-responsibility.
12. For a defense of the irrelevance of fault to rights-infringement, see Thomson 1990, 229–34. For a defense of the irrelevance of intention or fault to permissibility, see Thomson 1991, 294–96. I agree with these arguments, except that I would argue that autonomous agency is a necessary condition for both rights-infringements and impermissible actions (a claim that she denies elsewhere).
13. Goodin (1989) distinguishes between two kinds of compensation: *Means-replacing* compensation requires providing equivalent means for pursuing the same ends (e.g., a prosthetic leg for a lost leg), whereas *ends-displacing* compensation merely requires providing the means for offsetting the lost wellbeing whether or not it permits the equivalent pursuit of ends (e.g., a sum of money sufficient for achieving the same level of wellbeing, even if not sufficient to buy a prosthetic leg). Goodin defends the stronger, means-replacing, form of compensation, whereas I would argue in favor of the weak, ends-displacing form of compensation. What matters, I would argue, is offsetting the lost prospects for wellbeing, not necessarily restoring any particular capability (in the sense of Sen). For related argument, see Vallentyne 2005.
14. One argument for strict liability is based on the idea that (1) individuals fully own their bodies and various other things, and (2) full ownership includes the right to full compensation from the intruder. Although I agree that individuals fully own their bodies, I claim that full ownership is indeterminate with respect to compensation and enforcement rights (roughly, because they conflict with a full immunity to loss of rights). For elaboration, see Vallentyne, Steiner, and Otsuka 2005.
15. See for example, Thomson 1976; 1977; 1980; 1990, 91–8, for a defense of this view.
16. It's important to keep in mind that the justifying conditions for a right are based on the objective facts about the situation and not merely the evidence that the agent has. Thus, an agent can violate a right even though all her evidence suggests that it is permissible to infringe the right.
17. The main objection to the claim that agents who are not agent-responsible for wrongly intruding have a duty to compensate only for intrusion-harms for which they are agent-responsible is that it is *insufficiently demanding*. I here mention, but do not pursue, an objection that this view is *too demanding*. Suppose that the agent does not foresee how expensive it will be to compensate for the intrusion-harms for which she is agent-responsible. Perhaps she correctly foresaw a small intrusion-harm but did not foresee that it would be very expensive to increase the intrudee's wellbeing by that small amount (e.g., because the intrudee has some very unusual condition). For example, the intruder believed that the 10-unit loss of wellbeing would cost the usual $100 but in fact it will cost one million dollars. This raises the question of whether the duty to compensate should also be limited, on a responsibility view, by the cost of compensation that the intruder could have reasonably foreseen. I doubt it, but I don't see clearly.
18. My own view is that even intentional criminals suffer bad brute luck, and are eligible for compensation, when they have a reasonable but false belief that

the chances of their being punished are low. This, however, is a controversial view.

19. For insightful analysis of the tendency in American tort law to restrict duties of compensation to those whose legal rights were violated, see Zipursky 1998.
20. Coleman (1992, ch. 17; 1994) argues that one owes compensation for wrongful harms for which one is responsible. He understands a harm to be wrongful when it is either wrong *or* the result of an infringement of the harmed individual's rights. Thus, he agrees that one can owe third parties compensation for losses to their legitimate interests when one acts wrongly but without infringing their rights.
21. I would argue that there are no impersonal constraints. All impermissible acts wrong some being with moral standing. Here, however, I leave open the possibility of impersonal constraints, since I believe that they are conceptually possible.
22. In the previous section, I raised the possibility that those agent-responsible for violating rights are strictly liable to all victims—even if their rights are not intruded upon. If this is so, then it follows that they are strictly liable to those who rights they intrude upon in such cases. I tentatively suggested, however, that this was too draconian. It seemed more plausible that they would be liable to all victims, but only for the intrusion-harm for which they were agent-responsible. If this is so, then our question about our main case remains.
23. Unlike theories of retributive punishment, however, the point is not to impose a harm on the violator but rather to hold that the violator, rather than someone else, has a duty to bear the cost of the rights-violation. My proposal is thus, I believe, in the same spirit as the "justice-based" (McMahan 2002, 402) or "responsibility-based" (McMahan 2005, 394) accounts of liability to the use of force. I here focus on the duty to compensate, whereas McMahan focuses on liability to the use of force, but the general issues are, I believe, roughly the same.
24. For helpful comments, I thank Dani Attas, Ian Carter, Helen Frowe, Matt Kramer, Mike Otsuka, Hillel Steiner, and Jonathan Vertanen.

BIBLIOGRAPHY

Coleman, Jules. 1992. *Risks and Wrongs*. Cambridge: Cambridge University Press.

Coleman, Jules. 1994. "Corrective Justice and Property Rights." In Ellen Frankel Paul, Fred D. Miller, Jr., and Jeffrey Paul (eds.), *Property Rights*. Cambridge: Cambridge University Press.

Epstein, Richard. 1973. "A Theory of Strict Liability in Tort." 2 *Journal of Legal Studies* 151–204.

Fischer, John Martin and Ravizza, Mark. 1999. *Responsibility and Control: A Theory of Moral Responsibility*. Cambridge: Cambridge University Press.

Goodin, Robert. 1989. "Theories of Compensation." In R.G. Frey and Christopher Morris (eds.), *Liability and Responsibility*. Cambridge: Cambridge University Press, 1991).

Kramer, Matthew H., Simmonds, N. E. and Steiner, Hillel. 1998. *A Debate over Rights*. Oxford: Oxford University Press.

McMahan, Jeff. 2002. *The Ethics of Killing: Problems at the Margins of Life*. Oxford: Oxford University Press.

McMahan, Jeff. 2005. "The Basis of Moral Liability to Defensive Killing." 15 *Philosophical Issues* 386–405.
Otsuka, Michael. 1994. "Killing the Innocent in Self-Defense." 23 *Philosophy and Public Affairs* 74–94.
Perry, Stephen. 1992. "The Moral Foundations of Tort Law." 77 *Iowa Law Review* 449–514.
Hillel Steiner. 1997. "Choice and Circumstance." 10 *Ratio* 296–312.
Thomson, Judith Jarvis. 1976. "Self-Defense and Rights." In William Parent (ed.), *Rights, Restitution, and Risk: Essays in Moral Theory.* Cambridge, MA: Harvard University Press, 1986. Originally presented as 1976 Lindley Lecture at the University of Kansas.
Thomson, Judith Jarvis. 1977. "Some Ruminations on Rights." In William Parent (ed.), *Rights, Restitution, and Risk: Essays in Moral Theory.* Cambridge, MA: Harvard University Press, 1986. Originally published in *University of Arizona Law Review* 19 (1977).
Thomson, Judith Jarvis. 1980. "Rights and Compensation." In William Parent (ed.), *Rights, Restitution, and Risk: Essays in Moral Theory.* Cambridge, MA: Harvard University Press, 1986. Originally published in *Nous* 14 (1980).
Thomson, Judith Jarvis. 1984. "Remarks on Causation and Liability." 13 *Philosophy and Public Affairs* 101–33.
Thomson, Judith Jarvis. 1990. *The Realm of Rights.* Cambridge, MA: Harvard University Press.
Thomson, Judith Jarvis. 1991. "Self-Defense." 20 *Philosophy and Public Affairs* 283–310.
Vallentyne, Peter. 2008. "Brute Luck and Responsibility." 7 *Politics, Philosophy & Economics* 57–80.
Vallentyne, Peter. 2005. "Capabilities vs. Opportunities for Well-being." 13 *Journal of Political Philosophy* 359–71.
Vallentyne, Peter, Steiner, Hillel, and Otsuka, Michael. 2005. "Why Left-Libertarianism Isn't Incoherent, Indeterminate, or Irrelevant: A Reply to Fried." 33 *Philosophy and Public Affairs* 201–15.
Zipursky, Ben. 1998. "Rights, Wrongs, and Recourse in the Law of Torts." 51 *Vanderbilt Law Review* 1–100.

PART III
LEFT-LIBERTARIANISM

7 What Is Left In Left-Libertarianism?

Eric Mack

1. INTRODUCTION

This essay is a critical examination of key components of Hillel Steiner's left-libertarianism[1] as this doctrine is articulated in his most imposing An Essay on Rights (1994). The core of Steiner's left-libertarianism consists in the affirmation of certain original and universal rights—as does the core of standard rights-oriented libertarianism against which Steiner argues.[2] That standard libertarianism can be said to affirm only one original and universal right, viz., each agent's right of self-ownership.[3] It specifically denies that agents have any original right to particular extra-personal material or to shares of such material. In contrast, Steiner's left-libertarianism affirms both an original right of self-ownership and some original right with respect to extra-personal material. The left-ness of left libertarianism derives from this latter original right being a substantively equal right of ownership over the relevant extra-personal material.[4] Steiner's specifically left-libertarian affirmations of original rights is preceded by a meticulous and illuminating account of the nature of rights and their function within any wider moral theory; this account is itself a major contribution to moral and political theory.

One of the crucial tasks of left-libertarianism is to establish the coherence of a system which affirms both a robust right of self-ownership and a robust right to equal shares of extra-personal material. This reconciliationist task is complicated by the fact that self-owners live in and through the world of extra-personal objects. These agents appropriate, transform, reap the fruits of, and exchange raw material or transformed objects and, in doing so, they seem to place the stamp of their respective self-ownership on segments of the extra-personal world. For this reason, the implementation of a substantively equal right with respect to extra-personal material threatens to trespass upon the self-ownership of such agents. The natural strategy to avoid such a clash between self-ownership rights and original rights to extra-personal material is to restrict the latter rights to claims over *raw* material—material which has not been stamped by any self-owner. We should note here that Steiner plausibly maintains that abandoned objects return to the status of raw materials. Their abandonment removes the stamp of the abandoning agent's self-ownership. Throughout this essay, whenever I speak of raw materials, I should be understood to mean raw materials *and* abandoned objects, i.e., objects which have reverted to the status of raw materials.[5] In the remainder of this introductory section, I shall point to a series of criticisms I will be bringing against the left side of Steiner's doctrine. I begin the development of these criticisms after section 2's discussion of the point at which Steiner's left-libertarianism diverges from standard libertarianism.

The crucial opening claim on the left side of Steiner's doctrine is that there are original rights over raw material; more specifically, there are original rights which are constituted by a rule specifying the just initial distribution of raw material. (That the rule specifies an *equal* distribution is a further step in the argument.) I shall ascribe to Steiner three arguments on behalf of this opening claim. These are 'the conceptual argument,' 'the relinquishment argument,' and 'the proviso argument.' I will criticize the first two of these arguments in section 3 and the proviso argument in section 4.

A mark of a theory's incorporation of a robust right of self-ownership is that theory's accommodation of the Lockean idea that through their labour individuals acquire rights to the fruits of their labour. For this reason, Steiner is eager to affirm the rights-generating power of the exercise of (self-owned) labour. However, I shall argue in section 3 that, if one were to accept Steiner's conceptual and relinquishment arguments for the necessity of an original right to raw material, one would not be able to assign any independent rights-generating power to agents' exercise of their labour. In *An Essay on Rights*, Steiner endorses a modification of the claim that each individual has an original right to a specific equal bundle of raw material. The modification is that each agent has an original right that others leave *some* equal share for her. I shall discuss this modification in section 5 and argue that its unintended effect is to (further) undermine the conceptual and relinquishment arguments for there being an original right with respect to nature.

Prior to *An Essay on Rights*, Steiner explored various formulations of left-libertarianism in a series of intriguing articles published from the mid-1970s into the early 1980s.[6] One of the most interesting features of those essays was the way in which Steiner moved through a series of distinct left-libertarian positions as difficulties with already investigated positions became—or seemed to become—manifest (Mack 1983). There were two overall *tendencies* within that movement from one position to another. One was a shift from construing the original equal right with respect to extra-personal objects as a right of each agent to a discrete equal share to construing the original right as a right of equal joint-ownership. The other was a shift from taking the original right to range only over raw material to taking that right to range over (*non-abandoned*) man-made objects as well.[7] Both shifts heighten the prospects of a clash between the original right with respect to extra-personal goods and the original right of self-ownership.

The shift to equal joint-ownership portends a clash with self-ownership because it appears that self-ownership will be rendered nugatory if an agent must get permission from everyone else before she may do anything involving the world outside of her skin (Cohen 1995, 97–98). The shift to original rights over man-made objects portends a clash with self-ownership because it seems non-consensually to confer 'the ownership of (part or all) of one person's labour upon another' (Steiner 1980a, 249).

Neither of these transitions appear explicitly in *An Essay on Rights*. Nevertheless, I shall contend in section 5 that *An Essay* does contain an implicit movement from an original right to equal discrete shares to an original right of joint-ownership. Such an original joint ownership of nature threatens, as we have just noticed, to render nugatory the right of self-ownership and, thus, to defeat Steiner's basic reconciliationist project. However, I will also explain in section 5 how yet another implicit shift in Steiner's construal of original rights in *An Essay*—a shift which is *not* foreshadowed in his earlier essays—allows Steiner to avoid this undercutting of self-ownership. This is a shift from understanding rights as claims protected by property rules to understanding rights as claims protected by liability rules.[8]

Unfortunately, as I explain in section 6, the shift to construing rights as claims which are protected by liability rules is incompatible with Steiner's own core subscription to the Choice Theory of rights, according to which, to have a right is to be in position to chose whether another will remain under a duty to one or will be relieved of that duty. For instance, if I have a contractual right against Black that he pay me $5, I am in position to determine by my choice whether Black will be held to that duty or released from it. In section 6, I point out that Steiner has to choose between retaining the liability rule understanding of the original right to raw material and retaining the Choice Theory of rights. In the concluding section 7, I maintain that Steiner cannot retreat to a property rule understanding of that original right because under that understanding this right impinges severely on the right of self-ownership. Hence, the only way in which Steiner can avoid both such an impingement on self-ownership and the contravention of the Choice Theory of rights is to reject the original right to raw material.

There is a major complicating issue for Steiner's left-libertarianism which I simply try to skirt in this paper. Obviously, raw material is not merely held or rented by persons and used as sites for their activities; rather, it is usually consumed or converted into man-made objects. So questions arise about how persons who arrive on the scene relatively late are going to get their fair share of raw material and about whether, if they cannot get their fair share of raw material, they instead acquire a claim to some man-made objects. I shall try to avoid examining how Steiner deals (or fails to deal) with these questions by considering his views only insofar as they apply to situations in which all extra-personal objects are bits of raw material (or are abandoned man-made objects).[9]

2. PURE HISTORICAL ENTITLEMENT VERSUS ORIGINAL PATTERNED TITLES

Standard libertarianism of the rights-oriented sort endorses a purely historical conception of justice in extra-personal holdings. Self-owning individuals are understood to encounter a world of initially unowned raw material. Although G.A. Cohen describes this understanding as a 'blithe assumption,' it seems to be a pretty reasonable starting place for the theory of justice in extra-personal holdings. At the very least, the burden of proof seems to rest on those who would insist that the mere existence of raw material is sufficient for that material being owned, if there are persons around to own it. Standard libertarianism takes rights to particular extra-personal objects to appear only when an individual interacts with certain unowned raw material in special title-generating ways. The characteristic *Lockean* metaphor for these title-generating modes of interaction is that of mixing one's labour. Whatever the metaphor, the key Lockean intuition is that: (i) something which already belongs to the agent—her labour or energy or productive skill—is invested in some unowned raw material which is thereby transformed (in some intended way, for some purpose of the agent) and (ii) to take that transformed object from that agent without her consent is to violate her ongoing right to her invested labour, energy, or productive skill.[10] Individuals acquire initial rights to just those extra-personal objects which result from their respective interaction with unowned raw material in the specified rights-generating ways. Since what and how much each given individual will acquire in these ways will depend on that individual's skill, insight, initiative, energy, persistence, opportunity and luck and on how that individual chooses to employ or take advantage of these factors, only by accident will the resulting array of just initial holdings accord with any patterned theorist's favorite distributive norm.

Friends of purely historical justice in holdings go on, of course, to maintain that subsequent alterations of persons' respective just holdings are also not governed by any distributive principle. Through unilateral or joint action individuals may diminish or enhance their holdings in ways which preserve the justice of their holdings; and the justice of those resulting holdings will be independent of whether those diminutions or enhancements move the distribution of holdings toward or away from some sanctifying pattern. Such a conception of justice-preserving alterations and transfers is as essential a part of a purely historical theory of justice as the historical conception of justice in initial acquisitions. Nevertheless, critics of the purely historical theory concentrate almost entirely on the historical conception of justice in *initial* holdings.[11] People more readily challenge the justice of acts of initial acquisition because they more readily see one party's gain through her initial acquisition of some portion of the earth to be at the expense of other parties who are thereby excluded from acquiring that portion of the earth. Since 'natural resources' are thought of as both unchanging in quantity and more or less sitting there waiting to be (costlessly) acquired—like manna from heaven—it seems to many people that there must be some distributive rule which tells us how the objects of initial acquisition ought to be divided among us.

Steiner's constructive inquiry into the justice of extra-personal holdings can be seen as beginning with his *qualified* endorsement of Nozick's famous argument against all patterned theories of justice in holdings.[12] Steiner helpfully construes Nozick as arguing that no *unrelenting* patterned theory can deliver what it purports to deliver—viz., *just* distributions of holdings. Nozick invites any friend of a patterned doctrine to envision the institution of her favored pattern. That institution yields distribution d_1, which by hypothesis must be just. He then points out that, once d_1 is instituted, individuals acting in accordance with their diverse and innocuous choices about how to employ or dispose of their respective just holdings will almost certainly bring a different distribution d_2 into existence; and d_2 will almost certainly have to be deemed to be unjust by the unrelenting patterned theorist. For it will almost certainly be possible to redistribute some of what individuals come to hold under d_2 so as to produce distribution d_3 which would better realize the favored pattern than does d_2. But, according to Nozick and Steiner, if d_1 was really just, then d_2 must also be just. What are just distributions for except to specify what people have a right to dispose of according to their choice? To insist that, despite its pedigree, d_2 is not just unless it more conforms to the distributive rule that gave us d_1 than any other distribution into which d_2 may be converted is to *rescind* the judgment that d_1 was just. The same pattern will, of course, recur if we abide by the relentless pattern theorist's call in the name of justice to convert d_2 into d_3. Individuals will, through their diverse and innocuous choices, transform d_3 into d_4; but d_4 will be subject to conversion via redistribution into d_5 which better realizes the reigning distributive rule than does d_4. Yet to hold that justice demands the undoing of d_4 which (by hypothesis) arose from individuals non-harmfully deploying what was assigned to them in the name of justice is to rescind the claim that d_3 was just. There is, in short, an inescapable tension between the ambition of establishing just holdings and the ambition of maintaining or returning to a favored pattern in the name of justice.[13] All of this Steiner conveys in one of the best one-liners of political philosophy. Relentless patterned theories, he says, 'create rights to interfere with the exercise of the rights they create' (Steiner 1977b, 43).

Steiner's endorsement of Nozick's argument is qualified, however, because he immediately and correctly points out that the argument works only against what I have called the *relentless* patterned theorist. The argument only shows that, *if an initial distribution d_1 is just*, then a distribution d_2 which arises from d_1 by way of various innocuous deployments of the holdings sanctified in d_1 will also be just. It is entirely consistent with the argument to hold that the justice of d_1 derives from its comportment with some distributive principle, e.g., equality. The argument does not at all preclude that just initial holdings are constituted by some (egalitarian) starting-point distributive rule. Steiner's key departure from Nozick is his affirmation of such a rule.

3. THE CONCEPTUAL AND RELINQUISHMENT ARGUMENTS

In this section I consider and reject two Steinerite arguments for the crucial claim that just initial holdings of nature are constituted by some (egalitarian) starting-point distributive rule. These are the conceptual argument and the relinquishment argument. I contend that the conceptual argument has no persuasive force and that the relinquishment argument collapses into the non-persuasive conceptual argument. The kernel of Steiner's conceptual argument is the idea that for any action to be rightful or 'vindicable' its agent must antecedently possess titles to all the physical elements employed in or disposed of by that action. 'Vindicable titles imply previous vindicable titles from which they derive' (Steiner 1994, 103). In the case of an agent's initial appropriation of some natural material, the agent's action can be rightful or vindicable only if she already has title to that material. In *An Essay* Steiner writes that,

> . . . like all good things, every vindication chain must come to an end. All sequences of antecedent titles and duties must terminate in a set of *ultimately antecedent* titles and duties. I'm going to call this a set of *original* rights and duties. The vindicability of any current right or duty clearly depends upon the vindicability of its original antecedents (1994, 106–7).

Thus, 'the vindication of original rights and duties can involve no historical reference . . . ' (1994, 107). Instead, the vindication of original rights must appeal to a distributive principle which assigns to individuals ultimately antecedent titles. Steiner offered a clearer yet statement of this position in his 1977 paper, 'The Structure of a Set of Compossible Rights.'

> Chains of vindication must all terminate in original titles, which, therefore, cannot themselves have been created by exercises of rights. Those original titles are necessarily titles to objects the historical first uses of which constitute the earliest rightful actions performed with those objects. Thus, within the class of original titles required to vindicate any derivative title, there are some titles which—being necessarily nonderivative—are properly termed *ultimately original titles* (Steiner 1977a, 775).[14]

If an agent did not already have title to some raw object, no appropriation of it by her could be vindicated and, thus, no appropriative action on her part could generate a title to the object which is appropriated. Thus, entitlement with respect to extra-personal objects cannot be historical all the way down.

Why, however, should one believe that an appropriative action can be rightful or 'vindicable' only if the agent already possesses title to the material which she appropriates? It makes sense to believe this if and only if one is operating with a very strong sense of an action being rightful or vindicable. According to this very strong sense, one has a right to engage in an action only if *any* conduct by another party which is incompatible with one's performance of the action would violate one's right to engage in it. Only if one has rights over everything which would be a material component of one's action will it be true that *any* conduct by another party which is incompatible with one's performance of the action would violate one's right to engage in that action. Hence, only if one has rights over everything which would be a material component of one's action does one have a right to perform the action in this very strong sense. Unfortunately for the conceptual argument, there is no good reason to require of one's doctrine of original titles that it support the conclusion that agents have rights to appropriate in this very strong sense.

Here between Red and White is a nice, ripe, recently fallen acorn. Surely either of them may permissibly appropriate it as long as she or he does not violate various antecedent rights which the other actor has over *other* things. So, e.g., Red may appropriate the acorn as long as she does not proceed to do so by first breaking White's leg or slapping his grasping hand away from the acorn. Red need not have antecedent title to the acorn for her appropriative action to be rightful or vindicable in the weak sense of being permissible. Clearly a doctrine of original titles according to which there are no original titles to raw materials allows for appropriations of raw material which are rightful or vindicable in this weak sense. And, it is, of course, a central thesis of the standard libertarian that this same blithe doctrine allows for appropriations of raw materials which are rightful or vindicable in a stronger sense, viz., in the sense that those actions are permissible *and* generate titles to the appropriated objects. Steiner rejects that thesis; but that rejection largely depends upon the conceptual argument itself. That is, the rejection depends upon the thought that, if one appropriates raw material to which one does not have antecedent title, one must be appropriating raw material to which *someone else* has antecedent title and, hence, one's appropriation cannot generate an entitlement to the appropriated material. We are discovering, however, that there is no good reason to accept this conceptual argument.[15]

Might there be some *other* argument which undermines the pure historical story about how entitlement-generating initial appropriations are possible? Perhaps the historical entitlement-generation story can be undermined by arguing that, while its advocate needs to recognize a distinction between labour (or energy or productive skill) which is *invested* and labour (or energy or productive skill) which is *relinquished*, he will be unable to dismiss the hypothesis that the labour which he wants to say is invested is actually relinquished. This is the crux—or the apparent crux—of the relinquishment argument. This argument begins with Nozick's question about whether his mixing his few ounces of tomato juice with the ocean makes the ocean his property. 'But why isn't mixing what I own with what I don't own a way of losing what I own rather than a way of gaining what I don't?' (Nozick 1974, 174–75). Following up on Nozick's query, the question which Steiner raises is: When may one's mixing of one's labour with a bit of raw material or one's infusing one's 'expended energy . . . into parts of the external environment' or one's 'transforming their features in various ways' (1994, 233) be taken as an investment of one's labour, energy, or world-transforming skill and when may it be taken as a relinquishment of one's labour, energy, or world-transforming skill?[16]

According to Steiner, there are two easy sorts of case and an uneasy third sort of case to be considered. The first sort of easy case obtains whenever one is already the owner of all the physical components involved in one's actions. Thus, if one bleeds on one's own carpet, the now blood-soaked carpet is one's property; and we can say that the mixing of the blood was not a relinquishment of that blood (Steiner 1994, 234). Similarly, if one makes a wooden bench out of lumber and tools to which one already has title, one has title to the resulting bench; and we can say that one's labour has not been relinquished (1994, 234). The second sort of easy case obtains whenever one engages in an action some of the physical components of which are already owned by another. If I bleed on *your* carpet, I do not acquire title to the blood-stained carpet. If, without any contractual arrangement with you, I labour upon and restore *your* mildewed copy of the *Two Treatises*, my repairing the book will 'have constituted a relinquishment of my labour *since the book wasn't mine*' (1994, 235, emphasis added). Note that, in the book case, Steiner does not say that my labour is relinquished because it is mixed with something *which belongs to someone else*. Rather, he already says that it is relinquished merely because it is mixed with something which *does not belong to me*.

Steiner then goes on to consider the possibility that one may acquire title to 'a piece of land which belongs to neither you nor me nor anyone else' by bleeding on it or mixing one's labour with it. This is the third and uneasy sort of case. The friend of a purely historical doctrine of entitlements to extra-personal objects will say that one certainly can acquire title in such a case because a subsequent unconsented to seizure of the transformed land would include an unconsented to seizure of one's blood or labour. Since one has (and retains) a right to that blood or labour, the seizure of the resultant object violates one's right; and, thus, one has a right to the resultant objects. To this Steiner provides the tomato juice response that,

> . . . any claim, to the effect that [a piece of land is] being infused with my labour makes this land mine, can be met with the counter-claim

> that, in so infusing the land, I was relinquishing my title to that labour, *just as I did in undertaking the repair of your book* (Steiner 1994, 235, emphasis added).

He recognizes that someone might argue that there is no reason to believe that my (intentional, purposive) labour is relinquished in this case because labouring involves no trespass upon anyone else's property. Yet he offers two responses to this argument. First, he appeals to his account of why my labouring (without your permission) on your copy of the *Two Treatises* is a relinquishment of my labour, viz., it is relinquished 'since the book isn't mine' (1994, 235). But Steiner's interlocutor will reject this analysis; he holds that in the *Two Treatises* case the labour is relinquished precisely because the book is owned by someone else.

Consider then Steiner's second response to the claim that there is no reason to believe my (intentional, purposive) labour is relinquished in the case of labouring on unowned land. He reminds us that the wooden bench case is different from the cultivated land case because

> . . . the bench, unlike the cultivated land, is a product all the factors of which (being already owned by me) were ones which everyone else already had a duty to forbear from using, so my labour-mixing makes no difference in this case (1994, 235).

Postponing for a moment comment upon the striking last clause, Steiner seems here to be saying the following:

☐ There is a difference between the bench and the cultivated land case—viz., in the bench case, the agent already has title to everything which is a factor in the product of his labour whereas, in the cultivated land case, the agent does not already have title to everything which is a factor in the product of his labour.

☐ Therefore, there is *another difference* between the bench and the cultivated land case, viz., that, in the bench case, the agent has title to the product and has not relinquished his labour whereas, in the cultivated land case, the agent does not have title to the product and has relinquished his labour.

But, of course, the issue here is precisely whether the first difference makes for the second difference. Why should one believe that labouring upon a factor to which one does not already have title cannot generate a title to the product of that labouring? If Steiner is simply saying here that title to the product requires antecedent title to all the factors, then he is simply repeating the conclusion of the (already undermined) conceptual argument. If he is saying that labour is relinquished whenever it is applied to anything the agent does not already have title to, then we have a version of the relinquishment argument which resolves entirely back into the conceptual argument. Moreover, the basic claim of the conceptual argument—that one's labouring upon, expending one's energy upon, or exercising one's productive skills upon materials to which no one has antecedent title cannot generate for one a title to the resultant object—is simply intuitively implausible. The fact that this claim does imply that there must be ultimate original titles to all raw material (or to all raw material which can ever be an ingredient of any owned object) enhances its intuitive implausibility. Yet more reasons not to subscribe to this core claim derive from the difficulties which beset any attempt to specify more precisely to what those ultimate original titles to raw material amount.

Let us look back for a moment at the striking last clause of Steiner's remark about the difference between the bench and the cultivated land cases. Speaking about the paradigm case of the appearance of a title to a product, Steiner says, *so my labour-mixing makes no difference in this case* (1994, 235). What could this mean? I conjecture that it means what it says, viz., that the labour-mixing *itself* does not contribute to the agent's *title* to the bench. Against my conjecture, Steiner seems to hold that in the manufactured bench case the labouring agent's infusion of labour joins that agent's antecedent title to the physical material so as to yield the agent's title to the bench.

> To regard the manufactured bench as *not* belonging to me—to say that others are at liberty to dispose of it without my consent—is to deny my unencumbered antecedent titles to its production factors and/or my vested liberty to perform that labouring act. And these denials are *ex hypothesi* untrue (1994, 234).

It seems as though both ownership of the physical material and ownership of the infused labour are necessary conditions for the agent's right to the bench; and they are jointly sufficient. However, although there are other passages in *An Essay* in which an agent's labour comes in as one of a multitude of owned factors of production, this does not appear to be what Steiner is saying here. Here Steiner's invocation of the agent's 'vested liberty *to perform the labouring act*' (emphasis add) seems to me designed to rebut a different sort of challenge to the agent's title to the bench, viz., a challenge that the agent was not (robustly enough) at liberty to perform the labouring act. Perhaps the agent had contracted not to engage in such a performance. Saying that the agent had the vested liberty to perform the labouring act shows that the agent did not render himself ineligible to acquire a title to the bench. However, given the agent's eligibility, the title which arises seems to be based entirely on the titles to the antecedent materials. The title arises just as it would were the pre-alteration materials to transform themselves spontaneously into that wooden bench.

Certainly there are passages in *an Essay* in which Steiner treats an agent's labour as one of the product factors for a created object.[17] He tells us that '. . . you own whatever is begotten by what you own. You own the fruits of your labour because you own your labour' (1994, 239). Also, 'You justly own whatever your labour produces (*provided, of course, that the other factors entering into that production process are all things owned by you*)' (1994, 241, emphasis added). Indeed, Steiner's language suggests an agent's noticing that *somehow* a bit of her labour has hooked up with some other factors so as to beget a product. The agent's agency still seems to be as little involved as in the case of a spontaneous transformation of physical materials to which the agent has antecedent title. In any case, we have to ask whether this inclusion of an agent's title to his labour in the account of the agent's title to the product amounts to a significant incorporation of the idea that through their labour individuals acquire rights to the fruits of their labour. It is noteworthy that whereas the distinctive feature of Locke's understanding of a person having rights to the fruit of his labour is the non-necessity of his antecedent ownership of all the other factors,[18] the distinctive feature of Steiner's view remains the necessity of the person's antecedent ownership of all the other factors.

Consider one last time the contrast between the wooden bench and the cultivated land. We have here two cases in which one might well think there is a product to which an agent has title under the principle that one owns the fruits of one's (non-trespassing) labour. According to Steiner, what makes the difference between these two cases, i.e., what makes it true that only in the bench case does the agent genuinely have title to the fruit of her labour? Steiner's answer is that only in that case did the agent have antecedent title to all the (other) factors. Among all cases in which pre-theoretically one might well think an agent has title to the fruits of his labour, an agent actually has that title only in those cases in which he has antecedent rights to the fruits' (non-labour) factors. Indeed, if we recall Steiner's view that labour-mixing—as opposed to labour-relinquishment—occurs if and only if the labouring agent already has title over all the non-labour factors, we see that within Steiner's doctrine an agent's title to the product of her labour depends *entirely* upon her antecedent title to those non-labour factors. An agent's labour will count as mixed and not relinquished if and only if that agent has antecedent title to all the physical product factors. Hence, the right to the laboured upon object is settled by the right to the non-labour factors.[19] The agent's right to the fruits of his labour has no independent normative import. This is a major problem for Steiner who thinks that his subscription to persons having rights to the fruits of the labour is what marks his position off from the sort of socialism which subscribes to 'the right to subsistence' (Steiner 1994, 281).

4. THE PROVISO ARGUMENT

Let us turn to the third argument available to Steiner against purely historical initial acquisition and for original equal titles to raw material, viz., the proviso argument. After offering a few provisional points about what a

Lockean proviso is,[20] I will indicate what I take Steiner's proviso argument to be and why it is mistaken. A proviso is a sort of after-thought—Nozick says it is a bit of additional complexity—with respect to an entitlement theory of property rights (Nozick 1974, 174). An advocate of a proviso first identifies the procedures through which an individual acquires a property right to some holding. Actions which instantiate these procedures presumptively establish the individual's right to the holding in question. The individual's right to the property and the permissibility of his chosen deployment of his property obtain *unless* some rather special circumstance also obtains which rebuts or limits that right. Since, in the mind of the entitlement theorist, the individual's instantiation of entitlement-generating procedures does have the considerable moral significance of presumptively establishing his entitlement, only some rather remarkable ill-effect on another agent will negate that presumption and, thereby, rebut or limit that right. A proviso will, therefore, only protect individuals against some special possible ill-effect of the appearance of entitlements with respect to extra-personal objects—like the ill-effect of being made worse off than one would have been had such entitlements not appeared. It does not make sense to advance a *proviso* which immunizes individuals against an effect—like the effect of being left with less than an equal share—which is inherent or close to inherent in the entitlement-generating process which one's core theory endorses. For such a putative proviso would be no true *proviso*; instead, it would be a core element of an at least partially patterned theory of just holdings.

Consider the case of Locke who offers a core theory of how an agent may go about acquiring a property right. The agent may mix his labour with some raw material or he may trade the product of his labour-mixing for the fruits of another's labour, and so on. Locke also says that this process—especially, the initial acquisition phase of it—will not give rise to a property right if a special circumstance obtains, viz., that not 'enough and as good' raw material is left for others.[21] It is difficult to say precisely what Locke meant by this proviso and what motivated it.[22] Nevertheless, it is easy and important to see that Locke did *not* say that '*as much* and as good' must be left for others. It is easy to imagine individuals appropriating much more than an equal share of raw material while leaving enough and as good for others. So Locke's 'enough and as good' proviso does not reflect or reveal any commitment to an egalitarian distributive rule for defining original titles to raw material.[23]

When friends of a proviso begin to build their case, they do not start with examples in which some individual has more than the agent about whom they are concerned. Rather, they start with examples in which some individual has *everything*. Our agent is swimming toward the one island in a vast body of water only to discover that another individual has already done what is ordinarily sufficient for establishing a property right over that isolated island. Or our agent is stumbling toward the one waterhole in a vast desert only to discover that another individual has gone through procedures which are ordinarily sufficient for establishing a property right over that waterhole. Not only is some individual envisioned as owning everything, that individual is envisioned as exercising his ownership in a very specific way. The single owner is envisioned as simply entirely excluding the later arriving agent or as threatening such an entire exclusion so as to extract some onerous agreement from that agent. The advocate of a proviso begins with such an example because he believes that such an exclusion or threat of exclusion does constitute a special ill-effect which undermines the islander holder's right (or is *a rights-violating deployment* of his rightfully held island.)[24] The advocate goes on to attempt to give a general characterization of the ill-effect which is exemplified in this case and, hence, to identify the line between holdings (or deployments of holdings) which violate his proviso and those that do not. That line will be drawn so that many responses to the arrival of our agent far short of equal sharing—such as the island holder saying 'of course, there's a bit of land over there that you can occupy or, better yet for you, you could come to work for me for so-and-so wages'—will not trigger any complaint under the proviso.[25]

Steiner's proviso argument has two components. First, Steiner's cites reasonable affirmations of a proviso—by, e.g., Locke[26]—and construes these as reasonable affirmations of an egalitarian starting point rule. Second, following the lead of the early Herbert Spencer, he points to cases in which an individual would have a just complaint about being faced with exclusion from all of the earth and he takes the justice of that complaint to be a reflection not of the validity of some sort of proviso but, rather, of each agent's original equal title to the earth. Against Steiner, I maintain that affirmations of provisos are not affirmations of starting point distributive rules and that, contrary to both Spencer's and Steiner's understanding, the Spencerian cases point to a proviso, not to an original equal right to the earth.

Enough, I believe, has already been said to indicate why invocations by Locke (or by Nozick[27]) of a proviso should not be construed as invocations of a starting point distributive rule. I will only add one general reason against identifying provisos with starting point distributive rules. A proviso immunizes agents against certain ill-*effects* of the actions of others. Therefore, an agent who suffers what would count as such an ill-*effect* were it the result of others' actions does not have a just complaint under the proviso at hand if his unfortunate situation is not the result of others' actions. In contrast, if justice is a matter of agents' circumstances being in accord with some distributive rule, an agent's non-possession of what that distributive rules says is his fair share will itself be unjust whether or not it is the result of others' actions. An agent who has nothing because he lacks the physical ability to appropriate anything will have no just complaint against others under a proviso since this unfortunate agent would have nothing even if others were to appropriate nothing. However, under a distributive rule, this agent will have a just complaint about his having nothing.

What remains of the proviso argument are the Spencerian cases and their construal by Steiner (and Spencer) as an argument for equal original rights to the earth. Here is most of the passage from Spencer's *Social Statics* which Steiner presents in 'Slavery, Socialism, and Private Property':

> . . . if one portion of the earth's surface may justly become the possession of an individual, . . . eventually the whole of the earth's surface may be so held . . . Supposing the entire habitable globe to be so enclosed, it follows that if the landowners have a valid right to its surface, all who are not landowners, have no right at all to its surface. Hence such can exist on the earth by sufferance only. They are all trespassers . . . Should the others think fit to deny them a resting-place, these landless men might equitably be expelled from the earth altogether (Steiner 1980a, 251–52).[28]

In 'Capitalism, Justice, and Equal Starts,' Steiner presents a more abstract statement about what he takes to be the ill-effects of allowing (non-universal?) private ownership of the earth—a story which ends up slightly differently for the landless.

> Now what [the historical principle of initial acquisition of originally unowned raw material] does is to empower a subset of private individuals to create titles that necessarily deny to others the liberty to forebear incurring enslavement. These others—persons who arrive after the world has been appropriated—are unavoidably trespassers on one titleholder's property or another's. As trespassers, they lack the liberty to do anything (even commit suicide) on that owned property and are thus at liberty only to become part of it, to incur enslavement (Steiner 1987, 64).[29]

I think it is very striking how, once one differentiates between advocacy of a proviso and advocacy of a starting point distributive norm, one sees both of these passages as much more plausibly suggesting the former than the latter. These passages present each of a multitude of individual landowners excluding or threatening to exclude the latecomer just as the single owner of everything is presented as excluding or threatening to exclude the latecomer in the isolated island and waterhole cases. For this reason, these passages envision the latecomer undergoing the same sort of ill-effect as the proviso advocate seeks to guard against. (Advocates of a proviso themselves often begin with examples in which an agent is not so much excluded from appropriation or use but, rather, from movement (Nozick 1974, 55n; Mack 2002b, 246).) Thus, the attachment of a proviso to the entitlement theory under examination—e.g., a proviso which precludes latecomers being made worse off than they would have been had entitlements not been generated or one that precludes not enough being left for the use of latecomers—will suffice to explain the injustice of this treatment of latecomers and to immunize them against this treatment. A proviso advocate will also point out that the newcomer is in fact very unlikely to face even the threat of exclusion in a world of numerous landowners who are in competition with one another for employers or for leasers or purchasers of their land. It is the monopoly aspect of the isolated island or waterhole cases that raises the strong prospect of the latecomer suffering the sort of ill-effect against which a proviso offers protection. The privatization of Hong Kong, which certainly precluded latecomers from engaging in any *initial* acquisition of parts of that island, is precisely what made it possible for vast numbers of latecomers to arrive and do better for themselves than they would have had the privatization of that island not have taken place. Indeed, latecomers often benefit enormously from the trailblazing of the firstcomers. Thus, proviso advocates maintain that, in real private property regimes, individuals are unlikely to undergo the sort of ill-effects against which provisos are designed to protect.[30] However, the crucial point here is that no egalitarian original title to the earth is *necessary* to disallow the exclusions and threats of exclusion which Spencer and Steiner envision within their scenarios—since an attached proviso will suffice for that.

Nor will an egalitarian original title be *sufficient* to disallow the exclusions and threats of exclusion that concern Steiner. The passages from Spencer and Steiner offer us two alternative egalitarian original title proposals; neither of these suffice to deal with the problem which those passages depict. Spencer's proposal is that everyone is an equal joint-owner of the earth; everyone is an equal member of society which owns the earth. The obvious problem here is that this makes every individual subject to being declared *by society* to be a trespasser who had better clear out. In fact, under the joint-ownership proposal, individuals are much more likely to face the threat of exclusion because each individual is confronted by a monopoly owner, viz., society—as the swimmer is confronted with the island's monopoly owner. Steiner's proposal in 'Capitalism, Justice, and Equal Starts' (and seemingly in *An Essay*) is that an equal share of the earth be reserved for each individual. This will provide each individual with a place to reside and a basis for avoiding enslavement *if and only if* each individual can get to a share of the earth which is reserved for her without trespassing on any other individual's established share. And, of course, even individuals who do get to their own equal segment will pretty much have to hunker down there if other individual owners behave as Steiner depicts them as behaving. So no egalitarian original title to the earth is necessary for avoiding the difficulties depicted in the Spencer and Steiner scenarios and neither the joint-ownership nor the individual ownership of equal shares versions of an egalitarian original title to the earth is sufficient for avoiding those difficulties. In contrast, a proviso is necessary and sufficient for avoiding these difficulties.

5. TWO MODIFICATIONS OF THE ORIGINAL RIGHT TO EQUAL SHARES

I mentioned in the introduction an explicit movement within Steiner's earlier articulations of left-libertarianism from the position that the original equal right to raw material is a right to a discrete bundle of raw material to the view that this right is a matter of original equal joint-ownership over all raw material. This shift is largely motivated by the difficulty of specifying what counts as an equal portion of raw material. If agents are not to be allotted physically identical packages of raw materials, how is the equality of diverse packages to be determined? The natural suggestion is that each agent has title to a bundle of raw material which equals *in value* the bundles to which all others are respectively entitled. Unfortunately, this suggestion is problematic because the relative value of various raw materials will depend upon how raw materials are divided among individuals. Different divisions of raw material will engender different individual opportunities, preferences, plans and outlooks and, hence, very different concatenations of actions by and among individuals. How raw material is initially divided will make a difference in *how many* individuals will exist and *which* individuals with which endowments and needs. Different divisions will make a difference in which raw materials *become* 'natural resources' and, thus, count as things of value to be divided equally. Since all of these differences and also people's diverse anticipations of all or some of these differences will make for differences—indeed, radically unpredictable differences—in the relative value of different raw materials, there will be no distribution-independent specification of equal shares to serve as a guide for the initial equal division of raw material. Shifting to an understanding of the original right as one of equal joint-ownership circumvents the difficulty of identifying equally valuable shares.

The basic picture associated with the joint-ownership approach is that society, the collective owner, leases land to individuals; individuals are allowed to occupy sites only if they pay to the joint-owners the full rental value of those sites. The revenues from the lease of raw material to individuals are then equally divided among the joint-owners (or those revenues are used to finance essential governmental services available to all). One mark of the fact that the equal division and the joint ownership approaches are significantly different is that taxation is built into the structure of the joint-ownership doctrine—this is Henry George's 'single-tax'—while it is an open question whether an advocate of the equal division doctrine can go on to find any vindication for taxation.

Indeed, I believe that to this point I have understated the extent to which this joint ownership doctrine undermines self-ownership. For why shouldn't society set out to use its monopoly position to maximize the return to itself (and its constituents) which can be extracted from the labour, efforts, and talents of leaseholders? Why shouldn't society say to prospective leaseholders 'We are not going to engage in complex and contestable efforts to set the true rental value of the materials which we offer for lease. Instead, our terms are that all leaseholders will be subject to a revenue-maximizing progressive income tax regime. To become a leaseholder, you must agree to be subject to this regime which, if it is well designed, will leave you on net with just enough to motivate you to bring your labour, efforts, and talents to bear. Society's monopoly ownership of raw material should, in other words, enable it to get the naturally advantaged to agree that 'The naturally advantaged are not to gain merely because they are more gifted, but only to cover the costs of training and education and for using their endowments in ways that help the less fortunate as well' (Rawls 1971, 101–2).[31] That is to say, society will require all leasers to agree to their natural talents being treated as 'a common asset' (Rawls 1971, 101).

In *An Essay*, Steiner writes as though he has opted for equal discrete shares. ' . . . our equal original property rights entitles us to equal bundles of these [initially owned, i.e., raw or abandoned] things' (1994, 235). He tells us that he is no longer worried about the apparent difficulty of determining the equal value of physically non-identical shares of raw material (Steiner 1994, 271–72 n. 11). Moreover, Steiner offers an interesting argument against original joint-ownership (1994, 218–20). The argument purports to show that a regime of just ownership (e.g., of all apples) could only arise via consent from a regime of equal discrete ownership (of apples). Steiner argues that, if all extra-personal objects were apples and they were jointly owned,

> Your prevention of my using some apples would be both *permissible*, as an exercise of the enforcement power implied by your apples title, and *impermissible*, as a violation of your forebearance duty correlative to my apples title (1994, 219).

Unfortunately, this argument fails. For, in the relevant sense, your prevention of my using the apples does *not* violate my (purported) title to the apples. The reason is that your prevention of my using the apples does not require your use of the apples; it only requires your withholding your permission for me to use the apples. That withholding of permission is not something you use the apples to do. Hence, your prevention of my use of the apples does not violate my title to the apples—which consists in your not *using the apples* without my permission. Nevertheless, the presence of this argument supports the general impression that Steiner favors the equal discrete shares approach.

Steiner does not, however, embrace the implausible view that, for each right-holder, there is one specific equally valuable bundle of raw material to which that right-holder has the original moral title. If Red, White, Blue, and Black appear simultaneously as right-holders in an extra-personal world of twelve raw homogenous acres, it is not that Red has an original moral title to acres 1, 2, and 3 while White has an original moral title to acres 4, 5, and 6, and so on. Red need not pass up acres 4, 5, and 6 or acres 7, 8, and 9 and (somehow without committing a trespass) work her way over to acres 1, 2, and 3. Besides, how could a conscientious Red, who wishes to venture upon and appropriate only those specific acres which are antecedently hers, make even a reasonable guess about which of the three homogenous acres are antecedently hers? So 'no specific person originally holds a title to any specific such thing. Nevertheless, each is entitled to an equal portion of them (Steiner 1994, 268)'.[32] This introduces or reinforces a bit of terminological complexity.

> Does this mean that raw natural resources (sic) are not, after all, describable as 'unowned'? The answer, I suppose, is 'yes and no.' They're owned in the weak sense that a specified *proportion* of them belongs to each person. But they're unowned in the strong sense that none of them is specifically ascribed to any particular person as an item in a property title (Steiner 1994, 235, n.11).

This distinction between a sense in which raw material is originally owned and a sense in which it is not originally owned explains why Steiner feels free to speak of 'unowned' natural (or abandoned) objects over which, nevertheless, individuals have original titles. One of our two original rights is thus said to be a right 'to an equal share of initially unowned things (1994, 236)'.[33]

This modification of the original right to equal shares of nature is needed to avoid the implausibility that Red must enter upon and acquire only the three acres which are preordained for her. Unfortunately for Steiner, this modification undermines his claim that all vindications of actions as rightful must derive from the agent's antecedent titles to the objects utilized in those actions. It therefore undermines his general conceptual argument against entitlement being historical all the way down and in favor of there being a starting point distributive rule which constitutes our original rights over raw material. For, on this revised construal, individuals may permissibly appropriate even though they do not possess antecedent titles to what they acquire; and it is *through their permissible appropriation* that they acquire moral title to what they have appropriated (Mack 1983, 143–44). Perhaps an argument could be produced for the permissible and entitlement-generating appropriation of raw material being limited to the appropriation of equal shares of raw material. Nevertheless, Steiner can no longer argue that first titles to raw material must be constituted by some non-historical distributive norm and not by appropriative actions on previously unowned material.

Since, given this first modification, no three acres are pre-ordained for Red, Red must do something with respect to specific acreage to make or mark it as her own; she must do something to move that acreage from being weakly owned by her to being strongly owned by her. Suppose Red attempts to do this by spraying some of her tomato juice—or, better yet, some of her blood—over three of the available acres. How do we know when such a spraying will constitute a successful appropriation of those acres and when it will be a foolish dissipation of Red's juice or blood? Steiner's presumption here is that we can do at least a serviceable job at making this distinction. That may well be true; but, if it is, it is also reasonable to presume that the historical entitlement theorist can do at least a serviceable job at making the parallel distinction between invested and relinquished labour. If the historical entitlement theorist can do that, then the relinquishment argument against that theorist does not get off the ground.

I want now to point to a second and much more striking modification within *An Essay* of the original right to equal shares. This is a transition from original titles to nature being robust rights which are protected by property rules to their being relatively feeble rights which are protected by liability rules. This second modification is motivated by Steiner's need to deal with the fact that an undetermined number of further equal rightholders will be arriving at an undetermined rate. Suppose Red, White, and Blue are already present in a world of twelve homogenous raw acres. If they knew that no one else would be arriving, they could each appropriate four of those acres. If they knew that Black alone would (soon) be arriving, they could each appropriate three acres and leave as much for Black. But since they have so little idea of how many persons will be arriving and when, the proposal to reserve an equal share for later arrivals is a non-starter (so-to-speak).

> Perhaps if the number of all such [temporally overlapping] persons was knowable, it would in principle be possible for persons to limit their appropriations accordingly, leaving literally 'enough and as good' natural resources for others. As it's not, the dominant form of those original rights increasingly becomes, with the passage of historical time, a redress claim to their equivalent value. *What doesn't change is each current person's right to an equal share of their value* (Steiner 1994, 272, emphasis added).

Since Red, White, and Blue have so little idea how many others will be arriving and when, they may proceed to appropriate *as though no one else will be arriving.* Moreover, if and when Black does appear, those three need not retreat from one fourth of their respective holdings and, thereby, make one fourth of the raw material available to Black. Rather, *they each need only provide Black with something equivalent in value to one of their raw acres.* Perhaps this something would be a large enough supply of edibles—acorns and apples and aboriginal squash—which have been growing on their raw acreage. Alternatively, if Blue has cultivated his acres so that each of his developed acres now has a value *n* times that of a homogeneous raw acre, Blue may discharge his debt to Black by providing Black with 1/*n* of one of those acres (1994, 271).

Imagine that Black is not satisfied with the redress payments which Red, White, and Blue offer to him. Instead, he demands that Red, White, and Blue each retreat from one of the acres he or she has acquired. (Blue will be allowed to take with him whatever improvements he can move. The labour he has expended on improvements he cannot move will be relinquished labour.) Black magnanimously explains that he will not call for the punishment of Red, White, and Blue for their trespass upon his equal portion of the raw acreage in the interval between his becoming a right-holder and the present moment. He is not even going to demand rent from them for this interval. But as a right-holder who is equal in all relevant ways to them, he demands his equal portion of the land. Why, he asks, should the mere contingency that he has arrived later than Red, White, and Blue—through no fault of his own—introduce *any* difference between their rights with respect to the raw acreage and his rights. Black adds that, if his equal rights are not now respected, i.e., if each of the others do not now hand over to him an acre of the raw land, he just may rethink his willingness to stay the hand of retributive justice.

Here is the response of Red, White, and Blue to Black's demand:

> 'Black, we have *taken* the raw land to which in a sense you have every rightful claim. This taking on our part engenders in us only one obligation to you, viz., an obligation to make redress. We have no obligation not to take your share of the earth. We have no obligation to disgorge your share. Your right to an equal share of raw material *is* a right to due compensation should that share be taken (or withheld) from you. We are fully abiding by *that* right in this case when we retain possession of all the raw land but offer you a compensatory payment equal in value to what we have taken from you.
>
> 'Notice precisely what Professor Steiner has written. In the second sentence in the passage above, Steiner suggests that over time the character of one's right to an equal share of raw material changes. At first, it seems, it was a right to an equal share of that raw material. But then, 'with the passage of historical time,'—which seems to happen pretty quickly—the right becomes merely a right to redress. Indeed, Steiner's final sentence which is helpfully italicized by Mack strongly suggests that this change is more appearance than reality. For the core feature of each agent's right—that which does not change with the passage of historical time—is his claim to have (or have left for him) something which is *equal in value* to an equal share of raw material.
>
> 'When the only material which has value is raw land, then each agent's right to something of equal value amounts to a right to have (or have left for him) an equal portion of that raw land. However, even then the core right is not a right to a portion of land but rather a

right to something equal in value to that land. Somewhat surprisingly, given his earlier insistence on rights as titles to physical components of actions, Professor Steiner here construes equal rights with respect to raw materials as claims to an equal share of the wealth—the economic value—associated with raw materials. Since our taking of the raw acreage to which you claim a right is accompanied by due compensation to you, our taking does not violate your claim to that equal share of the wealth.

'According to Professor Steiner, it is entirely morally permissible for each of us to take more than an equal share of the raw land as long as the appropriater who takes more makes redress to others who end up with less. Indeed, as we explain this to you, we each have realized that any one of us could permissibly have appropriated *all twelve* of the raw acres had he or she been prepared to make due redress to all other equal rights-holders. Of course, as long as the only objects of value are raw acres, that redress must take the form of raw acres and, hence, the redress payments will bring us back to an equal sharing of the raw acres. But that simply obscures the fact that the unchanging core right with respect to raw material is, according to Professor Steiner, the right to an equal share of its total value.'

Were Red, White, or Blue familiar with the terminology, they might go on to say that, quite surprisingly and unknowingly, Steiner construes the right of each agent to an equal share of raw materials as a right protected by a liability rule rather than as a right protected by a property rule. Brown's right to the undershirt in his dresser draw is protected by a *liability* rule if others are merely restricted from taking that undershirt from Brown without making redress to Brown for having done so. Others are not required to elicit Brown's consent to the taking; they need only fulfill their liability to duly compensate Brown. In contrast, Brown's right to that undershirt is protected by a *property* rule if others are *forbidden* to take that shirt from Brown even if they are prepared to duly compensate him for that taking. If Brown's right is protected by a property rule, the choice of whether it remains with him or passes to another is Brown's. Another agent may come into possession of the undershirt only if Brown, by consenting to that transfer, chooses that the undershirt come into the other agent's possession. Property rules protect right holders' choices, not merely their enjoyment of the utility or wealth which the rightfully held object supplies. If Brown's right to the undershirt is protected by a property rule, he is doubly wronged if another absconds with the garment; he is wrongly deprived of the utility or wealth which he derived from possession of the garment and he is wrongly deprived of his choice about the disposition of the garment. Since, according to Steiner, Red, White, and Blue need only compensate Black for their appropriation and retention of that excess raw land, Steiner must be construing Black's right as one that is merely protected by a liability rule.

Steiner tells us that, 'Redress transfers are redistributions which, very broadly, *undo* the unjust redistributions imposed by encroachments on rights; they restore just distributions' (Steiner 1994, 266). Yet, a redress transfer does not consist in any actual return to a right-holder of the particular extra-personal object of which he was unjustly deprived. Redress *transfers*, instead, consist of redress *payments* to those who are said to have been the just owners. In this sense, Steiner's redress transfers do *not* undo—or even aspire to undo—'the unjust redistributions imposed by encroachments on rights.'[34] The redress transfers do *not* restore—or even aspire to restore—the antecedent just distributions if we understand those distributions as being composed of particular individuals being in possession of the specific extra-personal objects to which they respectively have title. The redress transfers only restore the distribution of utility or wealth which supervened upon (or would have supervened upon) that specific distribution of particular holdings.[35] We shall shortly see the benefits and costs of this shift.

6. A FINAL MODIFICATION OF THE EQUAL RIGHT TO THE EARTH

The third modification within *An Essay* of the original equal right to raw material is a shift to construing this right as a matter of original joint-ownership. Like the transition to construing this right as one that is merely protected by a liability rule, the shift to joint-ownership is not explicitly acknowledged. Nevertheless, is occurrence is strongly suggested by Steiner's transition in the latter part of his 'Epilogue: Just Redistribution' (1994, 266–82) to the language of leases, lease-holding, and rental payments and by his invocation of Henry George and the early Herbert Spencer in his final characterization of his own position. All occupiers of land (and other possessors of raw material) are taken to have a duty to pay the 'rental value' of the raw material which they occupy or possess into 'the global fund' (1994, 272). Steiner does continue to refer to the parties who pay into the global fund the rental values of the sites they occupy as the 'owners' of those sites (1994, 278). He even speaks of people 'looking to invest their money in the *purchase* of sites . . . ' (1994, 278, emphasis added); and he tells us that his scheme involves a 'global fund levy on the *ownership* of natural resources' (1994, 279, emphasis added). Still, we should remember that, according to Steiner, 'Titles to sites . . . amount to leaseholds . . . ' (1994, 272). Moreover, I believe that a closer analysis of Steiner's claims about what occupiers of sites are obligated to pay into the global fund supports my contention that Steiner migrates back to the joint-ownership understanding of original equal rights to nature. Consider this strikingly puzzling passage.

> . . . in a fully appropriated world, each person's original right to an equal portion of initially unowned things amounts to a right to an

> equal share of their total *value*. Correlatively, any person's possession of a just title to any such thing encumbers him with a duty to pay every person an equal share of its value (1994, 271–72).

Let us begin with the astonishing second sentence. How could it be that a person's 'possession of a just title' to this or that holding 'encumbers him with a duty to pay every person an equal share of its value?' Surely, if a person has just title to his or her possession, he *owes nothing* to others in virtue of that possession; and if others have just titles to their respective holdings, they *owe nothing* to the first party in virtue of their holdings. This sentence makes sense only if to have 'possession of a just title' means nothing but to have a just 'leasehold' from the collectivity each member of which has a claim to an equal share of the proceeds. How must we read the first sentence, for the second to present a correlative proposition? We have to read it as saying that each person's original right to an equal portion amounts to his right to an equal share of the total revenues from the 'leasing' of all raw materials. (The significance of the scare quotes will be clear shortly.) Individual possession of some portion of nature is not what the original right is about; rather, that right is about sharing in the payments that are due from possessors of sites—whether the possessed sites are greater or lesser than an equal share would be. If we picture those possessors as lease-holders, we can think that their possession encumbers them with duties to pay because those duties are conditions of their leases. If we picture those possessors as expropriators of raw material, we can think that their possession encumbers them with duties to pay as acts of redress for these unconsented to expropriations. Both pictures presuppose that the original title to what individuals occupy is held jointly by all persons.

Since there is no right of bequeathal within Steiner's scheme (1994, 248–58), just possessors can never be full-fledged owners; at most they can be lifetime leaseholders. Moreover, thinking in terms of *leases* rather than *sales* of natural sites and other raw material allows one to maintain focus on the mere occupation of natural sites and non-consumptive use of raw materials. For leasers and renters don't consume or destroy; they merely occupy or use what they rent and return it undamaged. Hence, one avoids encountering the vast complications which arise for a Steinerite theory when raw material is consumed or destroyed in the process of creating made things. Steiner's use of the language of leases and rental value is, of course, a strong indication that he has moved over to the joint-ownership conception of the original right to equal shares of the earth; and there is a further indication of precisely this shift. If one maintains that holdings of raw material up to an equal share are rightfully one's own, and only holdings beyond that encroach upon another's discrete rightful share, then one will call for rental/redress payments into the global fund only from those who hold in excess of an equal share. This is Steiner's stance at the beginning of his epilogue on just redistributions where he says that 'each particular over-appropriator owes redress equal to the amount of his over-appropriation' (1994, 268). But this is *not* the payment system which Steiner ends up proposing. Rather, his final proposal is that, no matter how little or how much one possesses, one must pay the rental value of all of those resources into the global fund. '... *each* such owner [i.e., *each* leaseholder] owes to the global fund a sum equal to *the site's* rental value ... '[36] (1994, 272, emphasis added). Only the construal of the original right as one of joint-ownership over raw materials makes sense of this proposal.[37]

The problem, as we noted in the introduction and in section 4's discussion of Spencerian joint ownership, is that original joint-ownership in raw materials seems to impinge radically upon original self-ownership. For original joint-ownership seems to require that every individual get permission from society—the monopoly owner of all raw material—before he can do anything whatsoever. Should we conclude that Steiner's third modification, viz., the shift to original joint-ownership of raw material, defeats the reconciliationist project because it renders nugatory persons' rights of self-ownership? Interestingly, Steiner's second modification, viz., the shift to taking rights to raw material to be protected merely by a liability rule, saves Steiner from this neutering of self-ownership. For, under the liability rule understanding of original joint-ownership, agents do *not* have to get the permission of society in order to occupy and make (non-consumptive) use of portions of the earth. They may proceed to such occupation and use without permission—as long as they make redress payments to society, i.e., as long as they pay into the global fund the rental value of what they occupy or use. The shift to understanding rights as claims protected by liability rules reduces society's right to the earth to a right to extract the rental value of portions of the earth from whoever has appropriated them. Society's right to the earth does not allow it to forbid any appropriation which it has not permitted. Thus, it seems that the original joint-ownership of nature does not render nugatory agents' self-ownership rights.

However, the appearance that self-ownership is preserved may be mistaken. For if the original right with respect to extra-personal material is merely a right protected by a liability rule, it seems reasonable to think that the original right with respect to persons, viz., *the right of self-ownership*, is also protected only by a liability rule. That would mean that *persons* are as subject to non-consensual occupation or use as raw material. Red, White, and Blue may, e.g., confine Black in a cage for a set period of time for their viewing amusement as long as they provide Black with payments equal to the full rental value of Black for that time! Let us assume that this rental value is what Black would agree to as payment for that confinement were there actual negotiations among the parties. And let us acknowledge that we often cannot say what Black would have agreed to except by seeing what he actually agrees to. Nevertheless, we can sometimes have pretty good reason to think that had Black been offered \$*N* he would have agreed to be confined for the period under consideration and, hence, \$*N* equals or exceeds the rental value of Black for the specified period. The implication of Black's self-ownership being protected only by a liability rule is that, if Red, White, and Blue correctly think that $*N* equals or exceeds an offer which Black would have accepted, then it is entirely permissible for them to confine Black in that cage for the specified time without his permission as long as they make a redress payment of $*N*.

Consider a variant on this case in which the confinement itself—i.e., aside from any side-payment to Black—is for Black's own good. Black is an alcoholic who is about to fall off the wagon; but confinement for this limited period will enable him to stay permanently sober. Assume that Red, White, and Blue correctly take this to be the situation. Then the implication of Black's self-ownership being protected only by a liability rule is that the caring paternalist trio may proceed to confine Black in that cage with no side-payment being required because preserving Black's sobriety is a redress payment in kind. If agents' self-ownership rights are protected only by liability rules, there is no room for the *principled* anti-paternalist claim that an agent must be allowed to engage in self-harming action even when coercive interference would genuinely protect him from self-harm. But it is clear that, just as Steiner wants a conception of self-ownership that allows individuals to engage in wrongful (but not rights violating) acts (1994, 215), he wants a conception that allows individuals to engage in self-harmful acts.

These difficulties point to a deeper yet problem for Steiner. The shift to an understanding of rights as claims protected by liability rules conflicts with Steiner's basic commitment to the Choice Theory of rights. The core element in the Choice Theory is the idea that to have a right is to be in a position to determine by one's choice how another may or may not act. 'According to the Choice Theory, a right exists when the necessary and sufficient condition, of imposing or relaxing the [moral or legal] constraint on some person's conduct, is another person's choice to that effect' (1994, 57–8). One has a right with respect to some extra-personal material if and only if, by one's choice, one can maintain another party's duty not to deprive one of that material and one can release that other party from this duty. If the Choice Theory is correct, no party P may permissibly deprive an agent A of extra-personal material M to which A has a right unless A has chosen to release P from his duty not to deprive A of M. However, according to Steiner's liability rule conception of the original right to raw material, agent A may be deprived of M to which A has a right without A having chosen to release depriving party P from his duty not to take M from A. More specifically, under the equal discrete shares construal, *Black* may be deprived of his equal share of raw material without his having released Red, White, and Blue from a duty not to deprive him of his equal share. And, under the joint-ownership construal, *society* may be deprived of its raw material without its having released individual appropriators from a duty not to deprive it of that raw material. If Steiner holds to either version of the liability rule understanding of the original right to raw material, he must abandon the

Choice Theory. If Steiner holds on to the Choice Theory, he must reject any liability rule construal of the original right to raw material.

7. CONCLUSION

The problem seems to lie with Steiner's shift to the liability rule understanding of the original right to raw material. Yet that shift is motivated by the need to avoid the severe impingement upon self-ownership which a property rule construal of the original right to the earth occasions—whether that right is taken to be a matter of equal discrete shares or joint-ownership. If an original right to equal discrete shares is taken to be protected by a property rule, all existing agents will have to leave enough equal shares for all reasonably anticipated latecomers—or, at least, they will have to be prepared to withdraw from the shares which latecomers lay claim to upon their arrival. (And latecomers will either have to leave equal shares for those later yet to arrive or be prepared themselves to withdraw from what becomes the just shares of later yet arriving agents.[38]) If present individuals have to leave equal shares for all reasonably anticipated latecomers, what will be available to present individuals for use and improvement through their self-owned labour will be radically restricted. If present individuals have to be prepared to withdraw from what becomes the just share of any later arriving agent, what it will make sense for present individuals to improve through their self-owned labour will be radically restricted. For if they were to mix their labour with raw material which becomes the just share of any later arriving individual, their redress transfer of that raw material to the new claimant would involve the loss of the labour which they have mixed with that material. Indeed, it seems that, were they to mix their labour with raw material which *subsequently* becomes the just share of a later arriving individual, that mixing either would be revealed to have been *relinquished* or would become *relinquished* [!] when the new just claimant to that material arrives.[39] If an original right of joint-ownership is taken to be protected by a property rule, then all must bow before the demands of society, the monopoly owner, before they permissibly do anything with raw material. And what they must bow to may be much more than what Steiner has in mind when he speaks of agents paying the rental value of the sites they are permitted to lease. (If they cannot permissibly arrange to bow, no appropriation or use will be permissible; and, as Locke points out, each person's due regard for others' rights will require that 'man had starved, notwithstanding the plenty God has given him' (Locke 1690, ii, para. 28).)

Whether it be understood as a right to equal portions or as a right of joint ownership, the equal right to the earth will severely impinge upon self-ownership unless the right to the earth is understood as being protected merely by a liability rule. Unfortunately for Steiner, the liability rule construal of rights conflicts with the Choice Theory of rights; and a liability rule construal of self-ownership clearly conflicts with Steiner's understanding of self-ownership. Thus, ultimately Steiner must choose between retaining an original right to the earth and retaining the Choice Theory of rights (and his own understanding of self-ownership). The standard libertarian urges him to exercise his right to choose the Choice Theory and robust self-ownership.

NOTES

1. This article was composed during my tenure as a Resident Scholar at the Liberty Fund, Inc. I am very grateful for Liberty Fund's generous support.
2. Robert Nozick's *Anarchy, State and Utopia* (1974) serves here and in Steiner's argumentation as the exemplar of rights-oriented standard libertarianism.
3. Other general rights—e.g., rights to life and liberty and to others' compliance with contracts made with one—will then be construed as aspects or implications of the right of self-ownership. Steiner too must assign this protean role to the right of self-ownership.
4. A position *properly* designated as 'right-libertarianism' would affirm a right of self-ownership and original rights among agents to substantively *unequal* shares of extra-personal objects.
5. Steiner also maintains that dead people have no rights and, most pointedly, no rights of bequeathal. Therefore, everything that persons possess at the time of their deaths is abandoned and, hence, reverts to the status of raw materials. Death replenishes 'the earth' to which all living persons have equal rights. See Steiner 1994, 250–58, which concludes, ' . . . the property of the dead thereby joins raw natural resources in the category of initially unowned things: things to an equal portion of which, as we've seen, each person has an original right' (1994, 258).
6. The Steiner articles I most have in mind are Steiner 1977a, 1977b, 1980a, 1980b. Steiner's 'Capitalism, Justice and Equal Starts' (1987) occupies a mid-point between these earlier articles and *An Essay on Rights*.
7. Original rights to *made* objects—and not merely those which have been abandoned—may enter the theory because made objects must substitute for raw materials as the former replace the latter in human history. See Steiner 1980a. Or original rights to *made* objects may enter the theory if it is thought that *all* private property rights require the consent of everyone who is called upon to respect them. Hence, the original and default position is that no one has a private right to any extra-personal object. See Steiner 1980b.
8. In this terminology, the distinction is developed in Guido Calabresi and Douglas Melamed 1972. I explain the distinction in section 5.
9. In this paper I also slide past what I think are difficult questions for Steiner about whether he can square his claim that *equality* is the fundamental rule of justice with a doctrine of self-ownership which assigns to individuals very unequal shares of personal endowments.
10. Rights-oriented libertarian theorists often include a right *of* property among persons' *natural* rights. A particular action will count as generating specific entitlements because it is an exercise of or is performed under the protection of this right of property. For one version of such a natural right of property, see Mack 1990. For another version, see the chapter on 'The Natural Right to Private Property' in Rasmussen and DenUyl 2005. Neither Nozick nor

Steiner think in terms of such a natural right of property and so I do not bring it into this essay's argumentation.

11. For a discussion of G.A. Cohen's objections to Nozick's (very skeletal) doctrine of justice in transfers, see Mack 2002a, 91–99.
12. See the section titled 'How Liberty Upsets Patterns' in Nozick 1974, 160–4. Here the term 'patterned' is understood broadly so that 'end-state' theories which specify a certain profile of holdings, e.g., equality among holdings and 'patterned' (narrower sense) theories which require that the distribution of holdings among persons track the distribution of some other feature among persons, e.g., virtue, both count as 'patterned' doctrines.
13. For a more detailed reconstruction of Nozick's argument, see Mack 2002a, 79–91.
14. Also consider the clear statement from Steiner 1987, 51: 'A historical and unpatterned conception of valid titles as derived titles logically presupposes a set of original titles which *ipso facto* cannot have been created by the exercise of titleholders' powers and liberties and is, in that sense, *not* historical'.
15. Even if Steiner's conceptual argument were correct, it would only show that *if* titles to appropriated or transformed extra-personal objects can arise, there must be original titles to raw material; it would not show that there are such original rights. This is simply an instance of the fact that Steiner's overall discussion of rights does not constitute an argument for the existence of rights.
16. Cf., 'Why not consider the labour to have been abandoned rather than the resource to have been privatized?' (Steiner 1987, 54).
17. In Mack 1983, 142–3, I argued that there was no room within Steiner's earlier formulations for the view that individuals acquire rights to the fruits of their labour through the exercise of their self-owned labour. I suggested there that Steiner might want to try counting the agent's labour as one of the ingredients of the manufactured object.
18. Indeed, Locke sometimes writes as though an agent's labour generates a title to its fruits even though others have (some sort of) antecedent title to what the agent labours upon. See Locke, *Second Treatise* (1690, ii, para. 27): '. . . it [the appropriated object] hath by his labour something annexed to it, that excludes the common right of other men.'
19. Would one have a right to the fruit of one's labour if one created that fruit *de novo*? Certainly Steiner wants to answer in the affirmative. See Steiner 1987, 57. But if there are no antecedently owned non-labour factors present *into which to deposit one's labour*, why isn't one's labour just fritted away?
20. My task here is complicated by the fact that I have a different understanding of precisely where and why a proviso should be inserted within a rights-oriented libertarianism. See note 24, below, and Mack 2002a, 99–103; Mack 2002b, 245–51.
21. Locke 1690, ii, para. 27. Locke adds a second proviso; one's property right to some good will be defeated if the good will spoil under one's continued possession (para. 31).
22. In Locke's case it *may* have been motivated by his invocation of the traditional doctrine that God had given the earth to all mankind in common; he certainly was motivated to invoke this doctrine to rebut Robert Filmer's claim that God had given the earth to Adam.
23. Locke's boldest assertion of something like the enough and as good proviso occurs in paragraphs 41 and 42 of the *First Treatise* (Locke 1690); yet Locke is there very far from asserting any egalitarian distributive rule for just holdings.

24. The parenthetical clause expresses my particular construal of a justified Lockean proviso. The Nozickian explanation of the injustice of the swimmer's exclusion is that the island holder does not really have a (full) property right over the island. My explanation for the injustice is that the island holder deploys *what he fully owns* in a rights-violating way—a way that violates the swimmer's correctly understood self-ownership. On my construal, the injustice done to the swimmer is like the injustice done when someone who fully owns a knife thrusts it into another's chest or threatens to do so. The injustice consists in the violation of the chest bearer's self-ownership, not in the knife holder's deploying something which is not (fully) his property.
25. A defender of a proviso must *justify* his claim that the special ill-effect which he identifies does rebut or limit the holder's property right or the holder's liberty to deploy his holding in the manner under consideration. Here I am only concerned about the *place* that a justified proviso would occupy within a theory of rights.
26. In Steiner 1994, 235–6, 236 n. 13. So strong is Steiner's tendency to equate these two affirmations that in Steiner 1980a, 253, he misremembers Locke as having said that '*as much* and as good' must be left for each (my emphasis).
27. See Steiner 1977b, 44, 45–6.
28. The passage is from the 1st edition of Spencer's *Social Statics* (Spencer 1851).
29. Steiner's statement is a bit hyperbolic. Steiner's latecomers are obligated to incur enslavement only if enslavement is the justified punishment for trespass.
30. Much more needs to be said about the character and rationale for any given proviso—especially about what the proviso 'baseline' is for inhabitants of a region or world much of the raw material of which was initially appropriated a long time ago.
31. I thank Leondidas Zelmanovitz for reminding me of this sort of implication of society's ownership of the earth.
32. Steiner's position here (and in Steiner 1987) is the one I indicated he might want to explore in Mack 1983, 142: 'Steiner could say that it is permissible for an agent to engage in any appropriation of previously unheld material as long as this appropriation does not provide him with more in total than an equal share of natural resources'.
33. ' . . . initially unowned things . . . ' are ' . . . things to an equal portion of which . . . each person has an original right (Steiner 1994, 258)'.
34. The violation of rights protected by property rules seems to call for a whole other mode of undoing. The return of the seized object undoes the loss of the object; the *punishment* of the absconder undoes—nullifies—the wrong of depriving the owner of his choice about the disposition of the object.
35. Steiner, as we have noted, takes Nozick's endorsement of a proviso to amount to an adoption of an original right to equal shares of nature. But he seems to think that Nozick then goes wrong in interpreting this original right '(along Benefit Theory lines) as one to whatever level of wellbeing we would have enjoyed in the absence of a resource's having been appropriated' (Steiner 1994, 236 n. 13). The irony is that these are precisely the lines along which Steiner comes to interpret this original right.
36. Steiner needs a solution to the problem of determining what portion of the rental value of a site is due to its raw (or abandoned) features and what portion is due to alterations of the site's raw (or abandoned) features. See Steiner 1994, 273 n. 14.
37. Steiner's stance on the germ-line genetic information which parents use in their production of children also manifests belief in original joint-ownership.

According to Steiner, because this information is jointly owned, parents who make use of bits of this information must made redress payments into the global fund in proportion to the value of the information that they use (as measured by the value of the children they produce) (Steiner 1994, 242–248). Notice that here too agents may utilize what is jointly owned *without antecedent permission*; the moral slate is clean as long as those agents compensate for their takings.

38. As David Schmidtz points out, this is not exactly a recipe for engendering a welcoming attitude toward later arrivals (Schmidtz and Goodin 1998, 83–84).
39. Cf. J.S. Mill's remarks in the selection from *Principles of Political Economy* (1848) that is reproduced in Vallentyne and Steiner 2000, 161: 'A holder will not incur this labour and outlay when strangers and not himself will be benefited by it. If he undertakes such improvements, he must have a sufficient period before him in which to profit by them; he is in no way so sure of having always a sufficient period as when his tenure is perpetual'.

BIBLIOGRAPHY

Calabresi, Guido and Melamed, Douglas. 1972. 'Property Rules, Liability, and Inalienability,' 85 *Harvard Law* Review 1089–128.

Cohen, G. A. 1995. *Self-Ownership, Freedom and Equality*. Cambridge: Cambridge University Press.

Locke, John. 1690. *Two Treatises of Government*. Ed. Peter Laslett, Cambridge: Cambridge University Press, 1967.

Mack, Eric. 1983. 'Distributive Justice and the Tensions of Lockeanism'. 1 *Social Philosophy and Policy* 132–50.

Mack, Eric. 1990. 'Self-Ownership and the Right of Property'. 73 *The Monist* 519–43.

Mack, Eric. 2002a. 'Self-Ownership, Marxism, and Egalitarianism. Part I: Challenges to Historical Entitlement', 1 *Politics, Philosophy and Economics* 75–108.

Mack, Eric. 2002b. 'Self-Ownership, Marxism, and Egalitarianism. Part II: Challenges to Self-Ownership', 1 *Philosophy, Politics and Economics* 237–76.

Mill, John Stuart. 1848. *Principles of Political Economy* (5th ed.). New York: D. Appleton & Co., 1909.

Nozick, Robert. 1974. *Anarchy, State and Utopia*. New York: Basic Books.

Rasmussen, Douglas and Den Uyl, Douglas. 2005. *Norms of Liberty*. University Park, PA: Pennsylvania State University Press.

Rawls, John. 1971. *A Theory of Justice* (1st ed.). Cambridge, MA: Harvard University Press.

Schmidtz, David and Goodin, Robert. 1998. *Social Welfare and Individual Responsibility*. Cambridge: Cambridge University Press.

Spencer, Herbert. 1851. *Social Statics*. London: John Chapman.

Steiner, Hillel. 1977a. 'The Structure of a Set of Compossible Rights'. 74 *Journal of Philosophy* 767–75.

Steiner, Hillel. 1977b. 'The Natural Right to the Means of Production'. 27 *Philosophical Quarterly* 41–9.

Steiner, Hillel. 1980a. 'Slavery, Socialism, and Private Property'. In J.R. Pennock and J.W. Chapman (eds.), *Private Property*. New York: NYU Press.

Steiner, Hillel. 1980b. 'Liberty and Equality'. 29 *Political Studies* 555–69.

Steiner, Hillel. 1987. 'Capitalism, Justice and Equal Starts'. 5 *Social Philosophy & Policy* 49–71.
Steiner, Hillel. 1994. *An Essay on Rights*. Oxford: Blackwell.
Vallentyne, Peter and Steiner, Hillel (eds). 2000. *The Origins of Left-Libertarianism: An Anthology of Historical Writings*. London: Palgrave.

8 Owning Persons, Places, and Things[1]

Michael Otsuka

I believe that the first correspondence I received from Hillel Steiner was an email in 1998 in which he generously praised a recently-published article of mine and added: 'I hope it's not presumptuous of me to say "Welcome to the wonderful world of left-libertarianism!"' The piece (Otsuka 1998) that prompted this unpresumptuous welcome was left-libertarian in spirit, as it was an attempt to reconcile self-ownership with equality. I was not yet convinced, however, that I was a left-libertarian, so it was not clear at the time whether my exploration of this world was as a curious and sympathetic visitor or as someone who had just begun a period of permanent residency. It turned out to be the latter, and Hillel deserves much of the credit for my settlement in this world that he had himself rediscovered in the 1970s and elegantly reshaped during the past three decades through his essays that lead up to, constitute, and develop and extend his marvellous *Essay on Rights* (Steiner 1994).

Over the past ten years, Hillel and I have had numerous exchanges, either in person or by email, on left-libertarianism. These became fast and furious when he, Peter Vallentyne, and I co-wrote a piece (Vallentyne, Steiner, and Otsuka 2005) on left-libertarianism. We discovered during this period that our mutual commitment to this version of liberal egalitarianism was more an overlapping consensus than a shared comprehensive doctrine. Our normative and conceptual disagreements were striking, and it was only after persistent efforts to persuade one another to our respective points of view and some artful papering over of the remaining differences that we were able to publish a piece to which the three of us could sign our names. In the remarks to follow, I explore some of the questions and points of disagreements regarding Hillel's views on the ownership of persons, places, and things that arose during these exchanges.

1. HOW STEINER'S ARGUMENT THAT PARENTS DO NOT FULLY OWN THE ADULT CHILD THAT ARISES FROM THE ZYGOTE THEY PLANT IN THE MOTHER'S UTERINE WALL IS UNDERMINED BY HIS COMMITMENT TO THE CLAIM THAT ONE CAN FULLY OWN THE FULLY-GROWN TREE THAT ARISES FROM AN ACORN THAT ONE PLANTS ON SOIL ONE OWNS

Steiner asks us to suppose that the first persons ever to exist, whom he names Adam and Eve, were the product of Darwinian evolution.[2] He then grapples with the question of whether Adam and Eve could come legitimately to have full ownership over their child Cain, where such full ownership is as extensive as that which slave masters have claimed over the slaves under their control. Steiner is committed to the proposition that if Cain were fully the product of his parents' labour, then Adam and Eve would fully own him in the manner that a slave master claims to own his slave.[3] Yet he maintains that:

> Cain is not fully the fruit of his parents' labour. For his production required them to mix their labour with natural resources in the form of *germ-line genetic information transmitted from his grandparents.* **Hence denying his parents full . . . ownership of him, . . . [t]hat is, encumbering their ownership is permissible** . . . [T]his encumbrance consists in the liability of their ownership, to expiry on the occasion of Cain's attaining his majority. Prior to the onset of majority—during his zygotic, foetal and minority phases—he is at their disposal. After that, he is a self-owner. And so are we (Steiner 1994, 248; italics in original, emboldening added).

Given Steiner's account of the conditions under which one can come to have unencumbered ownership, the emboldened sentence is, however, a non sequitur. To see why, let us consider the following analogy. Suppose that we have each rightfully enclosed equally valuable plots of land. Suppose, moreover, that some of the world has been left in common and that this commons consists of a grove of oak trees. Assuming, as Steiner does, the soundness of a Lockean account of just acquisition, I would legitimately acquire full ownership of, by gathering, one of the acorns that has fallen on commonly-owned ground if I manage to leave 'enough and as good for others'. Given Steiner's egalitarian interpretation of this Lockean proviso, I would leave enough and as good if my full appropriation of one acorn leaves everyone else with an opportunity fully to appropriate an equally valuable acorn.[4] If, having so left enough and as good, I plant this acorn on my privately-owned plot of land, then nobody could rightfully deny my full ownership of the tree into which this acorn fully grows (plus any other trees that sprout from the acorns that this tree eventually sheds onto my land). Nobody could rightfully deny me this even though, in gathering and planting this acorn, I have mixed my labour with natural resources in the form of germ-line genetic information transmitted from ancestral oaks.[5]

If scarcity makes it impossible to gather an acorn while leaving others with equally valuable opportunities to do so as well, I can, on Steiner's account, still come to have full ownership of an acorn and the tree into which it fully grows (plus future generations of trees on my land that arise from it), so long as I pay others a sum that makes them indifferent between their lesser opportunities to appropriate plus that sum and my greater opportunity to appropriate. Having paid that sum, I will, according to Steiner, have justly and fully acquired no more than an equal portion of unowned natural resources.

An oak tree is created by the planting of an acorn. Similarly a human being is created by the planting of a zygote in the uterine wall. What grounds, then, does Steiner have to deny that Adam and Eve can similarly come to have full (unencumbered) ownership of Cain by leaving enough and as good of the natural resources with which they mix their labour or by compensating others when they cannot literally leave enough and as good? If everyone is equally fertile, and the germ-line genetic information that Adam and Eve can combine to form an offspring is no more valuable than the germ-line genetic information that any other couple can combine to form an offspring, then Steiner's account of the conditions under which one can come to have unencumbered ownership implies that Adam and Eve have full ownership of their offspring, which is to say that they may rightfully exercise powers of slave ownership over their adult children. Even when the germ-line genetic information of some couples is less valuable than that of other couples, Steiner's account of the conditions under which one can come to have unencumbered ownership implies that couples can come to have full ownership of their offspring, so long as those who harbour more valuable germ-line genetic information pay sums of money to those who harbour less valuable germ-line genetic information, such that each couple is indifferent in a manner analogous to that described above.

The upshot of this discussion is as follows: Insofar as it rests on the significance of germ-line genetic information, Steiner's case for denying that self-owning parents can rightfully fully own their full-grown children is no stronger than the case for denying that we can rightfully fully own full-grown oak trees. Yet it follows from Steiner's account of the conditions under which one can come to have unencumbered ownership that there is no case for denying the latter.

2. ON THE COHERENCE OF STEINER'S CLAIMS THAT WE EACH OWN OURSELVES AND THAT WE ARE EACH ENTITLED TO AN EQUAL SHARE OF NATURAL RESOURCES

There is a tension at the core of Steiner's political philosophy between his claims that we each own ourselves and that we are each entitled to an equal share of natural resources. This tension arises because his view has the implication that nature's contribution to our mental and physical capacities can render our self-owned bodies natural resources to which everyone has an equal claim. To illustrate this tension, let us suppose that our primordial Adam has two good eyes and Eve is blind as a matter of genetics and that their holdings in resources external to their bodies is equal.[6] Steiner is committed to the claim that it follows from this disparity in their capacities that Adam and Eve possess unequal shares of natural resources, since the constitution of and disparity in their capacities is solely a consequence of the doings of nature.[7] If there is no way to alleviate or otherwise compensate for Eve's blindness other than by means of an eye transplant from Adam, then these shares would be rendered fair because equal in the only way possible (that is not Pareto-dominated by another fair and equal outcome) if each ends up with one good eye. Nevertheless, Steiner would also want to affirm that Adam's right of self-ownership stands in the way of Eve's coercively extracting one of his eyes and implanting it in order to redress an injustice of genetic inequality.[8] It is not, however, clear that Steiner can coherently maintain both that natural resources should be divided equally and that our rights of self-ownership should be respected, since these appear to issue conflicting claims regarding our rights of ownership in this case.

Now suppose that Adam and Eve are both fully sighted and they decide to conceive two children—Cain and Abel—who they know will be congenitally, genetically blind. On Steiner's view, any genetic inequality between Adam and Eve and Cain and Abel would be the first responsibility of the parents to redress. They would therefore each be obliged to donate an eye to one of their children, assuming that this is the only way to redress the injustice in the distribution of (genetic) natural resources to which their choice to conceive has given rise. Here such an obligation does not constitute an infringement of their rights of self-ownership, since it is plausible to maintain that Adam and Eve have forfeited their right to retain their eyes by choosing to bring Cain and Abel into existence.

Intergenerational compensation cannot, however, always be redressed in such a non-self-ownership-infringing manner, as it might be impossible to extract compensation from parents, because they have destroyed themselves and their estate, leaving their young children orphans. Steiner suggests that we deal in the following manner with cases in which it is impossible to collect from the responsible party: 'persons who decline to insure themselves, against the risk of suffering insufficiently redressable harm from others, are contributors to the adverse consequences they incur; see World Three [in which the victims bear the costs of such harms]' (Steiner 1997, 304n22). In other words, they've brought it on themselves, so they've made their own tough luck. But this solution does not apply to the case of those for whom it is too late to purchase insurance at the age of majority, since the harm will have already been done by then.

Following Dworkin (1981, § III), we might try to compensate such unfortunate individuals in a manner guided by what we each would have insured against on the hypothesis that we made our choice from behind a veil of ignorance. This, however, would imply that fortunate individuals would be liable to contribute to the provision of redress of the unfortunate even though they are not responsible for their misfortune.[9] Suppose that, at the same time that Adam and Eve came into existence, another couple of primordial persons—Adelaide and Everett—also came into existence. Assume, moreover, that, in order to escape their duty to compensate Cain and Abel, Adam and Eve destroy themselves and their estates. Adelaide and Everett had decided not to conceive, but a forced transfer of one eye from each of them to the blind Cain and Abel would make things equal. If duties to compensate are derived from hypothetical insurance choices, Adelaide and Everett would apparently be duty-bound to transfer one eye each, as a matter of redress of that to which they no longer have valid title (Steiner 1994, 266–7), as it would be rational, from behind a veil, to purchase insurance to guard against becoming totally blind at the cost of an equal probability of having one rather than two good eyes. Nevertheless, Steiner would like to affirm that such a result would be blocked by our rights of self-ownership.[10] For the reason I have offered above, it is not clear that he can coherently block this result in this manner.

Now suppose that everyone is genetically identical and possesses an equally valuable share of the earth yet some are less lucky than others because of an impossible-to-anticipate burst of radiation from which there's no refuge that envelops the earth and quantum indeterministically blinds half the population. It follows from Steiner's commitments that the two-eyed possess more than their fair share of natural resources, as the inequality in people's physical and mental constitutions is solely a consequence of the doings of nature. If we continue to assume that compensation via transfer of impersonal resources is impossible, then their shares would be rendered fair because equal in the only way possible (that is not Pareto-dominated by another fair and equal outcome) if everyone ends up with one good eye by means of a transfer of one from each of the two-eyed to each of the blind. Once again, Steiner would like to affirm that such a result would be blocked by rights of self-ownership, yet it is not clear that such a response is available to him.

Steiner might object to my stipulation that it is impossible, in all of the above cases, to compensate the blind via transfer of impersonal resources from the sighted. He might argue that this is an arbitrary and unrealistic stipulation and that, in more realistic circumstances in which such compensation is possible, he would advocate mandatory transfers of impersonal resources rather than mandatory eye transfers. What grounds, however, would Steiner have to prefer compensation via transfer of impersonal rather than personal resources to the blind when the former is possible, given that he appears to be committed to the claim that, in each case, what is at issue is the transfer of a natural resource to which each has an equal entitlement? The only grounds that I can think of would involve an appeal to the claim that our bodies are in fact self-owned *rather than* natural resources to which each has an equal claim. Suppose, not unrealistically, that a vast quantity of impersonal resources would have to be transferred from the sighted to the blind in order to make a blind person indifferent between being totally blind but possessing this sum of impersonal resources and having one good (transplanted) eye but no such impersonal resources. Suppose that this transfer of impersonal resources would need to be so vast that forced eye transplants would be a strongly Pareto superior means of realizing equality of natural resources when compared with such transfers. If Steiner resists eye transfers here, it must be because he cannot fully accept a proposition which he elsewhere insists upon: a proposition affirming that our bodies are natural resources (and hence resources to which we each have an equal claim) insofar as our physical and mental capacities—and variations in our physical and mental capacities—are solely traceable to the doings of nature.

3. A RESPECT IN WHICH STEINER'S LEFT-LIBERTARIANISM FAILS TO CONVERGE ON LUCK EGALITARIANISM

Steiner (1997, 296) maintains that his historical entitlement theory 'converges on conclusions quite similar to those of' the luck egalitarian position that people's level of advantage should be equal except insofar as any inequality is traceable to their own choices. More precisely, he maintains that his theory 'sustains . . . equal opportunity at least as well as Roemer's proposal' to equalize opportunity for advantage (Steiner 1997, 309). To be sure, Steiner's commitment to an egalitarian distribution of impersonal natural resources, plus his inclusion of germ-line genetic information within the compass of natural resources, go some way towards the equality to which luck egalitarians are committed. Steiner also presents an interesting argument against one large source of inequality that arises from voluntary transfers of impersonal resources—that of bequests.

Nevertheless, his case against bequests does not generalize to a case against gifts *inter vivos*. Moreover, Steiner describes 'the power to make gifts *inter vivos*' as 'an unimpeachable incident of natural property rights . . . If a living person (Blue) accepts a gift from another living person (Red), Blue clearly has a right to it and others are correlatively obligated not to interfere with her possession of it' (Steiner 1994, 253).[11] Suppose, for the sake of simplicity, that everyone's genetic endowment is equal and that people's shares of impersonal natural resources are initially equal as well. Inequalities in opportunity for advantage will nevertheless arise through voluntary transfers in the form of gifts *inter vivos*, since it is not entirely up to us and within our control whether we will be chosen as the recipient of such gifts, and hence some will have lesser opportunities for advantage in the form of gifts than others. On Steiner's view, there is no claim for redress of such inequality. This protection of a right to give and receive gifts *inter vivos* is a significant respect in which Steiner's theory fails to sustain equal opportunity by means of his just initial distributions of resources and entitlements to transfer these. Steiner therefore presses his claim of convergence on luck egalitarianism too far when he maintains that his 'historical entitlement structure . . . integrally embodies the requirements of the equal opportunity principle' (Steiner 1997, 311).

On my version of left-libertarianism, there would, by contrast to Steiner's, be no right to transfer interpersonal resources (of non-trivial value) in the form of gifts *inter vivos* (Otsuka 2003, 38–9). Steiner's and my contrasting stances regarding the giving of such gifts ultimately trace to our differing interpretations of the egalitarian requirement to which the Lockean 'enough and as good' proviso gives rise. He maintains that a ban on gift-giving would violate the full property rights in equally valuable shares of the world that his version of the proviso justifies, where shares of impersonal resources are equal insofar as they are of equal economic value at the outset of our adult lives. By contrast, I maintain that such a ban is necessary to ensure that the shares of impersonal resources we have appropriated are in fact egalitarian shares, as mandated by my version of the proviso according to which such shares are equal insofar as they secure our equal opportunity for advantage.

The salient difference between Steiner's version of the proviso and mine can be illustrated by means of the following simple example. Suppose a three-person world consisting of Alpha, Beta, and Gamma, whose capacities, including their productive talents, are equal, and who derive equal welfare per unit of resource consumed. Suppose, moreover, that they confront an unowned expanse of land of uniform quality throughout and that nobody is subject to brute luck arising from natural forces. On Steiner's version of the proviso, justice is secured if each appropriates full ownership of a plot consisting of one-third of the land that is available. These plots are of equal economic value, as can be shown by the fact that such a distribution meets Dworkin's envy-test (Dworkin 1981, § I): nobody prefers anyone else's holdings to his own. On my version of the proviso, such full ownership would violate the proviso. I maintain that shares are relevantly equal if and only if they ensure that each has the same opportunity as anybody else to secure greater advantage. Full ownership will not ensure this precisely because it permits asymmetrical transfers (that is, gifts rather than exchanges) from which not everyone has the same opportunity to benefit. Let us suppose, for example, that Beta and Gamma are siblings, and that Beta is so devoted to Gamma that he chooses to transfer a large share of his plot of land to him in the form of a gift. (Gamma does not reciprocate in kind.) Beta would, however, never dream of transferring land to Alpha in the form of a gift. Full ownership therefore ensures that shares are not relevantly equal, since such ownership fails to ensure that each has the same opportunity as anybody else to secure greater advantage. If, however, we maintain that each is entitled to acquire an equally large plot of land in this scenario, where the plots do not carry with them the right to transfer them as gifts (as opposed to exchanging them on an open market where the highest bidder always wins), then we will have secured a division of the world that ensures equality of opportunity for advantage.[12]

What grounds might Steiner have to prefer his proviso that allows for full ownership of impersonal resources such as the land to which Alpha, Beta, and Gamma lay claim, rather than my proviso that justifies only less than full ownership? Might he argue that his proviso should be preferred to mine on the grounds that his respects, whereas mine violates, a right of self-ownership? I would deny such grounds for preferring Steiner's proviso, since I have argued, as follows, that no right of self-ownership stands in the way of a ban on gifts *inter vivos* involving the transfer of impersonal resources:

> Recall the case discussed earlier of the individual whose income consists of the articles of clothing she weaves out of her own hair. Her being forbidden to give this clothing away to others might plausibly be regarded as a diminution of her right of self-ownership. And it might be equated with the partial confiscation of a wardrobe which she is entitled to give away. But this argument does not establish a right to give away one's income to whomever one pleases when this income has been generated through labour which involves the world as well as oneself. To see why it does not, consider the following variation of a case presented earlier. Suppose that a farmer's income consists of the crops that he harvests from the land that he farms. If he came rightfully to own this land by purchasing it on condition that he not give away any of his harvest, then it would not be any violation of his right of self-ownership if he were prevented from doing so in order to enforce the terms of his purchase. By parity of reasoning, a person's self-ownership would not be violated when he is constrained by the egalitarian proviso from engaging in the non-market transfer of income generated through interaction with the world. In this case as well as the previous one, a person's right of ownership over worldly resources does not extend to the right to give away income generated through interaction with these worldly resources. Hence, preventing someone from transferring these resources is a means of preventing him from doing things with the world that he has no right to do rather than an infringement of his right of self-ownership (Otsuka 2003, 39).

4. PROBLEMS IN DETERMINING WHAT COUNTS AS AN INFRINGEMENT OF SELF-OWNERSHIP[13]

Steiner (1997, 298) approvingly quotes the following claim of Gibbard's: 'Moral rules should be so constructed that, if the rules are obeyed, the acts of each person benefit or harm only himself, except as he himself chooses to confer or exchange the benefits of his acts' (Gibbard 1976, 84). Such moral rules do not, however, coincide with libertarian property rights, including that of self-ownership, since, among other things, competitive harms to third parties do not constitute infringements of such property rights.[14] If, for example, you invent a printing press that renders my skill in calligraphy obsolete, you have harmed me without my consent by rendering my talent worthless and depriving me of my livelihood, but you have not infringed my self-ownership.

How might a libertarian understand what it is to infringe someone's self-ownership other than by defining such an infringement as the harming of that person without his consent? Suppose he adopts Nozick's notion of a boundary-crossing or Thomson's related notion of a trespass or incursion (Nozick 1974, 57–8; Thomson 1990, chap. 8). The proposal that all and only boundary crossings are infringements must overcome apparent counterexamples such as the following:

(i-a) You freeze or remove the air you own that surrounds a person who faultlessly and unthreateningly occupies (though not at your invitation) your airtight chamber, thereby causing him to freeze or explode.[15] Here there is, apparently, no boundary crossing. There are, admittedly, causal chains that have an effect on things inside the skin of the person. But this isn't sufficient to constitute a boundary crossing, since the harm of economic competition has causal effects on things inside the skin of someone who is harmed (e.g., his serotonin levels), as does the non-self-ownership-infringing harm of telling someone a horrible lie—e.g., telling him that his child has just been killed. Do you infringe the person's self-ownership in the freezing and exploding cases? I think not. You do not infringe his self-ownership even if, as it would be natural to describe what you have done, you *kill* him rather than let him die.[16]

Insofar as the question of whether you infringe a person's self-ownership is concerned, these cases are relevantly similar to a case in which you have been heating the air on the edge of your rightfully owned property by building and maintaining a fire out of wood that is rightfully yours. You then pour cold water on this fire to put it out. But you are aware that this fire has attracted a person who had been huddling by it (just beyond the perimeter of your property) to keep warm (and who would have died in the absence of your fire). As the result of your dousing the fire, the air surrounding him grows colder, and he freezes to death. Do you thereby violate his self-ownership? Intuitively not.[17] My explanation of this intuition is that you do not cross his boundary, even though you do act in such a way that affects the air molecules surrounding him, which changes his body for the worse.

(i-b) You place very toxic smoke in the air adjacent to a person's mouth and nose between his intakes of breath.[18] Then he inhales, as he cannot help doing. Like the above cases, I would maintain that this isn't an infringement of his self-ownership, since it isn't a boundary crossing. Similar things can be said about a case in which you gas someone by removing the oxygen molecules that surround him by displacing them with carbon monoxide.

(i-c) You open a trap door on a bridge that you rightfully own, thereby causing someone to fall to his death onto the unowned jagged rocks below. This would again be no infringement of his right of self-ownership because it would involve no boundary-crossing. (This is not to deny that you infringe some other right of his.)[19]

In all of the above cases (apart from the one in note 19), you do something to property that is rightfully yours without thereby crossing anyone's boundary. Admittedly, your actions give rise to a causal chain of events that has a harmful physical impact on his body. But that's not enough to establish a boundary crossing that violates someone's self-ownership. These actions are all very different from the paradigmatic cases of stabbings and shootings which constitute incursions on the body that cross the boundary of an individual.

(i-d) But now consider a case in which you emit a very, very loud noise on your property, causing the rupture of someone's eardrums.[20] This is a hard case for the defender of the claim that only boundary crossings violate self-ownership. Intuitively, it seems like an infringement of self-ownership, but it is not clear that it involves any boundary-crossing. Perhaps it does involve such a crossing by virtue of the fact that it is analogous to a shooting of a bullet, except that you send dangerous sound waves rather than a bullet across the boundary of a person. (Compare a case in which you infringe someone's right of self-ownership by zapping him with a ray gun.)

(ii) You impose a significant risk of a boundary-crossing or incursion—e.g., you play Russian roulette on someone against his will, by spinning the cylinder of a gun in which two of the six chambers are loaded. The imposition of risk doesn't *in itself* count as a boundary crossing or incursion. Therefore, though one can condemn the shooting of someone as a violation of his self-ownership, one apparently cannot condemn the playing of such Russian roulette on someone as a violation of his self-ownership when the pulling of the trigger does not result in the firing of a bullet. That's a counterintuitive result. Perhaps we could nevertheless insist that one is duty-bound not to play

Russian roulette on someone, though this duty does not trace to the infringement of that person's self-ownership. Steiner (2006, 89 and 95) adopts this view. But it appears that a consequence, for Steiner, of such adoption, is that he is at a loss to explain why we are permitted to criminalize mere attempts.

(iii) It is also not clear how one can defend the claim that coercive gunman threats constitute violations of self-ownership if the threatened party yields to the threat. Suppose that the gunman doesn't grab his victim. (That would be a clear violation of self-ownership.) Rather, he merely points a gun and says that he'll shoot unless the victim hands over his money. Suppose that the victim rationally yields to this threat, and therefore the gunman doesn't shoot. We can't explain how this is a violation of the victim's self-ownership, on the incursion model. And, given Steiner's commitments, we can't explain why one has a coercively enforceable duty to refrain from issuing such coercive threats.

NOTES

1. I presented an earlier version of this paper in the Workshop in Political Theory at Manchester Metropolitan University in September 2007 and am very grateful to Hillel Steiner for the characteristically insightful and elegant reply that he delivered on that occasion.
2. Steiner writes: 'Consider a representative pair of primordial persons whom we'll uninventively call Adam and Eve. One thing we know from Darwin about Adam and Eve is that their parents were not persons. Nor, *ex hypothesi*, were they the products of persons' labour. So these parents (and their predecessors) were natural resources' (Steiner 1994, 247).
3. This is an implication of Steiner's claim that 'private ownership of labour-embodying things must be unencumbered by any liabilities other than contracted or compensatory ones' (Steiner 2002, 321).
4. Steiner writes: 'Self-ownership is, then, a sufficient basis for creating unencumbered titles both to things produced solely from self-owned things *and* to things produced from this equal portion of unowned things. We each own the fruits of our labour inasmuch as all the factors entering into their production are either things already owned by us or initially unowned things amounting to no more than an equal portion of them' (Steiner 1994, 236). But see § 3 of this chapter, where I question Steiner's claim that self-ownership is a sufficient basis for creating unencumbered titles to an equal portion of unowned things.
5. As Steiner writes: 'The first step in the production of *any* organism—plant and animal alike—occurs by virtue of the replicative and recombinant operations of the DNA strands within and between the nuclei of the germ cells or gametes supplied by other organisms' (Steiner 1994, 239).
6. In what follows, I shall refer to such resources as 'impersonal resources'.
7. Here I generalize from the following claim of Steiner's: 'One especially pertinent effect of the doings of nature is the constitution of individuals' genetic endowments. For these are determined by parental germ-line genetic information and mutational factors, both of which are products of nature. Such

endowments are themselves key factors in determining their bearers' overall levels of ability' (Steiner 1997, 305). I also draw on private email correspondences from Steiner in February and March of 2004.

8. Let us not try to figure out how Eve would manage this feat.
9. Compare Steiner's 'World One', as described in Steiner 1997, 304.
10. Self-ownership would not stand in the way of people *actually* purchasing insurance policies of this type. Yet it stands in the way of forcing such choices on individuals on the basis of their merely *hypothetical* choices.
11. See also Steiner 1997, 298–9, including the bottom of p. 299.
12. We will have secured such a division at least if we ignore those inequalities in opportunities for advantage that arise from unequal access to services and other purely personal interactions (as between friends and lovers) rather than from the transfer of impersonal resources. Here I bracket inequalities in opportunity that arise from such interactions. For a discussion of the latter, see Otsuka 2006.
13. Unlike the problems I have raised in the first three sections, the problems I raise in this section are not, I think, distinctive of Steiner's particular version of left-libertarianism. They are problems with which anyone who is committed to self-ownership must grapple.
14. For an account of various respects in which they do not coincide, see Arneson 1991.
15. If one maintains that it is impossible to own such air, then consider an example, suggested by Steiner in private correspondence, in which one freezes the water one owns in a pool in which someone sits.
16. Of course, it doesn't follow from the fact that you kill someone that you infringe his self-ownership in cases in which the person has *forfeited* his right of self-ownership—e.g., where you kill a culpable aggressor in justifiable self-defence. In the case under discussion, however, the person has done nothing to forfeit his right of self-ownership, as he is completely unthreatening and entirely without fault for being inside your chamber.
17. Intuitively, you don't kill him, either, in this case.
18. This case is inspired by Fried 2004, 78.
19. Now consider a case in which you push the person off the bridge, thereby sending him onto the jagged rocks. Here you violate the person's self-ownership. Yet the actual boundary-crossing (which, I shall stipulate, also includes boundary-touchings) is relatively minor. Is your violation of his self-ownership therefore minor too? I would say that it is. Nevertheless, by virtue of this minor violation, you can be held fully responsible for the extremely harmful foreseeable consequences of this violation. Your violation results in his body being torn to shreds. Although *you* cannot be said to have torn his body to shreds (as you could, by contrast, even if you tear him to bits, not with your bare hands, but with a sword), his death may appropriately be described as a rights violation (though not a violation by you of his right of self-ownership) for which you are responsible.
20. This case was inspired by Steiner's claim that a right of self-ownership explains, inter alia, why my right of free speech does 'not protect my liberty to shout in your ear' (Steiner 2002, 318).

BIBLIOGRAPHY

Arneson, R. 1991. 'Lockean Self-Ownership: Towards a Demolition'. *Political Studies*, 39: 36–54.

Dworkin, R. 1981. 'What Is Equality? Part 2: Equality of Resources'. *Philosophy & Public Affairs*, 10: 283–345.
Fried, B. 2004. 'Left-Libertarianism: A Review Essay'. *Philosophy & Public Affairs*, 32: 66–92.
Gibbard, A. 1976. 'Natural Property Rights'. *Noûs*, 10: 77–86.
Nozick, R. 1974. *Anarchy, State, and Utopia*. New York: Basic Books.
Otsuka, M. 1998. 'Self-Ownership and Equality: A Lockean Reconciliation'. *Philosophy & Public Affairs*, 27: 65–92.
Otsuka, M. 2003. *Libertarianism Without Inequality*. Oxford: Oxford University Press.
Otsuka, M. 2006. 'Prerogatives to Depart from Equality'. In A. O'Hear (ed.), *Political Philosophy*, Royal Institute of Philosophy Supplement, 58, Cambridge: Cambridge University Press.
Steiner, H. 1994. *An Essay on Rights*. Cambridge, Mass.: Blackwell.
Steiner, H. 1997. 'Choice and Circumstance'. *Ratio*, 10: 296–312.
Steiner, H. 2002. 'Self-Ownership, Begetting and Germ-Line Information'. In J. Burley and J. Harris (eds), *A Companion to Genethics*, Oxford: Blackwell.
Steiner, H. 2006. 'Self-Ownership and Conscription'. In C. Sypnowich (ed.), *The Egalitarian Conscience*, Oxford: Oxford University Press.
Thomson, J. 1990. *The Realm of Rights*. Cambridge, Mass: Harvard University Press.
Vallentyne, P., Steiner, H. and Otsuka, M. 2005. 'Why Left-Libertarianism is not Incoherent, Indeterminate, or Irrelevant'. *Philosophy & Public Affairs*, 33: 201–15.

9 Egalitarian Justice, Left-Libertarianism and the Market[1]

Philippe Van Parijs

The market mechanism consists of a number of buyers and a number of sellers interacting with one another in such a way that goods and services are exchanged at some price. It is endorsed, as a matter of justice, by all libertarians, including left-libertarians such as Hillel Steiner. It also seems to be condoned by all liberal-egalitarian conceptions of justice, i.e. all conceptions that try to combine a commitment to equal respect for the diverse conceptions of the good life to be found in a pluralistic society and a commitment to substantive equality in whatever makes our lives better lives. Why? The answers turn out to vary and, for a subset of them only, to overlap with one of two answers to be found in left-libertarianism.

1. RAWLS

Take first Rawls's theory. It interprets substantive equality in a lax, efficiency-sensitive way, in the sense that it allows some to have more than others because narrowing the gap would involve an unreasonable cost. The difference principle interprets this 'unreasonable cost' as a worsening of the situation of the worst off. If making the expectations associated with the various social positions less unequal would result in making the worst social position even worse—whether or not it would be occupied by the same people—, then more equality would come at an unreasonable cost. The fact that the less fortunate have less valuable opportunities than the more fortunate is justified by the difference principle. Does this then entail an endorsement of the market?

It does on the empirical assumption that the use of markets is so efficient, as regards both the allocation and generation of resources, that the index of social and economic advantages sustainably associated with the worst social position under the best feasible market arrangement is higher than under any arrangement that makes no use of the market. This is a purely instrumental, contingent, and highly conditional endorsement of the market economy. It is logically consistent with the possibility that countless market-based economic arrangements are less just than countless non-market-based arrangements. Moreover, the best market-based arrangement—some version of Rawls's 'property-owning democracy'—is bound to involve a tight regulation of the market, e.g. by tax, environmental and labour law, and possibly a partial or total insulation of some sectors of activity—security, education, health care, banking, media—from the grip of the market.

Is there no deeper Rawlsian justification for the market? One suggestion that there may be such a justification that rests on the role the difference principle gives to income and wealth. What could income and wealth mean in the absence of markets in which to use them? This second connection is real, but weak. Along with the other social and economic advantages that feature in the index used by the difference principle—powers and prerogatives, and leisure time—, income and wealth have been picked because they are primary goods. That is, in Rawls's initial definition, 'things that every rational man is presumed to want' (Rawls 1971, 62, 92) and, in his later definition, 'what persons need in their status as free and equal citizens, and as normal and fully cooperating members of society over a complete life' (Rawls 1999, xiii). Given the role income and wealth are thereby given, nothing forces us to interpret them as purchasing power on a market. Instead of being accessible as commodities, the goods we need as rational people or as free and equal citizens could conceivably be made available by some public agency, and still be incorporated into the index that aggregates the lifetime advantages associated with each social position. Working out such an index is no doubt greatly facilitated if income and wealth can be expressed as purchasing power, but no conceptual relationship to the market is presupposed.

A third connection between Rawls's conception and the market mechanism is suggested by his a priori rejection of central planning as a just social regime, in sharp contrast with the sympathy he expresses for 'liberal socialism', along with the form of capitalism he calls 'property-owning democracy'. Central planning and liberal socialism have in common that the means of production are publicly owned, and hence out of market reach. The key difference is that liberal socialism relies on a labour market, whereas central planning has to use public authority to allocate labour, and thereby violates the workers' freedom of occupational choice. Can it not be said, in this light, that the liberty constraint, rather than sensitivity to efficiency considerations, turns reliance on the market, at any rate for labour services, into a necessary feature of a just Rawlsian society? Not quite.

For it is possible to imagine a socialist society which neither curtails the workers' freedom of occupational choice nor steers their choices with differentiated market wage rates. But such a society would simply be so inefficient that it is unlikely to be sustainable, let alone able to beat liberal socialism or property-owning democracy using the standards of the difference principle. In other words, the absence of a labour market does not entail a violation of the liberty constraint but creates a dilemma between such a violation and making the worst off dramatically worse off. Consequently, this further suggestion of a deeper link between Rawlsian justice and the market fails just as much as the previous one. Whether and when the market is justified from a Rawlsian perspective is a contingent instrumental matter fully captured by the efficiency-sensitivity of the difference principle. The same cannot be said of Dworkin's theory of distributive justice, to which we now turn.

2. DWORKIN

Dworkin's theory of distributive justice is motivated by dissatisfaction with Rawls's theory on the ground that it is not egalitarian enough, not efficiency-sensitive enough, and not responsibility-sensitive enough. Rawls is not egalitarian enough, according to Dworkin, because his theory of distributive justice pays inappropriately little attention to the plight of the handicapped (Dworkin 1981, 339): some are simply excluded from consideration because they fall outside what Rawls calls the 'normal range', and even the others are granted no specific compensation on grounds of their handicap. At the same time, Rawls is not efficiency-sensitive enough, Dworkin claims, because gains, however small, for the worst off justify losses, however big, for everyone else (Dworkin 1981, 339–40). Thirdly, and most importantly in Dworkin's eyes, Rawls's theory is not responsibility-sensitive enough: it fails to pay appropriate attention to ambition (Dworkin 1981, 343–4). One might try to address each of these putative defects separately. What Dworkin proposes is an alternative theory of distributive justice that gets rid of all three in one sweep.

The core of his approach is captured by the conjunction of two 'twin principles' (Dworkin 2000, 324, 340) which he now also refers to as the two 'dimensions of dignity' (Dworkin 2006, 98 and 103–4). These are 'equal concern', or the idea that it is equally important to the political community that each person's life should go well, and 'personal responsibility', or the idea that the fate of each person should be sensitive to their own choices. From these principles it follows that distributive justice consists in making people's share of resources 'sensitive to their choices but insensitive to their circumstances' (Dworkin 2000, 322–23). To give these abstract demands a more precise expression, Dworkin uses two devices—a competitive auction and a hypothetical insurance scheme—which are meant to specify how the just distribution can remain ambition-sensitive while being made endowment-insensitive in the space of impersonal and personal resources, respectively. Or at least so it seems.

The first device requires us to imagine a situation in which a number of shipwrecked people arrive on a desert island. An auctioneer is put in charge of selling all the goods found on the island, each divided as finely as makes any sense. Each shipwreck survivor is endowed with an equal number of clamshells and instructed to use all of them, and nothing else, to bid publicly for these goods on the basis of all relevant information. The auction stops and the goods are distributed between the shipwrecked when each clamshell is committed and each good assigned to the highest bidder. The resulting allocation has three important properties. Firstly, it is *pareto-optimal*: no reallocation of the goods can make someone better off without making someone else worse off. Secondly, it is *envy-free*: no one prefers anyone else's bundle of goods to her own. Thirdly and most importantly, the bundle allocated to each person can plausibly be interpreted as having the same *value* as the bundle allocated to any other, in the sense that its *opportunity cost* to others is the same. What the auction proposes is 'that the true measure of the social resources devoted to the life of one person is fixed by asking how important that resource is for others' (Dworkin 1981, 288).

By thus making the amount of goods each receives responsive to how valuable they are to others, the auction can be said to make the distribution of the island's goods ambition-sensitive. By giving each of the shipwrecked an equal number of clamshells, it can be also said to make the distribution endowment-insensitive. Or at least it could be if only impersonal resources mattered. But what people will be able to achieve with the goods they are allocated will also depend on their personal resources, their talents. Dworkin's most impressive achievement consists in offering a solution for this problem. The key idea is that the availability of insurance turns brute luck—which endowment-sensitivity requires us to neutralize—into option luck—the consequences of which ambition-sensitivity requires each of us to bear. Brute luck is unchosen, whereas option luck is the outcome of a voluntary gamble. Those who take such a gamble and lose have no claim against those who win. And those who choose to abstain are owed nothing by those who gamble and win, nor owe anything to those who gamble and lose (Dworkin 1981, 292–5).

In the first-best version of his hypothetical insurance scheme, Dworkin asks us to imagine that we each know the distribution of all talents and handicaps among the members of our society. In addition we also know our own preferences, including our risk aversion, and are able to specify how much we would insure under such circumstances for each possible risk if the probability of having any particular talent or handicap were the same for everyone. This is done bearing in mind that the premiums to be paid if lucky will have to cover the indemnities to be received if unlucky, each weighted by the probabilities of the situations that trigger them (Dworkin 1981, 276–7). If it could be performed, this ingenious exercise would yield a set of person-specific vectors of lump-sum taxes and transfers, each corresponding to a possible endowment in personal resources of the person concerned. However, it involves a frightening amount of intellectual gymnastics, and moreover requires information that is unavoidably unavailable and, even it were available to some people, could not be expected to be truthfully revealed.

A first problem stems from the causal relationship between endowments and preferences. Can we make any sense of a thought experiment that requires us to abstract from our endowments while retaining preferences which we would not have had, had it not been for these endowments? Secondly, there is an unavoidable trade off between the specifiability of desirability and the specifiability of probability. For us to be able to determine how attractive or unattractive we would find a particular endowment of personal resources, the nomenclature of endowments needs to be pretty fine-grained. But the more fine-grained, the more difficult it is to assign probabilities to them. Thirdly, there is a formidable moral hazard problem. Even supposing people were able to determine the desirability, given their preferences, of all possible endowments, how can one expect them to honestly reveal these preferences? Is it not precisely against the absence of the talents they actually lack that they would say they would have insured?

Dworkin is aware of these difficulties. He falls back on 'what level of insurance of different kinds we can safely assume that most reasonable people would have bought if the wealth of the community had been equally divided and if, though everyone knew the overall odds of different forms of bad luck, no one had any reason to think that he himself had already had that bad luck or had better or worse odds of suffering it than anyone else' (Dworkin 2006, 115–16). The resulting rough approximation, Dworkin conjectures, will be a tax-funded scheme covering a number of specific risks. What sort of taxation? A progressive income tax rather than differentiated lump sum taxes on endowments because of the difficulty of identifying and assessing the value of a person's talents (see Dworkin 1981, 325–26, and Dworkin 2002, 126–29). Which specific risks? Mainly 'ordinary handicaps', such as blindness or deafness, with a level of premium and indemnity fixed by the average person (Dworkin 1981, 277–79), and the lack of sufficient skills to earn some minimum level of income no lower than the community's poverty line (Dworkin 2000, 335–38).

This is what Dworkin's hypothetical insurance scheme leads to as a rough practical approximation. But the insurance scheme, as understood so far, is meant to make the just distribution endowment-sensitive only as regards personal resources. As regards impersonal resources, it seems that it is the auction that should guide us. If this is right, the equal distribution of clamshells among shipwreck survivors suggests that Dworkin should favour a 100% tax on all gifts and bequests. However, he resists this implication, on the ground that it would amount to severely restricting the use people could make of their possessions: they could freely consume what they have but would be banned from giving it to others. In his original article, Dworkin cautiously left aside 'the troublesome issue of bequest' (Dworkin 1981, 334–35). When returning to the issue much later, he made a very different proposal. It is not the auction but a second, distinct hypothetical insurance scheme that should guide our effort to achieve insensitivity to impersonal endowments: 'we can imagine guardians contracting for insurance against their charges' having the bad luck to be born to parents who can give or will leave them relatively little' (Dworkin 2000, 347–84). This modification is subsequently corrected, when Dworkin proposes 'a different (and now I think better) description of gift and inheritance tax as insurance premium. On this different account, such taxes fall not on the donor, as my discussion assumed, but on the recipient of the gift or bequest' (Dworkin 2004, 353).

The upshot of this revision is that endowment-sensitivity is now achieved through a single hypothetical insurance scheme, with gift and inheritance lumped together with talents and handicaps among the dimensions of good and bad brute luck, to be transformed into option luck by the insurance scheme. In the first-best version of this scheme, we are asked to imagine all possible combinations of personal and impersonal endowments with their associated probabilities and to work out how high a premium we would be willing to pay or how high an indemnity we would want to receive in each of these possible situations. This is based on the assumption that we have the same probability as anyone else to be in each of them, and under the constraint that the premiums must probabilistically cover the indemnities.

Does this mean that the auction has no role left to play? Not at all. The auction is still there. But instead of arriving on the island with nothing that distinguishes them from one another, the settlers are now supposed to land each with a bundle of personal and impersonal resources, i.e. the endowments they owe to genetics and upbringing, to gifts and bequests. In this less simplified scenario, equality demands that the clamshells should be distributed not in equal amounts, but in the way determined by the hypothetical insurance. Those who, in their own judgement, regard themselves lucky will owe some amount of clamshells in tax. Those who regard themselves unlucky will be owed some amount of clamshells in subsidy.

The point of the auction parable is then simply to indicate what amount of goods it is fair that these clamshells should command, bearing in mind that the auction should now also concern the goods produced and the services offered by the settlers. The general equilibrium price structure that the auction is meant to elicit will determine how much each will be able to consume of the goods she desires, not only in the light of how scarce the initial supply of these goods is and of how widely and intensely the taste for them is shared, but also in the light of how much the labour each supplies will be valued by the auction, given the type and amount of labour others are able and willing to supply. If among two goods you could consume, one uses less valuable resources than another (given how scarce they are and how many people want goods produced out of them), it is fair—not merely efficient—that you should have less of the latter than of the former. If among two jobs you could do, one produces more valuable resources than another (given the direct and indirect demand for them), it is fair—not only efficient—that you should be paid less for doing the latter than for doing the former.

The role of the auction parable, in other words, is not to indicate how a just distribution must be made insensitive to impersonal endowments. It is rather to express the central role assigned to the market in the specification of the metric of justice. From his earliest formulation, Dworkin states boldly that the idea of a market must be at the centre of any attractive conception of equality of resources (Dworkin 1981, 284). Most explicitly: 'On my view a market in goods and services is indispensable to justice because only a market can measure what one person has taken for himself by identifying the opportunity cost to others of his having it, so only a market can allow people who enjoy a fair distribution of resources to preserve that fairness through their later decisions of occupation, investment, and consumption' (Dworkin 2004, 342). Both consumption and production choices are unequally expensive to society and a responsibility-sensitive conception of justice must take this into account: 'An efficient market for investment, labor and goods works as a kind of auction in which the cost to someone of what he consumes, by way of goods and leisure, and the value of what he adds, through his productive labor or decisions, is fixed by the amount his use of some resource costs others, or his contributions benefit them, in each case measured by their willingness to pay for it' (Dworkin 1983, 207).

For this reason, Dworkin, unlike Rawls, objects to socialism as a matter of principle, not only as a matter of empirical contingency. Whereas his principle of equal concern is perfectly compatible with a centrally planned economy, his principle of personal responsibility is not: 'A socialist society, for example, might assign jobs, fix wages and provide housing, health care, and other benefits in such a way that everyone has a roughly equal standard of living; in that way it might hope to meet the requirements of equal concern without relying on the taxation and redistribution of wealth as an important weapon. But a socialist society whose economy was so heavily controlled by collective decisions could not satisfy the further requirement that it respect personal responsibility. A community can respect that requirement only if it leaves its citizens very largely free to make their own decisions about work, leisure, investment and consumption, and only if it leaves fixing prices and wages very largely to market forces' (Dworkin 2006, 106).

Capitalism's actual markets are of course far from perfect revealers of opportunity costs. They frequently operate under highly imperfect information, under monopolistic conditions, and in the presence of a wide variety of positive and negative externalities. But this should not worry Dworkin too much. No perfect fit can be expected anyway in a technological, economic and cultural context that is constantly changing. Markets need to be regulated to keep monopolies under check and to ensure access to relevant information. And market prices need to be vigorously corrected in order to better approximate true costs through the internalization of externalities. The result will unavoidably be messy, but the use of markets is still the best possible way of making people pay and be paid in such a way that they bear responsibility for their preferences.

This justification for the market is nowhere to be found in Rawls. And this is precisely at the core of Dworkin's critique: Rawls fails to take personal responsibility seriously. By virtue of what the auction parable is meant to convey, the use of market prices as proxies for opportunity costs makes the very notion of equal endowments responsibility-sensitive by making people bear responsibility for the more or less expensive preferences they have and choices they make both as consumers and as producers. In particular, those who choose an unproductive way of life should pay the price of this choice by being denied an income. In contrast to what he takes to be Rawls's view, those who opt for 'idleness' cannot do so at the expense of the 'hard-working middle classes' (Dworkin 2000, 330–1). Rawls's conception of distributive justice, he claims, is unfairly soft on those who 'prefer to comb beaches' (Dworkin 2006, 104).

By contrast, Rawls's more contingent case for the market on grounds of efficiency is totally absent in Dworkin's approach. This is not because Dworkin does not care about efficiency. On the contrary, he considers that Rawls's maximin criterion, as used in his difference principle, countenances some unreasonable costs, i.e. does not take efficiency seriously enough. How egalitarian ex post can the distribution that emerges from the insurance scheme be expected to be? Suppose first that only income matters to people. Risk aversion in the mild sense entailed by the diminishing marginal utility of income will lead to redistribution from situations with high earning power (stemming from personal and impersonal endowments) to situations with low earning power. If real-world redistribution were costless, hypothetical insurance would lead to equal earning power. But administration costs and moral hazard make the real-life redistributive bucket leaky. Depending on how leaky it is, expected-utility maximization will fall short, indeed far short of equalizing earning power for each under all circumstances, i.e. irrespective of the combination of personal and impersonal resources each happens to be endowed with. If we now suppose that other things than income matter to people—for example, the pleasure they take in their work or other aspects of life irreducible to consumption—and that they do so to different extents for different people, deviation from equal earning power can obviously be expected to be even more pronounced. Consequently, from the standpoint defined by Dworkin's hypothetical insurance—in contrast to that defined by Rawls's difference principle—, inequalities in earning power that could be durably reduced in order to benefit the worst off can nonetheless be just: reducing them would involve an 'unreasonable cost'. The best real-life approximation of Dworkin's scheme can therefore safely be expected to endorse redistribution from the better off to the worse off on a scale more comparable to what a utilitarian would advocate than to what some sustainable maximin criterion would require.

In this sense, it could be said that Dworkin cares for efficiency more than Rawls since he is willing to diverge further from an equal distribution for the sake of a greater average benefit. But this has nothing to do with the reason why the market is essential for Dworkin. The question of the market is settled when efficiency considerations are allowed in. If it turned out that socialism was economically more efficient than capitalism, this would provide a relevant case against the market in a Rawlsian framework, but not in a Dworkinian one. For Dworkin, the market is needed because it provides a responsibility-sensitive metric of resources, not because it is needed to maximize the resources available for egalitarian redistribution.

3. STEINER

Let us now turn from responsibility-sensitive egalitarianism to so-called left-libertarianism, as best exemplified by Hillel Steiner's work. The point of departure is radically different. For egalitarians, the fundamental question is how a society's rules—including the structure of property rights—are to be shaped so that they can be justified to all the people expected to uphold them as equals. For libertarians, by contrast, the fundamental question is how a society's rules are to be shaped so that they can respect and protect a system of individual human rights, including property rights, supposed to be given in advance.

Any form of libertarianism, so characterized, can therefore be said to propose a historical, or backward-looking, or purely procedural, or entitlement conception of justice. But this strong sense of 'entitlement' must be sharply distinguished from a weaker sense in which Rawls's and Dworkin's theory also become entitlement theories. On any entitlement conception in this weaker sense, a state of affairs can only be assessed as being just or unjust in the light of how it came about, more specifically by examining whether the process that led to it respected or violated the rules that define a just social structure. Whether a price being paid for a particular good is 'just', for example, cannot be determined by just looking at the good, the amount of currency, the buyer and the seller. Rather, any price is 'just' provided the transactors act within the limits of the property rights they hold by virtue of a just social arrangement. The distinction between strong entitlement theories and egalitarian theories which are entitlement theories only in the weaker sense relates to the question of what makes a social arrangement just, as opposed to what makes a particular transaction or situation just.[2]

This difference leads to a justification of the market fundamentally different from the two discussed so far. Since private property rights over external objects are among the fundamental rights which libertarians believe a just arrangement needs to protect, markets, indeed capitalism, i.e. markets for means of production and the use of labour power, will arise—and persist—spontaneously out of individual's wishes to trade what they possess and produce for their mutual benefit. Consequently, whereas capitalism is necessarily condoned from a libertarian perspective, socialism, or the public ownership of the means of production, is necessarily condemned. Libertarians may also tend to believe that capitalism is more efficient than socialism, and that this fact has something to do with why it arises and persists spontaneously. But this is not what justifies capitalism in their eyes. Even if socialism turned out to be more efficient than capitalism, as some libertarians used to believe, capitalism would still be required by justice, because capitalism alone is consistent with respect for people's fundamental rights.[3] For egalitarians, this is of course nonsense: the structure of property rights is part of the output of equality-guided reasoning about just institutions, not part of the parameters within which this reasoning must operate. For efficiency-sensitive egalitarians à la Rawls, however, the social arrangement which this reasoning will lead to is most likely to ascribe a very significant role to the market, precisely because of the efficiency virtues that are irrelevant from a libertarian standpoint.

There is, however, a third type of justification of the market which is common to left-libertarianism à la Steiner and to responsibility-sensitive egalitarianism à la Dworkin. Whereas libertarians agree on the right of each private owner to use his property as he or she wishes, they sharply disagree on how one can become the legitimate owner of objects, typically natural resources, that previously belonged to no one. Right-wing libertarians adopt the principle 'first come first served' or, somewhat more mildly, some 'Lockean proviso' that stipulates that no one should be made worse off than he or she would have been in a state of the world without any private appropriation. Hillel Steiner, by contrast, interprets Locke's 'common ownership of the earth' as an equal right to all natural resources, and this is precisely what makes him a left-libertarian. The best operationalization of this equal right is a right to an equal share in the value of the natural resources. But how is this value to be assessed?

> Market value is thought to be both impartial and relevant because it imposes no canonical commensuration, either on the various qualities of a single object or on objects of different kinds. Rather, through the interplay of supply and demand, it conflates and subsumes the different commensurations of respective market participants and of nonparticipants, assuming the latter are not prevented from participating (Steiner 1987, 67).

This way of assessing the value of natural resources was put forward by Herbert Spencer and Henry George in the 19th century. Dissociating the value of unimproved land from the value of improvements raises a number of tricky issues which Hillel Steiner recognizes. As stressed by David Miller (1999, 191–7), they are made even trickier if one recognizes (as Steiner does, while Miller does not) that our culturally diverse world provides the scale appropriate for discussions of distributive justice. For the boundaries between what can be and cannot be produced, sold or used for profit can vary considerably from one culture to another, and this will unavoidably affect the market value of different types of natural resources. Nonetheless, Steiner assumes that 'proposals like those of Spencer and George—to distribute equally the pure rent of natural resources—are based on sufficiently relevant and impartial commensuration mechanisms for implementing the Locke solution' (Steiner 1987, 68). In his left-libertarian conception of justice, therefore, 'each right holder, when he or she becomes a right holder, is entitled to an equal portion of natural resource value' (Steiner 1987, 70). Moreover, it is not just nature that is commonly owned, but also the goods left without owner by the death of their owner. Hence, the stock of goods up for this sort of assessment and equal distribution can be handsomely expanded: unlike gifts *inter vivos*, bequests can and must be taxed at 100% of their market value (Steiner 1992).

It is important to stress the big difference between the two roles which left-libertarians thereby give to the market and the sharply divergent attitudes they correspondingly adopt to market prices. In the context of the first role, the just price is left completely undetermined: it simply is the amount of some currency which one agent voluntarily pays in order to acquire some good or enjoy some service while another agent voluntarily provides that good or service in exchange for receiving that amount. The price may have been settled in the light of very imperfect information, or on the background of a strongly monopolistic situation, or it may take no account of major externalities. Libertarians, left and right, do not care, providing both agents are the legitimate owners of whatever they exchange and do not violate anyone else's property rights. By contrast, the market prices to which appeal is being made by left-libertarians in order to determine what counts as an equal distribution of the value of natural resources—the market's second role—cannot be approached in such relaxed fashion. Quite analogously to what is required in Dworkin's auction, they must reflect the true opportunity cost to others of the relevant goods being appropriated by some, and this must be based on a fully informed aggregation of supply and demand under appropriate conditions.

There is more than just a conceptual convergence here. Taken by itself, as we saw, Dworkin's auction seemed to imply an equal distribution of the market value of all donations and bequests, just as Steiner's left-libertarian approach to distributive justice implies an equal distribution of the market value of all natural resources, possibly supplemented by the value of bequests. The left-libertarian interpretation of the Lockean common ownership of previously unowned resources amounts to giving each an equal number of clamshells with entitlements fixed by the competitive market prices of those resources. Whether Dworkin's egalitarian auction, taken on its own, or Steiner's egalitarian appropriation of unowned objects leads to a larger part of social or global income being distributed on an equal basis depends on the aggregate equilibrium market value of natural resources and gifts, respectively.

As we saw, however, there is not much point in speculating on this issue, since Dworkin has now (sensibly) reformulated his approach in such a way that the distribution of both impersonal and personal resources should be handled by his hypothetical insurance scheme. A hard, straightforward justification of an unconditional income at a level determined by correct market prices is therefore unavailable to (emended) Dworkin, even though, like Rawls, he may end up justifying it as part of the just institutional package on the basis of contingent factual considerations that relate, in particular, to the importance the 'average person' ascribes to leisure versus income.[4] Left-libertarians, instead, provide such a justification, be it at a relatively low level that depends on the relative scarcity of natural resources. Unlike right-libertarians and unlike egalitarians like Rawls and Dworkin, they therefore guarantee to every human being a small unconditional protection against having to sell their labour power to the market.

4. REAL LIBERTARIANISM

The account of distributive justice I proposed in *Real Freedom for All* (Van Parijs 1995) is not libertarian, nor therefore 'left-libertarian' in the sense used so far. Admittedly, the label I proposed myself in order to challenge the right's usurpation of freedom—'real libertarianism'—suggested otherwise, and some key aspects of the substance of what I propose can justify classification under some more broadly defined 'left-libertarian' umbrella (see Vallentyne and Steiner 2000; Reeve and Williams 2003). Instead, my 'real libertarianism' is yet another liberal-egalitarian conception of distributive justice. Yet, it seems to converge with Steiner's left-libertarianism by giving market prices the same roles as he does and by ending up providing a justification for an equal unconditional income as hard and straightforward as his, be it at a significantly higher level. How is this possible? Ultimately because it combines the instrumental, efficiency-guided attitude to market institutions to be found in Rawls with the recognition of the role the market could play for the sake of responsibility-sensitive evaluation, as exemplified by Dworkin and Steiner.

On the background of the earlier discussion, this point can most conveniently be spelled out by returning to Dworkin's theory. As noted above, Dworkin initially seemed to offer a dual conception of distributive justice, with the competitive auction covering impersonal resources, and the hypothetical insurance scheme covering personal resources. He subsequently moved the auction to the background and subjected both personal and impersonal resources to the insurance device. The approach developed in *Real Freedom for All* could be characterized as doing exactly the opposite. It amounts to expanding dramatically the scope of the auction, while relegating a functional analogue of the insurance scheme to a shrunk residual role. What motivated this move? Fundamentally the conviction that the opportunities we are given in life cannot adequately be conceptualized, as they are by Dworkin and in most liberal-egalitarian approaches to distributive justice (though not Rawls's), in terms of our endowments in personal and impersonal resources.

The underlying intuition is captured in emaciated format by so-called efficiency-wage theories of involuntary unemployment, as developed by Joseph Stiglitz, George Akerlof, Samuel Bowles and others. Through a number of distinct mechanisms, workers' productivity can be increased as a result of their employers paying them more than what they could get away with. The outcome is that the profit-maximizing wage exceeds the market-clearing wage and hence that involuntary unemployment will persist at equilibrium—in contrast to so-called 'Walrasian' models, where productivity is unresponsive to the pay level and where the equilibrium wage is therefore, of necessity, the market-clearing wage. Even in the most perfectly competitive circumstances—full information, costless entry and exit, no wage legislation or collective bargaining, etc.—, it thus appears, people endowed with exactly the same skills can be expected to be given very unequal opportunities.

What is captured in the highly purified air of these theoretical models is only the tiny and tidy tip of a massive and messy iceberg. In actual life, the opportunities we enjoy are fashioned in complex, largely unpredictable ways by the interaction of our genetic features with countless circumstances, from the smiles of our parents to the presence of older siblings, from our happening to have a congenial primary school teacher or imaginative business partner to our happening to have learned the right language or our getting a tip for the right job at the right time. Once we bear this fully in mind, it no longer makes much sense to try to imagine, as we are asked in Dworkin's first-best approach, all possible endowments of personal and impersonal resources we might have had and to determine how much we would have insured against having those we regard as unlucky. The alternative is to look directly at jobs and other market niches as incorporating very unequal gifts to which we are given very unequal access by a messy combination of factors. It is these gifts, and not only the much smaller amount that takes the form of donations and bequests that should be made the object of a Dworkin-like auction. This is the key distinguishing feature of the approach proposed in *Real Freedom for All.*

Needless to say, this assimilation of jobs to gifts is not uncontroversial. Is it not undermined, for example, by the fact that one generally needs to do something in order to get a job and keep it? This undeniable fact does not create a fundamental difference with donations or bequests. Attending politely your aunt's boring tea parties may be one of the necessary conditions for you not to get forgotten in her will. But this investment of yours does not make you 'deserve' the whole of the big chunk of wealth possessed by a person to whom you happened to be related. Similarly, the fact that one needs to go to the office every morning and busy oneself once there does not make one 'deserve' the whole of the salary one is able to earn by virtue of a combination of circumstances most of which are no less arbitrary than the fact that one of our parents happens to have a rich sister. In Dworkinian parlance, our ambition-driven choices and efforts, including those involving option luck, all operate on the background of massive brute luck. Whatever it was in the auction device that fed the presumption for taxing donations and bequests should be resolutely extended to the taxation of jobs, with the proceeds being distributed just as equally as Dworkin's clamshells. Moreover, this should not be misunderstood as an equalization of outcomes—a misunderstanding both as tempting and as serious here as it is in the case of Rawls's difference principle—but as an equalization of opportunities. What is being equalized is what people are given, not what they achieve with what they are given.

Is there no risk of overshooting the mark? How can one be sure that only the 'gift' component of jobs is taxed away? In the efficiency-sensitive egalitarian perspective for which *Real Freedom for All* proposes to settle, this is quite simple: just tax so as to sustainably maximize the tax yield, using nothing but predictable taxation, fully anticipated by all economic agents. More explicitly, taking efficiency considerations into account, as an efficiency-sensitive egalitarianism recommends we do, amounts to endorsing inequalities that are more than compensation for productive efforts-typically of greater magnitude than sipping the occasional cup of tea with one's aunt. It endorses higher rewards not only for those who happen to be endowed with more valuable talents, but also, for example, for those who happened to take advantage of unevenly spread information in an economy in permanent flux, or for those who are simply given more than their reservation wage because this is expected to boost their productivity. Trying to fully capture the gift component of jobs would involve an 'unreasonable' cost in the 'Rawlsian' sense of worsening the situation of the worst off. In the gift framework I propose, an efficiency-sensitive egalitarianism requires that the gift granted to those with the most modest gift should be as high as possible. How are the sizes of the gifts to be assessed?

This is where I side with Dworkin and Steiner: by using the metric of opportunity costs, i.e. in terms of the cost to others of what the gift commands, itself approximated by appropriate market prices. If and only if this metric is adopted, we get a strong presumption—in the context of a discrimination—free market economy regulated in such a way that prices track opportunity costs-in favour of a universal cash income unconditionally granted to all and paid for out of the predictable taxation of all market activities. At what level? At the highest sustainable one, my efficiency-sensitive egalitarianism recommends. This means that the tax bases—earnings, capital income, transactions, consumption, value added, etc.—as well as the tax rates and profiles—linear, progressive, regressive or some combination—must be chosen so as to sustainably maximize the yield of the tax, under the constraint that it be predictable. Predictability is essential in order to prevent the institutional structure (as distinct from extraneous option luck) from taking from an economic agent more than the value of the gift incorporated in his or her activity, and hence in order to secure that, subject to markets functioning properly, everyone gets at least the value of the universal basic income.

Should an equal amount be given to everyone in one go at a given age or should the amount be spread over people's lives, possibly with a lower level in childhood and a higher level in old age? For mildly paternalistic reasons, *Real Freedom for All* favours the latter, just as it favours giving part of the grant in kind, in particular in the form of free or heavily subsidized education and health care (see Van Parijs 1995, ch.2). How much and in what form? A thought experiment behind a veil of ignorance must provide guidelines for answering such questions: 'Supposing we had nothing but the universal basic grant and knew nothing about our life expectancy, health state and risks, how would we want it to be spread over our lifetimes and how much would we want ear-marked for specific expenditures?'

To this I added, in *Real Freedom for All*, a constraint of undominated diversity: justice requires that no particular person's comprehensive (i.e. personal and impersonal) endowment should be unanimously found worse than the comprehensive endowment of any other person. This concession to the mainstream endowment-based approach I felt was necessary to deal with egregious cases of handicaps which generate disadvantages only very partially captured by lesser access to jobs and other market opportunities. But I now believe this addition to be inessential. Once it is recognized that distributive justice must be defined in the first instance at the global level[5], the sort of thought experiment required to apply the criterion of undominated diversity becomes even trickier than it is in a domestic context, and even less likely to firmly justify significant transfers. To deal with non-pecuniary handicaps, one might as well rely on the nested veil-of-ignorance exercise mentioned above as a guide to devoting part of the universal grant to health care, bearing in mind that health care must be broadly construed as covering, for example, devices that facilitate the mobility of the blind or the disabled. Moreover, while the grant-based redistribution can and must be organized on the largest possible scale, this thought experiment can best be organized at a decentralized level so as to be sensitive to local circumstances and preferences. Thus, veil-of-ignorance exercises still have a role to play, but they are relegated to a subordinate function. In sharp contrast with the later Dworkin, an equal, or at least a fair distribution of all-purpose clamshells is the basic device. Fundamentally, justice is achieved by guaranteeing to every human being as high a minimal claim on the world's resources as is sustainable, in the form of a universal and unconditional grant presumptively given in cash.

In this light, the core of what *Real Freedom for All* proposed can be expressed as an articulation of four elements. Firstly, there is the ethical view, shared with Dworkin and Steiner, that the fair sharing of goods to which no one has a prior claim—such as those found by the shipwreck's survivors on (the early) Dworkin's island or the natural resources on (the left side of) Steiner's originally unowned earth, or scarce jobs in my non-Walrasian economy—requires valuation by suitable markets. Making people pay the true cost of what they appropriate is not only efficient but fair. Secondly, there is, shared with Rawls, the interpretation of efficiency-sensitive egalitarianism in terms of sustainable maximin. Equalization involves an unreasonable cost when it makes the worst off worse off. Thirdly, there is a stylized picture of society as a massive gift distribution machine, in contrast to Dworkin's community of unequally endowed individuals and Rawls's system of inter-linked social positions. It is these gifts that must be viewed as the substratum of people's opportunities. It is therefore their value that must be equalized across individuals, at any rate to the extent recommended by the efficiency-sensitive egalitarian maximin criterion. And fourthly, there is, reminiscent of Norman Daniels's (1985) or Ronald Dworkin's (2000, ch.8) approach to health care, a thought experiment about the concrete shape—lifetime profile, cash versus kind—which the highest sustainable basic grant should take.

These four elements combine to provide a theory of distributive justice, not a libertarian one like Steiner's relying on pre-institutionally given entitlements, but one expressing, like Dworkin's or Rawls's, a responsibility-sensitive, efficiency-sensitive conception of distributive justice. The key difference resides in the stylized picture of society which is needed to conceptualize inequalities and characterize justice. Dworkin opts for the mainstream perspective, shared by most of the economists and many of the philosophers who have been writing about distributive justice. The members of society are unequally endowed with talents, capacities, earning power, etc. and justice requires that inequalities in these internal endowments should be corrected through the distribution of external endowments. It is only in Walrasian general equilibrium, however, that internal and external endowments so defined exhaust the factors that determine people's life chances. In our messy real world, many other factors play a role that cannot be relegated to the margin as random noise. More than any specific feature, it is the inadequacy of this stylized picture that motivated my dissatisfaction with Dworkin's theory and other mainstream approaches.

Rawls proposed a radically different picture that does not suffer from this defect. People can settle in different social positions for all sorts of reasons, and people settled in the same social position achieve very different levels of the index of social and economic advantages over their lifetimes, also for all sorts of different reasons. However, the notion of social position is tricky. It works best in a society with a number of distinct stable occupations in which people tend to stay for most of their lives. To apply it worldwide (contrary to Rawls's own conception of world-level justice) and in a world in which people jump up and down from one position to another is not impossible. The Difference Principle simply asks us to focus on the index of social and economic advantages that can be expected by those spending their whole lives in the worst social position, as defined by the index. However, as soon as part-time work is involved, or interrupted careers, or long-term unemployment, we face head on the hard question of how to construct the metric in terms of which social positions are to be compared, within regimes and across regimes, in particular the question of how to weigh the components of the index which tend to be inversely correlated, in particular income and leisure. The solution proposed by Rawls himself is biased against leisure, and any welfarist resolution is unacceptable to him.[6]

The alternative I propose avoids, like Rawls's, the mainstream reduction of opportunities to endowments. At the same time, it side-steps both the need for a nomenclature of social positions and the need to provide an unbiased index that would make them comparable. Instead I propose focusing on the gifts we all receive, each measured by its opportunity cost as approximated by market prices. Maximizing the value of the smallest gift is a way of maximizing the power to consume of those with the smallest such power, but also the power to choose the sort of life they want to live by broadening their choice of occupation. It has, it must be admitted, limitations of its own, in particular the fact that it leaves out of the grasp of distributive justice all those gifts we receive—including no doubt some of the most important to our lives, such as the love of those we love—which are not taxable themselves nor mainly a way of accessing positions which yield in turn a taxable income.[7] But perhaps this is just as well. Perhaps a conception of justice that boosts the market power of those with least market power will serve us well enough, and will arguably serve us ever better, compared to the alternatives discussed, as mobility grows, globalization deepens and the market widens and tightens its grip. Even so much better—who knows?—that Hillel Steiner may discover that his honest, rigorous, patient quest for reflective equilibrium has turned him into some sort of liberal-egalitarian.

NOTES

1. Earlier versions of part of this paper were presented at the seminar 'Ethics, Economics and the Market' (Michael Sandel, Amartya Sen & Philippe Van Parijs, Harvard University, Spring 2008), at the conference 'New Approaches to Distributive Justice' (Washington University in St Louis, May 13th, 2008), at the Legal Theory Workshop (Yale Law School, September 18th, 2008) and at the annual meeting of the September Group (New York, September 21st, 2008). Special thanks to Sam Bowles, Jerry Cohen, Josh Cohen, Frank Lovett, John Roemer, Michael Sandel, Tim Scanlon, Amartya Sen and Erik Olin Wright for useful feedback.
2. See Van der Veen and Van Parijs 1985 for a clarification and further illustration of the distinction, partly inspired by Hillel Steiner's work and fully consistent with his recent discussion of the notion of a 'just price' common to all entitlement theories of justice, weak or strong (Steiner 2008).

3. See e.g. Wallich 1960.
4. See my discussion of Rawls on this issue in Van Parijs 2002, 218–22. Beyond Dworkin's reluctant pragmatic concessions (Dworkin 1983, 208; and Dworkin 2000, 309), a similar argument can be made on the basis of his most recent formulations in terms of an expanded insurance scheme.
5. See Van Parijs 2007.
6. See Van Parijs 1995, ch. 4
7. For further discussion of the dependency of my stylized picture of the world on the pervasiveness of the market, see especially Sturn and Dujmovits 2000 and my reply in Van Parijs 2001.

BIBLIOGRAPHY

Ackerman, Bruce and Anne Alstott. 1999. *The Stakeholder Society*. New Haven and London: Yale University Press.

Daniels, Norman. 1985. *Just Health Care*. Cambridge: Cambridge University Press.

Dworkin, Ronald. 1981. 'What is Equality? Part II: Equality of Resources'. 10 *Philosophy and Public Affairs* 283–345.

Dworkin, Ronald. 1983. 'Why Liberals Should Care About Equality'. In *New York Review of Books*. February 3.

Dworkin, Ronald. 1985. *A Matter of Principle*. Oxford: Oxford University Press.

Dworkin, Ronald. 1990. 'Foundations of Liberal Equality'. In G.B. Peterson (ed.), *The Tanner Lectures on Human Values*. Vol. XI. Salt Lake City: University of Utah Press.

Dworkin, Ronald. 2000. *Sovereign Virtue: The Theory and Practice of Equality*. Cambridge, MA: Harvard University Press.

Dworkin, Ronald. 2002. '*Sovereign Virtue* revisited'. 113 *Ethics* 106–43.

Dworkin, Ronald. 2004. 'Ronald Dworkin Replies'. In Justine Burley (ed.), *Dworkin and his Critics*. Blackwell: Oxford & Malden.

Dworkin, Ronald. 2006. *Is Democracy Possible Here? Principles for a New Political Debate*. Princeton: Princeton University Press.

Miller, David. 1999. 'Justice and Global Inequality'. In A. Hurrell and N. Woods (eds), *Inequality in World Politics*. Oxford: Oxford University Press.

Rawls, John. 1971. *A Theory of Justice*. Cambridge, MA: Harvard University Press.

Rawls, John. 1999. *A Theory of Justice*. Revised edition. Cambridge, MA: Harvard University Press.

Reeve, Andrew and Williams, Andrew (eds). 2003. *Real Libertarianism Assessed: Political Theory after Van Parijs*. Basingstoke: Palgrave Macmillan.

Steiner, Hillel. 1987. 'Capitalism, Justice and Equal Starts'. 5 *Social Philosophy and Policy* 49–71.

Steiner, Hillel. 1992. 'Three Just Taxes'. In P. Van Parijs (ed.), *Arguing for Basic Income*. London: Verso.

Steiner, Hillel. 2008. 'The Just Price', contribution to the conference 'The Ethical Status of the Market'. University of Reading.

Sturn, Richard and Dujmovits, Rudi. 2000. 'Basic Income in Complex Worlds: Individual Freedom and Social Interdependencies'. 22 *Analyse und Kritik* 198–222.

Vallentyne, Peter and Hillel Steiner (eds). 2000. *Left-Libertarianism and its Critics: The Contemporary Debate*. Basingstoke & New York: Palgrave.

Van der Veen, Robert J. and Van Parijs, Philippe. 1985. 'Entitlement Theories of Justice: From Nozick to Roemer and Beyond'. 1 *Economics and Philosophy* 69–81.

Van Parijs, Philippe. 1995. *Real Freedom for All*. Oxford: Oxford University Press.

Van Parijs, Philippe. 2001. 'Real Freedom, the Market and the Family: A Reply'. 23 *Analyse & Kritik* 106–131.

Van Parijs, Philippe. 2002. 'Difference Principles'. In S. Freeman (ed.), *The Cambridge Companion to John Rawls*. Cambridge: Cambridge University Press.

Van Parijs, Philippe. 2007. 'International Distributive Justice'. In R. E. Goodin, P. Pettit and T. Pogge (eds), *The Blackwell Companion to Political Philosophy*. Oxford: Blackwell, vol. II.

Wallich, Henry. 1960. *The Cost of Freedom: A New Look at Capitalism*. New York: Harper & Brothers.

PART IV
METHODOLOGY

10 Respect for Persons and the Interest in Freedom

Ian Carter

I begin this homage to my friend and mentor with two puzzles about his work on freedom. The focus of my essay will emerge through my discussion of these puzzles, so I beg the reader to indulge me in this rather lengthy introduction.

The first puzzle is this: when, almost twenty years ago, I embarked on a doctoral research project on the measurement of freedom, I assumed from the start that my first task must be to analyse the different ways in which freedom was valuable, where by 'valuable' I meant something like 'a good-making property of people's lives'. We are interested in measuring the degrees to which individuals are free, I thought, because freedom is (for whatever reason) a good thing, either for the individuals who possess it or for society as a whole. Liberal theories of justice tell us how to distribute burdens and benefits in a society, and they should, and often do, assume freedom to be one of the relevant benefits. Such theories therefore prescribe equal freedom or maximal freedom or 'maximin' freedom or a guaranteed minimum of freedom for all or yet some other distribution of freedom that is judged to be fair or efficient. Thus, in order to demonstrate an interest in measuring freedom, we need to show that freedom is indeed one such benefit. We need to know why it is better to have more freedom than to have less (at least *ceteris paribus*, and up to a certain level of satiation). And we need to reveal the relations of entailment between certain kinds of *reason* for valuing freedom and certain principles for the *distribution* of freedom (such as maximization or equality or a guaranteed minimum), each of which makes certain kinds of demands on our powers of measurement.

I eventually reached the conclusion that the need to be able to measure freedom is normatively pressing if and only if freedom has 'non-specific' value (Carter 1999, ch. 2). The non-specific value of freedom is that part of freedom's value which is independent of the content of specific freedoms.[1] The content of a specific freedom is determined by the specific thing that that freedom is the freedom to do. If freedom has non-specific value, it has value *not only* in virtue of this content—that is, *not only* in virtue of its being the freedom to do certain specific things—but also *as such*—that is, also in virtue of the simple fact of its being freedom. And if freedom has value as such, then any assessment of the overall value of a given set of freedoms must include an assessment of 'how much freedom' the members of that set together provide. I suggested that there are indeed good reasons for saying that freedom has non-specific value, or value as such. These reasons include the fact that the category of non-specific value is not, as one might at first have expected, exhausted by the category of intrinsic value. In other words, the term 'non-specific instrumental value' is not an oxymoron. For example, one might claim both that freedom is instrumentally valuable as a means to economic or social progress, and that our ignorance of the direction in which progress will take us makes it impossible for us to say which specific freedoms are valuable to this end. Thus, certain kinds of argument for the instrumental value of freedom are also arguments for its non-specific value, and therefore support an interest in having more freedom rather than less (at least *ceteris paribus* and up to a certain level of satiation).

At no point during this project did Hillel Steiner say to me: 'forget the value of freedom; just concentrate on the measurement issues'. And yet, I now think it safe to say that this is what my former teacher would have done had the project been his.[2] Steiner's earlier work on liberty,[3] which had originally inspired my own interest in the concept, discusses in some detail both the nature of individual freedom (what it is to be free to do something) and the problem of its measurement (on what basis we can say that one individual is freer than another), but almost wholly ignores the question of whether and, if so, why, freedom should be thought of as a good thing, either for those who possess it or for the society they live in or for any other individual or group. The question is also largely ignored in his monumental book *An Essay on Rights* (1994). While the problem of accounting for freedom's value has exercised the minds of a great number of liberal thinkers, from Humboldt, Mill and Spencer to contemporary libertarians and liberal egalitarians such as Hayek, Berlin, Rawls and Dworkin, it has not, apparently, troubled Hillel Steiner. This thought may be found puzzling, especially in light of the fact that Steiner's theory of justice is a liberal theory in which all moral rights are said to be derived from a fundamental right to equal freedom.[4]

I now turn to the second puzzle. Over many years and in a number of publications—not least in *An Essay on Rights*—Hillel Steiner has defended the thesis that '[a] universal quest for greater personal liberty is a zero-sum game' (Steiner 1994, 54). According to Steiner's 'Law of Conservation of Liberty' (LCL), within any given closed group of individuals there can be no absolute gain or loss in freedom, for any gain in freedom for one person will be exactly counterbalanced by a proportional loss in freedom for some other or others.

The intuition behind LCL depends on Steiner's conception of a person's liberty as consisting in her not being physically prevented by other persons from performing actions: I am free to do x if, were I to attempt to do x, I would not be prevented by any other person from doing x. This physical, interpersonal account of constraints on freedom—sometimes called the 'pure negative' account—entails that an agent's possession of freedom depends on her possession of (in the sense of *de facto* access to) physical objects (space or matter). For all actions have physical components, and the freedom to perform actions therefore requires access to such components. 'What I am free to do is a function of the things possessed by me, and what I am unfree to do is a function of the things possessed by others. My total liberty, the extent of my freedom, is inversely related to theirs. If I lose possession of something, someone else gains it and thereby gains the amount of freedom (whatever it is) which I've lost' (Steiner 1994, 52).

Despite its conceptual elegance, this zero-sum thesis has come under sustained attack from a number of quarters. Some of the criticisms can be discounted in the present context, because they presuppose a conception of freedom that is at odds with that of Steiner. LCL can of course be challenged quite easily if one simply adopts a different understanding of what it is to be free to do something. Others criticisms, however, are wholly internal to Steiner's pure negative conception of freedom, and appear to me to be unanswerable. Most importantly, it has been argued that LCL rests on a confusion of the number of *actions* that are compossible (that is, the number of actions that can all be performed in the same world) and the number of *freedoms* that are compossible (that is, the number of freedoms that can coexist in the same world) (Gray 1991, 159–62; Carter 1999, 261–63; Kramer 2003, 213–17. Cf. Cohen 1991). The number of actions that can be performed by means of a given set of physical objects (assuming certain human capacities to do so) depends only on the nature of that set of physical objects, and is therefore constant; the number of *pure negative freedoms* made available by that same set of physical objects depends, in addition, on the preventive dispositions of the agents who are free or unfree to use it. Such preventive dispositions depend on those agents' beliefs, desires and capacities, which are not themselves subject to anything like a law of conservation. Thus, in a world of three agents, it may happen that *each and every* agent has access to object *x*, even though *x* cannot be made use of by more than one person. Each and every agent will have access to *x* if it is true of each of the three agents that she neither wants to use *x* nor will attempt to do so. In such a world, it is true of *each* of the three agents that, *were* she to attempt to make use of *x*, she *would not* be prevented by any other agent from doing so. If, on the other hand, all three agents were to desire to use *x*, and consequently were to attempt to use *x*, only one would succeed in doing so. In this second world, unlike in the first, we can be sure that two of the agents are unfree to make use of *x*.

A generalized reduction in the disposition to perform preventive actions can indeed bring about an overall gain in freedom for a closed group of individuals. Moreover, we have every reason to anticipate that some institutional structures will be more efficient than others in discouraging the development of such preventive dispositions.

I shall not expand further on the reasons for rejecting LCL. Suffice it to say that I have yet to see a convincing answer to the argument given above. And yet Steiner has persisted in affirming LCL in a number of more recent writings (Steiner 2003a, 2003b, 2006).[5] This, then, is my second puzzle: why does Steiner persist in affirming a thesis that has undergone such sustained and plausible criticism? The reader of *An Essay on Rights* can be forgiven for interpreting LCL as an additional, interesting fact about individual freedom, rather than as a crucial premise in the author's own theory of justice. Nevertheless, Steiner's continued insistence on LCL suggests otherwise. It suggests that some essential element of his theory of justice hangs on the truth of LCL. Which element, exactly?

I shall argue in what follows that the solutions to these two puzzles are closely related. Sections 1 and 2 of this essay will be mostly interpretative, and will address the first and second puzzle respectively from Steiner's own perspective. In sections 3 to 5, I shall then ask how much of Steiner's theory of rights can be salvaged if LCL is rejected. I shall try to show that, although the falsity of LCL does indeed do considerable damage to Steiner's theoretical construction, the spirit of his theory of justice—in particular, the fundamental role he assigns to the right to freedom—can nevertheless be preserved if we substitute LCL with the thesis that freedom has non-specific value. The resulting account of the fundamental right to freedom will no doubt have implications for Steiner's account of property rights, including his requirement that all rights be compossible, but I shall not explore these implications here.

1. THE WILL THEORY OF RIGHTS AND THE VALUE OF FREEDOM

In attempting to solve the first puzzle, we should begin by noting Steiner's adherence to the so-called 'Will Theory' of rights (Steiner 1994, ch. 3; 1998).[6] According to this theory, a person's rights are essentially the choices she has about other persons' performance of correlative duties. Rights-bearers may exercise these choices at will—hence the expression 'Will Theory'. To have a right is to have the moral authority to constrain another (or not to constrain her) into doing (or not doing) something, for a right is, in Kant's words, 'the capacity to obligate others to a duty' (Kant [1797] 1965, 45). Will Theorists of rights therefore reject the so-called 'Interest Theory', according to which having a right means having an interest that is served by the performance of the correlative duty. For the Will Theorist, the basis of my right not to be the subject of violent behaviour is not my *interest* in bodily integrity (although, no doubt, I and many others do have such an interest), but the moral *authority* I possess, as a free and rational agent, to require (or, indeed, not to require) that others respect my bodily integrity.

What does the Will Theory of rights imply about our obligation to respect the freedom of others? A neat answer to this question was set out by H.L.A. Hart in his famous article 'Are There Any Natural Rights?' (1955). My having a right entails my having the moral authority to restrict the liberty of another person by 'obligating her to a duty'. A right therefore consists in a moral justification for such a restriction of another's liberty. But if such justifications are required, they must in turn presuppose a 'natural' right (a right not acquired through the exercise of other rights) not to suffer such restrictions of liberty, and such a natural right must be possessed by its holder simply in virtue of her being a moral agent. Thus, we arrive at a fundamental, natural right of all moral agents to be free. Along similar lines Steiner sees all rights as 'rights to impediment removals', and this fact leads him 'in the direction of understanding rights as claims to *freedom*' (1994, 209–10). For Steiner, to embrace the Will Theory is to accept that all rights derive ultimately from a fundamental right of each moral agent to a certain degree of freedom.[7] Notice, however, that neither Hart nor Steiner aims to supply a categorical reason for respecting the freedom of moral agents. Rather, their claim is that we must believe in a natural right to freedom if we believe in rights at all.

Given the role of the Will Theory in Steiner's analysis of justice, we can now see why it would seem inappropriate for Steiner to begin by saying why freedom makes people's lives go better. Saying why freedom is valuable in this sense appears to amount to saying why it is in people's *interests* to have freedom. Had Steiner embraced the Interest Theory of rights, such reason-giving would have constituted a necessary step in his argument for a fundamental right to freedom. But the whole idea of the Will Theory is that the nature and grounds of people's rights prescind from their interests: the rights one holds are powers over duties in others, not protections of one's interests. This point applies not only to a putative interest in bodily integrity or well-being or need-satisfaction, but also to a putative interest in freedom itself.

This solution to our first puzzle has itself left a number of theorists puzzled. Jeremy Waldron captures their sense of unease when he sets out the reason, as he sees it, for Hart's later rejection of his own deduction of the fundamental right to freedom as set out above. The trouble, Waldron says, with this transcendental argument 'is its abstraction from any plausible conception of human well-being. It proceeds on the purely analytic basis that rights provide justifications for coercion, which presupposes that coercion needs justifying, which indicates that coercion is prima facie wrong, which amounts in effect to a natural right to freedom. On Hart's present approach, an argument for rights must be more substantial, more full-blooded than this. Rights must be derived on the basis of a theory which accords importance to certain individual human interests rather than on the basis of the internal analytics of the language of rights itself' (Waldron 1988, 100–101).

To understand Steiner's resistance to such a 'full-blooded' appeal to human well-being or interests, we need to view his adherence to the Will Theory within the context of his overall approach to theorizing about justice. For Steiner, no appeal should be made to substantive moral values in the course of such theorizing. Justice is a truly freestanding concept: its meaning does not depend on any particular view of what constitutes the good life, be this a 'thick' view or merely a 'thin' view like the one assumed by John Rawls. In this sense, one can think of Steiner's theory as taking seriously (or as an extreme version of, depending on your point of view) the Kantian idea of the priority of the right over the good. Any appeal to substantive moral values in theorizing about justice is bound to violate the priority of the right over the good, so betraying the *raison d'être* of justice itself as an arbiter in disagreements over the good.

Rather than appealing to substantive moral values that might ground a particular interpretation of justice, Steiner seeks 'to derive the nature of justice from its microfoundations in the formal characteristics of moral rights' (1994, 188). He can acknowledge, of course, that justice is *itself* a value (that, after all, is why we are interested in analysing it). Similarly, he can acknowledge that rights are valuable in as much as they are constitutive of justice (they are 'the elementary particles of justice' (1994, 2)), and that a just principle for the distribution of freedom is itself valuable if rights are valuable (for rights are essentially normative distributions of freedom). The concept of freedom necessarily plays a part in a theory of justice because justice necessarily involves distributing freedom in a certain way. But it is one thing to claim that a certain distribution of freedom is valuable (because it is constitutive of justice); it is another thing to claim that freedom itself is valuable. Steiner does not need to make the latter claim in order to say what justice is.[8] Neither, for that matter, does he need to claim that *justice* is valuable in order to say what justice is. According to Steiner's methodology, the proper way to explicate the nature of justice is through analysis of the concept, and conceptual analysis does not itself require any substantive value judgements. This is why Steiner believes that, although he has shown justice to consist in a certain set of rights, he has nevertheless 'offered no reasons as to why we should *be* just' (Steiner 1994, 282).

Although an Interest Theorist might prescribe a right to freedom, there remains a fundamental difference between such a theorist and a Will Theorist. The difference can be usefully characterized as depending on whether one sees the prescription of freedom as entailed by a *concern* for persons or by an attitude of *respect* for persons (Steiner 2007). Showing concern for persons involves paying attention to their interests, and in this sense involves treating them as moral patients (even where the relevant interest is an interest in freedom), whereas showing respect for persons involves recognizing their dignity as moral agents. Showing concern for persons involves pursuing their ends (including their freedom, if freedom is one of their ends). Showing respect for persons involves treating persons as ends in themselves—as setters of ends or, alternatively put, as the points of origin of ends. I shall return to the notion of respect shortly.

2. THE LAW OF CONSERVATION OF LIBERTY

On the Will Theory of rights, the fundamental right to freedom can be derived without reference to a theory about human interests. However, this derivation does not itself generate a *determinate distribution* of freedom. According to the Will Theory of rights, if we believe there are any moral rights at all, then we must acknowledge the existence of a fundamental right to freedom and we must acknowledge that such a right is possessed by all moral agents. Nevertheless, the deduction of a fundamental and universal right to freedom is not yet enough to tell us which of the many possible distributions of freedom is prescribed by a just set of rights. This indeterminacy might be thought to lend support to Waldon's objection: without a theory of well-being that states why, and in what ways, freedom is good for individuals, how can we hope to justify assigning certain individuals *certain amounts* of freedom?

This brings us to the solution to our second puzzle. For it is in the derivation of a determinate principle for the distribution of freedom that the Law of Conservation of Liberty can play an important role. Indeed, it seems to me that LCL is a necessary premise in any such derivation that remains true to Steiner's exhortation to avoid appeals to substantive moral values when analysing justice.

Assuming the validity of LCL, an analysis of justice need not specify whether, or in what ways, freedom contributes to human well-being. If one embraces the Will Theory of rights together with LCL, one can indeed remain wholly indifferent over whether freedom is a good thing *or a bad thing* for those who possess it. If LCL is true, freedom is here to stay, and it is here to stay in a quantity that cannot be either increased or decreased. Freedom is ineliminable, regardless of whether it is an ineliminable good or an ineliminable bad. The most that can be done, and therefore the most that can be required of us, is to provide a rule stating how the constant sum of freedom is to be shared out among individuals. On this basis, Steiner is able to derive the justice of an *equal* distribution of freedom. His argument proceeds as follows. The only two alternatives available in sharing out a constant sum good (or bad) are an equal distribution and an unequal one. No unequal distribution can be justified without giving substantive moral reasons for privileging the ends (and hence the moral codes and values) of some individuals over those of others. Therefore, only an equal distribution of freedom can be deduced as one of the formal properties of a freestanding conception of justice. Equal freedom is entailed by justice because, by process of elimination, it can be shown to be the only distribution of freedom with which justice is not incompatible (Steiner 1994, 216). For future reference, let us call this derivation of the equal liberty principle 'Steiner's Derivation'.

To see the importance of LCL in the above argument, consider how that argument would fare if LCL were jettisoned. We could continue to affirm that only an equal distribution of freedom can be justified, but such a distribution of freedom would no longer be a determinate distribution. 'Equal freedom' does not imply a maximum or a minimum of freedom or any quantity of freedom in between the maximum and the minimum, so we would have no basis for preferring a distribution giving everyone a great deal of freedom to a distribution giving everyone very little freedom. Such a basis, it seems, would only be available if we were to introduce the substantive normative claim that giving people more freedom is (at least ceteris paribus) *better* than giving them less, and it is difficult to imagine justifying such a claim without reference to human *interests*, however conceived. In this case, people's interests would play a part in deciding what rights they have, and we would effectively have abandoned the Will Theory of rights in favour of its rival Interest Theory. This is not to say that the Will Theory itself depends on LCL. Rather, what is shown by the above argument is that LCL is needed in order to make the Will Theory do the work that Steiner wants it to do: without LCL, a purely formal analysis of the concept of justice (including a defence of the Will Theory of rights) will fail to generate a determinate set of distributive entitlements to freedom.

If LCL is valid, then, Steiner need not make the substantive claim that individuals have an interest in freedom in order to claim that justice entails a fundamental right to a certain amount of freedom. By resting his case on LCL, he can eschew that substantive claim and thus remain true to the Will Theory and to his view of justice as a wholly freestanding value. This conclusion solves both of our puzzles, as well as supplying the link between them.

The problem, however, is that LCL is almost certainly not valid. Thus, the question that now naturally arises is: Just how much of Steiner's theory of rights and justice can be salvaged if one rejects LCL—that is, if one attempts to reach a determinate distribution of freedom by replacing LCL with a substantive claim about the value of freedom?

3. RESPECT FOR PERSONS AND DEGREES OF FREEDOM

We have seen that the Kantian attitude of respect for persons is an important factor in motivating people to act justly in Steiner's sense. As Steiner himself points out, the Kantian imperative to treat humanity as an end in itself—where 'humanity' is to be understood as the human power of rational choice—'is generally interpreted as requiring one to respect the agency of others by performing no action that subordinates their sets of purposes to one's own', and 'actions that diminish one's freedom to less than that enjoyed by their perpetrators are pretty strong candidates for being described as actions subordinating one's set of purposes to those of others' (Steiner 1994, 221). Thus, according to Steiner, respecting others in the Kantian sense itself entails respecting the equal freedom rule.

In this section and the next, I shall argue that the deduction of the equal liberty principle from the ideal of respect for persons is valid even if LCL is not, and that such a deduction can be combined with an appeal to the non-specific value of freedom. This argument will require a closer examination of the notion of respect for persons. In the next section, I shall examine the way in which *equality* of freedom is derived from the ideal of respect for persons. In this section, I shall confine myself to examining the relation between respectful conduct and conduct aimed at promoting a certain *degree* of freedom.

Respect, in the sense of 'recognition respect' (Darwall 1977), is an attitude that one appropriately shows towards certain beings in virtue of their moral personality. Moral personality is a set of capacities, including 'the ability to reflect on one's desires and circumstances, to set ends for oneself, to form coherent plans' (Hill 2000, 87). Having these capacities gives one the authority to make moral claims on others and to hold them morally accountable. A respectful attitude to such authority involves recognition of these second-personal claims (Darwall 2006) which, following the argument of Hart set out earlier, can be shown to include a natural claim to freedom.

Given that the attitude of respect involves recognition of persons' capacity to make choices, it is reasonable to define respectful conduct as conduct that involves abstaining from performing actions that *direct the choices* of others, that is, actions that aim to affect the content of others' wills by means of changes in the array of options open to them.[9] For it is only by abstaining from such attempts to direct the choices of another that one is able to treat that other as a point of origin of ends. Although Steiner does not define respectful conduct explicitly in this way, its consistency with his conception of just conduct should be clear from his requirement that our principle for the distribution of freedom be 'untainted by tendentious instrumental considerations of *what that freedom is going to be used for*' (1994, 216, my emphasis), and from his explicit endorsement of Kant's view that justice is concerned not with the *content* of wills but only with the formal *relation* between them—that is, the compatibility of one person's freedom of action with that of another (Kant [1797] 1965, 24; Steiner 1994, 211). 'It is, if you like, their *purposiveness*—rather than their purposes—that is the proper object of the sense of respect that is clearly distinguishable from concern' (Steiner 2007).

What does respecting a person in the above sense entail for her entitlement to *a certain degree* of freedom? Given the identification of respect for persons with respect for their agency, and given the entailments that we have already established between respect, the Will Theory of rights and the right to freedom, it might be thought that increases or decreases in the respect owed to persons entail proportional increases or decreases in the freedom owed to them, and that 'fully' respecting a person entails according her as much freedom as possible consistently with a like freedom for others (that is, for those others who are owed a similar degree of respect). Despite first appearances, however, and *regardless* of the validity or otherwise of LCL, respectful conduct towards others does not, *in itself*, involve maximizing, or even aiming to increase or preserve, the degree of freedom of those others. For there is a conceptual difference between increasing or preserving the degree of choice available to others and abstaining from directing the choices that those others make in exercising their freedom. Similarly, there is a conceptual difference between restricting the choices available to others and directing the choices that those others make in exercising what choice is left to them. When I increase the freedom of another person I am not *necessarily* abstaining to a greater degree from attempting to direct the choices she makes in exercising her freedom, and when I decrease her freedom I am not *necessarily* abstaining to a lesser degree from such an attempt. There is, of course, often a strong contingent relation between these two forms of conduct: restricting another person's degree of choice is one tried and tested way of directing her conduct towards ends that one desires she choose (that is, of exercising power over her). But this is not the only motive I might have in restricting her choice. For example, I might claim that freedom as such is bad for a person, without making any reference to the ends that she might pursue in exercising that freedom in the various hypothetical scenarios in which she has more or less of it. In support of such a claim about the disvalue of freedom, I might suggest that having too much freedom is a direct cause of mental distress, and that such mental distress arises, at least in part, independently of the specific nature of the options that freedom offers us, being caused simply by the pressure of having too much information to process and too many choices to make. And I might add that this disvalue in terms of stress greatly outweighs any positive value that is generated by the fact of having more freedom rather than less. I can hold this position while remaining indifferent to the specific choices that agents make in exercising their freedom. Conversely, I might claim that having more freedom rather than less directly contributes to a person's sense of well-being, and is therefore a good thing in itself. Again, I can say this without referring in any way to 'what . . . freedom is going to be used for'.

Now the reasons I have just cited, for saying that freedom has disvalue or value, are, respectively, reasons for holding that freedom has *non-specific* disvalue or *non-specific* value. What allows us to distinguish between the two forms of conduct discussed above—that is, increasing or decreasing a person's freedom, and abstaining from or engaging in the direction of a person's choices—is exactly the fact that the former can be motivated by the non-specific value or disvalue of freedom, whereas the latter cannot. Thus, it is possible to respect a person fully (to treat her fully as a moral agent) *while also* actively promoting her interests (and in this sense treating her as a moral patient). The condition of that possibility is a particular characterization of the person's interests as resting on the non-specific value or disvalue of her freedom. Respectful conduct is *compatible* with conduct aimed at increasing (or decreasing) the freedom of others, *if and only if* it is motivated by the *non-specific* value (or disvalue) of their freedom. Showing a concern for the *specific* value (or disvalue) of a person's freedom is not similarly compatible with respect for that person, for it presupposes a concern for the choices she might make in exercising her freedom. When one exercises power over another person by manipulating her freedom or freedoms—when one changes the content of her will by substituting some of her specific freedoms for others, or by increasing or decreasing her overall freedom, *with a view to inducing her to make certain choices rather than others*—one allows one's concern for her freedom to depend on 'considerations of what that freedom is going to be used for'. In this sense, one fails to treat her fully as a point of origin of ends.

It might be suggested that, in the light of the above argument, respect for persons is compatible with a concern for the value of another person's freedom only when that value is *intrinsic* value. In support of this view, one might point to Steiner's previously cited rejection of '*instrumental* considerations' relating to a person's freedom. As I pointed out in the introduction to this essay, however, there is such a thing as 'non-specific instrumental value' (Carter 1999, §2.4). For example, I might value freedom because it tends, over the long run, to produce economic or social progress at the societal level, even though I do not at present know the particular ends in which progress consists. Because this concern for freedom's value remains non-specific, it remains respectful of persons' dignity as agents. It does not imply any attempt to influence the content of their wills, and it is therefore compatible with treating them as the points of origin of ends. Respecting a person is compatible with 'instrumental considerations' where such considerations relate to the ends that are (or might be) brought about by her *exercises of freedom as such* (her *purposiveness*). It is not compatible, on the other hand, with 'instrumental considerations' of '*what that freedom is going to be used for*'—that is, with considerations about what that person herself aims to achieve in exercising her freedom (her *purposes*).

The kind of respect for persons that motivates Steiner's Will Theory of rights is therefore compatible with a concern to promote greater rather than lesser freedom. In order to justify such a promotion of greater freedom, however, we must make a substantive liberal value judgement: we must judge freedom to be non-specifically valuable. Furthermore, we must judge, as liberals generally do, either that the arguments in favour of freedom's non-specific disvalue are unconvincing, or that they are outweighed by the many arguments in favour of freedom's non-specific value.

4. RESPECT FOR PERSONS AND EQUALITY OF FREEDOM

The argument of the previous section does not show that equal respect entails *equal* freedom, and it might indeed be thought to suggest otherwise. If it is possible to increase or decrease people's freedom while respecting them fully (in the sense of abstaining from directing their choices), is it not possible to accord people unequal degrees of freedom while nevertheless respecting them equally? To answer this question we need first to examine the basis for respecting persons equally.

Steiner's claim that universal respect for persons entails equal freedom depends for its validity on the assumption that the property of moral personality is possessed *equally* by all persons. The assumption of such an equality (and hence an equality of certain capacities of rational choice) is indeed a suppressed premise in the derivation of the equal liberty principle that I earlier called Steiner's Derivation: LCL and the Will Theory of rights are not in fact *sufficient* (even in conjunction) to generate a determinate (equal) normative distribution of freedom, even though, as we have seen, LCL is *necessary* for that purpose (in the absence of a substantive claim about the value of freedom). Respect is owed to persons in virtue of their possession of the capacities of moral personality. Therefore, if persons possess such capacities in *un*equal measures, it is appropriate to show them *un*equal respect: if A possesses the bases of respect (that is, the relevant capacities) to a greater degree than does B, then the obligation of each to avoid subordinating the other's ends to her own is presumably not symmetrical, but is possessed in a lesser degree by A and in a greater degree by B. Such an inequality of respect would be perfectly compatible with the Will Theory of rights, and would invalidate Steiner's Derivation.

Kant assumed all persons to have an equal power of rational choice on the basis of a transcendental conception of the self that few contemporary political philosophers are prepared to rely on explicitly. He was able to say that people are equals as moral agents because he assumed that moral personality had nothing to do with people's *empirical* capacities. If, however, we prefer to avoid such metaphysical assumptions (as do many contemporary neo-Kantians), and therefore interpret the relevant capacities (such as 'the ability to reflect on one's desires and circumstances', 'to set ends for oneself' and 'to form coherent plans') as empirical capacities of persons, we shall find that such capacities vary in degree from one person to another. Deriving the equal liberty principle is not, therefore, quite as straightforward as Steiner's Derivation appears to suggest.

This said, the problem of showing that persons are equal in the morally relevant sense is not one that I shall address here. I shall simply assume that the suppressed premise in Steiner's Derivation (the fact that individuals *are* equal in their possession of the property of moral personality) is true. Elsewhere, I have attempted to ground that premise in a way that does not depend on the Kantian transcendental conception of the self (Carter 2007b).

Having rendered explicit the egalitarian factual assumption behind the prescription of equal respect, we are now in a position to see why, although one can increase or decrease a person's overall degree of freedom without affecting one's degree of respect for them, equality of respect does nevertheless entail equality of freedom. If all persons are in equal possession of the capacities of moral personality—as they are, *ex hypothesi*—then Steiner's Derivation is correct, inasmuch as the only remaining way to justify an unequal distribution of freedom will be by assuming the greater value of one person's purposes over another's.[10] The only way to justify such an unequal distribution will be by assigning a greater value to one person's freedom than to that of another, and the only way to justify such an assignment of greater value will be through considerations having to do with the *specific* value of freedom—that is, through considerations of 'what . . . freedom is going to be used for'. If our concern is exclusively with the *non*-specific value of freedom (as it must be if we are constrained to respect persons fully), and if persons are equal in their agential capacities, we can find no reason for valuing the freedom of one person more highly than that of another. For example, if it is an end in itself that moral agents have freedom, and all persons are equally moral agents, then we have no basis for saying that one person's freedom has greater intrinsic value than that of another. Similarly, if freedom is non-specifically valuable as a means to progress, and if each person is equally capable of exercising freedom, we shall have no basis for saying that one person's freedom has a greater non-specific instrumental value than that of another. Precisely because respect for persons confines our concern for freedom's value to a concern for its non-specific value, then, equal respect entails equal freedom.

What *is* left open by the ideal of equal respect is the *level* of equal freedom. Equal respect is itself compatible with *minimal* equal freedom (if pursued on the basis of freedom's overall non-specific disvalue). The prescription of *maximal* equal freedom can only be generated by a substantive evaluative assumption about the degree to which freedom is non-specifically valuable.

5. AN INTEREST THEORY OR A WILL THEORY?

Let us now return to the difference between the Will Theory and the Interest Theory. Which of these two theories best captures the account of the right to freedom that emerges in the light of the above arguments? As should be clear by now, in terms of the purely formal properties of rights, the upshot of our analysis is that the Interest Theory must prevail: the right to freedom is indeed based on an interest in freedom (considered non-specifically). What the Will Theory correctly describes is the particular view of the content of rights entailed by an account of the relevant interests that rests solely on the non-specific value of freedom. '[I]f we believe that people should be able to choose what is for their own good, we will hold that rights should be secured to individuals in the form of choices. But that "liberal" view constitutes an argument about what the *substance* of rights should be; it does not make choice an *analytic* feature of rights' (Jones 1994, 35).[11] What we have arrived at, in other words, is the Interest Theory conceived as a *container for* the Will Theory, or, put another way, the Will Theory *embedded in* the Interest Theory. The Interest Theory correctly characterizes what rights essentially consist in, while the account we have given of people's interests provides us with a substantive account of rights that happens to be captured by the Will Theory.

At this point, the Will Theorist may express the worry that embedding the Will Theory in the Interest Theory will open the door to rights that are *not* captured by the Will Theory. For once one has admitted that the right to freedom rests on an account of human interests, appeals might be made to other interests in order to justify rights other than the right to freedom, so leading to a proliferation of conflicting rights. Indeed, once rights are seen to be based on interests, such an appeal to other interests (and therefore to other rights) might even seem to be *morally required*. After all, it is utterly implausible to claim that the interest in freedom is the only human interest. One of the motivations behind the Will Theory is the anti-inflationary belief that such rights-proliferation needs to be avoided if the currency of rights is not to be devalued and if rights are to do genuine normative work. If we accept the Interest Theory, on the other hand, such a proliferation of rights would seem to be unavoidable.

Another way of expressing the Will Theorist's worry is as follows. We can distinguish between the Interest Theory understood as a formal explication of rights (the Interest Theory as I have discussed it so far), and a substantive Interest Theory which includes an account of the relevant interests. And we can distinguish between two different ways in which the Will Theory might be embedded in such a substantive Interest Theory. Let us say that the Will Theory is *tightly embedded* in our substantive Interest Theory if, given our characterization of the relevant interests, the Will Theory fits *snugly* into its container theory, such that the substantive Interest Theory contains no further space for rights other than Will-theory rights. Let us say, on the other hand, that the Will Theory is *loosely embedded* in a substantive Interest Theory if, given our characterization of the relevant interests, the Will Theory fits into its container theory *with room to spare*, such that the substantive Interest Theory entails Will-theory rights *among others*. Where the Will Theory is tightly embedded, the set of Will-theory rights will be co-extensive with the set of Interest-theory rights supported by the relevant account of interests. Such tight embeddedness would be entailed by an account of the relevant interests as resting on freedom's non-specific value. Where the Will Theory is loosely embedded, on the other hand, the set of Will-theory rights will be only a subset of the set of substantive-Interest-theory rights. Such loose embeddedness would be entailed by the apparently more sensible view that there is a multiplicity of interests, of which the interest in freedom (considered non-specifically) is but one. The question we have to address, then, is whether any good reason can be given for favouring the tight embeddedness of the Will Theory over its loose embeddedness.

A positive answer to this question can be found in the view that respect for persons is constitutive of rightful conduct towards them. (This is not to say that respect is constitutive of all ethical conduct towards persons; only that it is constitutive of rightful conduct towards them, which in Steiner's view has lexical priority over other forms of conduct.) Human interests are indeed multiple and varied. However, if one holds respect for persons to be constitutive of rightful conduct towards them, then one must accept that justice is compatible with the pursuit of human interests *only* to the extent that those interests can be pursued *while also* treating persons as the points of origin of ends, for according to the Kantian maxim, one must treat humanity *never merely* as a means but *always also* as an end in itself. I have argued that the only human interest that can be pursued while also treating humanity as an end in itself is the interest in freedom considered non-specifically. Thus, if we hold that 'disrespect supervenes upon injustice' (Steiner 2007), and respect upon justice, we have a reason for singling out the non-specific value of freedom as providing that particular account of human interests that serves in determining our obligations of justice towards persons. On this particular interest-based account of rightful conduct, the Will Theory of rights is *tightly embedded* in a substantive Interest Theory.

The above argument leaves open the question of whether the tight embeddedness of the Will Theory is a characteristic only of rightful conduct *towards persons* or also of rightful conduct *in general*. For it is open to an Interest Theorist to accept a respect-based account of rightful conduct towards persons while also claiming that there is such a thing as rightful conduct towards non-persons (animals, children, the permanently comatose, and so on). On such a view, justice would be grounded not only on a concern for the freedom (valued non-specifically) of persons, but also on a concern for various other interests of non-persons, thus implying the loose embeddedness of the Will Theory in a substantive Interest Theory of rights considered more generally. On a more Steinerian interpretation of the above argument, however, all just conduct is necessarily characterized by respect for persons. On this view, rights just are rights of persons, and the Will Theory is therefore tightly embedded in a substantive Interest Theory of rights in general.

If we affirm the ideal of respect without affirming an interest in freedom, we fail to arrive at a determinate set of distributive entitlements. If we affirm an interest in freedom without insisting on respect for persons, we open the door to a proliferation of interest-based rights. If we ground our theory of justice both on respect for persons and on their interest in freedom, on the other hand, we can defend the libertarian and egalitarian spirit of Steiner's theory of justice in a way that avoids both of these consequences. However, this defence cannot be formulated coherently without also admitting to a methodological shift. While conceptual analysis can and should do a great deal of work in normative theorizing, it cannot, by itself, eliminate all rival theories of justice. Neither, therefore, can it generate a determinate theory of justice without taking a particular value perspective as its starting point.[12]

NOTES

1. For this reason, non-specific value can also be called 'content-independent' value (Kramer 2003).
2. Hillel Steiner was already my former teacher at that point. My PhD thesis was supervised by Steven Lukes.
3. I follow Steiner and most other contemporary political philosophers in using the terms 'freedom' and (non-normative) 'liberty' interchangeably.
4. I should emphasize that I am *not* here pointing to a difference between Steiner and myself over the possibility or appropriateness of measuring freedom without reference to its value. I follow Steiner in considering questions about the value of freedom (or of sets of specific freedoms) to have no bearing on questions about the existence either of specific freedoms or of degrees of overall freedom. We both favour a non-value-based approach to the measurement of freedom (Steiner 1983; Carter 1999, ch. 7). Our reasons for favouring such an approach are relevantly different, however. My own reason lies in freedom's non-specific value (Carter 1999, chs. 2, 5), whereas Steiner's reason lies in his belief that concepts like freedom and justice (which prescribes a certain distribution of freedom) can and should be analysed and defined without recourse to value judgements.
5. For earlier statements of LCL, see Steiner 1975, 1980, 1983.
6. More precisely, Steiner endorses the Kantian or 'classical' Will Theory of rights, which is essentially tied to the methodological stance discussed below. As N. E. Simmonds argues (1998), the Will Theory can also be defended in more moderate forms.
7. According to Steiner, this fundamental right should be interpreted as a universal right to *initial* (equal) freedom—a right that must be respected at the beginning of people's lives as moral agents, after which justice (understood as respect for rights) prescribes that they each take responsibility for their voluntary exercises of their freedom of action and of their power to alienate and acquire rights. I shall not discuss this 'luck-egalitarian' or 'starting-gate' aspect of Steiner's conception of justice in the present context, but will simply assume here that 'equal freedom' does indeed mean 'equal *initial* freedom'.
8. This said, Steiner does claim that 'freedom is a necessary condition of one's pursuing any purposes at all' (1994, 221; 2003, 123), apparently implying that freedom is instrumentally valuable. He also leads us to believe, at one point, that he sees freedom as having *intrinsic* value (2003a, 119). Joseph Raz certainly takes him to be saying as much (see Raz, 2003, 264, and the opening remarks in Raz's contribution to this volume). Nevertheless, in my

view both of these claims are superfluous to the argument Steiner constructs in favour of his own account of justice. As I have suggested, to rely on them would be to assume an interest theory of rights.

9. Making disrespectful conduct dependent on the manipulation of a person's freedom or freedoms allows us to classify certain forms of social power (for example, rational persuasion or the setting of examples) as not disrespectful. On the other hand, I do not mean to restrict actions that 'direct' the choices of others to *coercive* actions. I attempt an exhaustive analysis of the relation between pure negative freedom and the different forms of social power in Carter 2007a.
10. This negative conclusion is compatible with the prescription of a random distribution of freedom as well as with that of an equal distribution. But, as Steiner points out (1994, 217–18), any particular process of random distribution presupposes a prior distribution of entitlements.
11. The same point is made more extensively by N. E. Simmonds (1998, 187, 190, 213–14), but Simmonds unnecessarily combines the point with the rejection of a neutral metric for freedom (1998, 190). Such a metric can be justified without reference to Steiner's methodology (see note 4, above). Thus, Simmonds' rejection of the possibility of such a metric is in need of independent backing.
12. I am grateful to Matthew Kramer, Mario Ricciardi and Serena Olsaretti for their comments on an earlier draft of this essay. My concluding words are in line with the criticisms of Steiner's methodology presented in Kramer's contribution to this volume.

BIBLIOGRAPHY

Carter, Ian. 1999. *A Measure of Freedom*. Oxford: Oxford University Press.

Carter, Ian. 2007a. 'Social Power and Negative Freedom'. 24 *Homo Oeconomicus* 187–229.

Carter, Ian. 2007b. 'Respect and the Basis of Equality'. Paper presented at the conference on 'Equal Respect for Persons', University of Genova, December 2007.

Cohen, G. A. 1991. 'Capitalism, Freedom and the Proletariat'. In David Miller (ed.), *Liberty*. Oxford: Oxford University Press.

Darwall, Stephen. 1977. 'Two Kinds of Respect', 88 *Ethics* 36–49.

Darwall, Stephen. 2006. *The Second-Person Standpoint. Morality, Respect and Accountability*. Cambridge Mass.: Harvard University Press.

Gray, Tim. 1991. *Freedom*. London: Macmillan.

Hart, H. L. A. 1955. 'Are There Any Natural Rights?', 64 *Philosophical Review* 175–91.

Hill, Thomas. E. Jr. 2000. *Respect, Pluralism, and Justice. Kantian Perspectives*. Oxford: Oxford University Press.

Jones, Peter. 1994. *Rights*. London: Macmillan.

Kant, Immanuel. [1797] (1965). *The Metaphysical Elements of Justice*. Ed. J. Ladd, New York: Macmillan.

Kramer, Matthew H. 2003. *The Quality of Freedom*. Oxford: Oxford University Press.

Raz, Joseph. 2003. 'Comments and Responses'. In Lukas H. Meyer, Stanley L. Paulson and Thomas W. Pogge (eds), *Rights, Culture and the Law. Themes from the Legal and Political Philosophy of Joseph Raz*. Oxford: Oxford University Press.

Simmonds, N. E. 1998. 'Rights at the Cutting Edge'. In Matthew H. Kramer, N.E. Simmonds and Hillel Steiner, *A Debate Over Rights*. Oxford: Oxford University Press.

Steiner, Hillel. 1975. 'Individual Liberty'. 75 *Proceedings of the Aristotelian Society* 35–50.
Steiner, Hillel. 1980. 'Slavery, Socialism, and Private Property'. In J. R. Pennock and J. W. Chapman (eds), *Property*. New York: New York University Press.
Steiner, Hillel. 1983. 'How Free: Computing Personal Liberty'. In A. Phillips Griffiths (ed.), *Of Liberty*. Cambridge: Cambridge University Press.
Steiner, Hillel. 1994. *An Essay on Rights*. Oxford: Blackwell.
Steiner, Hillel. 1998. 'Working Rights'. In Matthew H. Kramer, N.E. Simmonds and Hillel Steiner, *A Debate Over Rights*. Oxford: Oxford University Press.
Steiner, Hillel. 2003a. 'Equality, Incommensurability and Rights'. In Lukas H. Meyer, Stanley L. Paulson and Thomas W. Pogge (eds), *Rights, Culture and the Law. Themes from the Legal and Political Philosophy of Joseph Raz*. Oxford: Oxford University Press.
Steiner, Hillel. 2003b. 'Evaluation and the Quantification of Freedom'. Paper presented at the conference on 'The Analysis and Measurement of Freedom', University of Pavia, September 2003.
Steiner, Hillel. 2006. 'A Famous Conflict'. Paper presented at the Colloquium in Legal and Social Philosophy, University College London, March 2006.
Steiner, Hillel. 2007. 'Bargaining, Exploitation and Respect for Persons'. Paper presented at the Conference on 'The Philosophy and Politics of Equal Respect', University of Pavia, June 2007. Italian trans., 'Contrattazione, sfruttamento, e rispetto per le persone'. In Ian Carter, Anna Elisabetta Galeotti and Valeria Ottonelli (eds), *Eguale rispetto*. Milan: Bruno Mondadori, 2008.
Waldron, Jeremy. 1988. *The Right to Private Property*. Oxford: Clarendon.

11 Games and Meanings

Norman Geras

In this paper I consider what games are. I examine, more particularly, a challenge to the Wittgensteinian approach to this question, a challenge which has lately won the praise of a number of philosophers. Near the beginning of the paper I register a contingent connection with the person who is the subject of the present festschrift. Otherwise, the paper does not directly engage with Hillel Steiner's work. However, it is animated by the ambition of analytical rigour that has been a hallmark of his writings, and it grapples with methodological issues which—in their general bearings—have occupied his attention. Moreover, my methodological focus aligns my essay to some degree with certain other essays in this volume. I start by describing four activities.

1. A man and a girl, respectively father and daughter, are playing at being two characters called Tree and Girl. Tree stands in the forest and Girl, who is wandering there, comes upon him and invites him to her house for tea. Tree explains that she'll have to uproot him first, which she does; she then shows him the way and helps him through the front door (he has to bend, being taller than the doorway). Girl gives Tree a cup of tea—and that's it. The routine may be repeated and usually is. It's me and one or other of my two daughters, many moons ago, playing what we called, unimaginatively, Tree and Girl.
2. A man and a girl again, this time me and my granddaughter, are sitting near the bottom of a staircase with a doll which is our child. Unlike the previous activity, this one has no official name and it doesn't run along the same fixed lines in every iteration. The man is sent off by the girl to shop for foodstuffs for the child—cereal, pasta, chocolate, broccoli. Sometimes he must phone back home to get further particulars. Other times she goes and he holds the baby. Yet other times he is a doctor, called to attend to the child. The two players improvise in their roles. In what follows I shall refer to this activity as Staircase.
3. The next activity used to involve four participants, one of whom was Hillel Steiner. They would take turns in a constantly repeated sequence. One of them would begin with the opening words of a story: for exam-

ple, 'Once upon a time, a tree stood in the forest.' The next participant would continue in any way she or he chose—such as 'The tree was called LBJ', or 'For a tree, it was remarkably knowledgeable about the work of C.B. Macpherson', and so on—producing stories of an unpredictable kind and with the aim of having some fun. This activity was known circa 1968, and for no logical reason, as Caractacus Potts.

4 The last activity I now invent out of a story which goes like this. There was once a philosophy department, twelve people strong, in which every year a most unwelcome chore had to be performed by one of them. At first, it was just given out more or less arbitrarily by order of the Head of Department; but so hateful was the task that it left those who were lumbered with it deeply resentful. One year a new HoD decided that henceforth the assignment of The Chore should be resolved annually by discussion at a departmental meeting. For several years, the meeting to consider the issue was a scene of terrible strife, and the bad feeling in the department increased as a result. The same thing when a subcommittee was formed with the job of assigning The Chore on the basis of weighing everybody's teaching and administrative contributions, with a view to handing it to the least burdened colleague. Finally, someone suggested that once a year the members of the department should sit around a table and be dealt, from a properly shuffled pack the seal on which had just been broken, four cards each—the deal to be administered by a non-participant known to all for her unbending honesty and incorruptibility. The player holding the most suits would have to take on The Chore; and in the case of a tie, the four-card procedure would be repeated until there was a unique loser—except that the procedure would be filmed from a hundred angles and any attempt to cheat disclosed by the cameras would override the state of the cards, the cheat becoming the loser and getting The Chore. This activity restored peace to the department.

I would be surprised if anyone reading this were surprised to learn that in the philosophy department of my story the procedure that finally brought peace to it came to be known as The Suits Game. I would be surprised, also, if they were surprised to learn that the other activities I've just described were referred to by their participants as games, and that the two involving me and my daughters and me and my granddaughter have been known to follow upon the suggestion 'Shall we play a game?' They are all, or so I have always thought, activities coming under the standard meaning of the word 'game'—along with other better-known examples of games, like chess, Monopoly, poker, golf, football, running races over various distances, charades, I Spy (With My Little Eye) and patience.

My thinking that all these activities are properly referred to as games was consolidated some 40-odd years ago by reading what Wittgenstein famously had to say about games in the *Philosophical Investigations* (31–32e):

> 'Consider . . . [he writes there] the proceedings that we call "games". I mean board-games, card-games, ball-games, Olympic games, and so on. What is common to them all?—Don't say: "There *must* be something common, or they would not be called 'games'"—but *look and see* whether there is anything common to all.—For if you look at them you will not see something that is common to *all*, but similarities, relationships, and a whole series of them at that. To repeat: don't think, but look!'

And Wittgenstein goes on to argue that, in looking at games 'we see a complicated network of similarities', and he invokes the idea of 'family resemblances'. Games belong to a family, one member of it sharing some but not other features with another member that in turn resembles a third member of the family by virtue of some traits, but which may also differ from that third member by lacking traits which it possesses. There is, Wittgenstein says, an 'overlapping and criss-crossing' of characteristics; but there is not anything common to all games.

I was and have remained persuaded, these many years, by his view: that 'game' is a family resemblance concept; and, furthermore, that the notion of family resemblance has wider application, to the meanings of other words as well.

Just recently, however, my attention was drawn to a book by Bernard Suits—*The Grasshopper: Games, Life and Utopia*—first published in 1978. It was drawn to my attention by a guest post on my blog by Nigel Warburton. Nigel was full of praise for the book. He reported, as well, on the laudatory opinions held of it by other philosophers—Simon Blackburn, Thomas Hurka and G.A. Cohen (Warburton 2008).

The Grasshopper's central thesis challenges Wittgenstein's view of games. To quote from Hurka's introduction to a new edition of the book: '[I]n giving necessary and sufficient conditions for playing a game [Suits is] doing exactly what Wittgenstein says can't be done . . . His book is therefore a precisely placed boot in Wittgenstein's balls' (Suits 2005, 11). I will pass over the aggressive nature of this metaphor, and merely say that after reading Nigel Warburton's post—which gives a brief account of Suits's definition of games—I couldn't wait to get my hands on a copy of *The Grasshopper*, and ordered it without delay.

Why I couldn't wait was partly just because, having been convinced for as long as I had that there was nothing all games have in common—a thesis I'd shared with my students from time to time in one connection or another, challenging them to refute it, which none of them ever successfully did—I was curious to see the shape and colour of that 'precisely placed boot' now earning high praise from some eminent philosophers. But it was more than this. Suits's definition of games, which Nigel's post on my blog had summarized, struck me as being, on its face, so obviously unsatisfactory that I was intrigued to see how he, Suits, had dealt with the predictable objections to it—as both Nigel Warburton and Thomas Hurka (in an online interview) reported he had indeed dealt with them, and most methodically at that (Warburton 2008; Hurka 2007). So the book arrived and I read it. I was disappointed.

Let me qualify this before I explain it. The book has an engaging style, dialogic much of the way, and is sporadically very funny. Its thesis is argued lucidly and with care. And Suits has some interesting propositions about games and utopia, which I'm afraid, despite my own (independent) interest in that conjunction, I'm going to have to ignore here altogether, other than to say that in the end I wasn't persuaded by them, finding that they include claims of a silly, and also a sinister, kind.

I want to concentrate exclusively, however, on Suits's argument about the meaning of the word 'game'. This—on which his book stands or falls—also hasn't persuaded me, and I am at a loss, I must confess, to understand why *The Grasshopper* has lately won the support amongst philosophers it has. That is why I have written this essay—to see if it might prompt anyone to help me identify what I've missed, if I *have* missed something.

I now give Bernard Suits's definition of what games are. To start with something short (what he himself calls the portable version): 'playing a game is the voluntary attempt to overcome unnecessary obstacles' (Suits 2005, 55).

In the full version, this definition has three elements—what Suits refers to, in turn, as the prelusory goal, the lusory means (defined, these, by the constitutive rules of the game), and the lusory attitude (which is an acceptance of those rules because they make the activity possible). So, using my own example . . . In football (soccer) the *prelusory goal* would be to put the ball in your opponents' net more times than they put the ball in your net. The *lusory means*, allowed by the rules, would be kicking the ball, heading it, passing it to other players in your team, and so on; but would exclude handling the ball, picking it up and just running across the goal line with it, shoving opponents out of the way, deliberately tripping them, knifing them. Thus, more efficient means of scoring and thereby winning are prohibited over less efficient means. And the *lusory attitude* is the willing acceptance of these various requirements and prohibitions in order precisely to be able to play the game as constituted. Or, for another, shorter example, Suits's own: a runner in a race isn't free to take a short-cut from the route over which the race is being run and so expedite his or her arrival at the finishing line; and he or she isn't free to use a bike. From which and from a fair bit more, Suits's full definition:

> 'To play a game is to attempt to achieve a specific state of affairs [prelusory goal], using only means permitted by rules [lusory means], where the rules prohibit more efficient in favour of less efficient means [constitutive rules], and where the rules are accepted just because they make possible such activity [lusory attitude]' (Suits 2005, 54–5).

Suits says of Wittgenstein that he did not follow his own 'unexceptionable advice': that is, to look and see whether there is anything common to all games. 'He looked, to be sure, but because he had decided beforehand that games are indefinable, his look was fleeting, and he saw very little' (Suits 2005, 21).

Now, how is one to decide on the accuracy or usefulness of this definition? And, as part of that undertaking, how judge it against Wittgenstein's view of games? First of all, I take it not to be a cogent objection in itself that we can think of uses of the word 'game' which are well understood but do not fit the definition. Thus the games referred to in 'Don't play games with me' (with the rough sense 'Don't lead me a song and dance') can be set aside as involving only games in a metaphorical usage. The fact that there are no constitutive rules with *such* games (rather the opposite, in fact) wouldn't damage Suits's case.

Equally, that an activity not standardly referred to as a game becomes one on his definition is not necessarily a problem. So, for example, mountain-climbing. It is, arguably, a game which, like patience, doesn't—or doesn't usually—involve competition against another participant trying to put obstacles in your way and to win against you, but it does involve the voluntary overcoming of obstacles. In the book, the main protagonist, Grasshopper, is challenged by his interlocutor, Skepticus, with the thought that the mountain-climber is *not* forbidden from using the most efficient means available (in the way of climbing equipment and so forth). Grasshopper responds by suggesting that Sir Edmund Hillary would not have regretted the trouble he took conquering Everest had he found someone else already at the summit who had got there by taking the escalator on the other side (Suits 2005, 85–6).

That we don't usually call mountain-climbing a game is no barrier to seeing that it has the features of some kinds of games—those, precisely, picked out by Suits's definition—and to being willing to recognize it as a game.

But how do we do this? I mean, how do we know when the 'fit' is good or when the lack of 'fit' doesn't matter? And how do we know when the lack of 'fit' *does* matter or when the 'fit' is bad? I'm not sure. Is it our old friend 'reflective equilibrium'? That is to say, we start with some rough and ready notion of what games are and then we look for a definition, or, if there is no strict definition, an account, of what they are and see what definition or account will work best. If we have to exclude, under the definition or account being considered, some secondary or marginal usages, that's one thing; but if we cannot accommodate some of the central usages, then that is more problematic.

I shall come back to this methodological point. I now go on to argue that Suits's definition is question-begging—both in itself and when read as a critique of Wittgenstein—and that this can be seen by his failure to deal persuasively with the sorts of activities known as games that I began with, as well as many others.

Tree and Girl, Staircase, Caractacus Potts and The Suits Game do not meet all of the three conditions of Suits's definition, so if they are properly called games these conditions can't be necessary conditions. In this situation it seems to me that there are two strategies of defence available to Bernard Suits.

(a) He could try to provide a convincing argument for these not *really* being games.
(b) He could show that, despite possible appearances to the contrary, they do in fact fit his definition.

A putative third strategy of defence that might be suggested is this:

(c) Suits could just acknowledge that his is a theoretical definition and as such revises the ordinary understanding of what a game is by narrowing the meaning of the word; and he could claim that it is therefore no problem for his definition if Tree and Girl, and a lot of other activities known as games, fall outside it.

But this third suggestion fails, in my view, because it amounts merely to stipulating what the word 'game' is to mean henceforth, and in that case his book, so far from being a boot placed where Thomas Hurka says it was, is more like a mislaid sock at the back of a shelf of philosophy books. Suits has recourse to both of strategies (a) and (b).

Strategy (a)—they're not really games. Faced with the suggestion that there is a class of children's games that do not fit his definition—Cowboys and Indians, Cops and Robbers, Ring Around the Rosie—Suits concedes (or, rather, Grasshopper does, for him) that children, teachers and others may refer to these as games, and goes on: 'But I think you will agree with me that Ring Around the Rosie is simply a kind of dance to vocal accompaniment, or a choreographed song. It is no more a game than *Swan Lake* is.' Similarly, of Cowboys and Indians and Cops and Robbers he writes: 'Aren't these things just ritual performances? . . . [If they] are games they strike me as being highly imperfect games, just as they did when I played them myself. For it was never quite clear what counted as a successful, or even legitimate, move' (Suits 2005, 89–91).

You can see how it works. By the same reasoning, Tree and Girl might be said to be simply a kind of dramatic performance, and Staircase likewise, though with more scope for improvisation; Caractacus Potts would be just a form of collective story-telling; and The Suits Game no more than a decision procedure.

But to say that some putative game is like something else which isn't a game doesn't establish that *it* isn't a game—unless you've assumed beforehand the truth of what you're seeking to demonstrate by argument. That the Zimbabwean political process in March and April of 2008 was like a dramatic farce doesn't mean that it wasn't still a political process.

The point is accentuated by something Thomas Hurka says in his introduction to *The Grasshopper.* On Suits's definition, games are still games when they are played by professionals—played, that is, primarily for money and whether or not for fun. Hurka writes (correctly, in my view), 'And it's essential for Suits's analysis to say this, since it would be absurd to deny that a pure professional golfer is playing golf' (Suits 2005, 15). By extension, it would be absurd to deny that it is games that professional sportsmen and women play.

Hurka knows this how? He knows it just by virtue of the circumstance that this class of games is so central in our thinking and talking about games that the definition, to be a credible one, has to fit it. But isn't it exactly the same with children's games? Children, like professionals, are amongst the first kinds of people we think of when we think about the human activity we call game-playing. They are games-players *par excellence* and the games they play are central to our usages in talking about games. It would be ironic, therefore, if a whole wide class of their games were to be excluded by what purports to be a definition giving the meaning of the word 'game'—ironic and, I contend, not credible.

Strategy (b)—some of them are, strictly, games. Suits, however, also devotes a considerable amount of space to explaining why at least one type of children's game—a type exemplified by Tree and Girl and by Staircase—do fall within his definition of games, at least when considered in more sophisticated versions: the type in question being games of make-believe or role-playing. He subsumes these under the model of an impersonation game, and the key point of his argument is that this type of game fits his definition because in impersonation the players deprive themselves of the most efficient means of doing what they set out to do. They deprive themselves because they play without a *script.* Suits writes: 'use of a script by players of make-believe games would be a more efficient—less risky—means for keeping a dramatic action going than is the invention of dramatic responses on the spot, which is what the game requires' (Suits 2005, 125).

Now, it should be said that this remark comes after thirty pages in which some quite subtle and refined examples of role-playing or impersonation games have been discussed, and it is arguable that with respect to *those examples* what Suits says has some force. I'm not altogether sure even of that; but in any case—and this I am sure of—what he says has no force with respect to the role-playing, make-believe games of very young children, and these are precisely the games his definition needs to fit, or *also* needs to fit, if it is to deal satisfactorily with a very large class of what are standardly called games.

The claim that children unable yet to read with facility, or to read at all, would play at make-believe games more efficiently with a script doesn't withstand a moment's scrutiny, and therefore the claim that games all involve the overcoming of unnecessary obstacles, the use of less efficient means than those that are available in principle, is not substantiated in this case. The same applies to the story-telling game I described—Caractacus Potts. The players could, I suppose, simply read from an amusing book, but while that might meet the objective of making them laugh, it wouldn't meet their objective of cooperatively creating their own story for the enjoyment of it. For this purpose, it's not clear that there *are* any more efficient means. The same applies, I think, to The Suits Game.

Is there a persuasive way of excluding such activities from the category 'games' that is not the result of the disputed definition (Suits's definition) itself? Note, first, that I am not committed by any philosophical principle to denying that there could be a definition of the kind he aims for (involving the specification of necessary and sufficient conditions). There are concepts that can be so defined, the concept of a triangle being one; and there are things in the world, like giraffes and other natural species, or capital cities, or Wednesdays in July, where we don't need to resort to the notion of family resemblance in order to say what they are. Note, also, that Bernard Suits says in the preface to *The Grasshopper*, that he for his part isn't committed to a principle of universal definability. 'It seems altogether more reasonable', he writes, 'to begin with the hypothesis that some things are definable and some are not' (Suits 2005, 22).

Yet when Skepticus proposes a counter-definition to Suits's own, to cover the role-playing games that his definition arguably does not, Suits has Grasshopper demur as follows: 'if there are two radically different kinds of game—role-governed and goal-governed—then we would have to give up our attempt to formulate a single definition of games' (Suits 2005, 91). Not wanting to give up on that enterprise cannot count, by itself, as a good enough reason for persisting with it when it appears to be failing. That would be question-begging—excluding by simple fiat those games that look unsuitable (*sic*).

Interpretative charity here should prompt us to understand Grasshopper as meaning, not that a single, unified definition *must* be found at all costs (for we know that Suits is not committed to the possibility of one always being findable), but only that the search for a single, unified definition is worth the effort. However, the requirement of charity notwithstanding, it looks to me as if begging the question is what Suits is in fact doing. In an essay written after *The Grasshopper* was published and which appears as an appendix to the new edition of the book, he writes as if there is an objective truth about what games are, such that his definition could fit this truth even against our linguistic usages, which have misled us. Suits writes:

> '[T]he question whether all things *called* games have something in common is very different from the question whether all things that *are* games have something in common. If, obviously, some of the things called games are called games metaphorically or carelessly or arbitrarily or stupidly, then there will predictably be nothing importantly common to all of them' (Suits 2005 162).

That appears to me to imply something like the following: we already know what games are, being guided to them, as to the species *giraffe*, by their shared properties; Suits's definition simply draws the boundary that is already there, and uses of the word 'game' to apply to other activities beyond the boundary have become 'metaphorical', 'careless', 'arbitrary' or 'stupid'. But another perspective on the same thing would be to say that his definition *picks out* from within the activities called games a subset, *stipulates* that only members of this subset are truly games and then disparages usages to the contrary with some bad-sounding words.

It is worth observing that what Suits is doing, so far from discomfiting Wittgenstein, was perfectly well understood by him:

> 'What . . . counts as a game . . . ? Can you give the boundary? No. You can *draw* one; for none has so far been drawn . . . We do not know the boundaries because none have been drawn. To repeat, we can draw a boundary—for a special purpose. Does it take that to make the concept usable? Not at all!' (Wittgenstein 1963, 33e).

And:

> 'If someone were to draw a sharp boundary I could not acknowledge it as the one that I too always wanted to draw, or had drawn in my mind. For I did not want to draw one at all. His concept can then be said to be not the same as mine, but akin to it' (Wittgenstein 1963, 36 e).

In any event, how can it be that games, a range of activities that we invent and name, are identifiable as a reality independently of our linguistic usages—such that one could say with Suits that there are things which *are* games as distinct from things which are merely *called* games? Games are not a natural kind. They are not like giraffes or planets or water, which would be what they are whatever we called them or if we ceased to be and so could not speak of them at all. They are also not like, say, democracies—concerning which there is, *de facto* and despite all other differences of understanding as to how the term 'democracy' is properly to be applied, some minimal level of definitional agreement, centred on the idea of a significant level of control by the governed over those who govern them.

(I interject, at this point, a caution to anyone who might want to infer from my defence of Wittgenstein on this specific question—the meaning of the word 'game'—that I have some more general commitment to anti-foundationalism. I do not. My philosophical commitments are, in fact, the opposite. But thinking, as I do think, that there are objective realities beyond language, and that not everything is constituted by discourse, in no way obliges me to believe that the meanings of words that we use for procedures or institutions created by ourselves must always be specifiable in terms of necessary and sufficient conditions. As we have seen, Bernard

Suits himself does not believe this, and the dispute about the meaning of the word 'game', consequently, has no general implication with respect to debates about anti-foundationalism and essentialism.)

Here's a thought experiment. An academic appointments committee dealing with a very large pile of job applications has agreed to draw up its shortlist from those applicants who appear from their application forms, CVs and references to satisfy three or more of four requirements, a, b, c and d. (In turn, say: some publications; some teaching experience; an expertise in theories of justice; an expertise in an immediately adjacent area.) An applicant who has fewer than three of the relevant characteristics doesn't make the cut. But anyone who does make the cut goes on to the committee's long list, this to be shortened in due course into a short list. By an emergent usage in the committee, such an applicant is called a *threeper.* (Collectively they might be referred to as *threeple.*)

I don't think it would make sense in this situation for a member of the committee to try and put her colleagues right by saying that in fact those whom they were *calling* threepers did not coincide with the group of applicants who *were* threepers; that some amongst the former were being called threepers carelessly or stupidly; that in reality, the threepers were the applicants with the two characteristics a and c (some publications and an expertise in theories of justice), this irrespective of whether they met the two other requirements. It wouldn't make sense to say so even in the circumstance that the dissident member of the committee had identified the two most important qualifications for the job. She would, in that case, have a good reason for trying to reorient the committee's deliberations so as to shape its long list in a more effective way. But she wouldn't thereby have hit upon the true meaning, or correct definition, of the word 'threeper'.

This seems to me analogous with the state of affairs regarding the meaning of the word 'games', though it is more formalized.

So far my argument has been that the three conditions laid down in Suits's definition as being necessary for some given activity to count as a game are not in fact necessary conditions. Are they, however, jointly sufficient in picking out what a game is? Some light may be thrown on this question by the following record of a conversation that has lately come into my possession.

L: Cheer up, GW. Why are you looking so depressed?

GW: Oh, hello there, Ludovic. I'm depressed because, as you know, I'm the Game Warden. It's my job to oversee the world's games and make sure there are enough of them. But I've just read this book by Bernard Suits. In it he puts forward a definition of games the effect of which is significantly to reduce the number of them. Tree and Girl (as played many times by Norman Geras and his daughters) I have always seen as a form of game, but if Suits is right, I was mistaken. The same with Caractacus Potts, Cops and Robbers and many other types of play.

L: Don't worry about it, GW. Even if Suits is right, which I doubt, it doesn't reduce the number of games being played.

GW: But how come, Ludie? It must do. The extent of the subtractions from the family of games that results from Suits's definition is considerable.

L: They are more than compensated for by the resulting additions, activities that no one would ever have thought of as games but for Suits's definition. Shall I give you an example?

GW: Yes, please do.

L: Well, there's this game that I play called Persuading My Wife. Now and again, she and I will disagree about something: what we should do for the evening, whether our neighbour, Hilly, has a good heart, this and that. My wife has two qualities—extreme stubbornness and a general willingness to believe what I say—that, together, tempt me towards using trickery to get my view to prevail; you know, telling the odd fib, taking an imaginary phone call in which I 'receive' a piece of information vital to deciding the issue at hand, and so on. But I have made a rule for myself not to lie and cheat when trying to persuade her. I love my wife and I am an honest man; I also enjoy seeing if I can persuade her without any trickery. In addition, I make it a rule not to try and influence her away from her view by offering her incentives to change her mind—such as that I'll do her share of the housework for a day or two. Would you like another example, GW?

GW: Yes, please.

L: I know a young man who is extremely hard up. He's in his first job, not very well paid, and really struggles to make ends meet. His mother is a wealthy woman. She could easily help him out and has offered to do so—by paying some of his utility bills and writing him a cheque now and again late on in the month. But he refuses to let her help. He's a proud fellow and he wants to make his own way. And even though it's a struggle for him—I've seen him hungry more than once—he *enjoys* managing on his means. He plays this game called Getting By, one of the rules of which is to accept no financial aid from anyone, and therefore not from his mother.

GW: These are interesting cases, Luders, but are they really games on Suits's definition? In Persuading My Wife, you want to persuade her for extraneous reasons—so you can spend the evening in the way *you* prefer to, so as to convince her that Hilly is not to be trusted, or whatever—and you eschew dishonesty and the offering of incentives because you don't think these are honourable means. It doesn't seem to me that you have what Suits calls the lusory attitude. Your self-limiting rules are not ones you have adopted merely to make the activity of persuading your wife possible. Similarly, the young man of your acquaintance wants to manage financially without his mother's help from a sense of his own dignity. His rule that he can't accept assistance may well be a rule of life for him but surely it doesn't create the game Getting By, if it is Suits's meaning of the word 'game' we are following here.

L: You're overlooking an important feature of these two activities, GW. It is true that I would feel bad about tricking or bribing my wife; and so I do have independent reasons for not doing that. It is also true that my young friend wants to manage without his mom's help because of a bid for adult independence (that's how he sees it, anyway). But as I explained, I also *enjoy* persuading my wife and I therefore have the constraining rules that I do in order to oblige me to succeed 'the hard way' even should I on occasion be tempted to resort to trickery. Likewise that young bloke . . . he *likes* the sense of achievement from managing to get by and so his no-financial-help rule keeps him to it. He, in playing Getting By, and I, in playing Persuading My Wife, accept rules that prohibit us from using more efficient means in favour of less efficient ones. Do you see what I mean?

GW: I think so, but while you were explaining it, something was bothering me and it led me to check on the precise terms of Suits's definition in my copy of *The Grasshopper* (which now accompanies me wherever I go). This speaks of 'using only means permitted by rules . . . where the rules prohibit more efficient in favour of less efficient means . . . and where the rules are accepted *just because* they make possible such activity'. I emphasized 'just because' in the way I read that. For couldn't Suits say, in response to your two examples, that they aren't examples of games under his definition, since the self-denying rules in the activities Persuading My Wife and Getting By are not accepted by you and your friend *just because* they make possible the persuading and getting-by activities which they govern? You and he, as you carefully explained to me, have additional reasons for respecting those rules: reasons of honour in your case, of independence, dignity, pride, in his.

L: No.

GW: I beg your pardon. Don't go getting all monosyllabic with me, Ludo. This is important. The size of the world's game population is at stake. What do you mean 'No'?

L: Sorry, Big G. It wasn't my intention to be short with you. I was catching my breath after a series of wordy explanations. But no, Suits could not say that. It is not a response that is available to him. In defending his view that professional games players are still indeed games players and playing games, he himself disallows an interpretation of 'just because' that would exclude the possibility of the player having extra reasons for accepting the rules, over and above the making-possible reason. If you'll just hand me your copy of the book, I'll find you the relevant passage. Thanks. Yes, here it is:

> 'Where A is some action and R is a reason for performing A, you, Skepticus, interpret the phrase 'A just because R' to mean: 1/ R is always a reason for doing A, and there *can* be no other reason for doing A. But I interpret the phrase 'A just because R' to mean: 2/ R is always a reason for doing A, and there *need* be no other reason for doing A. Thus, a player's acceptance of rules because 'such acceptance makes possible such activity' is the only reason he *must* have in playing a game, but it is not the only reason he *may* have' (Suits 2005, 131).

You see?

GW: Well, yes, I think I do see now. It's enough that the rules excluding more efficient means in favour of less efficient ones are accepted so that you can indulge in that particular exercise—here, persuasion without trickery, managing without financial help—but it's OK to have additional reasons for respecting those rules. Like Wayne Rooney, I suppose. He abides by the rules of football because he loves playing the game; but he's also not uninterested in the money he can earn by playing, so he accepts the rules for that reason as well, and what he plays doesn't cease to be a game because of this. Clear as pure water. I remain worried nonetheless.

L: But why?

GW: Because, my playful friend, Persuading My Wife and Getting By are a poor return for the loss of all those other games (children's games, make believe games, bags of them) demoted by Suits's definition. After all, how many people play Persuading My Wife and Getting By? Not very many, I'll wager—even if lots of people do try to persuade their spouses, of whatever gender, and quite as many struggle to get by. But they don't make a game of it, like you and young Go-It-Alone.

L: Aha, but this is short-sighted of you, mighty Game Warden. What you have failed to detect in my explanations is that they apply far beyond the two examples I've given you, which *were* only examples. They apply much more widely, for the simple reason that activities covered by one sort of description are always amenable to other descriptions, and these other descriptions may reveal to you the lineaments of what Suits categorizes as a game.

GW: For instance?

L: Reading. Why do people read fiction? Give me a few reasons. Naturally, I don't expect a comprehensive list, just some of the typical reasons.

GW: We're talking about novels, right? Well, they read for pleasure; they read to get a sense of other lives than their own, other places, times, situations; they read to learn about, or maybe just to 'see', the subtleties of human motivation; some of them read because they want to expand their acquaintance with the world's literature. I'll stop there.

L: Yes, that's enough for present purposes. But here is another reason why many people read, or at least why they continue with a novel once they've started it, always assuming that nothing in the early part of the book has put them off: they read on because they want to find out what happens. Even if this isn't true of everyone, it applies very widely.

GW: Fair enough. But what of it?

L: Can't you see? They're playing the game Reading to the End of the Book to Find Out What Happens.

GW: You've lost me.

L: Consider my own case. I read quite a bit but not nearly as much as my wife does. Nine out of ten of the novels I read she's already read; indeed I often read them on her say-so. The most efficient way of finding out what happens in most of the novels I read would be to ask Clarissa. Books she hasn't read I could look up on Wikipedia or in *The Oxford Encyclopaedia of Fictional Plots*. But I make it a rule not to. That rule makes it possible for me to find out what happens for myself—and that sure is a 'voluntary attempt to overcome unnecessary obstacles'. I have to read pages and pages—sometimes over 400 of them!—where I could find out just like that, by asking Clarissa or looking it up.

GW: But, Loodles, you enjoy reading for other reasons.

L: Indeed I do. However, you won't have so quickly forgotten Bernard Suits's specification of his 'just because' condition, GW? The only reason I *must* have for eschewing the shortcut is that I've adopted the rule against doing so; but it is not the only reason I *may* have. Reading to the End of the Book to Find Out What Happens is, consequently, a game on Suits's definition. You'll be familiar, I take it, with the concept of a 'spoiler'?

GW: Yes, I am.

L: It shows, I contend, that there are many players of this game, even if there are readers—I know one or two myself—who don't mind knowing in advance how things are going to pan out.

GW: But this is wonderful news. It means that, with Suits's definition, the population of game-playing episodes will be massively enlarged.

L: It's even better than you think, GW. It's not only reading. A lot of people have pretty much the same attitude to the movies they watch—they don't want to be told the denouement in advance. So there's the game Watching to the End of the Movie to Find Out What Happens. And there's also Watching to the End of the TV Series to Find Out What Happens.

GW: It's a game-playing explosion, Ludester!

L: You bet it is. Shall I tell you about the game Getting the Labour Candidate Re-Elected in a Totally Safe Seat?

GW: No, it's OK. I need to be getting back to work soon.

L: How about Composing a Letter to His Mother? Or (one I came across just the other day) Trying to Ensure That Sensible Decisions Are Taken at the Faculty Meeting?

GW: I feel I've thoroughly absorbed the point now . . . Oh . . . Oh . . . [*The Game Warden pauses. He appears to be assailed by an unwelcome thought. From a single line on his brow a troubled expression spreads downwards across his face.*] But hold on. What this all means, in fact, is that Suits's definition is busted. There's no explosion of episodes of game-playing after all.

L: I'm afraid not. Busted is right. Not only does his definition beg the question by being unable to account for a whole class of what we standardly regard as games, it also lets in, as being games, activities which not even Bernard Suits himself seems to have noticed for that status. If family resemblances give you imprecise boundaries in this matter, the 'voluntary attempt to overcome unnecessary obstacles' allows you to find games more or less at will. Still, as I began this conversation by saying: cheer up, GW. You're no worse off than you were before. You're left with roughly the population of games you previously thought you had. By the way, I have a spare copy of Wittgenstein's *Philosophical Investigations*. I'd be happy for you to have it.

To follow this long exchange, I make one other observation in concluding. Even if Bernard Suits's case had been compelling, as I have tried to demonstrate that it is not, he wouldn't have shown Wittgenstein to be comprehensively wrong. He would have shown only that Wittgenstein was wrong about the meaning of the word 'game', without thereby establishing that he was wrong about family resemblance concepts in general.

What are the necessary and sufficient conditions of something's being a table? Or of an act's being evil? There may be answers to these two questions, though if there are I would like to know what they are. But even if there are, I think that a certain sensitive area of Wittgenstein's anatomy remains secure against Bernard Suits's footwear so long as the family resemblance idea usefully accounts for a significant range of human meanings.

BIBLIOGRAPHY

Hurka, Thomas. 2007. 'Interview on Bernard Suits's The Grasshopper', at http://nigelwarburton.typepad.com/virtualphilosopher/2007/12/tom-hurka-on-be.html

Suits, Bernard. 2005. *The Grasshopper: Games, Life and Utopia*. Peterborough, ON: Broadview Press.

Warburton, Nigel. 2008. '*On The Grasshopper: Games, Life and Utopia* by Bernard Suits', at http://normblog.typepad.com/normblog/2008/01/writers-choic-1.html

Wittgenstein, Ludwig. 1963. *Philosophical Investigations.* Translated by G.E.M. Anscombe. Oxford: Basil Blackwell.

12 Consistency is Hardly Ever Enough

Reflections on Hillel Steiner's Methodology

Matthew H. Kramer

Hillel Steiner has enjoyed an illustrious career as one of the foremost political philosophers of his generation. Throughout the English-speaking world and well beyond, his writings have elicited admiration even from the many writers who have challenged his ideas. The present essay is no exception to that pattern. Although it takes issue with Steiner on certain methodological questions, it constitutes a tribute to his great acuity and originality as a philosopher and to his generosity as a person.

At every stage of his career, Steiner has endeavored to establish normatively rich conclusions on the basis of exiguous premises. In that respect, his ambitions place him in a broadly Kantian tradition of theorists who attempt to endow moral conclusions with the rigor and prestige of logic. His aim is to construct a detailed theory of justice through reasoning that is austerely focused on considerations of logical consistency. He believes that his theory will prevail if it avoids the incoherence that besets alternative conceptions of justice.

Logical consistency is obviously a key desideratum for any theory. However, that desideratum cannot bear the weight that Steiner places on it. Logical consistency is of course necessary for the acceptability of any theory of justice, but it is decidedly not sufficient in itself as a basis for selecting among rival theories. Steiner presumes otherwise because he thinks that very few accounts of justice do indeed partake of such consistency. My aim in this short paper is to contest his thinking on that point. Though this paper will not explore any theories of justice other than Steiner's, it will impugn his assumption that all or most such theories other than his are plagued by incoherence. For the purpose of rebutting that assumption, this paper will not need to look at those other theories of justice; instead, it will challenge Steiner's conception of incoherence.

Steiner proclaims his methodological austerity in the opening pages of his first book: "We unavoidably restrict one another's freedom. And justice is about how those restrictions ought to be arranged. What it's *not* about are the ends which might be achieved by that arrangement. Questions of justice arise precisely where the moral permissibility of one person's restricting another's freedom is not determined by the comparative merits of the ends to which they are respectively committed" (Steiner 1994, 1–2). Steiner proceeds to delineate the chief method which he will employ to answer questions of justice without passing any judgments on the merits of people's pursuits. He propounds what he designates as a "compossibility test": "A set of rights being a possible set is, I take it, itself a necessary condition of the plausibility of whatever principle of justice generates that set. Any justice principle that delivers a set of rights yielding contradictory judgements about the permissibility of a particular action either is unrealizable or (what comes to the same thing) must be modified to be realizable" (Steiner 1994, 2–3). Steiner declares that his compossibility test "does exemplary service in filtering out many candidate conceptions of justice," and he remarks that "[o]ur aspiration, obviously, is to pass through the eye of this needle with at least one theory of justice still intact" (Steiner 1994, 3).

Yet, far from being a stringent filter that singles out one theory of justice (or a very small number of theories of justice), Steiner's compossibility test is unhelpfully undemanding. It is satisfied by virtually every theory of justice that has ever enticed any estimable philosopher. Hardly any such theory generates the conclusion that some act-type or act-token is both morally permissible and morally impermissible.

Steiner takes a contrary view largely because of his adherence to a misconceived theorem of standard deontic logic, the Permissibility Theorem. That is, he presumes that the following proposition is true as a matter of logical necessity:

$$(\forall x)(Ox \rightarrow Px)$$

With the universally quantified variable "x" ranging over possible courses of conduct, and with "O" denoting obligatoriness and "P" denoting permissibility, this theorem in effect states that every obligatory course of conduct is permissible. Because Steiner subscribes to the Permissibility Theorem, he believes that any theory of justice is incoherent if it leaves room for situations in which people are legally forbidden to engage in legally obligatory courses of conduct. He elaborates and applies his compossibility test on the basis of that belief.

This essay will argue against the Permissibility Theorem, to which Steiner pertinaciously cleaves. It will thereby reveal that a genuine test for logical coherence is not adequate as a basis for selecting among theories of justice. By exposing the unsustainability of Steiner's methodology in that regard, this essay will contest his closely related assumption about the nature of the enterprise of analyzing key moral and political concepts. Hoping to rely exclusively on the compossibility test and a few other formal considerations for the vindication of his theory of justice, Steiner accordingly contends that a philosophical account of the notion of justice—and of connected notions such as liberty and rights—can and should be austerely analytical. Such an account will explicate the concept of justice without having to draw upon moral and political considerations, or so Steiner thinks. He dismisses the proposition that "analyses of the meanings of moral concepts are, ineluctably, a form of moral advocacy," and he retorts: "It's true that moral commitments frequently influence the choice of concepts to be analysed. . . . But there's simply no necessary connection between the factors motivating the choice of an analysandum and the content of its analysis. A misanthrope is perfectly capable of delivering a philosophically respectable account of benevolence, a coward of courage, and so forth. And it's difficult to see why the case of justice should be any different in this respect" (Steiner 1994, 4).

One shortcoming of the passage just quoted is that its penultimate sentence is a sheer assertion that provides no substantiation for the truth of its claim. As will be seen, that claim is indeed tenable—but only when it is construed in a manner that will lend no comfort to Steiner. An even more serious difficulty for him is that the passage just quoted is to a large degree an *ignoratio elenchi*. While rejecting his view that purely formal considerations such as logical consistency are sufficient as a basis for fixing upon an apt account of justice, Steiner's opponents need not and should not maintain that the values motivating one's choice of an analysandum must be the same as those that inform the substance of one's analysis. Instead, they should simply contend that any satisfactory analysis of a moral/political concept (such as the concept of justice) must draw centrally upon considerations of political morality. Anyone who professes to be able to do without such considerations and to rely instead on purely formal constraints is pursuing a chimera.

1. THE PERMISSIBILITY THEOREM

Throughout his work, Steiner upholds the Permissibility Theorem. He persistently asserts that "a duty to do an action implies a liberty to do it" (Steiner 1994, 86), and he likewise repeatedly insists that "obligatory actions form a subset of permissible actions" (Steiner 1998, 268 n55). He correctly observes that quite a few deontic logicians have affirmed the truth of the Permissibility Theorem and of the axiom that generates it. He is therefore confident that any account of justice which allows for states of affairs inconsistent with that theorem is an incoherent account.

I have impugned the Permissibility Theorem in a number of my past writings (Kramer 1998, 17–20; Kramer 1999, 52–53; Kramer 2001, 73–74; Kramer 2004, 280–83; Kramer 2005, 336–40; Kramer 2007, 125–27). Instead of rehearsing my previous criticisms, I shall here simply emphasize one point. Nobody should doubt that the Permissibility Theorem can be incorporated into a consistent system of deontic logic. There is nothing wrong with that theorem as a matter of its logical form. Rather, what is objectionable is the inadequacy and distortiveness of the Permissibility

Theorem—and of any system of logic which incorporates it—as a representation of the deontic relations which it purports to model formally. A coherent system of logic is of little or no value if it fails to capture accurately the formal features of the phenomena to which it purports to apply. Yet the Permissibility Theorem fails in exactly that respect. It ostensibly rules out states of affairs that can arise and sometimes do arise. Hence, instead of shedding light on the formal characteristics of legal and moral relationships, it obfuscates the nature of those relationships by classifying certain normative possibilities (and actualities) as logical impossibilities.

For Steiner's purposes, it does not matter whether conflicting duties—a duty of some person *P* to perform some action x at some time *t*, and a duty of *P* not to perform x at *t*—are owed to the same party or to different parties. Whether those duties are owed to the same party or not, they can never coherently coexist; or so Steiner maintains. Let us, then, briefly consider a scenario in which conflicting legal duties are owed by someone to different parties. We shall see that the coexistence of the conflicting duties is perfectly coherent and credible. (In Kramer 1998, 18–19, I have offered an example of conflicting duties that are owed to a single party.)

Suppose that Jeremy has formed a contract with Susan whereby he undertakes to be present at a certain location *L* on a certain day during a certain stretch of time. Suppose further that he subsequently forms—or has previously formed—a contract with Melanie whereby he undertakes not to be present at *L* on the specified day during the specified stretch of time. (Let us assume that Melanie fears that his presence at *L* would gravely upset somebody else who is scheduled to be there.) Each of his contractual partners has made costly arrangements in reliance on the undertaking received, and neither of them has any grounds for knowing of the contract formed with the other. Now, in these circumstances, the officials responsible for giving effect to legal requirements in the particular jurisdiction could undoubtedly handle the conflict between Jeremy's contractual duties by holding that in fact only one of those duties exists. They might, for example, declare that his first contract takes priority over the second. Nonetheless, although a conflict-resolving approach (of the sort just mentioned or of some other sort) would manifestly be feasible, the adoption of any such approach is a purely contingent matter rather than a matter of logical necessity. Moreover, in the envisaged circumstances, any conflict-resolving technique would most likely be unacceptably unfair to Susan or Melanie. In the absence of special mitigating factors, Jeremy should not so leniently be absolved of the burden of dealing with the quandary in which he has placed himself. His moral agency is not compromised by his being directed to live up to the obligations which he has incurred. Inevitably, of course, he will breach one of those two conflicting obligations. Either he will be present at *L* during the specified span of time, or he will not. Accordingly, regardless of how he acts, he will incur an additional legal obligation to remedy a breach of a legal duty (most likely through the payment of compensation). In the circumstances depicted, however, such an outcome is maximally fair to all parties concerned. In any case, more important here than the *fairness* is the manifest *possibility* of that outcome. Plainly possible is a situation in which the relevant courts decline to nullify either of Jeremy's contracts and in which they consequently require Jeremy to pay compensation regardless of whether he turns up at *L*. If he does turn up there at the agreed-upon time, he will have to compensate Melanie for the breach of his contract with her; contrariwise, if he does not turn up there, he will have to compensate Susan for the breach of his contract with her. A situation in which Jeremy cannot avoid compensatory liability is unmistakably coherent. That is, a situation in which the courts have left him under each of his two conflicting legal duties is unmistakably coherent. Hence, given that the Permissibility Theorem purports to disallow any such situation, that theorem is a specious logical principle rather than a genuine logical principle. No genuine principle of logic classifies patently possible states of affairs as impossible. (The speciousness of the Permissibility Theorem becomes especially plain when we recognize that that theorem putatively rules out contrary duties as well as conflicting duties. That is, it putatively excludes not only the coexistence of duties whose contents are starkly contradictory, but also the coexistence of duties whose contents are merely inconsistent. Suppose that, instead of contracting with Melanie to stay away from *L*, Jeremy has contracted with her to be in New York during the relevant period of time; and suppose that his being in New York precludes his being at *L*. Although Jeremy might breach both this duty to Melanie and his original duty to Susan, he cannot fulfill both of those duties. He will inevitably breach at least one of them. Hence, a state of affairs in which those contrary duties coexist is at odds with the Permissibility Theorem, just as much as a state of affairs in which Jeremy is under an obligation to be at *L* and an obligation not to be at *L*. Given that the actuality of contrary duties is even more common than the actuality of conflicting duties, the bankruptcy of the Permissibility Theorem as a logical principle can hardly be overstated.)

Thus, since the Permissibility Theorem is an untenable dogma masquerading as a logical constraint, it cannot rightly be invoked by Steiner as a criterion for differentiating between coherent and incoherent theories of justice. A theory of justice can countenance the existence of conflicting legal duties while remaining logically impeccable. Of course, any such theory that countenances the *pervasiveness* of such duties (as opposed to their *occasional* presence) is problematic. However, the dubiousness of such a theory lies not in logic but in substantive morality. As a substantive moral matter, principles of justice should not lead to the conclusion that people will very frequently be subject to legal penalties regardless of how they behave. Still, as the scenario of Jeremy and Susan and Melanie illustrates, there can sometimes arise a situation in which the shouldering of two conflicting legal duties by somebody is maximally fair to everyone involved. In any event, if Steiner disagrees with this claim about fairness, he will have to contest it on moral grounds. His hope of dealing with the issue on logical grounds is illusive.

2. FROM FORMALITY TO SUBSTANCE

Having just returned to the need for substantive moral reflection in order to select among theories of justice, we should look again at the passage in which Steiner dismisses any such need: "It's true that moral commitments frequently influence the choice of concepts to be analysed. . . . But there's simply no necessary connection between the factors motivating the choice of an analysandum and the content of its analysis. A misanthrope is perfectly capable of delivering a philosophically respectable account of benevolence, a coward of courage, and so forth. And it's difficult to see why the case of justice should be any different in this respect" (Steiner 1994, 4).

2.1 The Complications of Judgment-Internalism

The first main problem with the quoted passage is that the truth of its penultimate sentence is far from obvious. Steiner offers no substantiation of the claim asserted in that sentence, and the claim runs against a prominent line of thinking about the nature of moral utterances—at least if we assume that the analyses of ethical values which Steiner mentions are propounded sincerely. Specifically, his claim runs against the central doctrine of judgment-internalists, who submit that every sincerely held moral view is accompanied by an inclination to act in accordance with the tenor of that view. What these philosophers maintain is that, insofar as anyone genuinely harbors some moral conviction, he or she is disposed to conform his or her conduct to that conviction. If Tony is of the conviction that every act of torturing a baby for pleasure is morally wrong, he is disposed to refrain from performing any such act. Likewise, if he is of the conviction that keeping one's promises made to one's friends is morally obligatory, he is disposed to keep promises which he has made to his friends. Of course, unlike the strength of his disposition to refrain from torturing any baby for pleasure, the strength of his promise-keeping disposition is almost certainly not absolute. That latter disposition is susceptible to being overtopped by some of his other ethical dispositions in certain circumstances. Nonetheless, if he is not endowed with any disposition at all to keep his promises made to his friends — in other words, if he fails to fulfill his promises to his friends even when there are no significant ethical or prudential considerations that militate against his fulfilling them — then he is not sincerely of the conviction that keeping one's promises made to one's friends is morally obligatory. So these philosophers contend.[1]

Now, as has been conceded by some philosophers who are sympathetic toward judgment-internalism, the postulation of conceptual ties between moral convictions and motivations is unsustainable if such ties are presumed to align all positive moral verdicts with pro-attitudes and all negative moral verdicts with con-attitudes. There are undoubtedly some people who are altogether amoral, and the even more striking exceptions to ordinary moral valences are the outlooks of people who derive intense gratification from the knowing perpetration of wicked deeds. These latter people recognize that their acts are heinous, and they are impelled to perform those acts by precisely that recognition. Their awareness of the iniquity of their conduct is what drives them on with special delight. Hence, although there are links between their moral convictions and their motivations, the links are the opposite of what would normally obtain. These people's favorable moral assessments are connected to con-attitudes, while their unfavorable moral assessments are connected to pro-attitudes.

Simon Blackburn offers the example of Satan in Milton's *Paradise Lost*, who proclaims "Evil be thou my Good" (Blackburn 1998, 61). Vivid though the example is, it is not maximally illuminating. After all, Satan as a superhuman fallen angel is dauntingly far outside the range of ordinary moral agents. Fortunately, however, we can turn to Shakespeare for a literary example that is more realistic and thus more informative. On the one hand, Shakespeare's character Aaron in *Titus Andronicus*—who, when facing execution, declares "If one good deed in all my life I did, I do repent it from my very soul" (V.iii.189–90)—is not greatly more serviceable for my present purposes than is Satan. He is a thinly one-dimensional evildoer whose love for his son is the only leavening trait of his personality. On the other hand, however, we can more fruitfully turn to Shakespeare's greatest villain. Iago in *Othello* perfectly exemplifies the thirst for wickedness on which we are concentrating, even though he is also a full-blooded character. Capable of convivial discourse with men and women of various ranks, he identifies himself with Satan and repeatedly evinces his awareness of the monstrous knavery of his machinations. What drives him on to pursue his nefarious ends is, among other things, his firm sense that they are nefarious. In this respect, Samuel Taylor Coleridge's famous attribution of "motiveless malignity" to Iago is apt. Coleridge's wording should not be taken to indicate that Iago has no other reasons for carrying out his heinous plot against Othello and Desdemona.[2] Rather, what it correctly signals is that one of the powerful motivating factors impelling him to implement his plot is his sheer delight in evil for evil's sake. When he sincerely asserts that his conduct is demonic, he is specifying a feature of the conduct that strongly inclines him to engage in it. He does so, moreover, while remaining a credible and richly drawn character—one of the most fascinating characters in the whole of Western literature.

Iago is a telling counterexample to any claim that every sincerely held moral conviction is marked by a disposition to act in accordance with the terms of that conviction. Iago's sincerely held convictions concerning the turpitude of his own actions are marked by strong dispositions to act athwart the terms of those convictions rather than in conformity thereto. Note, furthermore, that judgment-internalists cannot successfully defend themselves against this counterexample by maintaining that Iago's apparent moral judgments are mere simulations or recapitulations of ordinary people's moral judgments. Ever since Richard Hare wrote about the ways in which ethical terms can be used in quotation marks or inverted commas (Hare 1952, 124–26, 164–65), judgment-internalists have been inclined to dismiss counterexamples to their doctrine by contending that moral judgments not appropriately connected to motivations are simply imitations or representations of veritable moral pronouncements. Those anomalous judgments are said to be similar to the reports of anthropologists (Prinz 2006, 38). Any such tack in response to the example of Iago would amount to a serious misunderstanding. Iago is not seeking to reproduce the moral judgments of ordinary people when in his soliloquies he utters his verdicts on the monstrousness of his own actions. When he declares to himself that his contrivances are diabolical, he is delightedly expressing his own view rather than anyone else's view. For his purposes, he needs to grasp what is morally right and obligatory; it is not enough for him to grasp what is thought to be morally right and obligatory. Only by apprehending what is actually right and obligatory can he fulfill his objective of acting in defiance of what is right and obligatory.

In short, if judgment-internalists' claims about the conceptual connections between moral convictions and motivations are construed to mean that every favorable moral assessment is linked to a pro-attitude and that every negative moral assessment is linked to a con-attitude, those claims are unsustainable. Judgment-internalists cannot blithely ignore Iago. Still, their position can be construed quite differently, in a manner that enables them to come to grips with Iago and any other counterexamples to the extreme rendering of their doctrine. What they should be taken to mean is that any sincerely held moral conviction not appropriately connected to a behavioral disposition is parasitic on the myriad moral convictions that are so connected.[3] In other words, had Iago not lived in a world in which people usually act in accordance with the terms of their moral judgments rather than athwart those terms, he would not have possessed the conceptual resources needed for the formation of his own moral judgments and inclinations. A world where all the moral convictions of everyone are not properly connected to motivations is no more a possibility than is a world where all the utterances by everyone are mendacious.

Only against a general background of truthful communications do people have opportunities to engage in prevaricative communications, since in the absence of such a background the people who undertake the prevaricative communications would not be presented with any established patterns of reference and meaning which they could distort for their own dishonest purposes. In that respect, mendacious utterances are parasitic on honest utterances.[4] Likewise, only against a general background of moral judgments appropriately connected to moral motivations does anyone like Iago have opportunities to arrive at moral judgments that are not so connected. In the absence of such a background, Iago would not be presented with the moral concepts by reference to which he pursues evil as such. He cannot identify evil as something to be pursued, unless he can differentiate it from moral goodness as something to be pursued and from evil as something to be shunned; and he cannot achieve that differentiation unless the sundry contexts of his life have supplied him with the requisite concepts. If everyone throughout those contexts were devoted to evil as such, then there would be no established patterns of perceived moral goodness (as something to be sought) and perceived moral badness (as something to be eschewed) from which the pursuit of evil as such could be differentiated. Only because there are those established patterns in the world in which Iago forms his identity, does he have any point of reference from which he can dissociate his own quest for wickedness. His quest is profoundly reactive. Its momentum is entirely that of a reaction against a regnant moral order. In that respect, his satanic perversity is parasitically dependent upon the sway of ordinary motivational patterns among other people. Because a satanic orientation like Iago's is parasitic upon the prevalence of appropriate connections between moral convictions and moral motivations, those connections can aptly be characterized as "quasi-conceptual." They are not invariably present, but they are not merely contingent. Without their general presence, moral discourse—including Iago's participation in it—would be impossible. We can and should acquiesce in the tenets of judgment-internalism, if those tenets are suitably reformulated to refer to quasi-conceptual connections along the lines just recounted.

2.2 What is the Upshot?

How might Steiner, with his remarks about misanthropes and cowards, respond to my discussion of judgment-internalism? One tack not open to him is any suggestion that the misanthropes and cowards sincerely endorse genuine ethical values but lack the strength of will to conduct themselves in accordance with those values in their day-to-day lives. If the misanthropes and cowards were of that type as they unfold their analyses of ethical concepts, they would not stand as counterexamples to the thesis which Steiner is opposing: namely, the thesis that such analyses necessarily involve ethical advocacy. So envisaged, the misanthropes and cowards would be ethical advocates—even though they would not practice what they preach.

Hence, Steiner must instead adopt either of two other tacks. He might contend that the misanthropes and cowards are relevantly similar to Iago, or he might contend that they are in some way insincere. That is, he might declare that they are sincere but perverse, or he might alternatively declare that they do not really believe what they are writing. According to the first of these two approaches—which is more plausible in application to a misanthrope than in application to a coward—the motive of a misanthrope for coming up with a sound analysis of an ethical value would reside in her aim of ascertaining how best to act athwart that value. According to the second of the two approaches, the motive of a misanthrope or coward for coming up with a convincing analysis of an ethical value would reside in some extraneous consideration such as the eliciting of approval from academic colleagues. (Note, incidentally, that an insincere analysis of an ethical value can take either of two broad routes. In keeping with Hare's reference to inverted commas or quotation marks, an insincere analyst might seek to report and elaborate other people's ethical views which she herself does not endorse. Much more likely, however, is that she will instead simulate the espousal of those views by expressing them rather than reporting them. Instead of attributing ethical doctrines to other people, she will articulate those doctrines—and expand on their corollaries—as if she believed in them.)

Either of the principal tacks that might be adopted by Steiner in response to my discussion of judgment-internalism is deeply problematic. After all, as has already been observed, he is guilty of an *ignoratio elenchi* in the methodological comments on which we have been concentrating. Each of the principal tacks just outlined will enable Steiner to show that the values underlying one's choice of an analysandum are not necessarily the same as those expressed in one's subsequent analysis. However, as has been remarked, his establishment of that point is decidedly insufficient for his purposes. What he needs to establish is not that point, but the much bolder claim that a satisfactory analysis of an ethical concept can draw solely on formal considerations (such as the constraint of logical consistency) to the exclusion of substantive ethical considerations. Far from *confirming* that bolder claim, each of the approaches adumbrated in the preceding paragraph *undermines* it.

If the misanthropes mentioned by Steiner are Iago-like deviants who explicate the concept of benevolence in order to determine how they can best act malignly, then their explications of that concept are squarely informed by substantive ethical considerations. As has been emphasized in my discussion of Iago himself, his perverse aims require him to focus on just such considerations. He needs to grasp what is morally right and obligatory, in order to set himself against what is morally right and obligatory. Much the same can be said about a misanthrope who plumbs the value of benevolence in order to furnish herself with knowledge that will sharpen her effectiveness in realizing her malevolent designs. Only substantive ethical reflection will deliver that knowledge. Ruminations on formal constraints such as logical consistency will be utterly insufficient. Indeed, Steiner himself would almost certainly accept that substantive ethical reflection is essential for analyses of benevolence by Iago-like misanthropes, since his own efforts to rely on purely formal considerations for selecting among theories are mounted solely with reference to theories of justice, and he emphasizes that justice does not exhaust the domain of ethics.[5] Thus, although the values that motivate the choice of benevolence as an analysandum by any Iago-like misanthrope are distinct from the values that are sincerely given voice in her analysis, that analysis must draw indispensably on principles of substantive ethics. Steiner cannot rightly adduce the example of the misanthrope in support of his own ambition to eschew any reliance upon such principles—and to resort instead to starkly formal constraints—in his quest for a theory of justice.

Even more problematic for Steiner is the second of the two approaches delineated in the antepenultimate paragraph above. A misanthrope or a coward who insincerely explicates the concept of benevolence or courage (perhaps in order to gain plaudits from academic colleagues) will have to advert to ethical factors when so doing, just as much as will any Iago-like misanthrope who expounds the concept of benevolence; moreover, in contrast with the Iago-like misanthrope, the insincere misanthrope or coward will not be setting her sights in a direction that can be countenanced by Steiner. Instead of focusing on what she believes to be genuinely benevolent or courageous, she will be focusing on what she believes to be perceived by other people as genuinely benevolent or courageous. To be sure, a full-scale analysis of the concept of benevolence or courage from her insincere perspective will involve her teasing out the implications of other people's views, rather than her simply rehearsing those views as they have already been unfolded. She will therefore be rendering ethical judgments, but those judgments pertain to ethical principles which she believes to be prevalently endorsed—rather than to ethical principles which she believes to be correct. Hence, the scenario of an insincere misanthrope or coward is doubly troublesome for Steiner. Such a misanthrope or coward is relying on non-formal considerations when she analyzes the concept of benevolence or courage, and the non-formal considerations on which she draws are not thought by her to be correct. Not only is she failing to address her questions in the manner favored by Steiner; in addition, she is not even asking the right questions.

3. CONCLUSION

In short, Steiner's methodology is to be rejected comprehensively. His Kantian dreams of educing an array of moral conclusions from austerely formal premises are indeed but dreams. The Permissibility Theorem, which constitutes the pivot of his methodology, is an unsustainable dogma that is falsifiable by a myriad of credible states of affairs. It is not formally defective, but it is woefully defective in its representation of normative possibilities and actualities. It cannot have any place in a system of deontic logic that models those possibilities and actualities accurately. Once we have rejected that theorem and the axiom from which it derives, we can apprehend that no formal constraint such as that of logical consistency will suffice as a criterion for selecting among theories of justice. Many plausible theories of justice clash with the Permissibility Theorem, but none of them clashes with any genuine constraint of logic. Thus, if we hope to select among plausible theories of justice, we shall have to have recourse to substantive moral argumentation. Steiner's endeavors to underscore the forgoability of such argumentation have proved to be fruitless. His examples have instead served to highlight the indispensability of substantive ethical factors and judgments in any analyses of ethical concepts. *Malgré lui*, Steiner has shown that—in the domain of ethics—austerity leads nowhere.

NOTES

1. For a lengthy discussion of judgment-internalism, with abundant references to the relevant philosophical literature, see the eighth chapter of Kramer 2009.
2. Iago suspects that he has been cuckolded by Othello; he resents the perceived slight of being passed over for promotion; he obviously envies Othello; and some of his utterances bespeak a racist animosity toward the Moor. (Jonathan Dancy correctly remarks that Satan in *Paradise Lost* is motivated by a lust for dominion over the world, but he incorrectly concludes that Satan is not also motivated by the prospect of evil for evil's sake. See Dancy 1993, 6.)
3. For a cognate view, see Blackburn 1998, 59–68. A similar view is also fleetingly broached in Harman 1996, 179. Note that, when I refer to moral convictions as "appropriately" or "properly" connected to dispositions, I am not necessarily suggesting that the convictions and dispositions themselves are appropriate. Rather, I am simply indicating that positive moral judgments are linked to pro-attitudes and that negative moral judgments are linked to con-attitudes.
4. For a corresponding observation about simulative statements such as those uttered by actors in plays, see Austin 1975, 21–22.
5. Steiner 1994, 62. Steiner inappositely presumes that the non-exhaustiveness of justice is due to the existence of duties that are not correlative with rights, but the general point about the non-exhaustiveness of justice can be salvaged from that faulty elaboration of it.

REFERENCES

Austin, J.L. 1975. *How to Do Things with Words*. Second Edition. Cambridge, MA: Harvard University Press. Edited by J.O. Urmson and Marina Sbisà.

Blackburn, Simon. 1998. *Ruling Passions*. Oxford: Oxford University Press.

Dancy, Jonathan. 1993. *Moral Reasons*. Oxford: Blackwell.

Hare, R.M. 1952. *The Language of Morals*. Oxford: Clarendon Press.

Harman, Gilbert. 1996. "Harman's Response to Thomson's Part II." In Gilbert Harman and Judith Jarvis Thomson, *Moral Relativism and Moral Objectivity*. Oxford: Blackwell.

Kramer, Matthew. 1998. "Rights without Trimmings." In Matthew H. Kramer, N.E. Simmonds, and Hillel Steiner, *A Debate over Rights*. Oxford: Oxford University Press.

Kramer, Matthew. 1999. *In Defense of Legal Positivism*. Oxford: Oxford University Press.
Kramer, Matthew. 2001. "Getting Rights Right." In Matthew H. Kramer (ed.), *Rights, Wrongs, and Responsibilities*. Basingstoke: Palgrave Macmillan.
Kramer, Matthew. 2004. *Where Law and Morality Meet*. Oxford: Oxford University Press.
Kramer, Matthew. 2005. "Moral Rights and the Limits of the 'Ought'-Implies-'Can' Principle: Why Impeccable Precautions are No Excuse." 48 *Inquiry* 307–55.
Kramer, Matthew. 2007. *Objectivity and the Rule of Law*. Cambridge: Cambridge University Press.
Kramer, Matthew. 2009. *Moral Realism as a Moral Doctrine*. Oxford: Blackwell.
Prinz, Jesse. 2006. "The Emotional Basis of Moral Judgments." 9 *Philosophical Explorations* 29–43
Steiner, Hillel. 1994. *An Essay on Rights*. Oxford: Blackwell.
Steiner, Hillel. 1998. "Working Rights." In Matthew H. Kramer, N.E. Simmonds, and Hillel Steiner, *A Debate over Rights*. Oxford: Oxford University Press.

13 Recalibrating Steiner on Evil

Stephen de Wijze

I first met Hillel Steiner in September 1997 when I began teaching political theory in the then Department of Government at the University of Manchester. His considerable reputation preceded him and I was rather apprehensive about meeting someone described to me as one of the best political philosophers in Britain. Fame and extraordinary talent in my experience can often be accompanied by a less than pleasant character or disposition. However, in this case my apprehension was entirely misplaced, since Hillel combines a prodigious intellect with an irenic and gentle manner which makes interaction with him a most interesting and enjoyable experience. My admiration for his abilities as a scholar grows with each passing year and I have benefited enormously from reading his work, being in reading groups with him, and especially from his careful questioning of my often-inchoate ideas. Hillel's uncanny ability to home in on the core issues at stake and quickly highlight just where an argument is at its weakest always leaves me a great deal clearer and wiser about a particular problem despite scrabbling for a way to salvage what I previously thought were unassailable arguments. I am continually surprised and delighted by the originality of his thinking, and even when I find his conclusions vastly counter-intuitive (as I often do), I applaud his ability and uncompromising Humean desire to follow an argument wherever it goes. It has been an invaluable learning process to work closely with Hillel over the past decade; a master class on how to do political philosophy with someone who not only has been a mentor and teacher but also a friend. I feel deeply privileged to be able to contribute to this collection of essays in his honour.

This paper seeks to examine an area of Steiner's work on which he has not written a great deal but highlights the key issues and the path to take if we are to understand the problem correctly. It is concerned with offering a secular account of evil, essentially the idea that certain immoral and terrible actions, characters, states of affairs, or persons, are properly and accurately described as evil. To refer to actions, characters, states of affairs, or persons as immoral or even extremely immoral fails to capture a *qualitative* difference that is of great importance in moral discourse. Steiner and I have had a considerable exchange of views on this topic and although we agree that a secular conception of evil is both possible and an essential part of our moral vocabulary, we disagree on its specifics. Steiner argues for a reductionistic, or what I shall call the 'Perverse Pleasure' (PP) account of evil[1], while I seek to defend a multi-faceted approach which I shall call the 'Non-Reductive Disjunctive' account (NRD).[2] My disagreements with Steiner's account stem from our different methodological approaches to understanding and examining moral concepts. Steiner's foundationalist and reductionist methodology forces him towards a substantive account that must systematically violate strong moral intuitions about how we understand and commonly use a secular notion of evil. My approach offers a more intuitively plausible account that employs a coherentist reflective equilibrium methodology, thus doing justice, I believe, to our moral reality. I begin the paper with some brief remarks on the recent revival of interest in a secular concept of evil. This leads to some important ground clearing in order to focus in on just what Steiner and I are seeking to do (and, importantly, not seeking to do) when defining a concept of evil. I then outline and evaluate Steiner's PP account of evil and the methodology that underlies its derivation, arguing that my NRD approach offers a more plausible account of evil that fits with our considered moral judgments. I conclude the paper by reiterating two insights that arise from the critique of Steiner's problematic account of evil and, in particular, the methodology he uses to derive it.

1. THE RECENT INTEREST IN A SECULAR ACCOUNT OF EVIL

Over the last decade there has been a revival of the use of the term 'evil' to characterise those actions, characters, states of affairs, or persons that are particularly egregious or depraved and demonstrate a deliberate and unashamed disregard for the value of life or for suffering generally. The terrible events of 9/11 combined with the subsequent 'war on terror' have undoubtedly given momentum to these debates. As Neiman (2002, xi) points out, it was not only the magnitude of destruction with nearly three thousand lives lost, but the motive and the evident delight at the destruction and death by those who planned and carried out the attacks. Just as in 1755 after the Lisbon Earthquake and after 1945 when the full extent of the Nazi Holocaust was becoming known, 9/11 raises the question of evil and our response to it. It was not simply the large number of people killed or the horrendous destruction that occurred on 9/11[3] that made it a watershed event with respect to raising the question of evil, but rather the fact that those who planned and carried out the attacks did so with the clear intention to cause as much death and destruction as humanly possible. The meticulous planning combined with the deliberate decision to turn civilian aircraft into missiles in order to kill tens of thousands of people using suicidal operatives, crossed a line into that realm of actions which most people would consider morally unthinkable. Al Qaeda violated every long accepted normative constraint on how enemies engage in conflict. They gave no warnings, made no demands that could plausibly be met, and aimed to kill and injure without discrimination. What is more, they boasted about and clearly gloried in what they had done. While millions recoiled in shock and horror, Al Qaeda vowed that this was just the beginning; that much more and much worse was to come.

Politicians, journalists and social commentators immediately began to talk of a 'post 9/11 world' evoking the term 'evil' to explain Al Qaeda, its actions, and those who supported them.[4] The subsequent wars in Afghanistan and Iraq, further terrorist attacks, the increase in suicide bombings, kidnappings, and other atrocities such as the massacre of school children at Beslan[5], further encouraged the search for an appropriate normative term that would properly or at least better describe these events. Merely to say that such actions were worse[6] than ordinary moral wrongdoing failed to grasp the *qualitative* difference that many people intuitively felt. Al Qaeda's actions were not just *very* wrong but in a different moral zone where the usual labels of right and wrong, good and bad were not adequate to the descriptive task. The term 'evil' was needed to fill this normative gap. Hence its new found attraction among those who previously rejected such talk as mere religious primitivism or superstition which explained nothing while provoking irrational hatred by demonising the enemy.[7] A secular notion of evil, however, makes strong intuitive sense when trying to identify and distinguish certain horrendous actions or states of affairs from everyday mundane, but all too common, immorality. The attacks of 9/11, the Nazi death camps, the horrific torture of fellow human beings, to mention just three examples, call out for a moral vocabulary that properly conveys the horror, disgust, and moral pollution that marks such events.

It would be an error to assume given recent events that this call for a secular account of evil is commonplace among moral philosophers. Its use and appeal sit far more comfortably with politicians, social commentators, journalists and the general public.[8] Moral theorists of all stripes are far more likely to reject a notion of evil, secular or otherwise, as crude and unhelpful. Indeed it is an issue on which both deontological and consequentialist moral theorists are often in agreement even if they see eye to eye on very little else. Put simply, a notion of evil, be it religious or secular, is not easily accommodated within modern and contemporary normative theories of right/good and wrong/bad. I do not propose to tackle their rejection or strong scepticism about the very possibility of a secular account of evil here, as it would take me too far away from my present concerns. Rather, I shall assume that there are strong arguments to support the pursuit of a secular account of evil or, at the very least, that we can bracket this judgment for the moment and examine one particular secular conception of evil and the methodology used to develop it. It may turn out that if we can offer a sufficiently plausible account of evil, then this analysis may go some way toward undermining the deep scepticism found among many moral theorists concerning the desirability and efficacy of a secular concept of evil.

So it is within the context outlined above that the following discussion of Steiner's work is situated. Steiner and I both agree that there is a need for a concept of evil and that it must be a secular account. We both reject the use of the term evil if it is derived from, or coupled to, a religious viewpoint. If it is necessarily so tied, then the concept is sufficiently problematic to make us better off without it. The metaphysical and theological problems that a religious notion of evil brings with it are such that its use would almost certainly bring greater normative problems than it would solve. The hope, then, is that a secular account can appropriately identify those persons and/or their acts which provoke a special horror and moral shudder within us. What is more, any such account ought to capture or resonate with the great majority of our strong intuitions about evil, and prove to be a useful explanatory concept. By 'explanatory concept' I mean, following Garrard (2002, 322), that a secular concept of evil provides 'an adequate account of what evil is' and can demonstrate 'why certain acts are to be categorised together under that heading' and 'why we respond as we do to them'. It might also provide some insights into why people do such acts.

Within these formal constraints, there can be many different substantive accounts of evil and indeed in the short time that work has been done on developing a secular account many different conceptions have been proffered, one of which is Steiner's PP account.[9] However, before examining the PP account of evil I need to make some further brief clarificatory points, specifically about what I will *not* be seeking to do. Firstly, I am not seeking to define or examine what are sometimes referred to as 'natural evils' such as earthquakes, tsunamis, and famines caused by drought.[10] A secular account of evil presupposes that persons (or groups of persons) were responsible for the actions under scrutiny and that at the time they acted they possessed the requisite levels of autonomy (agency), intellectual ability, and sense of morality. There is sometimes an issue of whether a particular agent did indeed have the prerequisites for making free choices,[11] but for the purposes of this paper I am concerned with the vast majority of cases where an agent is an autonomous adult with a sense of wrong and right and can be reasonably held accountable for his/her actions.[12]

Secondly, the conceptions of evil discussed in this paper focus on evil *acts* rather than what constitutes an evil person, or an evil character/disposition, or evil states of affairs. Some theorists have sought to examine what it is that defines an evil person (often interpreted as his or her character), presumably hoping that if this could be established then it would be relatively easy to distinguish evil from merely immoral actions.[13] Evil actions would then be defined as the actions of evil persons. However, this approach faces an obvious and persuasive criticism, that we often claim that a person committed an evil act without thinking of that person as evil. An evil act could be an aberration rather than the expression of a person's evil character. Evil actions, it seems, are not necessarily tied to evil characters although such characters are far more likely to exhibit a much higher incidence of evil acts.[14] However, if we can develop a credible account of what constitutes an evil action, then it may go some way to establishing what constitutes an evil person. Someone who continuously engages in evil actions may be properly referred to as an evil person, a person with an evil character. But this interesting puzzle is beyond the scope of this paper.

2. STEINER ON EVIL—THE 'PERVERSE PLEASURE' ACCOUNT (PP)

Steiner's PP account can be simply put.

> D1: 'Evil acts are wrong acts that are pleasurable for their doers' (Steiner: 2002: 189).

Steiner adds that we could plausibly offer a slightly more permissive account which weakens the affective requirement so that the agent need not feel pleasure from the immoral act but remains emotionally indifferent when he/she clearly ought not to be so. So expanding on D1 we can say:

> D2: 'An act is evil if (a) it is wrong, and (b) its doer does it either pleasurably *or with affective indifference*' (Steiner: 2002: 192 fn.10).[15]

Steiner's derivation of this definition is undertaken in two stages. Firstly, he engages in 'ground clearing' which involves drawing out four necessary properties attached to our common sense concept of evil as reflected in ordinary usage. A secular concept of evil must be derived from these properties if it is to have the right kind of explanatory power and become a useful addition to our moral vocabulary. The four properties drawn from ordinary usage are the following.

A secular conception of evil must:

1 not be 'synonymous with other terms of negative moral appraisal';
2 apply 'independently to acts, without logically committing its users to the existence of any connection between the evilness of those acts and evilness of either their perpetrators or their perpetrators' dispositions or the states of affairs resulting from their perpetration';
3 be understood 'as a wrong-intensifier in the aggravating or qualitative sense';
4 admit of 'quantitative variability', that is, evil acts can (in principle) be calibrated in that we can meaningfully refer to the 'lesser of evils'.[16]

Given 1–4 above[17] Steiner then seeks to explore their implications for 'assessing the extent to which evil acts are evil' (Steiner 2002, 185). His method of investigation is to compare and contrast evil acts with supererogatory acts, the latter being acts that are similarly puzzling from a normative point of view but which we generally accept as a useful part of our moral vocabulary. Supererogatory acts are those actions we consider especially good or right actions. They seem to involve a qualitative difference from ordinary morally good actions in that we consider them heroic and beyond normal ethical obligations.[18] Very few people ever engage in such actions and, when they do, we are astonished and admiring, since we acknowledge their rarity and appreciate how difficult they are for the doer. Steiner's hope is that if evil actions are indeed the negative counterpart to supererogatory ones, then we might be able to identify those shared features that place such actions in a different qualitative moral zone. He refers to this possible symmetry as the *Negative Counterpart Thesis* (NCT) and hopes that by 'closely scrutinising the possible grounds for NCT, we might hope better to illuminate the nature of our desiderated conception of evil' (Steiner 2002, 185).

Steiner's investigations utilise deontic logic to examine the 'axiological structures for the moral appraisal of actions' (Steiner 2002, 186) and he concludes that this modal interpretation of the NCT must be rejected since it cannot accommodate two of the four necessary properties required of a secular account of evil. While there is a negative symmetry in terms of axiological structures (supererogatory actions are highly valued while evil actions are disvaluable) the NCT fails to show why evil acts are qualitatively different from very bad acts and why evil acts are impermissible while supererogatory ones are beyond ethical obligation. However, Steiner does notice a negative symmetry in the *affective* properties of evil and supererogatory actions. While supererogatory actions are painful to perform and require much self-sacrifice, evil acts are pleasurable and involve self-indulgence. This affective interpretation meets the four necessary requirements, in particular providing a metric which enables the calibration of evil. Steiner argues that the scale for measuring evil actions would combine 'the scale for wrongness with that for pleasure' (Steiner 2002, 190). Given two persons, Adam and Bill, both engaging in acts of torture, we could declare, using Steiner's PP account of evil, that if Adam derives pleasure in carrying out this very wrongful action while Bill does not (or Adam derives more pleasure than Bill in doing so), then Adam's act is appropriately described as more evil.

It is important at this point to examine the methodological approach for deriving the PP account since it is vintage Steiner at work. Throughout his considerable corpus of work, he uses the same approach, that is, an attempt to derive powerful substantive normative conclusions from the barest or weakest foundational assumptions possible. This typically involves asserting some foundational, minimal, and largely uncontroversial (or widely accepted) normative content, which is then subjected to a rigorous logical analysis. Those inferences or conclusions that do not fall foul of logical inconsistencies or conceptual incoherence provide the best substantive normative conclusions achievable. The conclusions so derived are powerful, and ignored at the cost of irrationality even if at first glance they appear to be counter-intuitive.[19] What is more, this method provides a powerful criterion to assess, and where applicable dismiss, rival theories as inferior by demonstrating their inconsistencies and/or reliance on controversial normative content to support their different substantive conclusions. Steiner's *Essay on Rights* is a master class in just how to use this technique to find thought-provoking answers to the complex and important question 'what is justice?'. From the unproblematic, or at least very widely accepted assumption, that all persons have a right to freedom, Steiner employs the logical notion of 'compossibility' or mutual consistency to work up to his 'left-libertarianism', which is 'an historical entitlement conception of justice with some reasonably strong redistributive implications' (Steiner 1994, 5). Steiner states explicitly that he believes a sensible analysis of normative conceptions begins 'at the elementary particle level since big things are made from small ones' (Steiner 1994, 2). When seeking a conception of justice, Steiner uses the elementary particles of individual rights and subjects them to a rigorous logical analysis informed by the idea of compossibility. Similarly, with his search for a conception of evil, Steiner takes his elementary particles to be the four necessary properties derived from ordinary usage and, using his NCT, seeks to derive a criterion that will satisfy all four of these conditions. However, it is this very methodology that leads to deep problems with the PP account. As we shall see, a robust and plausible secular concept of evil may indeed encompass those cases where doers get perverse pleasure (or feel nothing at all) when they act immorally, but there is much more to a secular account of evil than this. How far Steiner's PP account falls short is the focus of the next section of this paper.

3. THE PROBLEMS WITH STEINER'S PP ACCOUNT OF EVIL

There are at least two serious problems facing Steiner's PP account. Both, in the final analysis, are problems that arise owing to his reductive methodology. While it may be possible to modify Steiner's PP account to deflect the first problem (which I call the 'Range Problem'), it is the second that deals the fatal blow. Steiner's PP account is unable to contend with actions that occur within *Weltanschauungen* which 'annihilate the moral landscape' and have a profound effect on ordinary commonplace activities. In such contexts, ordinary benign actions or projects are appropriately understood as evil. Consequently, the evil that is the Nazi worldview, for example, is not simply the 'agglomeration of countless acts performed by a sizeable number of actors' as Steiner suggests.[20] The reductive view that a complex notion is nothing more than the sum of its parts and therefore can be explained by examining its individual constituents is deeply problematic when it seeks to elucidate thick moral concepts that match our moral reality.[21] By contrast, my NRD approach attempts to take into account those conditions which warp or annihilate the moral landscape.[22] But before expanding on this point it is instructive to examine the 'Range Problem' and Steiner's possible responses to it, since it illustrates one of the inadequacies of his PP account.

The first problem is that the set of evil actions delimited by the PP account is at the same time both far too permissive and far too restrictive. The exclusive focus on the agent's affective state results in an account of evil that turns ordinary wrongdoing into evil acts while at the same time excluding cases which we typically and rightly think of as evil.[23] Consider the following two cases:

> E1. A teenager shoplifts items to the value of £50 from a large retailer. These acts give him great pleasure even though he knows that shoplifting is morally wrong. He enjoys the thrill of transgression and the street credibility it brings from his peers.[24]
>
> E2. From Chaim Kaplan's Warsaw Diaries. 'A rabbi in Lodz was forced to spit on a Torah scroll that was in the Holy Ark. In fear of his life he complied and desecrated that which is holy to him and his people. After a short time he had no more saliva, his mouth was dry. To the Nazi question, why did he stop spitting, the rabbi replied that his mouth was dry. Then the son of the 'superior race' began to spit into the rabbi's mouth and the rabbi continued to spit on the Torah.'[25]

Applying Steiner's PP account E1 is an evil action (wrongdoing which gave the doer pleasure), while E2 is not (if we assume that the Nazi carried out this humiliation from a sense of duty and gained no pleasure from doing so). If this classification of the two acts is correct, Steiner's PP theory is vastly counter-intuitive to say the least.[26] Very few people, if any, would class E1 as an evil act, while almost everyone would consider E2 as quintessentially so. The humiliation, viciousness, violation, inventiveness, symbolism, and sheer cruelty of the Nazi's actions rightly fill us with dread and horror. If any act ought to be classed as evil, then E2 is it.

To be fair to Steiner, adjustments can be made to the PP account to exclude E1 and include E2 despite first appearances. Steiner foresees the problem with including examples like E1 as an evil act and briefly alludes to a possible response.[27] Our reluctance to see such petty theft as evil, despite the doer's deriving pleasure from so acting, is due to our judgment that the wrong done is rather minor or trivial. Stealing £50 is not a serious wrongdoing compared with assault, murder, torture, and a host of other actions. So it seems that Steiner can exclude examples such as E1 by expanding his PP account to

> D3: 'An act is evil if (a) it is *sufficiently* wrong, and (b) its doer does it either pleasurably or with affective indifference'.

However, this addition of sufficiency comes at a very high cost. The PP account now faces the difficult task of providing appropriate thresholds. This issue becomes as important as, if not more so than, the condition of affectivity as the criterion that bears the weight for deciding the classification of wrongful actions as evil or otherwise. The PP approach is now in serious danger of collapsing into an account that simply claims that evil actions are those actions which are either especially harmful to others (the consequentialist route) or violate some very important moral prohibition (the deontological path).[28] And if this is the case, then there is no need to concern ourselves with the affective states that an agent may or may not possess while acting, since they are irrelevant and superfluous to the analysis. Steiner might reply that the sufficiency clause is only a necessary condition and that affectivity is still needed for the final judgment on whether a particular act is evil. But, as becomes clear when examining E2 below, some acts can be so harmful or so heinous that they are evil irrespective of the affective state of the agent. If this is true, then something besides the pleasure felt by the agent is doing the work in defining evil and at best the PP account is redundant, at worst a confusing distraction.

What of examples such as E2? Could suitable adjustments be made to the PP account enabling it to classify them as evil acts even if the agent derives no pleasure from his actions? Again, Steiner anticipates this concern when he argues that the set of evil actions can be enlarged by weakening the affective requirement through a more permissive formulation such as D2. The Nazi need not derive pleasure from his humiliation and abuse of the rabbi for his actions to be evil. It is enough that he lacked the requisite feelings of horror and disgust that ought to accompany such acts.[29] However, this permissive version of PP still doesn't go far enough. What would the PP account say of the Nazi if he acted out of a sense of duty and felt very badly about what he was doing, but did it nevertheless? What if he felt pain and horror in so acting? Would this make the action merely one of wrongdoing rather than evil? Steiner offers us the example of two Nazi doctors, one of whom enjoys performing gruesome experiments on Auschwitz inmates while the other does not.[30] The former, according to Steiner, is committing the more evil act. However, the Nazi who derives no pleasure from the task is still engaged in an indisputably evil action because what he does both easily crosses the threshold of sufficient wrongdoing and satisfies the clause of affective indifference. But it is not clear from this example that the first doctor commits a more evil *act* because he enjoys it. Perhaps a better way to characterise the situation is to say that the evilness of the acts is the same but that the doctor who enjoyed his work would be an evil person or would have an evil personality. At any rate, Steiner does not address the issue of the Nazi doctor who feels anguish and pain while performing the experiments. To think that because of this affective state the actions were merely wrong rather than evil is deeply mistaken, and this seems to be the inescapable conclusion if we use his PP account. Steiner himself notes in a paper where he poses the question of what it means to understand the evil of the Holocaust, that our abhorrence of Nazi views and actions is a fixed point on our moral compasses.[31] The Nazi in E2 who tormented the rabbi was engaged in a manifestly evil action whatever his affective state at the time and irrespective of his reasons for so acting.

The Range Problem takes much of the shine off Steiner's conception of evil, since the modifications needed to enable it to accommodate cases such as E1 and E2 come at some considerable cost. However, the second problem proves an even greater challenge for Steiner's account. The PP account cannot adequately explain horrendous events such as the Holocaust or the recent genocide in Rwanda, which we take to be paradigmatically evil. Although Steiner is trying to explain what, precisely, makes a wrongful act into an evil one, the PP theory cannot account for the important role of evil worldviews in this connection. An evil worldview can transform banal or innocuous acts into evil ones and when this happens a non-virtuous circle is created where evil acts and evil worldviews reinforce each other. Steiner's reductive account and foundationalist methodology focus exclusively on one of these two directions in this circle.[32] The PP account can only explain the evil of the Holocaust or the Rwandan genocide by pointing to the very many individual evil acts by 'a sizeable number of actors'. But this misses a crucial dimension of how to understand, explain, and identify evil acts.

What does it mean to hold a worldview that perverts or inverts the 'moral landscape'? I mean by 'moral landscape' those fundamental preconditions needed for the development and sustaining of a minimally civilised society and human interaction. Civilised conflict management requires, at the very least, a minimal level of respect and dignity between persons. Generally, these prerequisites are found in the international and local institutions within and between societies that involve the 'fair weighting and balancing of contrary arguments bearing on an unavoidable and disputable issue' (Hampshire 1999, 21). The 'moral landscape' also refers to the celebration and protection of life that is found in all moral theories that prohibit abuse, unnecessary harm and suffering, and require protection of the weak from the strong. It is the commitment to engender a world where suffering and death are minimised and where possible eliminated.

Those worldviews which invert or warp the moral landscape deliberately substitute force, violence and the fear of violence, for negotiation, compromise, and fair play. The goal of their protagonists is pure domination and the subjection of others where no outrage is forbidden and the constraint on their behaviour is limited only by what they are physically unable to do. As pointed out above, the Nazi worldview is a paradigmatic case of an ideology that warps the moral landscape. It is not just that the Nazis inflicted great harms on the Jewish people (although this would be more than sufficient) but that they dealt with all their enemies in a similar ruthless, cruel, and pitiless manner. They obliterated universal fundamental moral prohibitions common to all moralities making murder, torture, rape, massacres, slave labour, betrayal, theft, and much more into routine and legitimate activities. What is more, there was a conscious artistry and inventiveness to their cruelty and terrible abuse. For example, it was not enough to prevent Jews from living tolerable lives, but new and especially cruel ways needed to be found to humiliate and destroy them. The Nazi who spits into the rabbi's mouth to extend and continue the degradation and brutality, demonstrates a terrible inventiveness that we usually associate with an artistic consciousness.[33] An evil worldview embodies a form of malignant wickedness in that it seeks to take cruelty to new levels, inflict as much gratuitous suffering as possible, and to make its victims both aware of and complicit in their own destruction through acts of sadistic irony.[34] It is within such repugnant worldviews that ordinary activities can become evil activities. These ordinary activities cause a special kind of revulsion in part because their ostensible normality highlights the indifference to the terrible evil occurring all around them. Photographs of Nazi officers enjoying a picnic with their wives and children a few miles away from the horrors of a concentration camp is as troubling as, perhaps more so than, pictures of overt and terrible violence.

This dimension of evil, if I am correct, is not accessible to Steiner's PP account. It does not concern itself primarily with the intentions or consequences of individual acts and certainly does not refer to the affective states of agents. It highlights a twisted and perverted philosophical and socio/political ideology which can transform mundane acts and activities into evil ones.

4. REFLECTIVE EQUILIBRIUM AND THE NON-REDUCTIVE DISJUNCTIVE (NRD) ACCOUNT OF EVIL

In his seminal work *A Theory of Justice*, Rawls states:

> A conception of justice cannot be deduced from self-evident premises or conditions on principles; instead, its justification is a matter of the mutual support of many considerations, of everything fitting together into one coherent view' (Rawls 1971, 21).

I think that this claim is correct and applies equally to deriving a conception of evil. A useful and plausible account of evil needs both to depict and to justify our considered moral convictions; those presumed fixed points on our moral compass. I mean by 'considered moral convictions' those views which people, with the appropriate ability and motivation, come to hold when they consider moral issues under conditions where non-arbitrary judgments can be made. These moral convictions are held with the full awareness that they could be mistaken and are open to revision if a persuasive theoretical account of why they are wrong can be given. In this process, we revise particular moral intuitions at variance with a plausible set of general moral principles when the majority of our other strongly held intuitions are not at variance with those principles. Conversely, when the majority of our strongly held moral intuitions are at variance in some respect with our general moral principles, we revise the latter. In short, there is a process of 'reflective equilibrium' in play where our moral sensibilities inform our view of moral principles which in turn refine or adjust our moral sensibilities. This process, it seems to me, better reflects our moral reality, a balance between theoretical principles and deeply held moral convictions.

A wide 'reflective equilibrium' approach to developing a conception of evil draws on a non-reductive coherence method of moral justification, one which, following Nielsen,

> seeks to produce, and perspicaciously display, coherence among (a) our considered moral convictions, (b) a consistent cluster of moral principles, (c) a consistent cluster of background theories (including moral theories) about our social world and how we function in it, and (d) an empirically based, broadly scientific, conception and account of human nature (Nielsen 1994, 24).

The difference between a narrow and wide reflective equilibrium has to do with their relevance to justification. A narrow reflective equilibrium is concerned only with Nielsen's criteria (a) and (b), and as a result is a largely descriptive exercise best suited for engaging in a form of moral anthropology or hermeneutics. That is, a narrow reflective equilibrium reveals the principles underlying strongly held moral intuitions and vice versa in the same way that formal grammar reveals the unconscious internalised rules (and vice versa) by which we correctly use a particular language. A wide reflective equilibrium takes the method one step further by subjecting both our moral convictions and moral principles to Nielsen's criteria (c) and (d), and as a result provides a justificatory basis for accepting a particular set of principles as better than its rivals. This demanding process ensures that a particular coherence achieved between a set of intuitions and moral principles is such that reasonable persons would choose them over a range of competing theories. In this way, to claim that one particular conception of evil is better than another is to say that it coheres or fits within a wide reflective equilibrium.[35]

This approach stands in sharp contrast to Steiner's reductive and foundationalist methodology. Recall that he begins with four fixed conditions which he uses to explore their 'implications for assessing the extent to which evil acts are evil' (Steiner 2002, 185). A reflective equilibrium approach takes a markedly different route, one that enables the widest possible range of intuitions about evil actions to feed into possible principles. The process is one of a continual back and forth between strong intuitions and plausible principles until equilibrium is achieved. There is no attempt to develop moral principles from unassailable foundational beliefs in order to correct our intuitions.

As we saw from the 'Range Problem', Steiner's PP account throws up serious problems in dealing with examples that any compelling conception of evil must accommodate. It is laudable to follow an argument wherever the conclusion leads but in a context like this one, in which our intuitions are among the elements that have an indisputable and compelling role in guiding our assessments, if the conclusion is strongly counter-intuitive then it is quite likely unsound. Either there has been a serious error in the reasoning leading to the conclusion, or the method used to derive such a conclusion was inappropriate. Steiner's PP account falls foul of the latter problem. He adopts an inappropriate methodology for deriving thick moral concepts, in this case a secular conception of evil.

One way of supporting my claim would be to engage in a detailed critique of both reductive and foundationalist methodologies. However, space limitations prevent this, so I shall take a different, shorter, but nevertheless instructive route. I will offer my NRD account of evil, derived through a process of reflective equilibrium, and test it against examples E1 and E2 which cause such problems for Steiner's PP account. I contend that the NRD account offers a more plausible account of evil because it fits better with our strong intuitions.

My NRD conception of evil[36] can be stated as follows:

> Evil actions, projects or states of affairs are *always* wrongful actions, projects or states of affairs but *differ qualitatively* in that they fulfil one or more of the following conditions:
>
> A There is a *deliberate violation* of persons *with the intention* to *dehumanise* (that is deny basic respect and dignity to) those powerless to retaliate.
>
> B The action or project will gratuitously inflict, or bring about, one or more of 'The Great Harms'[37] to sentient beings with the relevant moral standing.
>
> C The action or project (or professed morality) seeks to annihilate the 'moral landscape'.

The first condition outlines the distinctive motive and intent underlying evil acts, while the second and third stress the special kinds of deprivation and context or social milieu which evoke a secular sense of evil. The three criteria are singly and jointly sufficient. At least one of the criteria must obtain (is necessary) for an evil action to be evil. The three conditions serve as a complex boundary within which a secular notion of evil can be understood. Condition A focuses on the intention of the agent which when linked to the dehumanisation of the weak, illuminates the qualitative difference from mere wrongdoing. Condition B picks up both on the intent (gratuitous infliction) and the terrible consequences that destroy a living being's ability to live a tolerable life. Finally C expresses our concern about the evil that is embedded in a particular kind of worldview which I have discussed in some detail in the previous section.

Now consider examples E1 and E2. The shoplifter who steals £50 and derives much pleasure from this wrongdoing does not satisfy any of the three conditions of my NRD account. He did not violate persons, nor seek to humiliate those powerless to retaliate. The stealing of £50, *ceteris paribus*, certainly does not inflict one or more of the great harms on anyone and such an action cannot plausibly be thought of as warping the moral landscape. The shoplifter is simply acting immorally and illegally. His affective state is irrelevant. Now consider E2. The Nazi who spits in the rabbi's mouth violates all three conditions. I call such acts quintessentially evil. The deliberate attempt to dehumanise the rabbi and gratuitously inflict a great harm are obvious. What is more, with respect to inverting the moral landscape, the Nazi is engaged in a project which demands the humiliation and eventual destruction of the Jewish people. The humiliation inflicted has an artistic consciousness to it, an inventive element that seeks to prolong and intensify the humiliation and abuse. Whether the Nazi felt pleasure in doing this is again beside the point when deciding if this is an evil act. It may be relevant in deciding if the Nazi is morally worse than other Nazis, but that is a different question.

Steiner's affective concern does home in on some strong intuitions we have about how to assess other peoples' characters. Individuals who derive inappropriate pleasure from the pain and distress of others, whether they were the cause or not, are thought of as callous at best. Feeling joy and happiness over another creature's pain and distress, all things being equal, is not a laudable character trait. The German term *schadenfreude*, the malicious joy at another person's misfortune, identifies a state of mind which we despise in ourselves and others. We think it cruel towards others and demeaning of ourselves to indulge in *schadenfreude*. However, a process of reflective equilibrium indicates that it is not the criterion for discovering evil acts but rather the description of an unpleasant, though in some circumstances perhaps evil, character.

5. CONCLUDING REMARKS

Steiner's PP conception of evil is seriously flawed. The difficulties arise owing to its foundationalist methodology. Its narrow focus on logic and formal considerations operating on minimal normative input proves to be an impediment to finding moral principles that resonate with our strong and cherished intuitive judgments about moral issues. What is more, our moral reality is complex, difficult, and often untidy and consequently sits uncomfortably with narrowly focused reductionistic principles that attempt to compress moral experiences into a linear explanation. My NRD approach with its three diverse conditions deliberately seeks to accommodate moral complexity, and although it lacks the neatness of the PP account it does fare far better when tested against our intuitions.

Of course, accommodating our intuitions and common sense perceptions of evil acts is only one virtue of a useful conception of evil (rigour, clarity, coherence, logicality are others), but it is a crucial one. Steiner looks for logical incoherence in order to sift out rival theories but this is only a necessary condition for deciding between options. It is possible for more than one option to pass this test, and then whether the principles resonate with our intuitions becomes hugely significant in deciding which account is more attractive and plausible. Principles that result in vastly counter-intuitive inclusions or exclusions within moral theory point to a deep problem that renders the account ultimately unstable and unhelpful.

I have been unrelenting in my criticism of Steiner's PP position on evil but I have been so while admiring his carefully argued and imaginative account. My disagreements with his views stem from a deep disagreement about the right way to obtain knowledge in axiological studies. However, there can be no doubt that—agree with Steiner or not—his PP account serves to clarify, inform, and invigorate this recently revived debate concerning the nature of a secular conception of evil.[38]

NOTES

1. Luke Russell calls Steiner's account the 'Sadist Account' of evil. See Russell 2007, 669–71.
2. Russell refers to my account as the 'Disjunctive Account' and I have partly adopted this label. See Russell 2007, 664–69.
3. Measured by the crude yardstick of the number of deaths and injuries, the attacks of 9/11 were not, by a large margin, the worst disaster to strike the USA, let alone the world. Many more people, for example, are killed and injured in road accidents in the United States every year. In 2004 there were 42,636 road deaths in the USA. See http://www.driveandstayalive.com/info%20section/statistics/stats-usa.htm (Accessed 29/06/08).
4. Although the term 'evil' was evoked by persons across the political spectrum, the most well known case is President George W. Bush's reference in his State of the Nation to those countries which formed an 'axis of evil' in their support and encouragement of terrorism. See http://www.whitehouse.gov/news/releases/2002/01/20020129-11.html (Accessed 24/06/08).
5. See http://www.guardian.co.uk/world/beslan (Accessed 29/06/08).
6. And by 'worse', here, I mean that such actions differ only in the intensity of wrongness, that is, by some *quantitative* measure.
7. See Card 2002, 28. Clendinnen (1999) strongly rejects the term 'evil,' as she argues that it does not have the requisite explanatory power for understanding why people act as they do. What is more, she insists that references to evil imply a sinister and metaphysical realm beyond human understand-

ing inhabited by monsters. Using the term 'evil' merely serves to exclude and polarise rather than enable understanding (86–7). I disagree. A secular account of evil offers an understanding of human action within moral discourse without resorting to mysterious religious or metaphysical entities. It seeks to provide the necessary and sufficient conditions for evil actions and capture an aspect of our normative sensibilities that is either ignored or denied by the standard moral theories. See Cole 2007, chapters 4 and 6 for a similar view to Clendinnen's.

8. In fact, one of the problems facing a philosophical attempt to precisely define a secular account of evil is that the term 'evil' is so often used without discrimination to refer to almost any unpleasant or bad event or set of actions. It is sometimes used as a mere intensifier, or for dramatic effect or because the issue is an emotional one. One of the central tasks of philosophical analysis is to bring some clarity and precision to this notion.
9. For example see Arendt 1963, McGinn 1997, Morton 2004, Garrard 1998, Neiman 2002 and others.
10. There is, of course, the issue of whether these natural phenomena are caused in part by human activities (consider the possible effects of global warming) or, if not, whether irresponsible humans cause the suffering and death to be very much worse by building on flood plains or allowing poorly constructed buildings in earthquake areas.
11. Children, the insane, the senile, the mentally impaired are categories of person who may not have the requisite autonomy and intellectual capacity required for moral responsibility. When such persons do terrible things their actions are better described as tragic rather than immoral, let alone evil.
12. There will also be controversy about where the boundaries for moral responsibility should be drawn. Do we, for example, think of children over the age of 10 as morally responsible for their actions? While a reasonable boundary will adequately distinguish between those who are responsible and those who are not, there will always be grey areas. Hence there is the need to be flexible when applying a boundary rule.
13. An excellent example of this is Haybron 2002. Haybron suggests that we 'understand the evil action in terms of its relation to the evil character: e.g., perhaps, an action is evil if it manifests profoundly deadened or perverted moral sensibilities—the sensibilities characteristic of an evil person' (Haybron 2002, 280).
14. Persons with evil characters or dispositions need not act evilly all the time.
15. In fact this more permissive account is essential for accommodating some very important intuitive cases of evil which would not be captured by D1. I return to this in my criticisms of Steiner's account.
16. Steiner 2002, 184–85.
17. Steiner does point out that although he assumes these four properties are foundational to a secular conception of evil, this does not amount to a 'monopoly licence from ordinary usage'. Nevertheless he does insist that it is 'indisputable that there is such a demand' in ordinary usage (Steiner 2002, 184–85).
18. Steiner does rightly point out that Kant, Bentham, and others rejected the notion of supererogatory acts in part because they are beyond duty and hence not obligatory (Steiner 2002, 186–87). No one can be morally blamed for not acting in a supererogatory manner, since such actions are not 'deontically obligatory'. However, evil actions are deontically impermissible just as any morally wrongful act would be.
19. Steiner is in good company using this methodological approach. Many of the great philosophers, such as Descartes and Kant, have used this method

to derive powerful substantive conclusions from minimal frugal formal premises. Kant's attempt to derive the fundamental principle of morality in the *Groundwork* begins with what he takes to be the unassailable assumption that the only thing that is good without qualification is a 'good will'. Many of Kant's moral claims are in the end deeply counter-intuitive since he excludes the consequences of actions as having moral significance. As he states: 'Every man has not only a right, but the strictest duty to truthfulness in statements which he cannot avoid, whether they do harm to himself or others. He himself, properly speaking, does not *do* harm to him who suffers thereby; but this harm is *caused* by accident. For the man is not free to choose, since (if he must speak at all) veracity is an unconditional duty'. See Kant 1898, 364.

20. Steiner 2002, 193 n. 14.
21. By 'moral reality' I mean the complex set of (sometimes conflicting and/or incompossible) duties, obligations, principles and intuitions that characterise how we understand our normative milieu. It involves much more than the issue of establishing a decision procedure for each and every conceivable moral situation. Rather, the task of moral theory also should be to seek to characterise normative situations we encounter so that they resonate with our considered moral convictions. I return to this when I discuss the reflective equilibrium methodology that underlies my NRD theory of evil.
22. Arendt's work on the banality of evil (Arendt 1963) picks up on an aspect of what I am alluding to here albeit from a different perspective and concern. Eichmann's bureaucratic activities were evil given the Nazi worldview in which he operated. Arendt's focus is on the character of Eichmann, his bureaucratic activities and, above all, lack of a personal morality which should have rejected the genocidal policies of his Nazi masters. Although Eichmann never personally killed anyone, his activities sent hundreds of thousands of people to their deaths. Eichmann argued that he was simply following orders with no malicious intent or desire to injure anyone. Unspeakably evil actions, it seems, can arise from the ordinariness of everyday activities given the right context and agent's personal morality or lack of it.
23. Russell (2007, 669–70) gives a similar criticism of Steiner's account of evil.
24. I am thinking here of the example used by Augustine at the close of book 2 of the *Confessions*. Augustine recounts an incident from his youth where he stole pears from a neighbour's tree. His actions were not motivated by hunger, need, or necessity and he so acted simply for the pleasure of doing wrong. As he puts it: 'I was willing to steal, and steal I did . . . I had no wish to enjoy the things I coveted by stealing, but only to enjoy the theft itself and the sin. . . The evil in me was foul, but I loved it. I loved my own perdition and my own faults, not the things for which I committed wrong, but the wrong itself' (St Augustine 1961, 47). Augustine believed that this form of wickedness is the worst kind since it is evil for evil's sake. I use the example ironically, to show that such wrongdoing is clearly not evil in a secular sense.
25. I take this example from Gaita 1991, 1.
26. Should we expect that the Nazis who carried out acts like E2 always derived some sort of perverse pleasure from them? If this were indeed the case then it would seem to support Steiner's claim that evil acts are those which give its doer pleasure. Whether the Nazis did indeed always feel pleasure in committing acts of this sort is an empirical question. It is not conceptually necessary that they had to feel pleasure or a lack of affect of any kind. However, this is not relevant to my argument since, as I make clear later in the paper, it is not

the *feelings* of the agent that make an action evil. Feeling pleasure indicates something about the person's character rather than what makes an action an evil one. I am grateful to Ian Carter for raising this point with me.

27. See Steiner 2002, 193 n. 13.
28. There is the added concern that it is not clear how or when the increase in the wrongness of an action tips over into a qualitative difference. Would stealing £1,000 exceed the threshold? Would stealing from the poor, even if it is a few pounds, be sufficiently wrong that the PP account applies? Would defrauding a leading bank of a large sum, say one million pounds, fail to cross the threshold since it is unlikely to have a serious impact on the viability or day-to-day activities of that institution?
29. This position gets very close to the 'Silencing Conception of Evil' developed by Eve Garrard. Garrard argues that an evil act is one in which the agent is completely unreceptive to the existence of reasons of the most important and weighty kind against his/her so acting. This is not merely a matter of allowing the important reasons prohibiting such actions to be overridden, but rather that the agent is profoundly unaware and cannot be made to see that there are these very important reasons which stand as a block to so acting. In short, an evil act is one performed by an agent with a profound cognitive defect. See Garrard 1998.
30. Steiner 2002,190.
31. Steiner 1995, 131.
32. It is interesting to note that some theorists insist that evil actions are almost wholly explained by the social context in which they occur. Zimbardo offers a psychologically based definition of evil and then focuses on what he calls the 'outer determinants' of human behaviour. His focus is heavily weighed towards social factors that facilitate evil actions and in the process underplays individual choice. Like Steiner's, this approach offers insights but fails to reveal the nature of evil in its full complexity (Zimbardo 2007, ch. 1).
33. I take these insights from Rosenbaum 2002.
34. Rosenbaum refers to the hideous irony of the words 'Arbeit macht frei' at the entrance to Auschwitz concentration camp. Another terrible example is the manner in which the Nazis used music in the death camps. As Fackler (2007) points out: 'It was by no means unusual for singing to provide the macabre background music for punishments, which were stage-managed as a deterrent, or even as a means of sadistic humiliation and torture. Joseph Drexel in the Mauthausen concentration camp, for instance, was forced to give a rendering of the church hymn "O Haupt voll Blut und Wunden" ("Jesus' blood and wounds") while being flogged to the point of unconsciousness. Punishment beatings over the notorious flogging horse (the "Bock") were performed accompanied by singing, and the same is true of executions'. URL http://www.music.ucsb.edu/projects/musicandpolitics/archive/2007-1/fackler.html
35. Space prevents me from discussing this method at length. For an extensive account of the reflective equilibrium method see Rawls 1971, Nielsen 1994, Scanlon 2002, and Daniels 1979. For a strong criticism of this approach see Brandt 1990 and Hare 1973.
36. For an extended discussion and derivation of these principles see de Wijze (2002, 217–30).
37. By 'Great Harms' I mean great physical suffering, torture, illness, starvation, death, destruction of home, and the misery of unrelenting terror and harassment.
38. I am indebted to Jeremy Barris, Ian Carter, and Eve Garrard for comments on an earlier draft of this paper.

BIBLIOGRAPHY

Arendt, Hannah. 1963. *Eichmann in Jerusalem: A Report on the Banality of Evil*. London: Faber.

Brandt, Richard. 1990. 'The Science of Man and Wide Reflective Equilibrium'. 100 *Ethics* 259–78.

Card, Claudia. 2002. *The Atrocity Paradigm*. Oxford: Oxford University Press.

Clendinnen, Inga. 1999. *Reading the Holocaust*. New York: Cambridge University Press.

Cole, Philip. 2007. *The Myth of Evil*. Edinburgh: Edinburgh University Press.

Daniels, Norman. 1979. 'Wide Reflective Equilibrium and Theory Acceptance in Ethics'. 76 *Journal of Philosophy* 256–82.

de Wijze, Stephen. 2002. 'Defining Evil: Insights from the Problem of "Dirty Hands"'. 85 *The Monist* 210–38.

Fackler, Guido. 2007. 'Music in Concentration Camps 1933–1945'. In *Music Politics* URL http://www.music.ucsb.edu/projects/musicandpolitics/archive/2007-1/fackler.html (Accessed 17/07/08).

Gaita, Raimond. 1991. *Good and Evil: An Absolute Conception*. London: Macmillan.

Garrard, Eve. 2002. 'Evil as an Explanatory Concept'. 85 *The Monist* 320–36.

Garrard, Eve. 1998. 'The Nature of Evil'. 1 *Philosophical Explorations* 43–60.

Haybron, Daniel. 2002. 'Moral Monsters and Moral Saints'. 82 *The Monist* 260–84.

Hare, R.M. 1973. 'Rawls' Theory of Justice'. 23 *Philosophical Quarterly* 241–51.

Kant, Immanuel. 1898. *Critique of Practical Reason and other Works*. Trans. Thomas Kingsmill Abbott. London: Longmans, Green and Co.

McGinn, Colin. 1997. *Ethics, Evil, and Fiction*. Clarendon Press: Oxford.

Morton, Adam. 2004. *On Evil*. New York: Routledge.

Neiman, Susan. 2002. *Evil in Modern Thought: An Alternative History of Philosophy*. Princeton: Princeton University Press.

Nielsen, Kai. 1994. 'Philosophy as Wide Reflective Equilibrium'. 43 *Iyyun* 3–42.

Rawls, John. 1971. *A Theory of Justice*. Cambridge, MA: Harvard University Press.

Rosenbaum, Ron. 2002. 'Degrees of Evil: Some Thoughts on Hitler, bin Laden, and the Hierarchy of Wickedness'. In *The Atlantic Monthly* (February) URL http://www.theatlantic.com/issues/2002/02/rosenbaum.htm (Accessed 15/07/08).

Russell, Luke. 2007. 'Is Evil Action Qualitatively Distinct from Ordinary Wrongdoing?'. 85 *Australasian Journal of Philosophy* 659–77.

Russell, Luke. 2006. 'Evil-Revivalism versus Evil-Skepticism'. 40 *Journal of Value Inquiry* 89–105.

Saint Augustine. 1961. *Confessions*. Trans. R. S. Pine-Coffin. Hannondsworth: Penguin.

Scanlon, T.M. 2002. 'Rawls on Justification'. In S. Freeman (ed.), *The Cambridge Companion to Rawls*. Cambridge: Cambridge University Press.

Steiner, Hillel. 2002. 'Calibrating Evil'. 85 *The Monist* 183–93.

Steiner, Hillel. 1994. *An Essay on Rights*. Oxford: Blackwell.

Steiner, Hillel. 1995. 'Persons of Lesser Value: Moral Argument and the "Final Solution"'. 12 *Journal of Applied Philosophy* 129–41.

Zimbardo, Philip. 2007. *The Lucifer Effect: How Good People Turn Evil*. London: Rider Books.

PART V

REPLY BY HILLEL STEINER

14 Responses

Hillel Steiner

"Ouch!!—and thank you", as a masochist might exclaim, confronted with a set of essays that so profusely supply not only generous comments but also, and especially, profound challenges. That I'm honoured and gratified at the efforts of the contributors goes without saying. Equally unnecessary is to say that I'm hard put to meet all those well considered arguments—and not due merely to the usual limitations of time and space. My failure to respond to some of them here should be taken as presumptive evidence that I currently lack a decent rejoinder. For many of the issues they so tellingly raise are ones that require considerable further reflection on my part: reflection which, I very much hope, will bear fruit in the preparation of the revised edition of *An Essay on Rights*.[1]

Accordingly, the responses that follow address only an embarrassingly narrow selection of those challenges to a range of views I've advanced or relied upon in some of my writings. As the following exchange perhaps suggests, I can't pretend that even this thereby restricted set of rejoinders is dispositive of the particular challenges it does address.

> *Student*: "But surely, Rabbi, *someone* gets to have the last word in an argument!"
>
> *Rabbi*: "Never".

Indeed, I'm painfully aware that some of the arguments addressed here are simply the latest instalments of debates in which their proponents and I have been engaged for many years. That said, it does seem to me that several of these are erroneous and that those errors sometimes rest upon assumptions which play no part in the structure of the 'project' I've pursued.

As Ian Carter's excellent introduction to this volume indicates, that project has been to derive a reasonably determinate conception of the demands of distributive justice—its 'anatomy'—from the purely formal or conceptual features of rights themselves and from the necessary conditions of such rights being mutually consistent or, to borrow a term from Leibniz, *com-*

possible.[2] This way of deriving those demands seemed to be recommended by the fact that much of the perennial contestation surrounding rival conceptions of justice has consisted in duelling with relatively free-standing moral intuitions. And the problem with such duelling is that the intuitions thereby deployed tend to be too uncomplex for what they're intended to accomplish:

> In particular, they don't respond well to problems where what is wanted is *not* some missing piece from a best world jigsaw puzzle, but rather some way of distinguishing the pieces of second-best worlds from those of third-best ones. Demarcating this elusive boundary is quintessentially a task of justice theories (Steiner 1994, 3).

Gnomic as this out-of-context bit of self-quotation may appear to be, what it gestures at are my beliefs (a) that justice makes sense only if construed as one amongst a plurality of mutually irreducible basic values or principles, (b) that the aforesaid intuition deployments often fail to take account of both that fact and, hence, the fact that those intuitions are themselves more readily associated with other members of that plurality, (c) that just rights are devices for resolving certain kinds of interpersonal conflict which are generated by conflicts between those other values or principles, and (d) that what principles of justice primarily distribute are rights to personal freedom.

Deriving justice from rights has also seemed warranted by a number of conceptual and empirical claims which enjoy considerable support from our ordinary pre-theoretical thinking about justice. Among these claims are:

(1) that moral rights are grounded in—are the elementary particles of—principles of justice;
(2) that principles of justice constitute the primary standard on which legal systems are morally assessed;
(3) that a legal system simply is that set of rules that enforceably dominate any other rules prevalent in a group of persons and that thereby determine who is free to do what;
(4) that, therefore, the demands of justice—of moral rights—are presumed to enjoy moral priority over those of any other value or principle.

So uncontested did at least the first three of these claims seem to me to be—as they still do—that they've figured as largely undefended assumptions in my work and, indeed, are only rarely articulated there. What that work does *not* assume, however, is that morality *must* be pluralistic or that principles of justice *should* constitute the primary standard on which legal systems are morally assessed. Nor does it offer reasons as to why legal systems—or individuals—should *be* just. So I do not join Rawls in his famous assertion that

> Justice is the first virtue of social institutions, as truth is of systems of thought (Rawls 1971, 3).

Rather, the spirit of the enterprise has been to say 'Look, *if* you ought to be just, here is what you must (not) do'. Indeed, I do not think there can be any (non-trivial, non-circular) reasons to be just. For that, after all, is what is standardly implied in describing any value or principle as irreducible or basic.

Obviously, then, a great deal of forensic weight has been placed on the nature of rights themselves. And here I must confess that it was not until the project had proceeded for some years that I came fully to appreciate that the general conception of rights with which I was working was both underarticulated and controversial:[3] it was a rudimentary version of the Will Theory, famously refined and expounded in its modern form by H.L.A. Hart, who clearly distinguished it from its traditional rival, the Interest Theory of rights. Accordingly, a major focus of my attention became the exploration of the Will Theory and the array of objections that have been levelled against it. However, since my development and defence of that theory (Steiner 1994, 59–73; 1998), are not challenged in any of the foregoing essays, I'll not rehearse them here. Nevertheless, I hope to show that several of the challenges that have been raised significantly rely upon premisses which are at odds with central tenets of the Will Theory.

A case in point is Matthew Kramer's trenchant attack on the Permissibility Theorem, as part of the foundation on which I've built my account of rights-compossibility. The Permissibility Theorem—that all obligatory acts are permissible ones—has widely been thought to be a logically necessary truth about any coherent set of normative statements.[4] Having this status, that theorem rules out the possibility of such a set entailing conflicting or jointly unperformable duties.[5] More recently, however, the balance of opinion among deontic logicians seems to have shifted against according this status to the Permissibility Theorem,[6] and for reasons which are well exemplified in Kramer's argument. Coherent sets of normative statements —or what I more simply call *codes*—can, without contradiction, generate duty-conflicts.

Three preliminary things, I think, need to be said in response to this. First, Kramer is quite correct in reporting that my recorded account of rights-compossibility invokes the Permissibility Theorem as part of its foundation.[7] Second: Does this matter? For it's plain that duty-conflicts are a Bad Thing and that leaving conceptual space for their occurrence is best avoided in the construction of any theory of duties. And if they do happen, it's obviously better if all but one of the conflicting duties involved can be shown, on closer analysis, not to be valid after all. But, more than that, it seems reasonable to suppose that most persons would regard codes that generate duty-conflicts as being, in some clear sense, deficient.[8] Contradictions, it's generally agreed, are fatal for any set of propositions. But duty-conflicts are bad enough. So why should we care whether the latter also entail the former? Third, however, subsequent reflection has led me to believe that my reliance on the Permissibility Theorem was, after all, unnecessary. For even if duty-conflicts in general do not—*pace* that theorem—signify the presence of contradictions, such conflicts between *correlative* duties (duties entailing rights) do. Why?

Consider the core example deployed in Kramer's argument here:

> Suppose that Jeremy has formed a contract with Susan whereby he undertakes to be present at a certain location *L* on a certain day during a certain stretch of time. Suppose further that he subsequently forms—or has previously formed—a contract with Melanie whereby he undertakes not to be present at *L* on the specified day during the specified stretch of time.

Evidently, Jeremy's (ostensibly) two contractual duties are not jointly performable: they conflict. Finding this a "patently possible state of affairs" and thereby rejecting the necessary truth of the Permissibility Theorem, Kramer claims that any resolution of this conflict is, ineluctably, determined by reference not to logical or conceptual considerations but rather to some substantive norm, such as a purely conventional first-contract-priority rule.

My rejoinder to this argument is, as suggested previously, that it rests implicitly on a rejection of the Will Theory of rights. The central tenet of that theory is that any person vested with a claim-right is also vested with the Hohfeldian powers of control over its correlative duty: that is, the right-holder is that person who has the authority to decide whether omission of the duty-act is permissible or impermissible and, if impermissible, whether its occurrence warrants redress. In the case of a right created by contract, one of the contracting parties (the duty-holder) has transferred to the other (the right-holder) the authority to make that decision. And that being so, it becomes easier to see why Kramer's duty-conflict example does indeed signify the presence of a contradiction. For if we suppose that Jeremy's contract with Susan vests her with a claim-right and thereby confers upon her the powers to decide whether Jeremy's absence from *L* at the appointed time is permissible or impermissible, we cannot *without contradiction* locate that same authority in Melanie (and *vice versa*). Either it is, or it is not, the case that these powers are held by Susan. Whereas Kramer's argument implies that both of these alternatives are true.

In *An Essay on Rights*, I observed that a key principle of an historical entitlement conception of justice, far from being an independent prescriptive rule, is merely a reflection of the conceptual properties which the Will Theory attributes to rights (Steiner 1994, 226). Jerry Cohen's challenge to that conception of justice seems to me to be equally reliant upon a rejection of the Will Theory. In his essay here, Cohen writes that

> "Whatever arises" says Robert Nozick, "from a just situation by just steps is itself just" (Nozick 1974, 151). Hence, so he argues, if we as-

> sume that the initial distribution in his famous Wilt Chamberlain story is just, then, unless, implausibly, we find some injustice within or surrounding the fans' decisions to pay to watch Wilt play, we must deem the resulting distribution to be just.

Against Nozick, Cohen maintains that the justification for that antecedent distribution cannot serve as the justification for the quite different subsequent distribution that may result from the various dispositive choices people severally make with regard to their entitlements under that antecedent distribution. That is, Cohen suggests that, if that subsequent distribution is different from its antecedent, it violates that antecedent's justificatory principle. Hence, its own justificatory principle (if it has one) must be different from that of its antecedent. That subsequent distribution might, for instance, be justified by a principle invoking freedom, but what cannot justify it is whatever principle—in this case, justice—mandated the antecedent distribution.

This argument, I believe, overlooks the Hohfeldian powers which the Will Theory attaches to rights. For the entitlements disposed of by Chamberlain's fans, in the movement from the antecedent distribution to its subsequent counterpart, simply are ownerships, and ownerships are composite entities. More precisely, they vest their holders with bundles of several Hohfeldian elements: a variety of claim-rights and immunities and their ancillary powers, which typically include powers concerning the transfer of those bundles to other persons, such as Chamberlain.

Of course, it's conceivable that (*contra* Nozick's example) these fans' antecedent bundles don't each include *all* the possible elements of ownership: that, for instance, the fans might not be the persons vested with the particular claim-rights and immunities to which those transfer powers are attached; or that, even if they are so vested, these transfer powers are restricted in various ways. But, if that's the case, it's necessary to ask where—in which other persons—those antecedent entitlements (or the Hohfeldian correlates of those restrictions) are vested. In effect, what such a proposal implies is that those bundles might be *jointly owned* by the fans and other persons. The point, however, is that nothing in the historical entitlement conception, *per se*, precludes such joint ownership.[9] Hence the plausibility of that conception's central contention: that, since the movement from antecedent distribution to subsequent one consists in nothing other than respective persons' exercises of their antecedent transfer powers, the very same principle that justifies that antecedent distribution of those transfer powers licenses their exercise.[10] To contend that this principle does not justify the distributional result of their exercise is to imply what is *ex hypothesi* false: namely, that those persons—Chamberlain fans or others—lacked the antecedent transfer powers which it does justify. Either that principle empowered them to make those transfers or it did not.

Within the barrage of powerful arguments advanced by Eric Mack's essay, at least one seems to me, again, to rest upon an incomplete understanding of the Will Theory. Mack claims to find a shift in my interpretation of the equal natural resources entitlement which my account of justice vests in each self-owner. This shift is characterised as one from a right constituted by a property rule to one constituted by a liability rule. Against resource appropriators and their successors, each person's right to be left an equal share of such raw resources, is said to be transformed into (merely) a redress claim to an equal share of the *value* of such resources. Mack's explanation of why this is problematic for my account runs as follows:

> These difficulties point to a deeper yet problem for Steiner. The shift to an understanding of rights as claims protected by liability rules conflicts with Steiner's basic commitment to the Choice [or Will] Theory of rights.[11] The core element in the Choice Theory is the idea that to have a right is to be in position to determine by one's choice how another may or may not act. 'According to the Choice Theory, a right exists when the necessary and sufficient condition, of imposing or relaxing the [moral or legal] constraint on some person's conduct, is another person's choice to that effect' (Steiner 1994, 57–8). One has a right with respect to some extra-personal material if and only if, by one's choice, one can maintain another party's duty not to deprive one of that material and one can release that other party from this duty. If the Choice Theory is correct, no party P may permissibly deprive an agent A of extra-personal material M to which A has a right unless A has chosen to release P from his duty not to deprive A of M. However, according to Steiner's liability rule conception of the original right to raw material, agent A may be deprived of M to which A has a right without A having chosen to release depriving party P from his duty not to take M from A . . . If Steiner holds to . . . the liability rule understanding of the original right to raw material, he must abandon the Choice Theory. If Steiner holds on to the Choice Theory, he must reject any liability rule construal of the original right to raw material.

Mack is correct in finding the aforesaid shift. But, in judging it to be inconsistent with the Will Theory, he neglects not only the classic legal maxim, *ubi jus ibi remedium*—no right without a remedy—but also its integral role in that theory, as well as its indispensability for any libertarian conception of justice.

The Will Theory does indeed vest A with the property rule choice of whether to prohibit or allow P to deprive A of A's M. But it's only ambiguously true that, according to my liability rule, "A *may* be deprived of his M without A having chosen to release depriving party P from his duty not to take M from A" (my emphasis). The aforesaid ambiguity is due simply to the equivocality of the English word 'may', which sometimes expresses possibility (as in 'It may rain') and other times expresses permission (as in

'You may leave the room'). The 'may' that pertains to liability in the Will Theory is one expressing possibility—not permission, as Mack appears to suggest. For that theory, in addition to vesting A with the choice of whether to prohibit or allow P to deprive A of A's M, also vests A with a further choice: namely, the liability rule choice of whether to prohibit or allow P to refrain from redressing A *in the event of* P's non-compliance with A's property rule choice. That is, the Will Theory entails *both* a property rule *and* a liability rule. It is not the case that a right-holder, having had his right violated, is given no further recourse by the Will Theory and is condemned by it simply to brood over his loss.[12] Indeed, the triad of principles constituting Nozick's historical entitlement conception of justice includes just such a liability rule, which he calls the 'principle of rectification'.

Nor can such a conception easily afford to dispense with the application of a liability rule when it comes to the just natural resource rights vested in each self-owner. For here we are confronted with the possibility—in our world, the actuality—of these self-owners being non-contemporaries: of their being members of different successive generations. And this possibility entails the further possibility—in our world, the actuality—of some historically later persons, As, arriving only after all natural resources have already been appropriated by Ps and have been transformed by Ps' self-owned labour. In the absence of the latter's waiver, such As would thereby owe what amounts to a *necessarily unperformable* duty of non-trespass to those Ps who are, accordingly, empowered to expel them—with all that this unfavourably implies for the compossibility of As' self-ownership rights with those of Ps. It is this possibility that (alone) motivates what Mack refers to as the 'shift' from a property to a liability rule with regard to As' natural resource rights. That shift, however, is one only in the conception of how those rights can be sustained against Ps in circumstances where simple reversal of Ps' over-appropriation is impossible. Because that shift still vests As with a choice—namely, the choice of whether to prohibit or allow Ps to refrain from redressing As—there is good reason to see those rights as Will Theory rights.

Not unrelatedly, Cécile Fabre's essay raises the issue of whether rights can be held against present persons by subsequent ones. Arguing that the Interest Theory of rights is far less friendly to this possibility than is commonly supposed, she also, correctly in my view, challenges Hart's attempt to block the claim that the Will Theory denies rights to those persons who are not yet agents. That is, although the Will Theory in no way undercuts the possibility of present persons having weighty moral duties to care for such non-agents, Hart's effort to construe these duties as correlative to Will Theory rights in them fails. In most of my work, I've tended to agree with Fabre on this implication of the Will Theory.[13] But more recently, and granting the weakness of Hart's resistance to it, I've been led to wonder whether that implication is entirely valid. Why?

Here, we need to distinguish, as Fabre does, between (a) those not-yet-agent persons, G_6s, who will never have any element of temporal concurrence with present agents, G_1s, from (b) those not-yet-agent persons, G_2s, whose existence will temporally overlap with that of G_1s—perhaps because those G_2s are the children or grandchildren of those G_1s. Now, I entirely agree with Fabre that rights in G_6s against G_1s cannot be Will Theory rights. Members of far future generations necessarily cannot exercise the powers, which the Will Theory vests in right holders, over the duties of members of present generations to ϕ in the present, which we'll call t_1. And, as she argues, it makes no sense to attribute powers to persons who necessarily—and not merely contingently—cannot exercise them.

However, when it comes to G_2s, the case is significantly different. For, although they too cannot prohibit or allow G_1s' omission of ϕ at t_1, there is no reason why they cannot—during their later shared period of temporal concurrence, t_2 —prohibit or allow G_1s to refrain from redressing G_2s for that omission. That is, as with the late arriving As in the preceding discussion of Mack's essay, it is possible to assign a liability rule choice to G_2s, even if they cannot be assigned a property rule choice. What I take this to imply, and what seems to be corroborated by some recent litigation, is that persons who suffer *enduring* injury at the hands of their abusive elders during their minority can be said, upon their attainment of agency, to have rights that empower them to sue those perpetrators for redress. And as in the Mack discussion, because those rights thereby vest G_2s with a choice—namely, the choice of whether to prohibit or allow G_1s to refrain from redressing G_2s—I'm inclined to see them as being Will Theory rights.

One of Mike Otsuka's challenges—his rebuttal of my claim that my left-libertarianism converges on luck egalitarianism—also seems to me to rest upon the neglect of an important feature of the Will Theory. Luck egalitarian theories aim coherently to combine egalitarian demands with responsibility-sensitivity, in determining the profiles of just distributions. Accordingly, a distribution is just, they claim, if what its rights equalise is not advantage or wellbeing *per se*, but rather *opportunities* for securing wellbeing or advantage: that is, wellbeing inequalities are permitted only insofar as they emerge from the choices of individuals whose opportunity-sets have been equalised. And the problem with my left-libertarianism is that its interpretation of the Lockean Proviso, as equalising persons' rights to only natural resource value (and the value of bequests), allows the opportunity-disequalising impact of *inter vivos* gifts to occur.

> On Steiner's view, there is no claim for redress of such inequality . . . He maintains that a ban on gift-giving would violate the full property rights in equally valuable shares of the world that his version of the proviso justifies, where shares of impersonal resources are equal insofar as they are of equal economic value at the outset of our adult lives. By con-

> trast, I maintain that such a ban is necessary to ensure that the shares of impersonal resources we have appropriated are in fact egalitarian shares, as mandated by my version of the proviso according to which such shares are equal insofar as they secure our equal opportunity for advantage . . . Suppose a three-person world consisting of Alpha, Beta, and Gamma, whose capacities, including their productive talents, are equal, and who derive equal welfare per unit of resource consumed. Suppose, moreover, that they confront an unowned expanse of land of uniform quality throughout and that nobody is subject to brute luck arising from natural forces. On Steiner's version of the proviso, justice is secured if each appropriates full ownership of a plot consisting of one-third of the land that is available. These plots are of equal economic value, as can be shown by the fact that such a distribution meets Dworkin's envy-test (Dworkin 1981, § I): nobody prefers anyone else's holdings to his own. On my version of the proviso, such full ownership would violate the proviso. I maintain that shares are relevantly equal if and only if they ensure that each has the same opportunity as anybody else to secure greater advantage. Full ownership will not ensure this precisely because it permits asymmetrical transfers (that is, gifts rather than exchanges) from which not everyone has the same opportunity to benefit. Let us suppose, for example, that Beta and Gamma are siblings, and that Beta is so devoted to Gamma that he chooses to transfer a large share of his plot of land to him in the form of a gift. (Gamma does not reciprocate in kind.) Beta would, however, never dream of transferring land to Alpha in the form of a gift. Full ownership therefore ensures that shares are not relevantly equal, since such ownership fails to ensure that each has the same opportunity as anybody else to secure greater advantage. If, however, we maintain that each is entitled to acquire an equally large plot of land in this scenario, where the plots do not carry with them the right to transfer them as gifts (as opposed to exchanging them on an open market where the highest bidder always wins), then we will have secured a division of the world that ensures equality of opportunity for advantage.

Is Otsuka correct in believing that a ban on Beta's gifting Gamma is required by a luck egalitarian theory that ensures equality of opportunity?

Let's suppose that the total expanse of land involved is nine acres, and that what Beta donates are two of his Steiner-allotted three acres to Gamma, resulting in a three-one-five division of the nine acres. Clearly, on both Otsuka's opportunity-egalitarianism and my own resource-egalitarianism, Beta has no valid complaint against this inequality, since the inferiority of his share was chosen by him: responsibility-sensitive theories permit no such complaint. Does Alpha have such a complaint? Evidently she would have, if there was any reason to believe that Gamma's now having five acres has diminished her—Alpha's—opportunities. But there's no such reason. For all those additional opportunities, which have now been made accessible to Gamma, are entirely identical with the opportunities now foreclosed to Beta by his own hand, leaving Alpha's opportunity-set entirely unchanged. Indeed, the three-three-three distribution mandated by a ban on gifts must be presumed to be *Pareto-inferior* to its unbanned counterpart, inasmuch as Beta's wellbeing is enhanced—and Alpha's wellbeing is unaffected—by the former satisfying his preference for gifting Gamma.[14]

Pareto considerations aside, however, there is a deeper conceptual problem besetting any gift-banning theory of opportunity-egalitarianism—a problem essentially similar to the one displayed in the previous discussion of Cohen's essay. Why? A ban on Beta's donation entails that he is encumbered with a Hohfeldian disability: he lacks the power to make that transfer. And the aforesaid problem is exposed when we ask who would hold the Hohfeldian immunity correlative to Beta's disability to transfer the two acres to Gamma and, more significantly, whether that immunity is *waivable*. For, if it *is* waivable, then whoever holds it can empower Beta to make that gift. And if it is not waivable, then that immunity-holder is, in turn, encumbered with a disability to which someone else holds the correlative immunity. Obviously, this disability-immunity chain could extend indefinitely but, if it is not to entail an infinite regress, it must terminate in an immunity which is waivable by whoever holds it. For although the Will Theory's central tenet—that rights (claims and immunities) are accompanied by ancillary powers—certainly doesn't exclude the possibility of such a chain, it does exclude that chain's termination in an unwaivable immunity. And the waiving of that terminal immunity can, through the relevant series of thereby successively licensed immunity-waivers, cancel all their correlative disabilities and, thus, empower Beta to make that gift. That is, since there simply cannot *be* absolutely unwaivable—inalienable—Will Theory rights (cf. Steiner 1994, 71–73; 1998, 252–255), a ban on gifts cannot be consistently sustained by any account of distributive justice employing Will Theory rights. Opportunity-sets having been distributed equally, any luck egalitarian theory must then allow persons to dispose of their assigned opportunities as they choose.

Like Otsuka's, Philippe Van Parijs's view of justice and my own converge in finding each individual to be vested with an equal and unconditional entitlement. But in Van Parijs's theory, that entitlement is at "a significantly higher level" because it is tax-funded not only by natural resource values and deceased persons' estates, but also by the value of gifts and, moreover, gifts which, highly innovatively, are interpreted to include *jobs*. Now, one rather blunt-edged response to this suggestion would be simply to invoke the foregoing argument against Otsuka's ban on gifts. If all persons are justly vested with rights to their self-owned labour, and if some are justly vested with rights to capital equipment, and if these rights respectively empower them to dispose of (only) those things on whatever terms they reach with one another, it's difficult to see not only how jobs can count as gifts (rather than exchanges) but also, and even if they can, how those terms—specifically, those wages—can be justly encumbered with a tax, as Van Parijs proposes.

One reason why this response is too blunt-edged is that, while Van Parijs shares Otsuka's view that the relevant *equalisandum* is opportunity-sets, his focus is on the implications of the empirical fact that ours is a non-Walrasian world where, like natural resources in *any* world, jobs—and hence, their concomitant opportunities—are scarce.

> The underlying intuition is captured in emaciated format by so-called efficiency-wage theories of involuntary unemployment, as developed by Joseph Stiglitz, George Akerlof, Samuel Bowles and others. Through a number of distinct mechanisms, workers' productivity can be increased as a result of their employers paying them more than what they could get away with. The outcome is that the profit-maximizing wage exceeds the market-clearing wage and hence that involuntary unemployment will persist at equilibrium—in contrast to so-called 'Walrasian' models, where productivity is unresponsive to the pay level and where the equilibrium wage is therefore, of necessity, the market-clearing wage. Even in the most perfectly competitive circumstances—full information, costless entry and exit, no wage legislation or collective bargaining, etc.—, it thus appears, people endowed with exactly the same skills can be expected to be given very unequal opportunities. What is captured in the highly purified air of these theoretical models is only the tiny and tidy tip of a massive and messy iceberg. In actual life, the opportunities we enjoy are fashioned in complex, largely unpredictable ways by the interaction of our genetic features with countless circumstances, from the smiles of our parents to the presence of older siblings, from our happening to have a congenial primary school teacher or imaginative business partner to our happening to have learned the right language or our getting a tip for the right job at the right time.

Accordingly, taxing wages looks like being at least a rough and ready way of capturing this portion of the opportunities pool, for equal distribution.

There is, of course, a serious difficulty besetting the capacity of *any* theory of distributive justice to determine the tax-and-transfer policies implied by its principles in non-ideal circumstances. The factors, listed by Van Parijs as contributing to those circumstances, appear to be so diverse as entirely to escape the reach of 'highly purified' theoretical models. And yet, we might have some reason to think that their reduction is not entirely unattainable within the parameters of the individual rights implied by such models. Reductions in imperfect information, in entry and exit costs, and in legislated wage levels, all seem to fall into that category. And perhaps the liability rule rights, broached in the previous discussion of Fabre, point in the direction of how differential childhood nurturing experiences—and even the impact of genetic inequalities (cf. Steiner 1994, 252–255; 1999)—can be similarly reduced. One thing that can be said is that, to the extent that processes like globalization bring the world closer to one where *ceteris* are *paribus*, I'm reasonably confident that Van Parijs would concur in thinking that the egalitarian fund's inclusion, of taxes on wages agreed between self-owning persons, will lack the corresponding degree of justifiability.

In regard to each person's equal rights in that fund, Serena Olsaretti raises a troubling point concerning the assignment of one of the costs associated with procreation: the *costs of added members*. Procreators produce claimants on that fund and hence, so it's alleged, are responsible for diminishing the size of every person's equal share. This is a problem because

> [T]hat position seems unstable as a result of a tension between Steiner's avowed views on just taxes—which support not holding parents responsible for all the costs of children—and his views about responsibility—which do seem to support holding parents responsible for all of them.

Since my theory purports to be a form of responsibility-sensitive egalitarianism, Olsaretti aptly challenges it with a passage from Eric Rakowski:

> [B]abies are not brought by storks whose whims are beyond our control. Specific individuals are responsible for their existence. It is therefore unjust to declare . . . that because two people decide to have a child, or through carelessness find themselves with one, *everyone* is required to share their resources with the new arrival, and to the same extent as its parents. With what right can two people force all the rest, through deliberate behavior rather than bad brute luck, to settle for less than their fair shares after resources have been divided justly?

This argument, persuasive as it appears to be, suffers from a misleading premise: namely, that it is procreators *alone* whose choices affect the number of claimants and diminish the size of everyone's fair—that is, equal—shares.

The basic thought underlying that argument seems to be as follows. In the absence of a procreative choice, the size of each person's share would be equal to d/n, where d represents the aggregate value to be distributed, and n represents the number of persons entitled to an equal share of d. A procreative choice causes that divisor to be greater than it otherwise would be, $n+1$, and thereby reduces the quotient to which others are entitled. Hence, it's suggested, a responsibility-sensitive account of distributive justice must be one which imposes that equal shares cost of a procreative choice solely on the procreators themselves. To maintain the value of each person's quotient, a procreator must have a just duty to contribute an amount, x, such that $d+x/n+1 = d/n$.

What this argument overlooks, however, is that there are *non-procreative* choices that equally reduce the value of *d/n* by causing that divisor to be greater than it otherwise would be. To put the point somewhat archly, the value of *d/n* is preserved in *d/n+(1-1)*. That is, whether the new arrival, consequent upon a procreative choice, increases the number of entitled persons, depends upon the number of new *departures*. And whether an entitled person departs is, more often than not, equally a matter of choice. For many, if not most, of the very ordinary and highly deliberate choices that we make from day to day are ones aimed at non-departure. I have in mind here such prosaic choices as those having to do with our nutrition, medical treatment and personal safety, as well as all the decisions that supply the economic and other material means for these ends. Call these choices *life-sustaining* ones. So the question is: Why shouldn't a responsibility-sensitive account of justice symmetrically impose the entire equal shares cost of *life-sustaining* choices solely on the life-sustainers themselves? For, were I *not* to make life-sustaining choices—were I to choose to depart—the value of *d/n* would not be reduced by a procreative choice on the part of others. It's my life-sustaining choices, as much as their procreative one, that are the cause of the divisor being *n+1* rather than *n*.[15]

Since virtually every entitled person is a life-sustainer, imposing that cost on them would necessarily abolish the equal shares entitlement altogether. So I take what amounts to this *reductio* to demonstrate that a responsibility-sensitive egalitarianism, though it must impose other child-care costs on procreators, cannot consistently impose on them Olsaretti's *costs of added members*.

Debates about the *reach* of distributive justice principles have, only relatively recently—and in my view, very belatedly—come to occupy a good deal of philosophical attention. Jo Wolff aims to steer a middle course between the cosmopolitan and nationalist protagonists in these debates, by abandoning what he sees as their shared assumption—that justice is uniform—in favour of the view that justice is relative to norms of co-operation. My response is simply that Wolff's view is itself, fundamentally, a form of cosmopolitanism.

Cosmopolitans start from the assumption that all individuals are morally equal.

> It has sometimes seemed that an irresistible consequence of such an assumption is that, in principle, one's duties to all other human beings have the same basis, and as a consequence all duties of justice are as extensive as duties to our fellow citizens. Consequently, whatever principles society adopts for 'domestic justice' must also apply across the globe . . . Some cosmopolitan theorists find this an acceptable, perhaps even welcome, consequence of their view (see, for example, Steiner 2005). Other political philosophers, however, find the idea of global distributive justice, modelled on their preferred theory of domestic jus-

> tice, unacceptable (Rawls 1999; Nagel 2005). There are various reasons why this might be . . . [C]ommonly the theory of global equality has been thought to be unacceptably demanding . . . One popular way of pursuing this more minimalist line is to argue that duties of justice only arise in a certain context, and that context is met in the domestic case but not in the global case. Strictly speaking, such theorists have argued, economic and social duties to those in other countries are not duties of justice. Perhaps they are duties of charity, or of humanity. This 'political' or 'nationalist' position allows the theorist to insist on stringent domestic duties of redistribution, but without also being committed to equally extensive duties of global redistribution (Rawls 1999; Nagel 2005).

Here we can leave aside the puzzling question of why nationalists are willing to acknowledge the global incidence of duties correlative to individuals' just *negative* rights (against, say, murder, assault, theft, and so forth), when they are unwilling to acknowledge the global incidence of their economic counterparts. What we should focus on instead is whether it's true that cosmopolitans are committed to the claim that "all duties of justice are as extensive as duties to our fellow citizens". For there are good reasons to believe that it's not.

There's a significant sense in which that mistaken claim, too, rests upon neglect of the Will Theory of rights. For that theory, as we've previously seen in the Cohen discussion, obliges us to distinguish between antecedent and subsequent rights, with the latter being *derivative* from the former by virtue of exercises of the powers attached to those antecedent rights. On conceptions of justice deploying Will Theory rights, each individual is vested with certain *ultimately antecedent*, or *foundational*, rights, the exercise of which serially generates further or subsequent ones for that individual and others. No other rights exist outside of this derivation framework, though we may well have weighty additional (non-correlative) moral duties, such as ones of charity and humanity.

To be sure, there is disagreement about the content of those foundational rights: Mack would say they consist solely in self-ownership; Otsuka and Van Parijs would claim that they are ones to both self-ownership and equal opportunity-sets; Steiner and (arguably) Dworkin[16] see them as ones to self-ownership and equal resources; and still other views are also conceivable. Such differences notwithstanding, however, those writers concur in the view that it's the dispositional choices that individuals make, with what is rightfully theirs, that alone determine what else is (then) justly owed to whom. And one such choice, which individuals very commonly make, is to enter into contracts with one another for the transfer of their goods and services. That is, by virtue of their *consent*, they confer rights to those things upon others. Those *derivative* rights, and their correlative duties, are as impeccably just as the rights exercised to create them.

Now, no cosmopolitan would suggest that, if I enter into such a contract with you, I must justly do the same with every other person in the world. The fact, if it is a fact, that you are my fellow citizen, has no bearing on whether the contractual duty I owe you is a just one. And if my fellow citizens and I choose to enter into more contracts with one another than we enter into with non-compatriots—to create, amongst ourselves, more of Wolff's 'norms of co-operation' than with others—the justice of that asymmetry would go entirely unchallenged by any coherent cosmopolitanism of which I'm aware. All that such cosmopolitans are concerned about—all that they need claim—is that each person's just *foundational* rights and the rights derived from them must be respected by everyone else, regardless of where in the world they are located, and that governmental policies on a vast number of issues must reflect that respect. If some cosmopolitans have claimed more than this, that is probably due to their not working with the Will Theory of rights.

Peter Vallentyne's essay presents us with some of the deeply troubling complexities that epistemic deficits pose for the application of a liability rule.

> Suppose, for example, that an agent intentionally shoots another in the leg because she reasonably but falsely believes that the other is a terrorist about to set off a bomb. She is agent-responsible for the foreseeable harm but not for violating the innocent person's rights (even though she does violate his rights) . . . Agent-responsibility for an outcome merely establishes that the outcome is suitably attributable to one's autonomous agency. I . . . suggest . . . that the duty to compensate depends in part on issues of agent-responsibility, and hence on what the agent knew or reasonably should have known. It's important to note that the appeal to agent-responsibility is for determining the extent of the *duty to compensate* . . . Strict liability, I suggest, holds if she is so agent-responsible but not if she is not agent-responsible for acting wrongly (e.g., was not acting autonomously at all or could not have known that she was acting wrongly).

From this position, Vallentyne proceeds to distinguish a range of permutations—of agent-responsibility, ancillary harms to third parties, morally justifiable rights infringements, and so forth—which are said respectively to warrant different apportionments of liabilities to make compensation.

On the standard view of strict liability, of course, such discriminations have been thought to be entirely out of place since, on that view, *causal* responsibility alone is not only necessary but also sufficient to incur full liability for all the compensation owed. And there is some reason to suppose that many libertarian writers and, indeed, perhaps Kant too, entertain just such a view.[17] Since, for them, just rights enjoy lexical priority over other values and are essentially claims to negative freedom, any encroachment on a person's rightful freedom—whether reasonably foreseeable or not—is one for which the encroacher alone should bear the full compensatory cost: no other person had any causal role in the bringing about of that encroachment. And yet, accepting that view of rights, and of strict liability as resting upon causal responsibility alone, I think that something along the general lines of Vallentyne's analysis can nevertheless be sustained.

Consider his example. Agent reasonably, but falsely, believes that in shooting X, she is preventing a terrorist from bombing (the rights of) others: Agent doesn't know that X is innocent of any such intention, and her ignorance is non-culpable. Non-culpable ignorance is, of course, an ineradicable aspect of the human condition.[18] Vallentyne appropriately describes the adverse consequences of actions informed by such ignorance as 'bad brute luck'. There are good reasons, I believe, to assimilate brute luck to the effects of what I've sometimes called the doings of Mother Nature (cf. Steiner 1997), and correspondingly good reasons so to assimilate our respective incapacities to be omniscient. If an unforeseen bad (or good) effect of an intentional action is not one which is reasonably foreseeable by the actor, nor by other human agents who may be interacting with him, it would be hard to lay the blame (or praise), for bringing that effect about, at the door of any agent other than Mother Nature. What other sort of (non-miraculous) factor could possibly be mobilised for the causal explanation of its occurrence? The fact that the specific natural causes of that effect cannot reasonably be known does not entail that there is none.

Unfortunately, compensation bills can't be sent to Mother Nature, and not merely because she lacks a postal address. But they can be sent to the *owners* of Mother Nature, just as the compensation bills for injuries caused by domestic animals are justly sent to their owners. Who are the owners of Mother Nature? Well, as the foregoing Mack and Otsuka discussions indicate, on my account of justice, they are everyone, severally and equally. That is, while only *some* persons are vested with those particular Hohfeldian elements of ownership bundles that give them control over permissible uses of their portions of nature, *every* person is vested with a claim to an equal share of the value of those portions of nature. If non-culpable ignorance is a product of nature, its (dis)value should thereby be shared equally. Accordingly, and greatly abridging the chain of reasoning that would convert this unduly metaphoric argument into a respectable one, I would suggest that liability for the compensation owed to X is justly apportioned equally amongst everyone. This conclusion seems to me to converge with Vallentyne's and thereby to align, as he wishes to do, strict liability with agent-responsibility. When Mother Nature acts, through our non-culpable ignorance—through our restricted epistemic capacities—to channel our intentional actions into the production of reasonably unforeseeable harmful consequences, it is she who is causally responsible for them and it is her owners who should be strictly liable for compensation.[19]

Ian Carter's essay raises the painful issue of my much criticised *Law of Conservation of Liberty* (LCL).

> Some of the criticisms can be discounted in the present context, because they presuppose a conception of freedom that is at odds with that of Steiner. LCL can of course be challenged quite easily if one simply adopts a different understanding of what it is to be free to do something. Other criticisms, however, are wholly internal to Steiner's pure negative conception of freedom, and appear to me to be unanswerable.

Whether they *are* unanswerable is, indeed, a question that continues considerably to exercise me. What I feel more certain of, however, is that Carter is mistaken in his estimation of the extent to which my construal of justice as equal freedom or liberty relies upon LCL. His account of that reliance goes as follows:

> Indeed, it seems to me that LCL is a necessary premise in any such derivation [of a determinate principle for the distribution of freedom] that remains true to Steiner's exhortation to avoid appeals to substantive moral values when analysing justice. This is because the Will Theory of rights depends on LCL in grounding a fundamental right to *equal* freedom. Assuming the validity of LCL, an analysis of justice need not specify whether, or in what ways, freedom contributes to human well-being. If one embraces the Will Theory of rights together with LCL, one can indeed remain wholly indifferent over whether freedom is a good thing *or a bad thing* for those who possess it. If LCL is true, freedom is here to stay, and it is here to stay in a quantity that cannot be either increased or decreased . . . The most that can be done, and therefore the most that can be required of us, is to provide a rule stating how the constant sum of freedom is to be shared out among individuals. On this basis, Steiner is able to derive the justice of an *equal* distribution of freedom. His argument proceeds as follows. The only two alternatives available in sharing out a constant sum good (or bad) are an equal distribution and an unequal one. [Since there are many conceivable unequal distributions], no unequal distribution can be justified without giving substantive moral reasons for privileging the ends (and hence the moral codes and values) of some individuals over others. Therefore, only an equal distribution of freedom can be deduced as one of the formal properties of a freestanding conception of justice. Equal freedom is entailed by justice because, by process of elimination, it can be shown to be the only distribution of freedom with which justice is not incompatible . . . Let us call this derivation of the equal liberty principle 'Steiner's Derivation'.

And the flaw in this derivation is said to be one of *indeterminacy*. For if LCL were jettisoned, "we could continue to affirm that only an equal distribution of freedom can be justified but there would be any number of equal distributions of freedom, and we would have no basis for preferring a distribution giving everyone a great deal of freedom to a distribution giving everyone very little freedom."

Is this charge of indeterminacy warranted? Is it true that, under the auspices of the equal liberty principle, we could give everyone either a great deal of freedom or very little? It seems to me that a perfectly natural question to ask here is this: If we give everyone only very little freedom, *what happens to the rest of it*? Can it really make sense to say, under that dispensation, that we—the givers—are no more free than everyone else? Are not we, the givers, in denying everyone an otherwise available greater amount of freedom, *ipso facto* in possession of some greater amount ourselves? Observe that, if this argument is correct, then there simply cannot be an equal distribution of freedom that is not also an equal distribution of *maximal* freedom. And hence, there would be no indeterminacy in the equal liberty principle, even if LCL is jettisoned.

But even if that argument, for the *impossibility* of a sub-maximal equal distribution, is incorrect, this would still not impugn the determinacy of the equal liberty principle as mandating an equal distribution of maximal freedom. The reason is that any sub-maximal equal distribution suffers from the same fatal forensic deficiency as that which, as Carter notes, besets any unequal distribution of freedom: namely, that it cannot "be justified without giving substantive moral reasons for privileging the ends (and hence the moral codes and values) of some individuals over others".[20] In this case, those who are restricting the freedom of others, and of each other, to an equal but sub-maximal amount (for instance, some puritanical ruling oligarchy), can justify their doing so only by invoking the ends which that restriction subserves. Whereas no such subservient relation obtains between any particular ends and a maximal equal distribution.

This argument, concerning the equal liberty principle, has a direct bearing on the claim famously advanced by Joseph Raz and further defended in his essay here: that distributional equality can have no intrinsic value. I have, for the most part, agreed with Raz. That is, I agree that, in almost all cases, it is implausible to believe that our reason for increasing the amount of a valued good possessed by someone with an inferior share of it is to achieve a less unequal distribution of that good. The exception, I believe, is liberty.

As Raz correctly remarks:

> Necessarily, egalitarians are value pluralists. It makes no sense to believe in the equality of what is itself of no value . . . If the distributive equality of anything is intrinsically valuable it must be something which is itself of value (or disvalue) or something necessarily related to what is intrinsically valuable.

And, clearly, liberty *is* valuable: this is true whether we construe that value along the lines of Carter's 'non-specific value' or simply as consisting in the fact that being free to secure our intrinsically valued ends is a necessary condition of our doing so. Why, then, would an equal distribution of liberty itself be *intrinsically* valuable?

My original argument to this effect was heavily reliant on LCL (Steiner 2003). But even prescinding from that disputed entity, I think that an equal distribution of liberty can possess intrinsic value. For something to possess intrinsic value, it must be valued for its own sake, so to speak, and not for either its causal role in bringing about something which has intrinsic value or its being an incidental side-effect of such causation. Raz is right to suggest that the value which much egalitarianism mistakenly attributes to equal distributions of both those types is intrinsic value. In fact, however, if we distribute bread equally, we do so not because that distribution is good in itself, but rather because that distribution is likely to achieve, or to be a side-effect of, the greatest attainable level of hunger alleviation—which is, itself, intrinsically valuable.

But no such instrumental or side-effect quality can be attributed to the equal distribution of liberty: there is nothing (else) of intrinsic value that can be so associated with everyone's having the same amount of it.[21] For what that distribution's consequences would be is entirely contingent on how persons would severally choose to exercise their respective portions of liberty. Indeed, were the incidence of indifference, to other intrinsically valuable things, to be sufficiently widespread, we might well expect that their realization would actually suffer under such a distribution. In that event, it might perhaps be arguable that liberty's equal distribution should give way to a distribution of it that is more consonant with the demands of those other valuable things.[22] Such an argument would, however, no more impugn the intrinsic value of liberty's equal distribution than a demonstration—say, that hunger alleviation frustrates autonomy enhancement —would impugn the intrinsic value of those two ends. We know, from the preceding Carter discussion, that the value of any particular *un*equal distribution of liberty must be non-intrinsic. One of the virtues of construing its equal distribution as intrinsically valuable is, indeed, that doing so lends corroboration to Raz's insistent contention that there is a plurality of intrinsically valuable things. Justice—equal liberty—just is a member of that plurality.

Perhaps unwisely, I once accepted an invitation to stray beyond the confines of my normal concerns and contribute to a collection of papers on the subject of *evil*. Several of the arguments in Steve de Wijze's essay have pretty much convinced me that I strayed too far. The principal object of that contribution, entitled "Calibrating Evil" (Steiner 2002), was to supply an account of evil acts that would underwrite the quantification implicit in such familiar expressions as 'the lesser of two evils', *without* construing evil as being merely what some have called a 'wrong-intensifier': that is, without its being simply synonymous with 'very wrong'. De Wijze and I agree that ordinary usage—and not only ordinary *theological* usage—seems to sustain such a conception of evil, along with many others, of course.

His critique places the blame, for the failure of my analysis adequately to capture his quite compelling counter-examples, squarely on what he sees as that analysis's reductionist and foundationalist tendencies. In its place, he advances an account which employs a coherentist reflective equilibrium methodology and which, he believes, more closely corresponds to our moral reality. For what he aptly labels my *Perverse Pleasure* (PP) theory of evil, in

> trying to explain what, precisely, makes a wrongful act into an evil one . . . cannot account for the important role of evil worldviews in this connection . . . [It is] unable to contend with *Weltanschauungen* which 'annihilate the moral landscape' and have a profound effect on ordinary common place activities. In such contexts, ordinary benign actions or projects are appropriately understood as evil . . . This dimension of evil, if I am correct, is not accessible to Steiner's PP account. It does not focus primarily on the intentions or consequences of individual acts and certainly does not refer to the affective states of agents. It highlights a twisted and perverted philosophical and socio/political ideology which can transform mundane activities into evil ones.

What is wanted instead, de Wijze contends, and what he offers, is an account of evil informed by the more holistic approach embodied in Rawls's conception of wide equilibrium, whereby coherence is achieved among our considered moral convictions, a consistent cluster of moral principles, a consistent cluster of background theories (including moral theories) about our social world and how we function in it, and an empirically based, broadly scientific, conception and account of human nature.

Readily conceding my analysis's inability to meet several of his arguments, I suggest that a difficulty with this alternative holistic account is that it fails to satisfy one of the two parameters of the exercise I was undertaking. For while it undoubtedly yields a much richer conception of evil acts, and one that can accommodate his telling counter-examples, what it seems to be resistant to is their *calibration*. How can we know, of two acts that are both strongly informed by worldviews that 'annihilate the moral landscape', whether—and if so, which—one is the lesser of those two evils? What is the nature of the metric on which we could scale different such annihilations? Since our moral reality unquestionably sustains a conception of evil whereby one act can embody more of it than another, such a metric is clearly needed. The certain fact that PP theory cannot supply it should serve as a further incentive, to those with more holistic views, to do so.

I'm delighted to be reminded, by Norm Geras's essay, of the bygone days when we used to play *Caractacus Potts*.[23] Indeed, *play* is the operative term here. For, while disavowing any more general commitment to anti-foundationalism, what he nonetheless offers is a critique of Bernard Suits's classic attempt to refute the famous claim advanced by Wittgenstein: namely, that the diverse activities which we call 'games' are so called not because their respective descriptions each satisfy one and the same set of necessary and sufficient conditions, but rather because they more loosely bear something like family resemblances one to another. I take this, more precisely, to mean that no particular triad of games need have any features in common.

Notwithstanding Geras's suggestion, like de Wijze's, that my own work is informed by foundationalist tendencies, I feel like a bit of an interloper in this dispute. For although I readily plead guilty to harbouring such tendencies, I've never really examined their causes, beyond my holding the simple belief that any form of philosophical *analysis* must, to some extent, be driven by them. So rather than being drawn into a debate that I'm probably not competent to conduct, I'll venture one thought about a portion of Geras's argument that seems to me open to question.

> [Suits's argument] appears to me to imply something like the following: we already know what games are, being guided to them, as to the species *giraffe*, by their shared properties; Suits's definition simply draws the boundary that is already there, and uses of the word 'game' to apply to other activities beyond the boundary have become 'metaphorical', 'careless', 'arbitrary' or 'stupid'. But another perspective on the same thing would be to say that his definition *picks out* from within the activities called games a subset, *stipulates* that only members of this subset are truly games and then disparages usages to the contrary with some bad-sounding words . . . In any event, how can it be that games, a range of activities that we invent and name, are identifiable as a reality independently of our linguistic usages—such that one could say with Suits that there are things which *are* games as distinct from things which are merely *called* games? Games are not a natural kind. They are not like giraffes or planets or water, which would be what they are whatever we called them or if we ceased to be and so could not speak of them at all . . . [T]he three conditions laid down in Suits's definition as being necessary for some given activity to count as a game are not in fact necessary conditions. Are they, however, jointly sufficient in picking out what a game is?

To this latter question, Geras's answer is also 'no'.

To be sure, games are not a natural kind. But there may be something about natural kinds that make them more like what Suits takes to be true of games. What I have in mind here is that the conditions, whether necessary or sufficient, for being a thing of a certain natural kind are sometimes *scalar* in nature. Geras's giraffes, say—in view of the possibility of cross-breeding or genetic mutation—are subject to this possibility. In which case, the analyst is confronted with a choice between (a) allowing that collections of apparently very diverse things nonetheless constitute one and the same kind of thing, and (b) insisting that such diversity is constitutive of a plurality of kinds. I think the analytical tradition favours the pluralist option: that multiplying distinctions is analytically preferable to diminishing them. Ordinary usage, it's true, sometimes resists such multiplication. However, and reverting to the primary focus of the earlier parts of this essay—namely, rights—I note that it was Hohfeld's meticulous dissection of that usage's tendency to agglomerate several logically very different normative relations under the common term 'rights' that is the reason why his work is credited with bringing so much clarity and coherence into that domain of discourse. Perhaps a corresponding caution is warranted in regard to the agglomeration of what are called games.

In conclusion, let me say just this. Nothing, I think, can be more gratifying for a scholar than to have other scholars—very gifted scholars—grapple with his work. And for some of them to take the time and trouble, to organise those grapplings into a collection like the present one, creates a debt of gratitude that is, to say the least, not easily repaid. Ian, Matt and Steve have, with characteristic insight and consummate skill, accomplished that task superbly. I here extend to them my heartfelt thanks.

NOTES

1. Oxford University Press, forthcoming.
2. Which is not to say that this derivation rests upon on *no* normative premises whatsoever. Its sole normative premise, as far as I can see, is that justice extends its rights, thus conceived, to *everyone* who can consistently be said to have rights (though this claim is itself supported by the non-normative claim that no reason is consistently available for restricting that extension).
3. I owe that realization to arguments pressed on me by Brian Barry, Derek Parfit and Nigel Simmonds. Its absence from my earlier work is well reflected in some of the arguments advanced in Eric Mack's contribution here.
4. Cf. Hughes and Cresswell 1972, 301: '"Whatever is obligatory is permissible" remains a sound principle'; similarly Prior 1962, 220 ff; and Prior, 1967.
5. Thus Hilpinen (1971, 16) says: 'The principles of deontic logic determine conditions of consistency for normative systems. By a "normative system" we understand here simply any set of deontic sentences closed under deduction. When is a set of deontic sentences consistent? It seems natural to require that at least the following "minimal condition" should be satisfied: . . . [that] all obligations in this set can be simultaneously fulfilled, and that [an act] is permitted only if it can be realized without violating any of one's obligations'.
6. I'm indebted to Paul McNamara for this piece of information.
7. See, for example, Steiner 1998, 268.
8. In my view, that deficiency is best understood as consisting in their violation of the rational choice axiom of *completeness*.
9. And a *full* specification of the antecedent distribution would take account of any such ownership fragmentation and dispersal.
10. For it's self-contradictory to say that X is vested with both a Hohfeldian power to do A and a Hohfeldian disability to do A.

11. 'Choice Theory' is H.L.A. Hart's name for the Will Theory, and one which I too used in *An Essay on Rights*.
12. Of course, any sensible liability rule will assign priority to simply reversing the effect of P's non-compliance, by having that redress take the form of (at least) returning M to A. But, in the event of such simple reversal being impossible—say, because P has destroyed or otherwise transformed M—it's unlikely that A would be given no further recourse by that rule and would have to resign himself merely to brooding over his loss. That is, the rule would mandate redress in the form of something as nearly equivalent in value to M as possible.
13. Though see Steiner 1999.
14. Can her right, in which an Alpha complaint could be grounded, be construed simply as a right that *all* opportunity-sets be *continuously* equal? One problem with this *time-slice* construal of opportunity-egalitarianism is its levelling-down implication that an Alpha-Beta-Gamma distribution of one-one-one is as just as a three-three-three distribution: that is, such a right is morally indifferent as between mandating a gift-ban and mandating a post-gift reduction, in the size of Alpha's as well as Gamma's opportunity-sets, to that of Beta's.
15. Indeed, one of the standard arguments for legally prohibiting voluntary euthanasia—a prohibition which is precluded by the right of self-ownership—is that licensing that practice creates incentives to refrain from making life-sustaining choices.
16. In his concern with 'the slavery of the talented'.
17. On Kant, see Steiner 1994, 211–213, 220–223; 1998, 275–283.
18. To avoid adding another epicycle of complexity here, I'll assume that non-culpable ignorance includes ignorance for which *no one*—not merely Agent—is causally responsible: her ignorance of the fact that X is not a terrorist is not due to her having been misled by anything that anyone else did or failed to do.
19. Symmetrically (and equally consonant with luck egalitarianism), when Mother Nature correspondingly acts to channel our intentional actions into the production of reasonably unforeseeable *beneficial* consequences, it is she who is strictly responsible for them and it is to her owners that those benefits should accrue.
20. The explanation of why this is a fatal forensic deficiency is simply that, if those substantive privileging reasons were shared by the parties to a practical conflict, they would each lack any reason to invoke their rights—their entitlements to liberty—at all. I don't sue people who agree with me about what is the best thing to do. Unequal distributions of liberty are justified only instrumentally.
21. That such a distribution of liberty is not a means to enhancing autonomy is, for instance, inferable from Rousseau's *Emile*, where a wise tutor develops his tutees' capacity for leading autonomous lives. *Conscripting* such tutors to perform such tasks would constitute both a reduction in their liberty and a means to bringing about an overall enhancement of autonomy.
22. Though note 20 above enters a caveat on the validity of such a move.
23. Potts, I should remind readers who have somehow forgotten, is the central character in the 1968 film, *Chitty Chitty Bang Bang*, based on the Ian Fleming children's novel of the same name.

BIBLIOGRAPHY

Hilpinen, Risto (ed.). 1971. *Deontic Logic: Introductory and Systematic Readings*. Dordrecht: D. Reidel.

Hughes, G.E. and Cresswell, M.J. 1972. *An Introduction to Modal Logic*. London: Methuen.
Prior, A.N. 1962. *Formal Logic*. Oxford: Oxford University Press.
Prior, A.N. 1967. "Deontic Logic." In Paul Edwards, (ed.). *The Encyclopedia of Philosophy*. New York: Macmillan, vol. 4, 509–13.
Rawls, John. 1971. *A Theory of Justice*. Cambridge, Mass.: Harvard University Press.
Steiner, Hillel. 1994. *An Essay on Rights*. Oxford: Blackwell.
Steiner, Hillel. 1997. "Choice and Circumstance", *Ratio*, X, 296–312; reprinted in Matthew H. Kramer (ed.). *Rights, Wrongs and Responsibilities*. London & New York: Palgrave, 2001.
Steiner, Hillel. 1998. "Working Rights." In Matthew H. Kramer, N.E. Simmonds, and Hillel Steiner, *A Debate over Rights*. Oxford: Oxford University Press.
Steiner, Hillel. 1999. "Silver Spoons and Golden Genes: Talent Differentials and Distributive Justice." In Justine Burley (ed.), *The Genetic Revolution and Human Rights: 1998 Oxford Amnesty Lectures*. Oxford: Oxford University Press. Reprinted in David Archard and Colin Macleod (eds), *The Moral and Political Status of Children*. Oxford: Oxford University Press, 2002.
Steiner, Hillel. 2002. "Calibrating Evil". *The Monist*, 85, 183–193.
Steiner, Hillel. 2003. "Equality, Incommensurability, and Rights." In Lukas H. Meyer, Stanley L. Paulson and Thomas W. Pogge (eds.), *Rights, Culture and the Law: Themes from the Legal and Political Philosophy of Joseph Raz*. Oxford: Oxford University Press.

Contributors

Ian Carter is Associate Professor of Political Philosophy at the University of Pavia, Italy. His principal books include *A Measure of Freedom* (1999) and *La Libertà Eguale* (2005). He and Hillel Steiner and Matthew Kramer have recently edited *Freedom: A Philosophical Anthology* (2007).

G.A. Cohen is Chichele Emeritus Professor of Social and Political Theory and a Fellow of All Souls, Oxford. He is the author of *Karl Marx's Theory of History: A Defence* (1978; expanded edition, 2000), *History, Labour, and Freedom* (1988), *Self-Ownership, Freedom, and Equality* (1995), *If You're an Egalitarian, How come You're So Rich?* (2000), and *Rescuing Justice and Equality* (2008).

Cécile Fabre is Professor of Political Theory at the University of Edinburgh. She is the author of *Social Rights under the Constitution* (2000) and *Whose body is it Anyway? Justice and the Integrity of the Person* (2006).

Norman Geras is Professor Emeritus of Government at the University of Manchester. He is author of *The Legacy of Rosa Luxemburg* (1976); *Marx and Human Nature: Refutation of a Legend* (1983); *Literature of Revolution: Essays on Marxism* (1986); *Discourses of Extremity: Radical Ethics and Post-Marxist Extravagances* (1990); *Solidarity in the Conversation of Humankind: The Ungroundable Liberalism of Richard Rorty* (1995); *The Contract of Mutual Indifference: Political Philosophy after the Holocaust* (1998).

Matthew H. Kramer is Professor of Legal & Political Philosophy at Cambridge University; Fellow of Churchill College, Cambridge; and Director of the Cambridge Forum for Legal & Political Philosophy. Among his many books, the most recently published is *Moral Realism as a Moral Doctrine* (2009).

Eric Mack is Professor of Philosophy at Tulane University and a faculty member of Tulane's Murphy Institute of Political Economy. Among his more recent publications are: 'Self-Ownership, Marxism, and Egalitarianism: Part I. Challenges to Historical Entitlement' and 'Self-Ownership, Marxism, and Egalitarianism: Part II. Challenges to the Self-Ownership Thesis', in *Politics, Philosophy, and Economics*; 'Libertarianism and Classical Liberalism' (with Gerald Gaus), in *A Handbook of Political Theory*, ed. G. Gaus and C. Kukathus; and 'Prerogatives, Restrictions, and Rights', in *Social Philosophy and Policy*.

Serena Olsaretti is Senior Lecturer in the Faculty of Philosophy at Cambridge University, and a Fellow of St. John's College, Cambridge. She is author of *Liberty, Desert and the Market* (2004), and has edited *Desert and Justice* (2003).

Michael Otsuka is Professor of Philosophy at University College London. He is the author of *Libertarianism without Inequality* (2003).

Joseph Raz has recently retired as Professor of the Philosophy of Law at Oxford University. He is currently a Professor at Columbia University Law School. His publications include *The Authority of Law* (1979); *The Concept of a Legal System* (2nd ed., 1980); *The Morality of Freedom* (1986); *Practical Reason and Norms* (2nd ed., 1990, reprinted 1999); *Ethics in the Public Domain* (revised paperback edition, 1995); *Engaging Reason* (1999) and *Value, Respect and Attachment* (2001).

Hillel Steiner is Professor of Political Philosophy at the University of Manchester and a Fellow of the British Academy. His current research concerns the concept of 'the just price', and the application of libertarian principles to global and genetic inequalities.

Peter Vallentyne holds the Florence G. Kline Chair in Philosophy at the University of Missouri-Columbia. He is editor of *Contractarianism and Rational Choice: Essays on David Gauthier's Morals by Agreement* (1991); *Equality and Justice: Desert and Entitlement* (2003); *The Origins of Left Libertarianism: An Anthology of Historical Writings*, edited with Hillel Steiner (2000); and *Left Libertarianism and Its Critics: The Contemporary Debate*, edited with Hillel Steiner (2000).

Philippe Van Parijs holds the Hoover Chair in Economic and Social Ethics at the University of Louvain-la-Neuve, Belgium. He joined Harvard's Philosophy Department on a part-time basis in January 2005. His many publications include *Marxism Recycled* (2003), *Real Freedom for All: What (if Anything) Can Justify Capitalism?* (1995), and (with B. Ackerman and A. Alstott), *Redesigning Distribution: Basic Income and Stakeholder Grants as Cornerstones for an Egalitarian Capitalism* (2005).

Stephen de Wijze is Senior Lecturer in Political Theory at the University of Manchester. Among his recent publications are 'Defining Evil – Insights from the Problem of "Dirty Hands"' in *The Monist* (2002); 'The Political Limits of Reasonableness' in *Imprints* (2002); 'Tragic-remorse – the anguish of dirty hands' in *Ethical Theory and Moral Practice* (2004).

Jonathan Wolff is Professor in the Philosophy Department at University College London. He is author of *Robert Nozick: Property, Justice and the Minimal State* (1991), *An Introduction to Political Philosophy* (1996), *Why Read Marx Today?* (2003) and, with Avner de-Shalit, *Disadvantage* (2007).

Index

For Product Safety Concerns and Information please contact our EU representative GPSR@taylorandfrancis.com
Taylor & Francis Verlag GmbH, Kaufingerstraße 24, 80331 München, Germany

www.ingramcontent.com/pod-product-compliance
Ingram Content Group UK Ltd.
Pitfield, Milton Keynes, MK11 3LW, UK
UKHW022117190926
475702UK00013B/1485

* 9 7 8 0 4 1 5 7 5 4 3 6 1 *